2nd Edition

Mr. Cheap's®
Chicago

Michelle Roy Kelly
and
Jennifer M. Wood

Editorial Assistants
Michelle M. Lang
Elizabeth Washer

Previous edition written by Mark Waldstein

Adams Media Corporation
Holbrook, Massachusetts

Published by Adams Media Corporation
260 Center Street, Holbrook, MA 02343. U.S.A.

Mr. Cheap's® is a registered trademark of Adams Media Corporation.

ISBN: 1-58062-374-3

Printed in Canada.

J I H G F E D C B A

Library of Congress Cataloging-in-Publication Data
are available from the publisher.

Product or brand names used in this book may be trademarks or registered trademarks. Any use of these names does not convey endorsement by or other affiliation with the name holder.

Every effort has been made to ensure that all material in this book is current as of the time of this writing. However, this information is subject to change. Readers should check with the individual services and products to find up-to-date information, such as current prices, fees, and features.

This publication is designed to provide accurate and authoritative information with regard to the subject matter covered. It is sold with the understanding that the publisher is not engaged in rendering legal, accounting, or other professional advice. If legal advice or other expert advice is required, the services of a qualified professional person should be sought.
—From a *Declaration of Principles* jointly adopted by a Committee of the American Bar Association and a Committee of Publishers and Associations.

This book is available at quantity discounts for bulk purchases. For information, call 800/872-5627 (in Massachusetts, 781/767-8100) or email at jobbank@adamsmedia.com.

Visit our Website at www.adamsmedia.com

Also in the Mr. Cheap's® Series:

Mr. Cheap's® Atlanta   ISBN: 1-55850-292-0

Mr. Cheap's® Boston   ISBN: 1-55850-556-3
    2nd Edition

Mr. Cheap's® New York   ISBN: 1-58062-271-2
    2nd Edition

Mr. Cheap's® San Francisco   ISBN: 1-55850-388-9

Mr. Cheap's® Seattle   ISBN: 1-55850-445-1

Mr. Cheap's® Washington D.C.   ISBN: 1-55850-415-X

To order books, please send check or money order
(including $4.95 for postage) to: Adams Media Corporation,
260 Center Street, Holbrook MA 02343.
(Foreign orders please call for shipping rates)
Discounts available for standing orders.

Ordering by credit card? Just call **800/USA-JOBS**
(In Massachusetts, call **781-767-8100**). Fax: **800/872-5687**.
Please check your favorite retail outlet first.

Visit our Website at www.adamsmedia.com
or send an e-mail to mrcheap@adamsmedia.com

TABLE OF CONTENTS

MANY THANKS...

First and foremost, we would like to thank Mr. Mark Waldstein, the original author or *Mr. Cheap's® Chicago,* for laying the groundwork for this (still) vast undertaking. It is because of his initial parsimony that this second edition has been made possible.

Thank you to all the business owners, managers, and employees who were so willing to share their stories and information with the authors, making this book as comprehensive as possible.

Thanks to the many Chicagoland Barnes & Noble locations who were kind enough to let us use their stores as a platform for communication between the authors and the readers of this series. A special thank you goes to the many Barnes & Noble patrons who helped in making these contests work.

Our extreme gratitude also goes out to the many dedicated readers who took the time to write us with leads, feedback, and support. Keep it coming!

Finally, a very special thank you goes out to James L. Menzies, who so graciously volunteered his time and gourmandise as he and the author rambled about this toddling town.

THANK YOU!

THE *MR. CHEAP'S*® PHILOSOPHY

Ultimately, the world can be divided into two types of people: those who have money to burn, and those who don't. Being of the latter species (and let's face it, most of us are), we have spent considerable time and energy assembling this book, with both the frugal and the frivolous in mind. Even if you *do* have a money tree germinating in your backyard, we are all united in the fact that nothing feels better than getting something for less!

Before taking a hasty glance at this book and dismissing it simply because you think "Me? *Cheap*? Never!," please bear with us for a moment while we explain that the term "cheap" – in no way – should be understood to have a negative connotation. Here are a few synonyms for our own definition of cheap: frugal, thrifty, cost-conscious, economical... the point is, while a "cheap" person may be understood as someone who reuses paper plates and plastic utensils, and brings to mind visions of Ebenezer Scrooge, a *Mr. Cheap's*® reader is someone who only expects or accepts the highest quality products and the highest caliber services, at budget-friendly prices. Again, this does not mean that you insist on paying under $10.00 for *any* article of clothing, or *any* entertainment must be free; Mr. C never sets such stringent guidelines. *Mr. Cheap's*® simply believes that everyone, no matter what their lifestyle, *can* and *should* be getting things for less.

If you prefer to wear an Armani suit to work, or are strictly all-Donna Karan-clad, that is fine. *Mr. Cheap's*® will let you know the best places to buy. But, if you prefer to buy your clothes by the pound at the local thrift store, *Mr. Cheap's*® is here to aid you in *your* search as well. No matter what your preference or your budget, this book can help you. And no matter what you're looking to buy, eat, or do, we've got you covered.

Spend the weekend at a ritzy hotel, take in a show, shop 'til you drop, eat 'til you explode – then come back tomorrow and do it all over again. Don't worry about the cost, with the money you'll be saving the first time around, you can afford to be excessive. So grab a cup of coffee ($.87 at **Coffee & Tea Exchange**), slip into something comfortable (sleepwear purchased 60 percent off at **Carson Pirie Scott**), bury yourself beneath the covers (bought dirt cheap at the **Crate & Barrel Outlet Store**) and let *Mr. Cheap's*® show you how to conquer the Windy City!

WEBSITES

While Mr. C and his staff try their hardest to bring you the best and most in cheap fun, food, and fashion around the city, there's always more to be uncovered. Therefore, if you've read this book cover to cover (and you definitely should) and you still can't find exactly what it is that you are looking for, the following list of Websites might provide you with some useful information. Enjoy!

⌂ CENTERSTAGE CHICAGO
http://centerstage.net
The Lowdown: This can be your one-stop guide to the city. Centerstage Chicago is particularly good for those new to the city, but also has some useful information for natives. Here you will find hundreds of reviews that may help you make a decision about where to get the best buy for your buck. The site also includes reviews of theater productions, a directory of golf courses, a "Virtual El Line", and links to book hotel rooms, search fllights, and make a rental car reservation.
***Cheap* Tip:** There is a special section for student travelers on this site that includes information on what to do in Chicago on a budget.

⌂ CHICAGO CITYSEARCH
http://chicago.citysearch.com
The Lowdown: This extensive Website offers information on every aspect of life in the Windy City. Explore detailed listings in the areas of arts & entertainment, special events, restaurants, bars, and shopping. The site includes articles and reviews as well as links to additional reviews on other sites.
***Cheap* Tip:** The "City & Visitor's Guide" should be of particular interest to visitors and natives alike; this link provides information on all sorts of free things to do, and how to get great discounts on some of the city's best hotels.

⌂ CHICAGO CONVENTION & TOURISM BUREAU
http://www.chicago.il.org
The Lowdown: As you may have guessed, this site is geared toward business travelers. After all, Chicago is touted as the Convention Capital of the World. However, all visitors can use this site as a guide to popular attractions in the city. Included is information on what to do and see, as well as historical facts about the city. Business travelers can find out what conventions are happening during their stay.
Cheap Tip: If you plan to shop 'til you drop, then be sure to refer to the listings of Discount/Outlet Stores and Consignment Stores for tips on where to find cheap buys.

⌂ CHICAGO HOTELS ONLINE
http://www.chicagohotelsonline.com
The Lowdown: This is *the* site for finding an affordable hotel in the city, quickly and easily. You can check availability and rates for a limited number of hotels in the downtown area. When you

find the place that suits your needs and your budget, simply make a reservation online. (Of course, Mr. Cheap's always recommends calling the hotel to make sure that the reservation is in order before you arrive).

Cheap Tip: The nice part about this site is that you can compare the rates between a bunch of different hotels; rather than having to search each one individually.

⌘ CHICAGO MAGAZINE
http://www.chicagomag.com

The Lowdown: *Chicago Magazine* traverses every corner of the city and reports back to its readers. There are sections on people, entertainment, dining, news, and getaways. They've got the latest news in current events, entertainment, dining, people, and a few getaway suggestions. My favorite features are the Unofficial Neighborhood Guide (with thorough descriptions of area stores and the type of goods they sell) and an article on finding the best public bathrooms in the city.

Cheap Tip: First date jitters have you shakin' in your boots? Have no fear, *Chicago Magazine* will plan the date for you. All you have to do is answer a few simple questions, submit them to the editors, and they will create a plan for a memorable evening on the town.

⌘ CHICAGO-SCENE
http://www.chicagoscene.com

The Lowdown: If you are a mover and a shaker, this is your site. Chicago-Scene keeps you up-to-speed on the city's best hotspots. Whether it's the restaurant, nightclub/bar, fashion, or music scene that interests you, Chicago-Scene will let you know what's going on, when, and where. If you're tired of the nightclub scene, check out the Event-Party-Festival Database. Here you'll find the latest on public parties, charity events, and fundraisers.

***Cheap* Tip:** Become a Chicago-Scene VIP member to get discounts on admission to events and trips; advanced notification on openings; and access to restricted areas of the Website. The cost is $100.00 for a year or $175.00 for two years. It's a little steep, but well worth it if you are interested in serious networking.

⌘ CHICAGO SUN-TIMES
http://www.suntimes.com

The Lowdown: Yes, this in the online version of the award-winning newspaper. So you can expect to find the latest news stories, as well as coverage of entertainment, sports, business, and other related items of interest.

Cheap Tip: You can open a free email account through this site. Replace some of those long distance phonecalls with free email. Did I mention this is free?

⌘ CITY SPIN CHICAGO
http://www.cityspin.com/chicago

The Lowdown: Yet another Website predominantly designed for the tourist. City Spin Chicago has a Best Bets link which should serve as a trusty guide for the leisure traveler. It outlines popular attractions to visit in the city. The shopping section can be particularly helpful since it lists shops by type, name, and location, and it also includes such often overlooked shopping venues as button stores and furriers.

Cheap Tip: Kill two birds with one stone by searching for restaurant options within the hotel section. Whether you are staying at the Hyatt Regency or the Palmer House you can find a place to get a bite that is close by and reasonably priced.

⌖ CITYPASS
http://www.citypass.net

The Lowdown: If you've ever visited a big city, chances are you've heard of CityPass. With one quick CityPass purchase, you will gain admission to six of Chicago's biggest attractions. The Art Institute of Chicago, The Field Museum, The Museum of Science and Industry, Adler Planetarium, Shedd Aquarium, and the Sears Tower Skydeck are all on the Chicago CityPass lineup. Adult passes are $30.50, $25.00 for senior citizens, and kids under 11 are $22.75.

Cheap **Tip:** In conjunction with several of Chicago's most popular hotels, CityPass can also help make rooms affordable. Browse through their "Hotel Packages" to find a deal that suits your budget (CityPass is included, of course).

⌖ ENJOY ILLINOIS
http://www.enjoyillinois.com

The Lowdown: As the official site of the Bureau of Tourism, Enjoy Illinois is one place you can count on to lead you in the right direction. The Website has eight main divisions: Attractions, Accommodations, Camping, Events, Food, Golf, Outdoors, and Shopping. In Attractions, you'll find everything from amusement parks to historical sites. Find an accommodation that is kid-and/or pet-friendly. If you want to spend some time camping, pick a site that offers your favorite activity, like hiking or fishing. Once you have typed in your criteria, you'll be faced with an extensive list of places to go and things to do, complete with directions, maps, hours, and admission prices. What's more, the site offers a trip planner service so that, once you have viewed the listings you can add it to your trip planner and print out the itinerary when you are done.

Cheap **Tip:** The Bureau of Tourism offers free brochures, travel guides, and maps which you can order through the Website.

⌖ GREATER NORTH MICHIGAN AVENUE ASSOCIATION
http://www.themagnificentmile.com

The Lowdown: You're probably wondering why Mr. C would even bother mentioning the Magnificent Mile to his fellow cheapsters when it is known for high-cost boutiques and restaurants. Well, this Website is probably *the* most comprehensive guide devoted to this one mile stretch of the city. About 750 companies located here are members of the Greater North Michigan Avenue Association. You'll find shops and restaurants with contact information, direct links to homepages, and brief descriptions of each.

Cheap Tip: The GNMAA hosts several events throughout the year for the general public to enjoy, such as the Magnificent Mile Lights Festival and the Magnificent Mile Crystal Carnival.

⚘ HOT ROOMS
http://www.hotrooms.com

The Lowdown: Hot Rooms provides a sizable list of hotels with contact information, ratings, and price lists. Hot Rooms even tells you the extra person charge and parking fee, and sheds some light on the hotel by providing a brief description.

Cheap Tip: Hot Rooms lists the full price for a hotel room compared to the rate they offer. I was thrilled to find a recognizable hotel for about $100.00, but as I continued looking I eventually found one as low as $59.00 per night.

⚘ METROMIX
http://www.metromix.com

The Lowdown: Another favorite of mine, Metromix has a lot of information about entertainment connections. If I haven't said it enough; take advantage of the search engine. If you choose this method, you'll find that Metromix not only reviews your chosen venue, it also provides extra information you may want to know like admission price, parking fees, hours, etc. Anytime you click on one of the subject hyperlinks, Metromix provides a list of related articles. Definitely glance at these articles, as some of them are for the budget-minded. I looked under Stage and was lead to an article about the best seats and best deals in town. The site listed a number of theaters, provided the seat numbers for the best view in the house, and included a few deals that pertained to that particular venue.

Cheap Tip: Under Visitor Information be sure to check out the listing of museum free days. You can save some dough by visiting museums on designated days.

⚘ NEWCITY CHICAGO
http://www.newcitychicago.com

The Lowdown: Like Metromix, Newcity Chicago has enough entertainment connections to keep you stirring from the early morning to late night. Check out the Special Events section which lists events, mostly free or under $10.00.

Cheap Tip: By far the best asset of Newcity Chicago is "Best of Chicago", which lists the greatest of everything you can imagine.

⚘ ONLINE MAITRE D' RESTAURANT SEARCH
http://www.searchchicago.com

The Lowdown: Everyone loves a good meal, but sometimes the experience doesn't live up to the expectations. However, armed with advice from this Website, you'll know whether a four-star, upscale restaurant is worth its high prices and hype, or if it is worth your while to tackle the buffet line at a local eatery. The Website provides addresses and phone numbers of featured restaurants, type of cuisine, what meals are served, price range, hours, and a brief description.

Cheap Tip: To narrow your search, choose the neighborhood you'll be eating in, then enter "Under $20" as the price range.

SHOPPING

Books & Magazines

AFTER-WORDS
23 East Illinois Street, Chicago IL 60611. 312/464-1110. **World Wide Web address:** http://www.abebooks.com/home/afterwords. **The Lowdown:** If you're anything like me, collecting books is just as important as buying them. There's nothing greater than finding a gorgeous old hardcover edition of one of your favorite stories. For this reason, After-Words is a really great bookstore. What would you be willing to pay for a 1969 hardcover edition of F. Scott Fitzgerald's *The Last Tycoon* (complete with author's manuscript notes)? Here, it's just $9.00. A 1932 copy of William Faulkner's *Sanctuary* was seen for just $4.00; as was a copy of Norman Mailer's *Tough Guys Don't Dance* (in excellent condition). And what about those wonderful stories you read over and over as a child? For just such a nostalgic reader, Mr. C spotted a hardcover copy of Jack London's *White Fang*, in great condition and a handsome addition to any library, for just $6.00. After-Words specializes in out-of-print searches, special orders, and personalized stationary and printed items. They do sell new books as well, but it's their selection of used books that keeps bibliophiles coming back. Open Monday through Thursday, 9:00 a.m. - 9:00 p.m.; Friday, 9:00 a.m. - 11:00 p.m.; Saturday, 10:00 a.m. - 11:00 p.m.; Sunday, 12:00 p.m. - 7:00 p.m.

BARGAIN BOOKS
49 East Chicago Avenue, Chicago IL 60611. 312/642-6416. ♦ 12 North Wabash Avenue, Chicago IL. 312/578-8328. **The Lowdown:** They sure aren't lying when they say that their books are bargains. Unlike many other stores that offer books at discount prices, Bargain Books is divided into sections, so you may actually be able to find what you're looking for. Reference, business, computers, travel, bestsellers, fiction, entertainment... all genres are represented. The back of the store even has a great children's book section with lots of new and classic titles. Books come direct from the manufacturer, which means unbeatable bargains. Most of them are returns or overstocks, but all the books are new and in fantastic condition. Expect to save anywhere between 50 and 90 percent.

BOOKLEGGER'S
2907 North Broadway, Chicago IL 60657. 773/404-8780. **World Wide Web address:** http://www.bookleggers.com. **The Lowdown:** You may have heard about bootlegging in Chicago, but what about booklegging? Since the 1979 opening of their tiny store in East Rogers Park, Booklegger's has long been part of the Chicago community. Booklegger's carries more than 10,000 used books, all in great condition. And since all the book jackets are covered in plastic, you can be sure that they've tried hard to maintain this condition. While they do carry all genres, lovers of literature, philosophy, and art may find this store a particular treasure. They also carry a decent selection of used CDs, tapes,

books on tape, and videos, but it's with the books that you'll have the most fun. Open daily, 12:00 p.m. - 9:00 p.m. *$Cash Only$*

BOOKMAN'S CORNER

2959 North Clark Street, Chicago IL 60657. 773/929-8298.
The Lowdown: Bookman's Corner carries thousands of books, all crammed onto the floor in stacks or atop the 12-foot-high shelving. Because the number of books seems to exceed the amount of available room, they offer great sales almost weekly. When I visited, everything on the shelves was being discounted by an extra 40 percent. The store is well organized by section, and they've often got more than one copy in stock. Nothing I saw was in less than excellent condition. They offer a particularly good selection of art books, with lots of artist compilations for as little as $10.00 (they'd sell for $30.00 and up anywhere else). Local interest and history books are specialties of the store. If you've got a specific title, edition, etc. in mind, Bookman's Corner may impose a timely challenge to you. It's a much more enjoyable place if you enjoy digging to uncover a forgotten treasure. Open Sunday, 12:00 p.m. - 6:00 p.m.; Monday through Saturday, 12:00 p.m. - 8:00 p.m.

BOOKSELLERS ROW

404 South Michigan Avenue, Chicago IL 60605. 312/427-4242.
The Lowdown: One of Chicago's favorite used bookstores, Booksellers Row gives booklovers a chance to build their collections for pennies on the dollar. The stock turns over constantly; among the used books, Mr. C spied a paperback copy of Aeschylus' *The Oresteia* for $3.25, and a mint-condition hardcover of William H. Pritchard's *Randall Jarrell: A Literary Life* for $15.00 ($10.00 off the original price). Thomas Pynchon's *Gravity's Rainbow*, a heavy 750 pages worth, was buoyed by a price of only $6.45. In children's books, a new copy of Maureen Galvani's *Me And My Dog* was seen marked down to $3.98. The remainders section may yield up a brand-new copy of Merrill Schleier's *The Skyscraper in American Art 1890-1931*, reduced from $12.95 to just $4.98; and David E. Greenberg's *The Construction of Homosexuality*, listed at $35.00 for the hardcover, was $6.98. In their $.99 section, they had a used copy of *The Chicago Daily News Cookbook*, dating from about 1935, in excellent condition. Open Sunday, 11:30 a.m. - 7:30 p.m.; Monday through Thursday, 10:30 a.m. - 7:30 p.m.; Friday and Saturday, 10:30 a.m. - 8:30 p.m.

BOOKWORKS

3444 North Clark Street, Chicago IL 60657. 773/871-5318.
E-mail address: TheBookworks@msn.com. **The Lowdown:** Another of Chicago's great used bookstores, Bookworks is for the bookworm in us all. If you usually avoid used bookstores because of the often chaotic and haphazard arrangement, this place may just change your mind. Its shelves are impeccably arranged and (could it be true?) totally dust-free. The majority of the stock is used, but there are also some new volumes thrown in for good measure; all of the books offer significant discounts. For

example, a new copy of Jack Kerouac's *All Sizes*, listed at $8.95, was seen for $8.05. The store's cookbook section is huge, with lots of interesting titles on vegetarian and ethnic cooking. How about *The Complete Cookbook of American Fish and Shellfish* by Jean F. Nichols, in hardcover, for $8.00 (originally listed at $19.50)? The fiction and literature sections are overwhelming with innumerable cheap buys abounding. A practically new-looking copy of *High Fidelity*, Nick Hornsby's paperback was seen for $5.00; Penelope Niven's account of Carl Sandburg's life was selling for $17.50, half its original price. The extensive animal book collection yielded more great buys, like *Peterson's Field Guide to Western Birds* for $8.00 (it would sell for twice that if new). Used children's books like the Disney Golden Book favorites are also half off retail. Mr. C even saw a leather-bound volume of John Milton's works for $22.50, and The Franklin Library's leather-bound copy of *Moby Dick* for $12.50. The store offers domestic shipping services for a modest charge. Open Sunday, 12:00 p.m. - 6:00 p.m.; Monday through Thursday, 12:00 p.m. - 10:00 p.m.; Friday and Saturday, 12:00 p.m. - 11:00 p.m.

O'GARA & WILSON BOOKSELLERS, LTD.

1448 East 57th Street, Chicago IL 60637. 773/363-0993. **The Lowdown:** Founded in 1937, O'Gara & Wilson offers a wide range of used, rare, and out-of-print books. Literature, history, and the arts are the main focus here, with plenty of philosophy and religion sprinkled in. Mr. C enjoyed leafing through *100 Masterpieces of the Art Institute of Chicago*, with lots of color plates, selling for half its original price at $30.00. The literary collection *Steinbeck: A Life in Letters*, edited by Steinbeck's wife, was available in both hardcover ($12.50) and paperback ($7.50). And, like any good used bookstore, there are plenty of paperback mystery and crime novels for $1.00. Open Sunday, 12:00 p.m. - 8:00 p.m.; Monday through Saturday, 9:00 a.m. - 10:00 p.m.

SECOND EDITIONS

4923 Oakton Street, Skokie IL 60077. **Toll-free phone:** 800/694-6531. **E-mail address:** Second Edn@aol.com. **World Wide Web address:** http://www.secondeditions.com. **The Lowdown:** True bibliophiles won't mind a 20 minute trek north of the city to visit Second Editions. Their mission statement says it all: "Second Editions is the place for people who love to read." Second Editions offers an enormous selection of new and used paperbacks and other book necessities such as bookmarks, covers, and clips. New paperbacks are generally sold at 10 percent below retail; but it is with the used books that the best bargains are buried. Discounts of up to 50 percent are given on used paperbacks on all sorts of topics. If you're not really sure what you want to read, don't be afraid to ask for help. Owners Hope and Fran and the rest of their entourage will be more than happy to offer suggestions if you tell them a couple of your favorite books, authors, or genres. To further accommodate book-lovers, Second Editions offers a number of in-store discussion series. Readers from all over come to join in these enlightening, educational, and – most of all – fun discussions.

Topics range from Oprah's latest book of the month to the most recent romance novel. If you haven't read the book du jour, Second Editions will be happy to sell you a copy at 25 percent off the retail price. It's a great way to keep up with your reading, even when you're on a budget. Just be sure not to leave Second Editions without saying hello to Merlyn, the store's real owner. If you don't recognize him from the store's logo, he's the guy up front purring and wagging his tail.

THE STARS OUR DESTINATION

1021 West Belmont Avenue, Chicago IL 60657. 773/871-2722. **E-mail address:** stars@sfbooks.com. **World Wide Web address:** http://www.sfbooks.com. **The Lowdown:** As you may gather from the name, this bookstore is solely devoted to the science fiction/fantasy genre. Alice Bentley, a die-hard fanatic herself, created this shop and runs it with a meticulous hand. Although she sells new *and* used books, Mr. C was primarily interested in the used section, which may be the largest in town for sci-fi. There are three separate sections of used hardcovers and paperbacks lining the walls. The first is a section of books in fair condition, as well as book club editions. Next comes the average section, offering better quality and more well-known authors, such as Asimov, Heinlein, Clarke and Bova. Then there is the section of very recent used titles, in which prices are a bit higher. Bentley knows that there may be some collector's editions mixed in on these shelves, but she doesn't try to price them at market rates. Not only would this require a lot of extra effort, but she also prefers to keep the stock moving. Used paperbacks are uniformly sold at half the cover price (or a $1.00 minimum). For those who do want to follow the collector's market, she does provide a reference section of the latest price guides. Open Sunday, 12:00 p.m. - 6:00 p.m.; Monday through Saturday, 11:00 a.m. - 9:00 p.m.

WALDENBOOKS

127 West Madison Street & South LaSalle Street, Chicago IL 60602. 312/236-8446. **The Lowdown:** In addition to discounting the company's top 10 hardcover bestsellers, Waldenbooks offers its customers a Preferred Reader discount card. Show it at the cash register whenever you buy something in any branch of this national chain and you'll be entitled to an additional savings of 10 percent off of your entire purchase (excluding magazines, newspapers, and gift certificates). Plus, for every $100.00 you spend during the course of a year, you'll get a $5.00 savings certificate toward a future purchase. How much to enjoy all these wonderful perks? You can pick up your Preferred Reader card for just $10.00; sign up in any one of their stores or call Walden-by-Mail at 800/322-2000. Another way to save money is to look for Waldenbooks' selection of publishers overstocks and remainder books. These are available frequently throughout the year and always offer significant discounts.

'ZINES & BEANS

934 West Webster Avenue, Chicago IL 60614. 773/755-2681. **The Lowdown:** 'Zines & Beans combines two of Mr. Cheap's

favorite activities: reading and coffee-drinking. If you think you're an expert on any particular subject, think again. 'Zines & Beans carries more than 4,500 magazines in their vast library. Whatever your favorite subject, they've got a magazine to satisfy your curiosity. Chefs may have a subscription to *Bon Appetit*, but wouldn't they want to read about *Vegetarian Times Natural Remedies*? Sure it might be easy for horror-lovers to find the latest issue of *Fangoria*, but how often do you come across a copy of *Shivers*? The collection at 'Zines & Beans is obviously one of the largest around. You can satisfy your caffeine-craving as well as your curiosity with a sampling of their coffee and tea offerings from around the world.

CDs, Records, Tapes, & Videos

AUDIO-VISUAL

2449 North Lincoln Avenue, Chicago IL 60614. 773/871-1928. **The Lowdown:** Though the name of this video store is a bit listless, the selection at Audio-Visual is anything but! They like to refer to their selection as "wide, weird, and wondrous." Mr. C would have to agree. Audio-Visual buys, rents, and sells videos of the non-mainstream variety. It's the kind of place you would go when seeking a rare independent, foreign film, or cult classic; the kind of place where *The Toxic Avenger* (the man and the movie) would feel right at home. What I like most about this store is their sense of humor. You don't come into Audio-Visual to find a horror film, you come in to find some splatter gore; instead of a drama, you can opt for a medical melodrama or a samurai saga; skip the film noir, and head straight for the female revenge section; and be sure that you know the difference between gangster flicks and gangsta flicks. Not yet feeling the holiday spirit? Might I suggest *Santa Claus Conquers the Martians* and a gallon of egg nog to do the trick. Of course, at any time of year, films like *Alice in Acidland* and *Swamp Woman* are sure to keep you entertained. With even the tiniest bit of information to go on, the film-crazed staff can help you find a film (or remember the name of that one, you know, with that actor.). Audio-Visual offers a film search service and also does mail order. Whether you're looking to rent *or* own that lost campy classic, Audio-Visual is a great place to begin your search. Open Sunday, 12:00 p.m. - 8:00 p.m.; Monday through Saturday, 12:00 p.m. - 10:00 p.m.

BEVERLY RECORDS

11612 South Western Avenue, Chicago IL 60643. 773/779-0066. **E-mail address:** info@beverlyrecords.com. **World Wide Web address:** http://www.beverlyrecords.com. **The Lowdown:** Since its humble beginnings in 1967, Beverly Records has become one of the Chicago area's most respected (and visited) record stores. Just make sure you set aside an hour or two before you visit, as you'll want to stay and browse through the stacks and racks of old vinyl treasures. From the 1920s to current favorites, Fats Waller to Fats Domino, The Beatles to The Parliament Funkadelic, Beverly Records carries all genres from all time periods. 45 rpm reissue albums are a mere $3.49 apiece, while original records start at just $4.00 a pop! Not too shabby. They've also got lots of other music-related paraphernalia, like posters, displays, and autographs. For the music-lover in your life, Beverly Records offers a handsome and unique birthday gift idea; you give them the name and the birth date of the recipient, and they'll give you a framed record of the number one song that day and year. Prices range from $20.00 - $60.00, depending on the condition and rarity of the record. Beverly Records also offers a record search service, for that rare album you've been looking for. Even if you're not in the market to buy anything, a trip to Beverly Records is like a stroll down memory lane. Come on in and browse! Open Sunday, 12:00 p.m. - 4:00 p.m.; Monday through Thursday, 9:30 a.m. - 7:00 p.m.; Friday and Saturday, 9:30 a.m. - 6:00 p.m.

DISCUS CD EXCHANGE
2935 Broadway, Chicago IL 60660. 773/549-6815. **E-mail address:** chicago@discus-cdexchange.com. **World Wide Web address:** http://www.discus-cdexchange.com. **The Lowdown:** It's no gimmick when Discus refers to themselves as a "CD Exchange." One of the best ways to save money while shopping here is to go through your own supply of CDs at home first. You're bound to find more than one CD that you could use as a trade-in. If you want to go by Mr. C's philosophy "If you've forgotten you own it, it's ripe for the selling." Come on, when was the last time you actually popped in Air Supply's *News From Nowhere*? With so many people trading in different CDs every day, the 15,000+ inventory is ever-changing. Discus carries all musical genres from classical to jazz to the latest top 40 hits. Even if you haven't got any CDs to sell, Discus CD Exchange is still one of the best and cheapest used music stores in the city. Still, the name doesn't say it all. Discus also carries a large selection of used DVDs. These are mostly new releases, hot off the rental shelves. Again, all genres are well-represented from classic to comedy and drama to horror. If you're looking to spruce up your home entertainment options, Discus CD Exchange is the place to do it cheaply. Open Sunday, 12:00 p.m. - 6:00 p.m.; Monday through Saturday, 10:00 a.m. - 10:00 p.m.

DR. WAX
2523 North Clark Street, Chicago IL 60614. 773/549-3377. ♦ 1203 North State Street, Chicago IL 60610. 312/255-0123. ♦ 5225 South Harper Avenue, Chicago IL 60615. 773/493-8696. **World Wide Web address:** http://www.drwax.com. **The Lowdown:** Although Dr. Wax is becoming well known as an independent online music source, you would be missing out if you did not stop by one of the three locations. Part of the thrill of shopping here is rummaging through new and used records and CDs, and finding that rare, out-of-print, independent label that you couldn't find anywhere else. They carry all sorts off memorabilia, new releases, and classic vinyl selections. But above all else, Dr. Wax is devoted to indie labels of all types of music, be it country, rap, or jazz. Each store has its own distinct identity and strengths, so call ahead or visit them all. Of course, if you're too busy to get the full shopping experience, then the Website will serve your purpose just fine.

DUSTY GROOVE AMERICA
1180 North Milwaukee Avenue, 2nd Floor, Chicago IL 60622. 773/645-1200. **E-mail address:** rick@dustygroove.com. **World Wide Web address:** http://dustygroove.com. **The Lowdown:** I think the proprietors describe their store best when they say that they cater to the "discerning rare groove enthusiast." Dusty Groove America specializes in all sorts of rare and alternative

sounds including soul, jazz, funk, hip-hop, Latin, Brazilian, lounge, and reggae. The inventory comprises new and used CDs and almost everything is in mint condition. As you might expect, the rarer the album the higher the pricing: An original pressing of James Brown's *Ain't it Funky* sells for just under $50.00 while the reissue goes for $8.99. Overall, prices are as fantastic as the selection. What's best about this place is that – when you take the time to browse – you'll always find something exciting. Mr. C spotted a near mint condition of Chuck Berry and The Steve Miller Band *Live at the Fillmore* for $11.99 and Eddie Bo & The Soulfinders' *Hook and Sling* for $8.99. Jazz in all its many forms – acid, soul, avant garde – is an especially well-represented category. A great selection of Dizzy Gillespie CDs and LPs start at a mere $6.99. Dusty Groove sells a variety of books and magazines too, from song books to biographies to critiques. Rare and old copies of *Downbeat*, *Grand Royal*, and *Straight No Chaser* provide a particularly interesting browsing experience. Posters and videos seem to lean heavily toward blaxploitation flicks; a brand new *Shaft* poster was selling for $11.99 and the accompanying videos (*Shaft in Africa*, *Shaft's Big Score*) were seen for $11.99 apiece. Other movies included *Super Fly*, *Watermelon Man*, and just about every Pam Grier flick ever made (pre-1990s that is)! The story of Dusty Groove is a rare one. They opened up their doors online and, to meet the demand of local customers, actually built a retail store later. Usually, you see companies closing their doors because of a booming Web business. It just goes to show they care about customer satisfaction. Open Friday, 12:00 p.m. - 8:00 p.m.; Saturday, 12:00 p.m. - 6:00 p.m.; Sunday, 12:00 p.m. - 6:00 p.m.

GRAMAPHONE RECORDS

2663 North Clark Street, Chicago IL 60614. 773/472-3683. **E-mail address:** gphone@gramaphonerecords.com. **World Wide Web address:** http://www.gramaphonerecords.com. **The Lowdown:** It's no wonder Gramaphone has been the shopping mecca of some of the city's funkiest DJs. With an enormous selection of new and used CDs and vinyl, Gramaphone genres know no boundaries. Hard and deep house, hip-hop, and techno offerings encompass some of the store's best deals. Mr. C spotted a bunch of records – including Mary J. Blige's *Beautiful*, Groove Collective's *Everything is Changing*, Robert Hood's *Psychic*, and Plastikman's *Africa* – for $6.39 apiece. Tapes like Juice's *The Man* start as low as $3.99. Acid jazz staples like Blackalicious, East Flatbush Project, and DJ Vadim are all in stock as well. But it's not all about funk here; Gramaphone Records carries a noteworthy selection of perennial club favorites by the likes of Grandmaster Flash & The Furious Five, The Sugar Hill Gang, and KC and the Sunshine Band. Shake your booty on over and see if they've got your favorite. Open Sunday, 12:00 p.m. - 6:00 p.m.; Monday through Friday, 11:00 a.m. - 9:00 p.m.; Saturday, 10:30 a.m. - 8:30 p.m.

JAZZ RECORD MART

444 North Wabash Avenue, Chicago IL 60611. 312/222-1467. **E-mail address:** jazzmart@delmark.com. **World Wide Web**

address: http://www.jazzmart.com. **The Lowdown:** For those of you thirsting for good and affordable jazz at an ultra-reasonable price, there's no place like Chicago's Jazz Record Mart. They're so popular, in fact, they've started up their own Website in addition to their booming mail order service. You, however, can get the authentic experience by stepping foot inside this jazz haven for yourself. The Jazz Record Mart's owner, Bob Koester, a man who was at the forefront of the mid-sixties blues revival, the first to record adventurous jazz artists affiliated with Chicago's AAMC, and the owner of the Delmark Records label – a label who has produced the works of such greats as Junior Wells and Mighty Joe Young. What you'll find in this store is a virtual shrine to all that is jazz and blues. Hard-to-find albums and out-of-print titles are not so hard to come by in this store. Jazz Record Mart features tens of thousands of titles – both new and used – in all sorts of formats (LP, tape, compact disc). You'll also find lots of jazz and blues paraphernalia, like posters and T-shirts, too. If ever there were a store to make that hard-to-buy-for jazz enthusiast happy, this is the place. Throughout the year, Jazz Record Mart hosts a number of in-store performances that attract some of the genre's most talented local and touring musicians. As Koester has always provided a warm and welcoming environment to musicians in the past, it's no wonder they still continue to flock to his place. Even if you're just starting out on your jazz journey, the staff here can certainly help you. Plus, they often stock many must-have jazz and blues titles on their own rack, so you'll have no problem knowing where to begin. Prices are good, even on rare titles, and the selection is incomparable. A free quarterly magazine is available by contacting the store. Open Sunday, 12:00 p.m. - 5:00 p.m.; Monday through Saturday, 10:00 a.m. - 8:00 p.m.

RECKLESS RECORDS

3157 North Broadway, Chicago IL 60657. 773/404-5080. ◆ 1532 North Milwaukee Avenue, Chicago IL 60622. 773/235-3727. **The Lowdown:** Here's a full-service rock music store, with good prices on new recordings (including lots of imports and EPs) and a big selection of lower-priced secondhand discs. They also sell videos, posters, books, T-shirts, and other memorabilia. Used CDs start as low as $1.00. Used cassettes are mostly under $5.00. Record albums make up a good portion of the store. A sticker on each LP rates its condition.

RECORD EMPORIUM

3346 North Paulina Street, Chicago IL 60657. 773/248-1821. **The Lowdown:** Record Emporium has got everything you could ever need for a relaxing night of music-listening: thousands of LPs, 45s, 78s, and CDs are in stock as well as lots of great magazines, memorabilia, and collectibles. Much of the music is rare or hard-to-find, so it pays to check the stock here before scrounging the rest of the city in search of a particular title. Each Saturday, they even offer an in-store performance, perhaps allowing you to broaden your musical horizons. Open Sunday, 12:00 p.m. – 6:00 p.m.; Monday through Saturday, 11:00 a.m. – 7:00 p.m.

2ND HAND TUNES

2604 North Clark Street, Chicago IL 60614. 773/281-8813.
• 2449 North Lincoln Avenue, Chicago IL 60614. 773/871-2328.
• 1377 East 53rd Street, Chicago IL 60615. 773/684-3375.
The Lowdown: These second-hand music stores stock LPs, cassettes, and CDs up to the ceiling. In addition to carrying some of the latest albums below retail price, 2nd Hand Tunes has an impressive display of Broadway show tunes, soul, and disco. On the record side of things, in addition to rock 'n roll, there's a comedy and an international section; and there's lots of LPs and 45s selling for under $1.00. The store also carries lots of boxed sets and even 8-track tapes.

SEE HEAR MUSIC

217 West North Avenue, Chicago IL 60610. 312/664-6285.
The Lowdown: The shop might be tiny, but the savings are huge! See Hear Music offers fantastic prices on both new and used CDs. While the number of new CDs definitely outnumbers the amount of used discs, the prices are equally good. They carry all musical genres and virtually every artist you can imagine is in stock. See Hear Music also carries an always-growing selection of DVDs at a discount. Items can also be mail ordered at the same great prices, and they are always more than happy to answer your requests. Open Sunday, 11:00 a.m. - 5:00 p.m.; Monday through Saturday, 10:00 a.m. - 9:00 p.m.

SHAKE, RATTLE & READ BOOK BOX

4812 North Broadway, Chicago IL 60640. 773/334-5311. **E-mail address:** mags@rockmag.com. **World Wide Web address:** http://www.rockmag.com. **The Lowdown:** Here's a funky combination store selling old magazines, used books, and used records, tapes, and CDs. If you're a collector looking for that hard-to-find old issue of *Life*, or if you're in search of an old Bob Dylan record, get yourself over to this Uptown shop. The vintage prices can't be beat here. Open daily, 12:00 p.m. - 6:00 p.m.

TOWER RECORDS

2301 North Clark Street, Chicago IL 60614. 773/477-5994.
World Wide Web address: http://www.towerrecords.com.
The Lowdown: Nocturnal music lovers can't beat Tower, located at Clark and Belden in Lincoln Park. After all, this national mega-chain stays open until midnight every single night of the year. Your favorite artists can often be found discounted in just about every department. There are usually a good range of CDs for $11.99 and under. And be sure to check the cut out bins in Tower's classical music department, where overstocks are always drastically reduced. Open daily, 9:00 a.m. - 12:00 a.m.

VIDEO BEAT

2616 North Clark Street, Chicago IL 60614. 773/871-6667.
E-mail address: videobeat@aol.com. **The Lowdown:** They can't fool Mr. C with that misleading name; I know they've got more than just videos in there. Video Beat offers a large selection of used movies, records, tapes, and CDs (kind of filling out every niche this chapter stands for). Prices, for whatever it is you're

looking for, start as low as $1.00 - $2.00. That's right, whether it's a Hollywood hit or Chicago crooner you're looking to take home, just a few dollars can make that happen here. The videos, mostly shows of rock bands, are used and sell for $8.00 - $10.00 each. Video Beat also boasts a truly vast selection of used records, tapes, and CDs. The record section is a jazz lover's dream. Priced from $1.99 and up, the bins are packed with Sinatra, Coltrane, the Crusaders, and more, going all the way up to Kitaro. Records are labeled with notes like Not Perfect and Very Rough Shape, to alert you to their condition, and the friendly guys behind the counter will be happy to play any disc to further evaluate the sound quality. Prices are based on the album and the sound quality. No matter what, you're sure to save a few bucks here by buying used music. Open Sunday, 12:00 p.m. – 8:00 p.m.; Monday through Saturday, 11:00 a.m. – 8:30 p.m.

Clothing: Bridal Wear

DAVID'S BRIDAL

4512 North Harlem Avenue, Harwood Heights IL 60706. 708/583-1740. ◆ 7706 South Cicero Avenue, Oak Lawn IL 60459. 708/636-6100. ◆ 421 East Roosevelt Road, Lombard IL 60148. 630/932-7333. ◆ 500 East Golf Road, Schaumburg IL 60173. 847/884-8990. **World Wide Web address:** http://www.davidsbridal.com. **The Lowdown:** Since it's founding in 1950, David's Bridal has grown into one of the nation's largest and most recognized bridal wear discounters. The store offers the same designer gowns you'll see in all the fashion magazines at a fraction of the cost. It's really a one-stop bridal destination as they've got bridesmaid, mother of the bride, and flower girl gowns as well. They'll even outfit you with all the necessary bridal accessories. As an added incentive to buy, they'll even give you a great financing option that includes no money down, no payments, and no interest for 90 days. While the Windy City doesn't have a David's Bridal of their own, there are plenty of outlets close by. Call for specific location hours.

HERE COMES THE BRIDE

190 North Swift Road, Addison IL 60101. 630/261-9950. **E-mail address:** herecomesthebride@hotmail.com. **World Wide Web address:** http://www.herecomesthebrideinc.com. **The Lowdown:** Sure it's a little ways outside of Chicago, but a once in a lifetime occasion like this merits the drive for savings like these! This bridal outlet couples big designers with little prices, making you one happy bride-to-be. Everything is sold at prices 30 - 70 percent off retail. But don't think you're coming to some huge warehouse to get lost in the racks; part of the beauty of Here Comes the Bride is the personalized attention. Shopping is by appointment only. You can feel and look like a million bucks... at a fraction of the cost. Dresses start at just $199.00 and include famed bridal designers like Richard Gasgow and Ulla Maija. With savings like these you can afford to be a bit excessive with the rest of your wedding plans.

I DO DESIGNER BRIDAL CONSIGNMENT

6742 West Belmont Avenue, Chicago IL 60634. 773/205-1234. **World Wide Web address:** http://www.idobridalconsignment. com. **The Lowdown:** I'm not sure what more I can tell you about this store as the name says it all! I Do is a bridal consignment shop offering a fabulous array of designer gowns. They've even got the Midwest's largest selection of vintage gowns along with hundreds of headpieces and veils for as little as $50.00. For extravagant taste on a *Mr. Cheap's* budget (dresses start as low as $200.00), I Do is one place that can certainly help make The Big Day a perfect occasion. In fact, it is because of the owner's own search for that perfect affordable dress that the store was even opened. Kelly Hamilton decided that buying a once-worn gown was the way to go, as have the hundreds of women who have entered through her doors. To ensure personalized service, it is suggested that you make an appointment before stopping in. Open Tuesday through Friday, 12:00 p.m. - 8:00 p.m.; Saturday and Sunday, 12:00 p.m. - 6:00 p.m.; closed Monday.

MARIA'S PAYLESS BRIDAL
4938 West Irving Park Road, Chicago IL 60641. 773/283-1731.
The Lowdown: Maria's is a Mr. Cheap's pick because you'll always pay less! Best of all, they've got lots of designer names like Alfred Angelo and Mori Lee, and they carry an enormous amount of inventory in every size available. Open daily.

PAYLESS BRIDAL HOUSE
4632 North Harlem Avenue, Chicago IL 60634. 773/237-6389.
♦ 4866 West Dempster, Skokie IL 60077. 847/679-7960. ♦ 2942 West 95th Street, Evergreen Park IL 60642. 708/422-6383.
World Wide Web address: http://www.bridal1directory.com/payless.htm. **The Lowdown:** Here's another great bridal shop that urges you to pay less. Luckily for you, they've got three locations in the area. For more than 15 years, Payless has offered brides-to-be great discounts on gorgeous gowns by well-known designers. They've also got tons of clothing that will perfectly outfit your entire party, from tuxedos for the groom and ushers to dresses for the bridesmaids, flower girl, and mother of the bride. Discounted accessories – including shoes, handbags, and jewelry – will help complete the outfit. The Chicago location is open Sunday, 12:00 p.m. - 5:00 p.m.; Monday through Thursday, 12:00 p.m. - 8:30 p.m.; Friday, 4:00 p.m. - 8:30 p.m.; Saturday, 10:00 a.m. - 5:00 p.m. The Skokie location is open Sunday, 12:00 p.m. - 5:00 p.m.; Monday through Friday (except Wednesday), 11:00 a.m. - 8:00 p.m.; Saturday, 10:00 a.m. - 6:00 p.m.; closed Wednesday. The Evergreen Park location is open Sunday, 12:00 p.m. - 5:00 p.m.; Monday through Thursday, 1:00 p.m. - 9:00 p.m.; Friday, 12:00 p.m. - 6:00 p.m.; Saturday, 10:00 a.m. - 6:00 p.m.

Clothing: Children's & Junior's

CHILDREN'S WEARHOUSE
2640 West Pratt Boulevard, Chicago IL 60645.
773/761-3572. **The Lowdown:** This resale shop
has got everything for child and mother alike. Tons of children's clothing, juvenile furniture, and baby equipment are all in excellent condition. Stock up early (before the baby arrives) and moms can take advantage of their inexpensive selection of maternity clothes. It's a great way to save money on things that will be outgrown in a matter of weeks.

THE FAMILY SHOPPER
5555 North Broadway Street, Chicago IL 60640. 773/271-6655.
The Lowdown: No fancy brand names here, but a good selection of basic new clothing, primarily for young girls. You'll find good prices on everything from casual separates and ensembles to party outfits and communion-style dresses. There is clothing for the little guys, too. Open Sunday, 11:00 a.m. - 6:00 p.m.; Monday through Saturday, 10:00 a.m. - 7:30 p.m.

ONCE UPON A CHILD
2908 North Ashland Avenue, Chicago IL 60657. 773/281-9957.
♦ 5316 North Milwaukee Avenue, Chicago IL 60630. 773/594-1705. **The Lowdown:** As anyone with a child knows, it seems like before you even get their clothing in the washing machine, kids have outgrown it. That's what makes dressing your young ones such a costly task. Yet, with the number of children's resale and consignment shops that keep popping up all across the country, dressing your child stylishly and affordably is becoming a much more feasible reality. With more than 200 stores in North America, Once Upon A Child is the nation's largest and most-respected chain of children's resale shops. In addition to the two locations in Chicago, they've got locations in Bloomington, Bolingbrook, Chicago Ridge, Downers Grove, and Fairview Heights. Like many other companies involved in the resale industry, Once Upon A Child considers their merchandise "gently used," as it's all in excellent condition. They even carry a selection of new, brand-name products. Unlike other stores, you'll find much more than just clothing here. Once Upon A Child sells furniture, bedding, and baby equipment like strollers and car seats. They've also got a huge selection of toys, books, puzzles, and games at prices that can't be beat! And Once Upon A Child is not just about making a quick sale; they're interested in protecting your children. Unlike other resale shops, Once Upon A Child is a completely recall-free environment. They even maintain up-to-date lists on product recalls so that you can be sure your kids are safe at home. Clothing is sold from newborn to size 7 and all articles are in pristine condition; toys and games are checked to ensure that all pieces and parts are in place. Inventory includes top brand names like Little Tikes, Playskool,

Fisher Price, Step 2, and Century. Most importantly, Once Upon A Child is a fun place to shop! They often have special events where storytellers and other entertainers are invited to come in and impress the little ones. Kids will be amazed by the entertainment while you'll be amazed by the prices. And how about this for a cheap tip? If you're looking to save even more money, why not gather up some of the clothes and toys your own child has outgrown? As long as they are current styles and in great condition, you can sell them to the store. When you then turn around and buy up all the new goodies you've just found, you've hardly spent a penny! Open Sunday, 11:00 a.m. - 4:00 p.m.; Monday through Friday, 10:00 a.m. - 7:00 p.m.; Saturday, 10:00 a.m. - 5:00 p.m.

THE SECOND CHILD

954 West Armitage Avenue, Chicago IL 60614. 773/883-0880. **World Wide Web address:** http://www.2ndchild.com. **The Lowdown:** The Second Child advertises itself as an upscale resale children's boutique. The racks are crowded with adorable outfits, all name brands, all previously worn, but not worn out, by any means. The Second Child accepts only current fashions. For expecting moms, a pair of Guess? maternity overalls were only $20.00, and would probably sell for at least $80.00 if new. A plaid jumper by ReCreations was only $15.00, and a knit sweater/skirt set by Lanz was $32.00. A gingham dress, perfect for the office, was only $38.00. For the baby, Gerber one-piece sleeper outfits may cost as little as $1.00. Snowsuits for tiny tots are priced in the $15.00 - $20.00 range. For little girls, a striped cotton top by Esprit was $6.00, and a velvet Rare Editions party dress was $18.00. A boys' Osh Kosh oxford was seen for $12.00. The store is overflowing with shoes, and among those noted were girls' leather slip-ons by Capezio ($5.50), and other styles by names like Nike and Sam & Libby. Boys' black suede lace-ups by Playskool were only $8.00; and Sporto winter boots for kids were about $10.00. A pair of little girls' rollerskates was also found for $10.00. The store also sells accessories like strollers and car seats here, as well as maternity clothes. Strollers by Graco, regularly selling for $100.00 and up, are priced in the $60.00 - $75.00 range.

THE WEAR HOUSE

222 Merchandise Mart Plaza, Suite 216, Chicago IL 60654. 312/836-0612. **The Lowdown:** One visit to The Wear House and you're guaranteed to find major bargains on children's outerwear for every season, though off-season purchasing offers the best buys. Most merchandise is first quality and in perfect condition. For the handy and creative customer, it's worth your while to check out the occasional "as is" merchandise they vend: while the merchandise is damaged, it is most always wearable and/or repairable. Open Monday through Friday, 9:00 a.m. – 6:00 p.m.; Saturday, 10:00 a.m. – 5:00 p.m. Because Saturday hours are subject to change, it is best to call ahead first!

Clothing: Consignment & Resale

ABSOLUTELY FABULOUS

2821 North Halsted Street, Chicago IL 60657. 773/244-2330. **The Lowdown:** Well, they certainly got the name right. Absolutely Fabulous offers a great selection of women's clothing for all occasions. Whether it's a formal affair, an important business meeting, or a lazy Sunday you're looking to dress for, Absolutely Fabulous has got the names and styles you want. I found some really amazing stuff on my visit: silk shirts by Donna Karan (in several different colors and styles) for $25.00; casual and dressy sweaters by The Gap and Free People for as little as $15.00; Gap jeans for under $20.00. Absolutely Fabulous is a particularly great place to shop for those just starting out in the work world; they've got a great selection of appropriate suits and dresses. Mr. C saw some great little dresses by Banana Republic, J. Crew, Emanuel, and Ann Taylor for $35.00 and under. This upscale resale shop has also got an "absolutely fabulous" array of accessories. Absolutely Fabulous is also blessed with a completely organized display of clothing; merchandise is arranged by size and color, and different clothing styles are separated onto different racks. Let me assure you that it's difficult to walk out of this store empty-handed. Open Sunday, 12:00 p.m. – 5:00 p.m.; Tuesday through Friday, 11:00 a.m. – 7:00 p.m.; Saturday, 11:00 a.m. - 6:00 p.m.; closed Monday.

BELLA MODA

947 North State Street, Chicago IL 60610. 312/642-0330. **The Lowdown:** Bella Moda is one of the many great consignment shops dedicated to designer couture. Bella Moda carries the best names in high fashion including Escada, Karl Lagerfeld, Ungaro, Calvin Klein, Chanel, Jil Sander, Giorgio Armani, and Donna Karan. They've also got lots of great accessories, like bags, belts, and jewelry at a fraction of the retail cost. Scarves by Hermes are just one of the many bargains to be found here. While the prices here aren't decidedly cheap, they are certainly great for anyone who loves and buys couture clothing. Bella Moda accepts designer clothing and accessories Monday through Saturday. Open Monday through Friday, 10:00 a.m. – 6:00 p.m.; Saturday, 10:00 a.m. – 5:00 p.m.; closed Sunday.

BUY POPULAR DEMAND

2629 North Halsted Street, Chicago IL 60614. 773/868-0404. **The Lowdown:** In this store's packed showroom, better designer suits, shoes, and jackets for women are sold on consignment. Buy Popular Demand only accepts clothing that is less than two years old. Items sell here for about one-third of their average original price; and anything that hasn't sold after four weeks in the shop is further reduced until it does. Rita Code, one of the owners, showed Mr. C a number of great bargains. There's lots of stuff for the office, like a two-piece Liz Claiborne rayon suit with peplum waist, in barely-worn condition, going for a remarkable $40.00; or a set of Ann Taylor sarong-style, silk-print shorts and top for $15.00. Formal evening gowns by Victor Costa tend to sell in the $60.00 - $120.00 range. Ms. Code also pointed out a two-piece, woman's Armani suit (retailing at $1200.00) with a barely-noticeable fabric distortion selling for an incomparable $100.00. The shoe selection includes dressier styles by Calvin Klein, Naturalizer, and Ferragamo for as low as $15.00. Some of the belts and costume jewelry border on outlandish, but more conservative styles can always be found among the selections. Designer handbags range from $10.00 - $60.00. Buy Popular Demand is one of the few consignment stores that sells men's clothing as well. There isn't nearly as much to choose from, but Mr. C did see an Yves St. Laurent suit for $150.00, and a Missoni Uomo sport jacket for $100.00. For even further bargains, don't miss their end-of-summer and end-of-winter sales; that's when everything in the store suddenly goes to half-price. Call or stop in to find out when the next sale is on. Open Sunday, 11:00 a.m. - 5:00 p.m.; Monday through Saturday, 11:00 a.m. - 7:00 p.m.

CACTUS TRADE

2040 North Halsted Street, Chicago IL 60614. 773/472-7222.
The Lowdown: Cactus Trade is a small, handsome shop selling new and used designer clothing for women. Like many such stores, it's run by a former model who is using her wardrobe, experience, and contacts to good advantage. Resale makes up the majority of the racks, but you'll find new items mixed right in. Although some of the clothing is fancy, the emphasis here is on the casual side. Items spotted here included a zip-up cardigan from Ann Taylor for $26.00 and a wrap top and skirt by Armani (originally $220.00) for just $95.00. The store looks like any upscale boutique; clothing is arranged by size and color and everything is in the most pristine condition. There's a great selection of shoes and handbags, many of which are new and at discount. Mr. C saw a pair of like-new Paloma heels for just $24.00. Cactus Trade also has a lovely selection of hand-crafted jewelry which is definitely new; it's made by local designers. Though the men's side is definitely a bit smaller than the women's, they offer the same fantastic deals on top name designer suits and casual wear. The service is friendly and always helpful, which can make your visit that much more pleasant. As part of the Chicago Upscale Resale Connection (along with Cynthia's Consignments and The Daisy Shop – see separate listings), you can be sure you're getting the highest quality clothing at the best possible prices. Open Monday through Friday, 11:00 a.m. - 7:00 p.m.; Saturday and Sunday, 11:00 a.m. - 6:00 p.m.

THE CHICAGO FUR OUTLET

777 West Diversey Parkway, Chicago IL 60614. 773/348-FURS.
The Lowdown: This shop specializes in previously owned (or,

what they like to call "pre-furred") fur and leather jackets for men and women. Some of the merchandise is bought from shops that have gone out of business, some is consigned by individual owners and stores, and other coats are closeouts or bought outright from other fur stores. To give you an idea of the savings, a dyed, sheared mink coat from Denmark sells here for $600.00. Swing coats, so popular in recent seasons, are fully stocked; so are those with detachable liners and fur collars. The store also packs in suede coats, fur hats, slippers, and boas. Yet this store is as much about service as it is savings; their de-furred payment plan and zero percent financing are very helpful options for those on a budget. Open Monday through Friday, 11:00 a.m. - 6:00 p.m. (until 7:00 p.m. on Mondays and Thursdays); Saturday, 11:00 a.m. - 5:00 p.m. During prime fur season (October - March), The Chicago Fur Outlet is also open Sunday, 12:00 p.m. - 4:00 p.m.

CYNTHIA'S CONSIGNMENTS LTD.
2218 North Clybourn Avenue, Chicago IL 60614. 773/248-7714.
The Lowdown: Cynthia is a former model (and one-time Miss Illinois) who has gone into the consignment business. So, you know she's got fashion sense and connections. From her own closet, and those of other models, she fills this bright, spare shop with lots of great used designer clothing. None of it is over two years old, and much of it is quite stunning. A blue suede skirt and top set by Peggy Martin was selling for $98.00; a two-piece plaid suit by Ann Taylor was $52.00; and a pair of Liz Claiborne houndstooth slacks was just $32.00. Shoes — in fine condition — included a pair of Escada grey linen-finish pumps for $32.00 and a pair of brand-new suede flats from Bloomingdale's private label for $18.00 (the original price tag, still intact, was asking $59.00). Some of the merchandise here is brand new, coming directly from manufacturers and designers. These tend to be overstocks from current lines, like an Anne Klein navy blue suit for $72.00; or a Biba skirt suit, originally $600.00, selling for (are you sitting down?) $62.00. Other great names you're likely to find here include Donna Karan, Calvin Klein, Chanel, Prada, Gucci, and Versace. Cynthia likes to keep prices at the low end, preferring to get clothes out of her store and onto her customers. There's also a bargain table, where you may see a yellow Polo sweater for $10.00, or a pair of Esprit print shorts for $8.00. There are lots of fancy dresses and formal gowns too, many of which can be rented as an inexpensive alternative to buying. The store also has one of the city's largest selections of designer bridal gowns with names like Vera Wang and Jim Hjelm gracing the racks. Gowns that sell for anywhere between $3,000 and $5,000 at the Ultimate Bride on Oak Street can be found here for as little as $550.00. Consignments run only 60 days, so the selection is always changing. Open Monday, 11:00 a.m. - 7:00 p.m.; Tuesday through Saturday, 11:00 a.m. - 6:00 p.m.; Sunday, 12:00 p.m. - 5:00 p.m.

THE DAISY SHOP
67 East Oak Street, 6th Floor, Chicago IL 60611. 312/943-8880.
E-mail address: daisyshop@aol.com. **World Wide Web**

address: http://www.daisyshop.com. **The Lowdown:** The Daisy Shop has got classy clothes to complement a classy neighborhood. Don't let the impeccable clothing or gorgeous boutique surroundings intimidate you; while The Daisy Shop has all the makings of a brand new clothier, they are actually a resale shop. The merchandise is comprised of both contemporary and vintage clothing and accessories and includes a great assortment of both fine and costume jewelry. All clothing has been barely worn and is in excellent condition; they wouldn't sell it here otherwise. Armani, Vera Wang, Ungaro, Krizia, Gaultier, Escada, and Chanel are just a few of the top-name designers you might stumble upon. But with price tags reflecting savings of up to 80 percent off retail, The Daisy Shop makes them affordable. While the prices here may not please the bargain-hunting masses, they are distinctively good for women who enjoy swaddling themselves in couture clothing. A large selection of Hermes scarves were seen for just over $200.00 apiece with another collection by the equally-notable Yves St. Laurent starting at just $65.00. Accessories are a particularly good bargain at The Daisy Shop; a classic Fendi shoulder bag was selling for under $150.00. A fantastic selection of vintage jewelry and accessory pieces were really priced right; Mr. C spotted a vintage ceramic pin from the 1950s for just $64.00. If you're looking to heat up that winter ensemble with a little bit of style, Mr. C saw the perfect thing: a pair of white vintage leather gloves for just $50.00. Even the cheaper of the department store chains don't afford such great savings. If you can't make it to the store itself, you can visit their Website and view several pages of online bargains. Unlike many resale shops that are cash only, The Daisy Shop accepts all major credit cards, making it a bit easier for you to enjoy the savings. The Daisy Shop claims that this is "where very gently worn, noble items find a second home." Perhaps they're referring to your home! Open Sunday, 12:00 p.m. - 5:00 p.m.; Monday through Saturday, 11:00 a.m. - 6:00 p.m.

DISGRACELAND

3338 North Clark Street, Chicago IL 60657. 773/281-5875. **The Lowdown:** Disgraceland is a college student's dream. The main attraction here is jeans – they've got 'em in all styles, shapes, and sizes. But, aside from the jeans, what they carry is used clothing from some of the stores most popular with the trendy young set including Banana Republic, Gap, and J. Crew. All of the clothing is in great condition, and would not be selling here otherwise. They've got clothes for men and women in styles to suit a night out on the town or a Friday workday. Disgraceland also carries new and used accessories (jewelry, scarves, purses, shoes, and belts). Open Sunday, 12:00 p.m. – 6:00 p.m.; Monday through Saturday, 11:00 a.m. – 7:00 p.m.

DUOMO MEN'S DESIGNER RESALE

2906 North Broadway, Chicago IL 60657. 773/325-2325. **The Lowdown:** While this chapter is usually overrun with shops strictly for women, it's nice to see that there are some consignment shops that specialize solely in men's clothing. Whether the lack of consignment choices is due to supply or demand, we'll never know, but at least we know there's one place where these generalities don't apply. Duomo carries high-end brand name clothing for work or weekends at prices that are pretty hard to beat. Brand names you're likely to come across include Giorgio Armani, Dolce & Gabbana, Ralph Lauren, and Prada. As the price of suits is probably one of the most costly expenses for a man in corporate America today, prices at Duomo can be particularly pleasing. Owned by the same folks who brought you Cynthia's Consignments (see separate listing), you can be sure that clothing is current and in fabulous condition; Duomo only accepts clothing that has been cleaned and pressed, and nothing in the store is over two years old. Much of the merchandise even comes directly from some of the city's most popular high-end men's retailers; it's brand-new, end-of-season merchandise that was not sold in the original store. Open Sunday, 12:00 p.m.- 5:00 p.m.; Monday through Saturday, 11:00 a.m. - 7:00 p.m.

ELLIOTT CONSIGNMENT
2465 North Lincoln Avenue, Chicago IL 60614. 773/404-6080.
The Lowdown: Like Hubba-Hubba (see separate listing), Elliott Consignment has the unique distinction of being operated by a mother-daughter team of owners. They carry lots of top name designers and, though they specialize in women's wear, they've got a nice selection of men's clothes too. In addition to clothing, you can also find an array of furniture and collectibles at fantastic prices. A free parking lot lets you start saving as soon as you pull up. The best place for a true Cheapster, however, is in the back room where already-low prices are reduced even further. Open daily, 10:00 a.m. - 9:00 p.m.

McSHANE'S EXCHANGE
815 West Armitage Avenue, Chicago IL 60614. 773/525-0282. ◆
1141 West Webster Avenue, Chicago IL 60614. 773/ 525-0211.
The Lowdown: In 1988, when pioneer Denise McShane Caffrey opened her eponymous stores, the idea of buying resale moved into the mainstream. Now considered one of Chicago's ultimate closets, she continues her innovations to this day. McShane's Exchange is a one-stop wardrobe destination for the ultra-high-power set. Denise is devoted to her customers. "I consign for women who really love to shop and resale and have everything, so I have to think about what will seduce them" says she. Her taste is impeccable, with offerings from such tasteful designers as Armani, Chanel, Gucci, Hermes, Kors, Prada, TSE, and Ungaro. Still, there's also lots of stuff from The Gap and the like, so there's surely something to fit everyone's budget. Items sell at one-third their original cost, with weekly sales that further reduce the prices by 10 - 90 percent. Mr. C spotted a number of great bargains like a butter-soft suede skirt by Dolce & Gabbana (with a retail price of $468.00) selling for $168.00. Also seen was a $2,800.00 cashmere/wool suit by Jil Sander for $88.00 and a Ralph Lauren sweater for an unbelievable $1.00! Denise certainly does mean what she says when she claims that her 'ridiculously low prices won't make you choose between getting dressed or paying the rent. So, again in the words of Ms. McShane Caffrey,

"If you can't afford your own designer wardrobe, buy someone else's." McShane's Exchange certainly affords you, the bargain-hungry, to do just that! Open Monday through Friday, 11:00 a.m. - 7:00 p.m.; Saturday, 10:00 a.m. - 6:00 p.m.; Sunday, 12:00 p.m. - 5:00 p.m.

MILLENNIUM CONSIGNMENT STORE
1545 North Wells Street, Lower Level, Chicago IL 60614. 312/664-4021. **The Lowdown:** Shopping at Millennium Consignment is a sheer joy. From the moment you descend the stairs and enter this winding shop, you'll be subjected to pleasantries and personal service not often seen in a city as bustling as this one. Walk in and the bargains just jump out at you. I spotted a variety of funky picture frames, elegant candleholders, and pretty home furnishings, all for under $10.00. While most of the store is dedicated to women, they do carry a good selection of men's clothes too. For women, there are plenty of suits, casual and dressy dresses, shoes in a variety of styles, and great inexpensive accessories. The men's section carries a slacks, shirts, suits, and coats. A particularly good bargain was a great ¾-length leather coat, in perfect condition, for $199.99. Millennium Consignment is starting to get a lot of vintage items in, and looking forward to receiving more. Like any consignment shop, there's definitely some searching involved to find the styles and sizes that complement you. But, with new merchandise arriving all the time, it pays to check back often. Call for hours.

RECYCLE IT!
1474 North Milwaukee Avenue, Chicago IL 60622. 773/645-1900. **The Lowdown:** Recycle it! is a designer resale boutique featuring fabulous men's and women's designer apparel at a fraction of the original cost. Located in the über-hip Bucktown/Wicker Park neighborhood, Recycle it! features "gently worn" clothing by contemporary designers including Prada, Diesel, and Gucci. There is something for everyone from the traditional to the eclectic. And while, for the most part, Recycle it! is considered a resale boutique, they carry a huge selection of brand-new merchandise from some of the area's hottest retailers at savings of up to 70 percent. If that kind of discount doesn't get you in a recycling kind of mood, I don't know what will! Open Sunday, 11:00 a.m. - 5:00 p.m.; Monday through Saturday, 11:00 a.m. - 7:00 p.m.

SELECTIONS
2152 North Clybourn Avenue, Chicago IL 60614. 773/296-4014. **The Lowdown:** An upscale resale shop featuring both consignments and designer samples, Selections is a fantastic place to buy anything from an office outfit to an evening gown at greatly reduced prices. It's also one of the few such shops which carry a good range of used men's designer clothes. The stuff is fancy; even fur coats are sold here, in season. As a matter of fact, this store has so much stock, they display only the appropriate clothing for each season. Men's fashions may include such items as a double-breasted Armani wool suit for $320.00; or brand-new silk ties, valued at $65.00 - $95.00, selling for

$16.00 - $20.00. Mr. C saw a sharp-looking dress shirt from Saks Fifth Avenue for just $14.00. Women have a much larger selection to choose from than the men. Mr. C was shown a Kasper linen skirt suit for $48.00, an Anne Klein II blazer in mustard and rust plaid for $60.00, and a white merino wool sweater by Henri Bendel for $28.00. Ladies will no doubt enjoy the good variety of shoes and accessories too, which include a pair of Via Spiga flats or Evan Picone dress pumps for $28.00; a Louis Vuitton bag, originally $300.00, reduced to $55.00. And there's a long display case of costume jewelry, like a pair of Austrian crystal earrings for $12.00. As you can see, things are priced to move. If they don't move after one month, prices are cut further and twice in their second month. All sales are final, and the store firmly maintains that prices are not negotiable. Open Tuesday through Thursday, 11:00 a.m. - 7:00 p.m.; Friday, 10:00 a.m. - 6:00 p.m.; Saturday, 10:00 a.m. - 6:00 p.m.; Sunday, 12:00 p.m. - 5:00 p.m.; closed Monday.

SUITSMART

115 North Wabash Street, Chicago IL 60602. 312/236-7848. ✦ 388 East Golf Road, Arlington Heights IL 60005. 847/290-8008. **World Wide Web address:** http://www.suitsmart.com. **The Lowdown:** Owner Dan Hooson had the idea of a shop that would cater to businessmen, in the business district, saving them big money on their business attire. This store combines all of the current trends, from recycling to computerized marketing analysis and a return to good old fashioned personal service. Suits and sportcoats by Bill Blass, Brooks Brothers, Givenchy, Ralph Lauren, Giorgio Armani, and many others sell here at bargain prices. If they were new, of course, they would each go for hundreds of dollars more; the amazing thing about Suitsmart, though, is that everything in here has been so well-kept that it all looks new. In fact, some shoppers don't even realize that these are used clothes. There are some new items, closeouts on smaller things like silk ties. Dress shirts, hosiery, and other accessories are here too. Suitsmart even offers bargain rates on alterations, having worked out a deal with a semi-retired tailor from Italy who prefers a relaxed workload. Hooson also buys used fine clothing from those willing to sell them. Open Monday through Wednesday, 9:00 a.m. - 6:00 p.m.; Thursday and Friday, 9:00 a.m. - 7:00 p.m.; Sunday, 11:00 a.m. - 4:00 p.m.; closed Saturday.

ULTIMATELY YOURS

2931 North Broadway, Chicago IL 60657. 773/975-1581. **The Lowdown:** This Lincoln Park resale shop offers top name designer clothing (Donna Karan, Armani, et al) at a fraction of what you'd pay at some fancy department store. Like many of the other shops listed in this chapter (Cactus Trade, Cynthia's Consignments, Duomo Men's Designer Resale – see separate listings), Ultimately Yours is part of the Chicago Upscale Resale Connection. The goal of C.U.R.C.? To provide resale customers with the highest quality clothing and best names at the lowest possible price. It's certainly a philosophy that works for me! While the store does carry clothing for both of the sexes, it's the racks of women's clothing that cover the most floor space. In addition to clothing, Ultimately Yours carries a great selection of shoes, jewelry, and other accessories. For men, Ultimately Yours has got the workday in mind; mostly what you'll find is a few racks of big name suits. While these prices can still be a bit high, it's the name that you're paying for. Are you willing to dish out a little extra cash to get the designers that people clamor for? That decision, my friend, is Ultimately Yours. Open Sunday, 12:00 p.m. - 5:00 p.m.; Monday and Thursday through Saturday, 12:00 p.m. - 6:00 p.m.; closed Tuesday and Wednesday.

Clothing: Men's & Women's

A & M FURS

620 West Roosevelt Road, Chicago IL 60607. 312/663-4305. **The Lowdown:** West of the Loop, this block of Roosevelt is sort of a discount district, with a little bit of everything, even furs. A & M Furs imports and makes some of its own merchandise, selling primarily to department stores; but you can save a bundle by shopping here directly. There are high-quality furs of every color and style for men and women, along with some leather fashions as well. A full-length men's mink coat imported from Finland, for example, was seen here for $2,500.00; in other stores, it may sell for as much as $7,000.00. In leather, Mr. C saw a black bomber jacket from Argentina, reduced from $1,250.00 to $495.00. There's also a half-price rack, for even better bargains. More importantly, the friendly folks in here are willing to negotiate a bit on their prices; you may be able to create a hot deal on a warm coat. Layaway plans are available, too, and A & M does storage, cleaning, and repair work on the premises.

BUY-A-TUX

615 West Roosevelt Road, Chicago IL 60607. 312/243-5465. **The Lowdown:** A member of the retail trade told Mr. C he considers this shop to be perhaps the only one of its kind in town - if not the entire country. Certainly, anyone who has more than one formal occasion in a year can benefit from buying a tuxedo rather than renting one repeatedly. Especially when you can save as much as 40 percent off the prices found in fancier specialty stores. These are snazzy duds indeed, including designer formal wear and the largest selection of formal accessories probably found anywhere. For example, a Jhane Barnes tuxedo was seen here for only $600.00. Joseph Abboud, Cole Haan, and other famous makers are well represented in this large store which, unlike most others on the block, is not a no-frills bargain joint. If those designers are fast company for you, even at reduced prices, don't despair. Buy-A-Tux offers quality tuxedos, complete with a cummerbund and bow tie, that start as low as $169.95. Buy-A-Tux also carries lots of shoes, cufflink and stud sets, and other accessories also at discount prices. They also have fashions for slightly less formal situations, and since they carry sizes up to 68XL, you are sure to find the perfect fit. Open daily.

CONCEPT FOR MEN

628 West Roosevelt Road, Chicago IL 60607. 312/341-0727. **The Lowdown:** Their slogan is "where quality exceeds price." Now that's a concept that more than just men can get used to. Concept for Men carries a large selection of discounted clothing from a stable of worldwide designers like Atlantic Connection, Versace, Medici, and Tundra. In addition to clothing, they carry a wonderful supply of hats and other accessories. Open daily.

FOX'S
2150 North Halsted Street, Chicago IL 60614. 773/281-0700.
♦ 9444 Skokie Boulevard, Skokie IL 60077. 847/673-8516.**World Wide Web address:** http://www.foxs.com. **The Lowdown:** A true Cheapster would probably walk right by the window of Fox's, not believing that – past the trendy storefront – there could lie a bargain or two. But sure as I am frugal, Fox's is all about – to put it in their words – "catching the thrill of a great buy." Fox's offers everyday fantastic prices on top designer clothes. For the most part, the labels have been removed (just a formality), but any true fashion maven will know who they're buying. Clothes are all completely in-season and in perfect condition. Prices are generally 50 - 70 percent off retail. Their enormous selection will surely suit any occasion or function whether it be work, leisure, travel, or something special. The Chicago store is open Sunday, 12:00 p.m. - 5:00 p.m.; Monday through Friday, 11:00 a.m. - 8:00 p.m.; Saturday, 10:00 a.m. - 6:00 p.m. The Skokie location is open Sunday, 12:00 p.m. - 5:00 p.m.; Monday through Wednesday, 10:00 a.m. - 6:00 p.m.; Thursday and Friday, 10:00 a.m. - 8:00 p.m.; Saturday, 10:00 a.m. - 6:00 p.m.

GINGISS FORMALWEAR OUTLET
542 West Roosevelt Road, Chicago IL 60607. 312/347-9911. **The Lowdown:** It pays to live in such a big city, especially when that city is the geographical center point of the business world. Tons of businesses choose to house corporate headquarters and large retail outlets in the Windy City because it is easily accessible for the rest of the country. Gingiss Formalwear, one of the nation's most reputable names when it comes to men's formal wear, has strategically placed an outlet right in the downtown area (you know all those Loop businessmen, they've got plenty of formal soirees to attend to). And what better way is there to make an entrance than in a fully paid-for tux? While Gingiss does carry a number of new tuxedos, it's the used ones where you'll find the best bargains. As they carry both name brands and names that are not so familiar, prices can flux accordingly. Open Sunday 11:00 a.m. - 4:00 p.m.; Monday through Friday, 10:00 a.m. - 6:00 p.m.; Saturday, 9:00 a.m. - 5:00 p.m.

HUBBA-HUBBA
3309 North Clark Street, Chicago IL 60657. 773/477-1414. **The Lowdown:** While the prices at Hubba-Hubba may sometimes be a bit pricier than at other local boutiques, the clothing is always on the cutting edge of fashion. That's because Ellen Freedman and Julie Schneider, the mother-daughter team that owns the store, are always on the lookout for the new "it" designer. They have inaugurated the careers of a number of up-and-coming designers who have gone on to make quite a name for themselves in the fashion world. And customers will benefit from this keen sense of fashion. With displays changing daily, there is always something new to see at Hubba-Hubba. They carry a great mix of new, retro-inspired, and selected vintage clothing, as well as a great selection of jewelry. Even if you're in a last-minute bind, you can always find a fantastic party outfit the night of the event, with great accessories to complement. Mr.

C spotted a great selection of shawls from $26.50 - $82.50. Repeat customers will benefit even more from some of the in-store promotions at Hubba-Hubba. Hubba dollars are generated with each buy and can be used (just as real money) toward future purchases. If it's your birthday (yes, they will ask for I.D.), they're also willing to throw in an extra discount for you. Now that's what I call customer loyalty.

IRV'S MEN'S STORES

431 North Orleans, Chicago IL 60610. 312/832-9900. ✦ 2841 North Laramie Avenue, Chicago IL 60641. 773/286-7293. ✦ 610 Milwaukee Avenue, Prospect Heights IL 60070. 847/459-8060. ✦ 7511 Lemont Road, Darien IL 60641. 630/910-1333. **E-mail address:** email@irvsmensstores.com. **World Wide Web address:** http://www.irvsmensstores.com. **The Lowdown:** This family-run business offers the best in current styles menswear at some of the city's best prices. Irv's refers to themselves as a price cutter. I say that Irv's is a bargain hunters dream come true. The service is attentive, friendly, and (as clothing retail has been in their blood for years) extremely knowledgeable. The enormous selection at Irv's offers shoppers an awful lot of styles and sizes to choose from, at prices that are 30 - 50 percent less that big-name department stores. They carry lots of brand names like Bill Blass, Chaps, Pierre Cardin, and Calvin Klein. You can pick up an all-wool suit for as little as $185.00. Separately, you can purchase sports coats and slacks in all your favorite materials: wool, gabardine, silk; Irv's stocks only the highest-quality fabrics. Slacks start as low as $55.00 and blazers can be had for just $125.00. For weekends and leisure time, Irv's carries a large selection of casual wear. For those cooler months, Irv's offers lots of outerwear at unbeatable prices, like leather coats for $250.00 and overcoats for $135.00. To complete the outfit, don't forget to check out the full line of accessories including ties, shoes, gloves, and scarves. Shoes start at under $40.00 a pair. For those little guys who are longing to be just like Dad, Irv's offers a boy's department (with just as wonderful savings) in their Prospect Heights and Darien stores. Also, for some extra special savings, walk up to the second floor of the Laramie Avenue location (a.k.a. Irv's Attic). Here, you'll find additional savings of 60 - 80 percent off Irv's already low prices! Call for specific location hours.

MARK SHALE OUTLET

2593 North Elston Avenue, Chicago IL 60647. 773/772-9600. **E-mail address:** mso@markshale.com. **World Wide Web address:** http://www.markshale.com. **The Lowdown:** Located in the Clybourn Corridor is the outlet store for this popular men's and women's clothier. It is as bright, fashionable, and well-stocked as any full-price store; the only difference is in the prices. In addition to its own lines, the Mark Shale Outlet mixes in bargains from other well-known brands. The styles here are mostly casual, for folks who are young and active... or who at least for those who want to project that image. Great prices can be found on items like men's wool sweaters and spring dresses for women, just a few months past their prime selling season.

There are some dressy and professional looks here as well: linen blazers for women were seen here for $100.00 off the original price. An Everything $9.00 table was laden with shirts, belts, socks, and silk ties. Toward the rear of the store is the Bumped, Bruised, and Dented area, with final sale merchandise at 50 percent off and more. While much of the merchandise is past season, there are also some damaged and irregular pieces. Mark Shale helps you out by clearly tagging the item as irregular, and documenting the flaw with a diagram. Also helpful is the large erasable sign over the cash register, highlighting the store's newest arrivals. And each week brings loads of special discounts for men and women. New merchandise is arriving all the time, so if you don't find something wonderful the first time around, don't be afraid to pop back in next week. In addition to weekly and monthly promotions, twice a year the outlet offers a "20 percent off everything in the store sale." Plenty of free parking only adds to the money-saving experience. Open Sunday, 12:00 p.m. - 5:00 p.m.; Monday through Friday, 10:00 a.m. - 8:00 p.m.; Saturday, 10:00 a.m. - 6:00 p.m.

THE MEN'S WEARHOUSE

48 East Walton Street, Chicago IL 60611. 312/482-9303. ◆ 25 East Washington Street, Chicago IL 60602. 312/263-2306. ◆ 2070 North Clybourn Avenue, Chicago IL 60614. 773/525-5942. **World Wide Web address:** http://www.menswearhouse. com. **The Lowdown:** Okay, okay so they might be one of those immediately recognizable chain discounters, but because men have such a hard time going out to shop in the first place, maybe the savings here will be an incentive. The Men's Wearhouse carries designer clothing and shoes at the very best prices. Suits by designers like Evan Picone, Chaps by Ralph Lauren, Pierre Cardin, and Oscar de la Renta can be found at 20 percent - 30 percent less than you would find in department and specialty stores. Designer 100 percent wool blazers cost $170.00 - $180.00. Been attending too many charity events (or proms for you younger chaps)? Instead of getting suited up every year for a tux and dishing out a decent amount to use it for one night, it might be worth your time and money to buy your own. At The Men's Wearhouse, 100 percent wool tuxedos start at $200.00, about as much as you would spend to rent it on three separate occasions. If you're job is following the trend of "business casual" days, then you may need to spruce up your wardrobe instead of rolling into work in shredded jeans and a T-shirt. You'll find wrinkle-resistant cotton twill pants for $30.00 and 100 percent cotton collar shirts priced $30.00 - $50.00. And don't forget shoes. Brand-name shoes like Bostonian, Dexter, Timberland, and Florsheim start around $70.00. Shopping at The Men's Wearhouse does pay off though. Should you gain or lose any weight in the future, have no fear about squeezing into that suit of yours. The Men's Wearhouse offers free re-alterations for any seam previously altered by them. They also provide on-premise tailoring and free lifetime pressing of clothing. What more could a guy ask for? Open Monday through Friday, 10:00 a.m. - 9:00 p.m.; Saturday, 10:00 a.m. - 6:00 p.m.; Sunday, 11:00 a.m. - 5:00 p.m.

MORRIS & SONS
555 West Roosevelt Road, 2nd Floor, Chicago IL 60607. 312/243-5635. **The Lowdown:** Morris & Sons is a goldmine of current-season couture, designer sportswear, suits, dresses, and accessories. Prepare to be astonished by the discounts and selection, and pleased by the knowledgeable, friendly service. This family-run business has been around for over 40 years, and specializes in Italian merchandise. For many prominent Italian designers, in fact, this is the only current-season discounter in the United States. Morris & Sons sells clothing from 30 - 70 percent below current, regular prices. How can they do that, you might ask? It's for a variety of reasons: One, because they buy direct; two, because of their low-rent location; and three, because they offer no tailoring services. Morris & Sons stocks over 4,000 men's suits alone, in everything from wool blends to cashmere. Dress shirts by famous designers are more than 50 percent off their retail prices, and athletic shirts are discounted by at least 30 percent. Men and women's leather and wool coats are similarly priced. Some of these are salesmen's samples, barely used, at even greater discounts. Mr. C spotted a women's two-piece suit marked down several hundred dollars from its retail price. At Morris & Sons, you can also save 50 percent on dress shoes, in traditional styles. For even better buys, visit their large clearance section where skirts regularly selling for $100.00 in department stores were slashed to just $25.00. If you've lived in the Windy City all your life or are a frequent visitor and never heard of this place, don't feel slighted; Morris & Sons saves more on its costs by not advertising. Trust me, they do enough business strictly through word-of-mouth. Once you spend $500.00 or more in the store, you'll be added to the mailing list and allowed into their private annual clearance sale.

MORT COOPER'S
161 North State Street, Chicago IL 60601. 312/332-8410. **The Lowdown:** At Mort Cooper's, you can look spiffy for just a few cents... well, almost! By not advertising, this Loop shop can afford to sell high-quality clothing for men, both career and casual, at inexpensive prices. The store has survived this way since 1921, operating mostly by word-of-mouth to draw in new customers. Free alterations, in addition to the personal attention given to shoppers, keeps them coming back. Not all of the brands here are well-known designers, but all of the looks are sharp and all of the quality is outstanding. While average-sized men will find a bonanza at Mort Cooper's, big and tall sizes can be hard to come by in this shop. None of the shirts I looked at had sleeves longer than 35 inches. Still, if you don't need such specifically-designed clothing, you can certainly find a trip here worth your while. Open Monday through Saturday, 9:00 a.m. - 5:15 p.m.

RAGSTOCK
812 West Belmont Avenue, Chicago IL 60657. 773/868-9263. **E-mail address:** ragstock@ragstock.com. **World Wide Web address:** http://www.ragstock.com. **The Lowdown:** While everyone has their own preference as to what type of stores they like to shop (new, used, vintage), Ragstock has secured all three

niches by making this an all-in-one store. For women, there are always-wearable tank tops for $4.99, ¾-sleeve T-shirts and peasant tops for $9.99, hooded zip-up sweatshirts for $18.99, and brand-new French cuffed blouses for $13.99. While a plaid miniskirt would go great with any of the above tops, Ragstock also had short velour skirts and long crêpe skirts for more formal settings. But don't think you can brave all four seasons with that wardrobe; don't forget to choose from a variety of wool and cotton sweaters ($19.99 - $24.99). Ragstock's coat department afforded great savings to both men and women: For women, brand-new ski parkas were selling for under $40.00; men should be thrilled to wrap themselves in a new bomber jacket for just $19.99 or a motorcycle-style jacket for just $10.00 more. If you're planning to make the nightclub scene, you can afford to order one more martini if you shop here. An array of funky shirts – perfect for a night of clubbing – were priced between $20.00 and $30.00. Open Sunday, 12:00 p.m. - 7:00 p.m.; Monday through Thursday, 10:00 a.m. - 9:00 p.m.; Friday and Saturday, 10:00 a.m. - 10:00 p.m.

RAINBOW SHOPS

2539 West Cermak Road, Chicago IL 60608. 773/376-8031. ◆ 4607 North Broadway, Chicago IL 60640. 773/271-0069. ◆ 3434 South Halsted Street, Chicago IL 60608. 773/927-8043. ◆ 201 East 47th Street, Chicago IL 60653. 773/373-2144. ◆ 1601 West Chicago Avenue 60622. 312/226-5799. ◆ 5619 Belmont Avenue, Chicago IL 60657. 773/889-7383. ◆ 2947 West Addison Avenue, Chicago IL 60618. 773/478-7901. ◆ Several other locations. **World Wide Web address:** http://www.rainbowshops.com. **The Lowdown:** This trendy chain carries a large selection of kids, juniors, and plus-sized apparel (up to size 24). Still, the clothes would probably be more befitting of a teenage daughter than a young-at-heart mom. Chunky-heeled sandals, shoes, and boots retail, on the average, between $10.00 and $20.00. Mr. C saw a pair of knee-high stretch boots for just $29.99. There was a large selection of more formal dresses, priced between $14.99 and $23.00. Junior and plus jeans in a variety of styles were priced under $25.00. For the kids, character tees were seen for $12.99, and Mr. C spotted a Mickey Mouse top and jean set for just $14.99. Rainbow Shops also carries a variety of equally-well-priced accessories including jewelry, hosiery, and bags. Get there during clearance time and you can find a range of clothing and accessories for under $5.00.

SAGRANI CLOTHIERS

540 North Michigan Avenue, Chicago IL 60611. 312/644-0604. **E-mail address:** SagraniCT@aol.com. **The Lowdown:** Sagrani Clothiers – located on the second floor of the Marriott – has been offering men some pretty generous discounts on well-known labels from around the world since 1972. Best of all, they cater to the hard-to-fit man and do lots of custom orders at prices that are still quite reasonable. Open Monday through Friday, 10:00 a.m. - 7:00 p.m.; Saturday, 10:00 a.m. – 6:30 p.m.

Clothing: Vintage Shops

BACKSEAT BETTY'S
1530 North Milwaukee Avenue, Chicago IL 60622. **Toll-free phone:** 877/222-5732. **E-mail address:** solyan@backseatbettys.com. **World Wide Web address:** http://www.backseatbettys.com. **The Lowdown:** Since old styles continue to resurrect themselves with each passing fashion season, shopping at a vintage store is a cost-effective way to stay trendy within a budget. Backseat Betty's offers a large selection of vintage clothing, accessories, and items dating back to the 1920s onward. Backseat Betty's carries some great selections from the early 20th century, like lots of fine silk and velvet eveningwear for under $200.00. That's a heck of a lot cheaper than you'll find at the local department stores, even with a sale! How about a gorgeous little black dress, covered in sequins, for just $60.00? Or a fabulous layered lace cocktail dress, for $35.00? Designer duds abound too; a velvet evening dress by Anne Klein was $50.00. A rack of lots of colorful dresses from the 1950s, in a variety of fabrics and styles, were seen starting at $25.00. Other great finds included strappy platform sandals, that have made a comeback as of late, dressy enough for even the most formal occasion and priced right at $30.00. A fantastic wool coat with fur collar and cuffs was seen, completely in-season, for $100.00. A collection of cashmere sweaters, in pullover, cardigan, and henley styles, were $45.00 - $55.00. Even in the dead of winter, Backseat Betty's keeps the dream of summer alive with an enormous selection of bathing suits in all your favorite styles including triangle top, halter, hip hugger, and zip-front. With prices between $20.00 and $35.00, you can afford to get a head start on summer. Backseat Betty's men's collection is sure to satisfy all types of dressers. They carry lots of suits and sport coats for as little as $50.00 apiece; vintage Adidas items for those who spend their time pumping iron; and great vintage leather items. Accessories include straw and Stetson hats for between $25.00 and $35.00, cashmere fedoras for $45.00, and a fun selection of bow and neckties. Women will love the enormous selection of eyeglass and sunglass frames, as well as lots of vintage handbags in hard-to-find fabrics like snakeskin. Open Sunday and Monday, 11:00 a.m. - 7:00 p.m.; Tuesday through Saturday, 10:00 a.m. - 9:00 p.m.

FLASHY TRASH
3524 North Halsted Street, Chicago IL 60657. 773/327-6900. **The Lowdown:** No matter what you call it (flashy trash, shabby chic), there's no denying that vintage clothing makes a statement. To make a statement of your own, a trip to Flashy Trash may be just the ticket. Designers and celebrities alike have been known to scout the racks here, looking for that one oh-so-special piece. But with prices like these, why not stock up? Flashy Trash carries an equal mix of contemporary clothing and vintage

finery. With clothing for both men and women, a trip to Flashy Trash is certainly an activity you can enjoy with anyone. Flashy Trash carries a variety of popular name brands like Diesel, Free People, Bulldog, Andrew Christian, and Lip Service. They carry a great selection of jewelry and accessories too, dating back to the early 1900s onward. If you like to make an entrance, Flashy Trash is the place to find an inexpensive outfit that will help you do just that! Open Sunday, 11:00 p.m. - 6:00 p.m.; Monday through Saturday, 11:00 a.m. - 8:00 p.m.

SILVER MOON
3337 North Halsted Street, Chicago IL 60657. 773/883-0222.
The Lowdown: Silver Moon could fit into the bridal wear category just as easily as vintage clothing. Though they are predominantly a vintage clothing shop, they carry enough unique wedding and evening gowns to make even the most popular of bridal shops jealous. In addition to the wedding and formal gear, they carry a good selection of designer vintage and antique clothing for both men and women. They also boast a fantastic supply of antiques and other vintage furnishings. Whether you're looking to decorate yourself or your home in styles and pieces that are truly unique, Silver Moon can offer you some fantastic and inexpensive options. Open Tuesday through Sunday, 12:00 p.m. - 6:00 p.m.; closed on Monday.

STRANGE CARGO
3448 North Clark Street, Chicago IL 60657. 773/327-8090.
The Lowdown: One of the few vintage stores in town that carries as much clothing for guys as it does for gals, Strange Cargo is a goldmine of clothes, shoes, accessories, and other neat and unusual toys and trinkets. Lots of men's vintage pants (including hard-to-find Levi's Sta-Prest) and women's dresses and shirts still have their original tags. For men, a black leather jacket, worn, but still sharp looking, is a steal at $69.00. If you can't afford a vacation to the islands this year, new and vintage Hawaiian shirts will make you look like you've been there. They even have muumuus and leis. If cold weather gear is what you need, they have plenty of hats, gloves, and scarves for under $10.00. A pair of genuine leather combat boots are just $30.00. Ladies will be impressed by the eclectic collection of dresses, from a '60s psychedelic go-go dress to a new red leopard-print slip dress. The perfect little black dress, be it vintage or brand new, can be found for less than $30.00, which will leave you plenty of money to buy a pair of shoes to match. New leather Converse sneakers are a mere $8.00, and a pair of black Mary-Janes were seen for only $10.00. There are also never-worn, vintage platform shoes from the '70s, even in men's size 14! Strange Cargo is a good bet for that perfect '70s outfit, (if there is such a thing), from a sexy silver jumpsuit to a big collar leisure suit. Jewelry and other accessories are plentiful too. Leather belts are $14.00, and there is an array of bags and purses from $9.00 to $19.00. Men's and women's sunglasses (including rhinestone cat's eyes and gold Elvis shades) are only $10.00. There is also a lot of neat stuff to decorate your home, such as beaded curtains and posters; or how about a Mexican wrestling

figure with a bobbing head? Most of the items that fit into the neat stuff category are under $5.00 - that includes Pez, trading cards, magnets, and even a *Dukes of Hazzard* watch. Now, there's an ensemble for you.

UNA MAE'S FREAK BOUTIQUE

1422 North Milwaukee Avenue, Chicago IL 60622. 773/276-7002. **E-mail address:** unamae@enteract.com. **World Wide Web address:** http://unamaes.com. **The Lowdown:** While it *is* listed under "Vintage Shops," Una Mae's Freak Boutique has enough new merchandise to place this listing elsewhere. But, regardless of the age of the clothing, there's no denying that this stuff is funky! The store carries clothing for both men and women, plus a variety of accessories and great gift items. Styles – for both men and women – range from everyday streetwear to special occasion formalwear. The clothing at Una Mae's is definitely geared toward the younger set. Whether the look you're going for is definitive James Dean or pure Tony Manero, Una Mae can help get that perfect outfit on your back. A wide range of accessories and gift items include beautiful beaded bags, sunglasses, stylish belts, gorgeous cufflinks, and vintage flasks and lighters. There is also a wonderful selection of scented candles and incense from Japan, India, and Tibet.

WACKY CATS

3109 North Lincoln Avenue, Chicago IL 60657. 773/929-6701. **E-mail address:** wackycats@hotmail.com. **World Wide Web address:** http://www.wackycats.com. **The Lowdown:** Selling funky vintage dresses, suits, undergarments, and shoes from the 1940s through the 1970s, this Lake View shop sells boutique-like vintage clothing at non-boutique prices. The store caters mainly to women, but there are some great men's suits and overcoats here, too. A men's lined leather bomber jacket, for example, was seen for only $55.00, and a snazzy sharkskin suit for $75.00. For the ladies, a metallic silver and black tank dress was just $19.00. You may only have to pay $9.00 for a pair of Levi cut-offs, or $18.00 for a wool houndstooth jacket by h.i.s. Wool stirrup pants, with the Carson Pirie Scott label, were seen for a trifling $19.00. To go with the pants, an Italian mohair and wool blend sweater will keep you warm for only $21.00. Open Sunday, 12:00 p.m. - 5:00 p.m.; Monday through Friday, 12:00 p.m. - 7:00 p.m.

Discount Department Stores

BENNETT BROTHERS, INC.
30 East Adams Street, Chicago IL 60603-5676.
312/621-1600. **Toll-free phone:** 800/621-2626. **World Wide Web address:** http://www.bennettbrothers.com. **The Lowdown:** Bennett Brothers was originally founded in 1884 as a jewelry store. Today, Bennett Brothers carries an enormous selection of merchandise at prices that will be hard to beat no matter where you shop. Bennett Brothers made their name when, after introducing *The Blue Book* catalog, businesses across America became Bennett Brothers customers. While they deal mostly in mail order, the Bennett Brothers warehouse and distribution center (located in The Loop) is open to the public five days a week. In addition to the jewels that started it all, Bennett Brothers now carries a varied selection of electronics, appliances, sporting goods, furniture, and collectibles. In a single visit you are likely to find sparkling white diamonds at cut-rate prices, freshwater pearl necklaces for under $100.00, and 14-karat gold watch (men's and women's) by top designers like Jules Jürgensen at half their original price. Great collectibles, like the adorable Precious Moments collection, can be found for as little as $14.95 apiece. It's no wonder Bennett Brothers has been serving the corporate gift market for so long; with high-quality goods, at some of the lowest prices around, and a large enough selection to match anyone's taste, Bennett Brothers is a truly inexpensive one-stop shopping experience. Open Monday through Friday, 8:15 a.m. – 5:00 p.m. (with extended holiday hours during December).

BLOOMINGDALE'S
900 North Michigan Avenue, Chicago IL 60611. 312/440-4460.
The Lowdown: If you've ever read any of the other *Mr. Cheap's* books, you probably know that one of my favorite pastimes is bashing stereotypes. When it comes to department store shopping, many stores can easily earn an "expensive" reputation, simply because they carry high-quality goods and fashions. I have worked very hard to get to the truth of the matter and let you know – honestly – which department stores you can and cannot afford to shop in. I will start the dispelling of stereotypes with Bloomingdale's for two reasons: One, it is one of my favorite big-name stores in which to hunt for bargains; and, two, it starts with the letter "B" so, in the alphabetical progression of things, it comes first. In any city or town in any state in the country, there never seems to be a small Bloomingdale's! Floor after floor, you continue to find more and more merchandise. This 900 North Michigan anchor is no exception; the store never seems to end. Because of the store's enormity, it takes a ridiculous amount of clothing to fill the racks; and, because the store prides itself on carrying the latest fashions, the stock is ever-changing. Henceforth, as new merchandise is constantly coming in one

door, it needs to be going out another. At any time of year, with every turn of the corner, you'll be faced with Bloomingdale's sale racks. You can expect to find anything and everything on these racks, at prices that will make your jaw drop. A recent visit found extraordinary bargains in every department; in the home store, towels by the likes of Calvin Klein and Ralph Lauren were selling for $9.99 apiece while everything in the luggage department was practically being given away at prices 25 – 60 percent below retail. Racks upon racks of clothing, in all sizes, were on sale at prices up to 65 percent below the original tag price. Ralph Lauren, Tommy Hilfiger, and Adidas are names that are sure to please even the most discerning kids; men will love saving on Calvin Klein, Ralph Lauren, and DKNY; women won't be able to choose a favorite maker with discounted offerings from such prestigious brands as BCBG, Max Studio, Laundry, Vivienne Tam, and Easel. Handbags are another great area where women can save big; while bigger names like Kate Spade might be impossible to come by cheaply, there are always lots of purses and bags by Donna Karan and Calvin Klein that are bargains just waiting to be purchased. Bloomingdale's is one of the biggest when it comes to size, selection, and savings.

BURLINGTON COAT FACTORY
4520 South Damen Avenue, Chicago IL 60609. 773/254-0054. ♦ 7340 West Foster Avenue, Chicago IL 60656. 773/763-6006. **World Wide Web address:** http://www.coat.com. **The Lowdown:** If you're not too familiar with Burlington Coat Factory, don't make the mistake of many first-timers: they offer more than just coats! Since its founding several decades ago, Burlington Coat Factory has grown into one of the nation's largest (and most prolific) brand name discounters. While each store varies in selection, you're bound to find more than just a jacket or a pair of slacks. Everyday discounts of 25 - 60 percent keep customers coming back time and time again. When Burlington Coat Factory says they cater to every member of your family, they mean it! They offer clothing for infants, children, juniors, and grown-ups, and in a range of typically hard-to-fit sizes as well. They've got your fashion week covered with new and trendy looks to keep you looking your best in a board room, bar room, or ballroom. If you live outside of Chicago, there are plenty of suburban locations as well, so it would be a good idea to check your local phone book. Call for specific location hours.

CARSON PIRIE SCOTT
One South State Street (at Madison Street), Chicago IL 60603. 312/641-7000. ♦ 120 South Riverside Plaza, Chicago IL 60606. 312/744-5380. ♦ 7601 South Cicero Avenue, Chicago IL 60652. 773/581-5555. **The Lowdown:** Once again, we find a big name department store stocking lots of affordable goodies. Throughout the store, big *SALE* signs should lead you right to the bargains. In the luggage department, a random sale had a five-piece set by Ricardo Beverly Hills (originally $500.00) for $149.99. And this isn't a clearance deal, with only one set left, no siree. Just as if you were paying full price, you have full reign to choose color, etc. Many other luggage pieces, single and in sets, were 50

percent off original prices. In the shoe department, Mr. C spotted a sale so unbelievable, I had to pinch myself to be sure I wasn't dreaming. Carson Pirie Scott's full line of Dr. Martens was 25 percent off. If you don't know to "ooh" and "ahh" at that simple fact alone, let me explain a little something: Dr. Martens *NEVER* go on sale. Sure, you can find them at several discount shops with a reduced price tag, but they never actually go on sale!! Since the store is comprised mainly of clothing, there were plenty of reduced prices in these departments as well. On average, prices were slashed 30 – 60 percent. For women only, several racks of Calvin Klein pajamas and nightgowns were reduced by as much as 60 percent. A bin full of gorgeous neckties by designers like Donna Karan sported reductions of 30 percent or more. As department stores like Carson Pirie Scott carry just about everything you could possibly want or need, it pays to check prices here when scouting out the best

VALUE CITY
4701 North Harlem Avenue, Harwood Heights IL 60443. 708/867-6011. • 8716 South Cicero Avenue, Oak Lawn IL 60453. 708/857-1080. • 1101 West North Avenue, Melrose Park IL 60160. 708/345-2686. • 9000 West Golf Road, Niles IL 60714. 847/635-5000. **World Wide Web address:** http://www. valuecity.com. **The Lowdown:** When a word like *value* appears in the company name, Mr. C heeds extra special attention. For every room and body in the home, Value City has got the brands you love. Best of all, merchandise is discounted 30 - 70 percent from what other retailers charge. In addition to clothing, shoes, and accessories for the entire family, you'll find discounted home furnishings too. Plus, a sporting goods department will ensure you good physical fitness as well as good financial fitness. With more than 100 stores across the country, it's no wonder this department store is becoming a household name. I think their slogan says it best: "It's your money. Get more for it." I couldn't have said it better myself. Call for specific location hours.

WORLD DISTRIBUTORS
3420 North Milwaukee Avenue, Chicago IL 60641. 773/777-2345. **E-mail address:** info@worlddist.com. **World Wide Web address:** http://www.worlddist.com. **The Lowdown:** This is a wholesale distributor of everything from socks to stereos, priced at cost so that you can enjoy the same prices that dealers get. The products are all first-quality, in current models and styles. A men's Rolex-style watch originally selling for $75.00 was recently priced under $14.00. Lots of other jewelry can also be found including 14 karat gold and sterling silver. You'll also find a great variety of small appliances, such as a rechargeable shaver for under $5.00. You want more? Well, World Distributors has baby furniture, toys, sporting goods, leather wallets and purses, luggage, tools, car accessories, Christmas decorations, and tons more, all stocked right there on the showroom shelves. It's all at wholesale prices, meant for other stores to purchase in quantity, but also available to you without any membership deals or special rules. Pick up a catalog. Open Monday through Saturday, 9:00 a.m. - 6:00 p.m.; Sunday, 11:00 a.m. - 5:00 p.m.

ZEMSKY'S
2740 West Cermak Road, Chicago IL 60608. 773/247-4600.
- 3539 West 26th Street, Chicago IL 60623. 773/522-1222.
- 1700 West 18th Street, Chicago IL 60608. 773/226-6230.
- 4181 South Archer Avenue, Chicago IL 60632. 773/247-1422.
- 7601 South Cicero Avenue, Chicago IL. 773/585-8270.

The Lowdown: Since its founding in 1958, Zemsky's has been offering a large selection of clothing for the entire family at affordable prices. They're one of the largest supplier's of Dickie's brand apparel. While they specialize in school uniforms for children, they also carry a large selection of everyday wear for Mom, Dad, and junior! Zemsky's also carries a large selection of home furnishings that are priced well enough to leave a little money left over in your pocket. Call for specific location hours.

Electronics

AUDIO CONSULTANTS
839 North Clark Street, Chicago IL 60611. 312/642-5950. **E-mail address:** clarkstreet@ audioconsultants.com. **World Wide Web address:** http://www. audioconsultants.com. **The Lowdown:** One option that often goes overlooked when it comes to making an audio/video purchase is buying used equipment. We immediately conjure up ideas of broken equipment and irreplaceable parts, but this is not always the case. At Audio Consultants, you can purchase the highest quality name brands and products (that have been used) at prices that won't break the bank. Most of the merchandise is either trade-ins or demo equipment. If you love those open box sales that many big chains love to have, this is pretty much the same deal. And all merchandise comes with some sort of guarantee (though the number of days varies from product to product). Where else could you find a deal like a Pioneer 50-disc changer (originally $450.00) with a two year warranty for $275.00? A demo model of a Sony minidisk player (originally $350.00 and in good condition) with a one year warranty was seen for $249.00. The sales staff will be happy to help you and will let you know (honestly!) what kind of condition the equipment is in. They carry everything from speakers to amplifiers to surround sound equipment. If you're looking to beef up your home theater, this is one place where you could do it for a reasonable price. Sometimes, it just doesn't make sense to buy new... especially when you've got a store like Audio Consultants in the area. Open Tuesday through Saturday, 10:00 a.m. - 6:00 p.m. (until 9:00 p.m. on Thursday); closed on Sunday and Monday.

CENTRAL CAMERA COMPANY
230 South Wabash Avenue, Chicago IL 60604. 312/427-5580. **Toll-free phone:** 800/421-1899. **The Lowdown:** Open since 1899, Central Camera Company is a third generation, family business, and it definitely does know what it's doing. Selling both new and used cameras, along with scads of lenses and other equipment, it's a heaven for both amateur and professional photographers alike. The selection of used equipment offers great bargains, with stock changing constantly. Most used items also include a one-year Central Camera warranty. A 35 mm Olympus OM-10 camera with a 50 mm lens was seen for $150.00; and a Canon FTb with a 50 mm lens, was priced at $180.00. Central Camera also maintains an impressive selection of used Leicas. Even secondhand, these are still pricey; but they last a lifetime, and Leica fans find them worth every penny for those silent shutters. Used Canon zoom lenses are priced in the $100.00 - $200.00 range, depending on age and condition. Pentax and Konica lenses are also well-represented, as is Oriental paper (25 sheets of the 8x10 portrait paper runs about $11.00) as well as printing papers by Kodak, Agfa, Ilford, and Forte. They also carry a wide selection of magnifiers, binoculars,

scanners, printers, and digital cameras. Best of all, if you make your purchase through the power of plastic (credit cards, that is) you can get free shipping to almost anywhere in the United States.

CHICAGO COMPUTER EXCHANGE

5225 South Harper Avenue, Chicago IL 60615. 773/667-5221. **E-mail address:** ccex@ripco.com. **World Wide Web address:** http://www.ccexchange.com. **The Lowdown:** It's a little tricky to find this place, located in the planned community of Harper Court just below Hyde Park Boulevard. But once you find it and make your way inside their solid blue front door, it's a lot of fun to wander around the cluttered shop, where every square inch is piled high with various bits of old computers. Chicago Computer Exchange is one of the few stores in all of Chicago selling new and used computers, a relatively new retail arena and an important one for those who think they'd have to refinance their car in order to get into computing. Well, just like a used car lot, this store sells older machines that have been reconditioned (with warranty!) and still have plenty of life left in them. If you don't need a computer with all the latest bells and whistles, you can save a lot of money this way. For example, if all you want is something basic for word processing, spreadsheets, and the like, you can get an older IBM system complete with keyboard, monitor, and dual floppy disk drive for $500.00. It's not fancy. But if you only intend to write a college thesis, or want an inexpensive starter system for your children, this will do quite nicely. Something more recent you might find could be a Macintosh LC II system, with a 40-megabyte hard drive and 4MB of RAM (apologies to non-techies) for $850.00. You may even come across some used laptops; Mr. C saw a Toshiba 3200SX laptop here for just $750.00. Used printers start around $75.00; a used HP Laserjet printer may go for only $300.00. All used items carry a 90-day store warranty. If you already have a computer, you may want to check out Chicago Computer Exchange for its stock of used innards. Their service department can even upgrade your old model to the very latest specifications for a lot less than buying new components. Service is really the name of the game here; even if you want to buy a new computer, they will discuss your needs, check around with national distributors, and piece together a complete system at the lowest possible price. Open Monday through Thursday, 10:00 a.m. - 7:00 p.m., Friday and Saturday, 10:00 a.m. - 5:00 p.m.; closed Sunday.

COMPUTER DISCOUNT WAREHOUSE

315 West Grand Avenue, Chicago IL 60610. 312/527-2700. **Toll-free phone:** 800/829-4CDW. **World Wide Web address:** http://www.cdw.com. **The Lowdown:** CDW offers great prices on computers, peripherals, disk drives, memory, software, floppy disks, and pretty much anything else you could ever want or need. They are authorized resellers for major brands like Toshiba, NEC, Texas Instruments, Hewlett Packard, and Panasonic, though they do not sell Macintosh products. Desktop personal computers (not including monitor) start at under

$600.00; get a complete package, or design your own system. CDW carries loads of laptops, printers (both laser and inkjet), scanners, projectors, and digital cameras. Whatever your home or office computing needs, CDW has got it at a great price. Everything they sell goes for way below retail. CDW is great in that it combines a discount approach with a retail store atmosphere, where you can talk to knowledgeable salespeople and see everything before you make a decision. There is a very good selection in all areas, with over 15,000 products in stock. All of the latest software titles are here at discount as well. CDW has a full support staff, including a free technical helpline for its customers. You can order by phone and online, too. Most orders are shipped the same day. CDW has been doing right by consumers for more than 15 years, and has been favorably written up in such prestigious publications as PC *Magazine* and *The New York Times*. Open Monday through Friday, 8:00 a.m. - 7:00 p.m.; Saturday, 10:00 a.m. - 5:00 p.m.; closed Sunday.

HELIX CAMERA AND VIDEO

310 South Racine Avenue, Chicago IL 60607. 312/421-6000.
• 233 North Michigan Avenue, Chicago IL 60601. 312/565-5901.
• 1515 East 53rd Street, Chicago IL 60615. 773/532-3030.
• 11040 South Kedzie Avenue, Chicago IL 60655. 773/238-6464.
E-mail address: info@helixphoto.com. **World Wide Web address:** http://www.helixphoto.com. **The Lowdown:** There's no doubt you've probably heard of Helix Camera and Video: it's one of the nation's largest discount photography stores. While mail order and the Internet have allowed Helix to gain this reputation, the only place you can actually step inside a retail location and browse around is in Chicago and the surrounding suburbs. Luckily for you, there's plenty to see here. Helix's main store (on Racine Avenue) offers eight floors of photography and video equipment. In addition to 35mm and video cameras, Helix carries a large selection of darkroom equipment, camera accessories (bags, film, etc.), lighting, and binoculars. If you're planning on doing a little underwater filming or picture-taking, Helix has got everything you need at the right price. They carry an especially impressive selection of used equipment, affording you even further savings. You'll find such sought-after names as Canon, Konika, Leica, Pentax, and Tamron. Call for specific location hours.

INTERNATIONAL VIDEO & ELECTRONICS

2355 West Devon Avenue, Chicago IL 60659. 773/338-9033.
The Lowdown: One trip to this 3,000-square-foot showroom and I guarantee you won't go home empty-handed. As the name suggests, most of the products here are from overseas manufacturers. What the name doesn't tell you is that in addition to all that "Video & Electronics" implies (televisions, VCRs, video cameras, stereo equipment), they also carry an enormous selection of small and large appliances. At International Video & Electronics, you can find great deals on kitchenwares, washers and dryers, and refrigerators. International Video & Electronics also offers electronics repair services.

JOHN'S ELECTRONICS
5322 North Broadway, Chicago IL 60640. 773/878-3716.
The Lowdown: Panasonic, Yamaha, Technics, JVC, Sony, and Minolta are among the big names available at reduced prices at this shop. You'll find anything from small to large here, from a Sony cordless phone for $39.95, to a big screen projection television, also by Sony, selling for $1,159.00. A Yamaha EQ-70 model graphic equalizer was seen here for $149.00. One boom box, with a double tape deck by Sony, was $59.00; another, by JVC, combined a CD player with a double tape deck for $129.00. Put some Maxell XLII 90 Gold blank tapes in; they're $1.49 each. John's even sells Sony Beta Max VCRs, which you *really* can't find anywhere else. And with lots of high-end electronics, they're sure to have the latest technology. In the camera department, Mr. C found a Minolta Freedom 202 35mm camera, with automatic features, for just $59.00; and a Canon Sure Shot Telemax 35mm camera, with a zoom lens, for $149.00. John's is also a good place for budget-priced cameras, like the Minolta Memory Maker, a fully automatic 35mm model. It comes in a kit which includes batteries and film, for $39.95. Good prices on film and accessories, too. Open Monday through Saturday, 10:00 a.m. - 7:00 p.m.

SATURDAY AUDIO EXCHANGE
2865 North Clark Street, Chicago IL 60657. 773/935-8733. **Toll-free phone:** 888/553-8733. **World Wide Web address:** http://www.saturdayaudio.com. **The Lowdown:** Saturday Night is alright for something like shopping at Saturday Audio Exchange. High-fidelity buffs, listen up. Beginning years ago as a resale shop for used stereo equipment, Saturday Audio Exchange now sells a large variety of new, used, and second-quality new audio components, all at low prices. And they carry many of the finest names in the business, such as Kef, Onkyo, Kenwood, Monitor Audio, and NHT. A new Harmoan Kardon 5-disc CD changer (still in the box) was recently spotted for under $300.00. Other equipment included a discontinued NAD receiver for $169.00 (list price $299.00) and discontinued PSB speakers for $299.00/pair (list price $500.00). However, the specialty at Saturday Audio Exchange is turntables. The stock changes weekly and often includes tons of used and one-of-a-kind pieces of equipment. This place is even pleasant for the casual browser, since salesmen are knowledgeable and helpful, but not paid on commission. The limited hours at Saturday Audio Exchange help keep the business brisk and the overhead low; hence, the great deals. Open Thursday, 5:30 p.m. - 9:00 p.m.; Saturday, 10:30 a.m. - 5:30 p.m.; Sunday, 12:00 p.m. - 4:00 p.m.

TRIANGLE CAMERA
3445 North Broadway Street, Chicago IL 60657. 773/472-1015.
The Lowdown: This Wrigleyville store does a lot more than sell film. Triangle Camera sells a complete line of new equipment and accessories at very competitive prices; many items are sold at or near cost. Owner Linda Ogata doesn't see fit to keep needling with her prices; she'd rather have the business, and sell out the current stock at a low price. So, you never know what hidden

bargains may be here. But there are other ways to save here, too. One option is the used camera department, where you may find all kinds of goodies at up to half their original prices. There are usually several used flash units and lenses available too. Used equipment carries no store warranty, but what you can do is rent these cameras and apply the rental fee to the cost of buying. Some of the cameras in this section may even be unused, discontinued models; these are sold at dealer cost, and still carry the full manufacturer's warranty. For the serious photographer, the Triangle Camera Club entitles you to discounts on film processing, studio darkroom rates, plus bulk prices on new film. Open daily.

20TH CENTURY TV & STEREO CENTER
1615 West Montrose Avenue, Chicago IL 60613. 773/528-1728. **The Lowdown:** Husband and wife technology wizards, Mitch and Ursi Lewczuk, run the sort of sales and repair shop that is quickly dying out in this age of shopping malls and chain stores. They buy and sell high-quality new and used components. You can get a new Sansui Vintage amplifier for $795.00, originally priced $1250.00, or a Tascam cassette deck for $695.00, originally priced at $1,600.00. If you're still lagging behind the times in technology, then you may need to replace the belt on your record player, in which case, 20th Century TV & Stereo Center can help. Mitch believes passionately that it is better to buy something that's built to last, even if it's an older, used piece; and why not buy it from these folks who can keep it going forever? After all, they have a staff of certified electronic engineers. They have the service manuals for everything ever made, which they've acquired as other stores have gone out of business. And they have 15,000 replacement needles for phonograph cartridges. They've got it all. Open Sunday, 12:00 p.m. - 6:00 p.m.; Monday through Saturday, 10:00 a.m. - 8:00 p.m.

Flea Markets

ASHLAND SWAP-O-RAMA

4100 South Ashland Avenue, Chicago IL 60609. 708/344-7300. **The Lowdown:** Expect to encounter at least 20,000 people if you hit Ashland Swap-O-Rama on any given weekend, particularly in the summer. The flea market is open year-round and generally holds about 600 vendors inside and, in warm weather, 400 vendors outside. Any type of knick-knack or gadget you can think of is sold here at some point. For just a $1.00 entrance fee, it's worth the risk that you won't find what you're looking for. Open Thursday, 8:00 a.m. - 7:00 p.m.; Saturday and Sunday, 7:00 a.m. - 4:00 p.m.

BUYER'S FLEA MARKET

4545 West Division Street, Chicago IL 60651. 773/227-1889. **World Wide Web address:** http://www.chicagofleamarket.com. **The Lowdown:** As one of the largest indoor/outdoor flea markets in the Chicago area, Buyer's Flea Market is also one of the most popular. Since 1980, Buyer's Flea Market has been serving up some of the sweetest deals in town on clothing, jewelry, electronics, and collectibles. After you've worked up an appetite from all that shopping, Buyer's Flea Market has got a great food court that offers more than just the standard fast-food fare you might expect. With more than eight acres worth of goods, Buyer's Flea Market is sure to make a buyer out of you! They offer a large parking lot with plenty of free parking, and there's a CTA bus that will practically drop you on their doorstep. Open Saturday and Sunday, 8:00 a.m. - 5:00 p.m.

KANE COUNTY FLEA MARKET

Kane County Fairgrounds, Route 64 & Randall Road, St. Charles IL 60174. 630/377-2252. **World Wide Web address:** http://www2.pair.com/kaneflea. **The Lowdown:** If you're serious about flea marketing, then a trip to St. Charles' Kane County Flea Market is definitely a good idea. Though the flea market is more than an hour outside of Chicago, it is one of the best and biggest in the Midwest. This is the place where you can find just about anything. Antiques and collectibles are just the beginning, there are all sorts of odds and ends. Food is served all day and the flea market is never cancelled. Admission is $5.00 per person, free for children under 12. Kane County Flea Market operates the first Sunday of every month and the preceding afternoon. Open Saturday, 12:00 p.m. - 5:00 p.m.; Sunday, 7:00 a.m. - 4:00 p.m.

NEW MAXWELL STREET MARKET

Canal Street (between Taylor Street & Depot Place), Chicago IL. 312/922-3100. **The Lowdown:** For more than 100 years, Maxwell Street Market has been one of Chicago's most treasured traditions. Their new location on Canal Street (hence the "new" in their name) and scaled down size hasn't slowed them down a bit. Every Sunday, more than 400 vendors that come here to hawk their wares to the throngs of customers. You'll find everything from clothing to food to toys. As the market has kind of an ethnic flair, you'll also find lots of unique and inexpensive ethnic arts. In better weather, you can even shop to the sounds of some great blues musicians playing in the background: regular performers include Willie James' Band, David Lindsey's Band, and Piano C. Red's Flat Foot Boogie Band. Open every Sunday, 7:00 a.m. - 3:00 p.m. *$Cash Only$*

WOLFF'S INDOOR FLEA MARKET

2031 North Mannheim, Melrose Park IL 60160. 847/524-2180. **The Lowdown:** Each week, more than 7,000 people cross over the old Chicago cobblestone entryway to shop at Wolff's Indoor Flea Market. With 350 vendors selling their wares, there is always an enormous assortment of quality antiques, collectibles, and new and used merchandise to choose from. Wolff's Indoor Flea Market has a huge supply of sports cards and Beanie Babies. To further entice the collector, Wolff's Indoor Flea Market brings sport card and collectible toy shows to the grounds the second and fourth weekend of every month. Located just a half hour outside of the city, it's a short drive and a worthwhile one at that. Free parking is just one of the many amenities at Wolff's Indoor Flea Market. At the time this book went to press, the Wolff family was eagerly awaiting the completion of their Antique Mall and Flea Market (open daily). By the time these words reach your eyes, it should be open. Call for more information. Shop for gifts, shop for necessities, shop for yourself, shop for fun! Admission is $1.00 for adults, $.50 for seniors and children, and free to children under six. Open Saturday and Sunday, 8:00 a.m. - 4:00 p.m., year-round.

WOLFF'S OUTDOOR FLEA MARKET

6920 North Mannheim (between Touhy & Higgins), Rosemont IL 60018. 847/524-9590. **The Lowdown:** Just six miles from Wolff's Indoor Flea Market in Melrose Park (and bordering Chicago's O'Hare Airport) is Wolff's Outdoor Flea Market. Owned and operated by the Wolff family for more than 10 years, this well-known flea market is a familiar sight to those traveling I-90. A wide variety of quality new, used, antique and collectible merchandise is what you'll find here including clothing, furniture, jewelry, electronics, books, crafts, and tools. There's even lots of stuff to keep the kids entertained; Wolff's Outdoor Flea Market offers a great selection of toys, beanbag toys, and sports cards. Plus, they'll be astonished as they watch the planes take off and land at O'Hare. With more than 450 dealers to haggle with, there's bargains to be had by all! Plus, there's plenty of food and free parking. Admission is $1.00 for adults, $.50 for seniors and children, free to children under six. Open Sunday, 7:00 a.m. - 3:00 p.m. April through October.

Flowers & Plants

ALY'S POSEY PATCH
654 West Diversey Parkway, Chicago IL 60614. 773/281-7455. **Toll-free phone:** 800/875-BUDS. **The Lowdown:** The only thing cuter than the name might be their slogan: "Nice Flowers From Nice People at Nice Prices.'" Aly's specializes in flowers from Holland; and they offer same day delivery, 7 days a week. In addition to flowers, they carry a great selection of balloons and reasonably-priced fruit and gourmet baskets. Aly's phone lines are open and ready to take your order 24 hours a day.

FLOWER BUCKET
1100 West Belmont Avenue, Chicago IL 60657. 773/935-9773.
* 158 West Washington Street, Chicago IL 60602. 312/346-9773.
* 1375 East 53rd Street, Chicago IL 60615. 773/955-5700.
* 1164 North LaSalle Street, Chicago IL 60610. 312/943-9773.
Toll-free phone: 888/271-1300. **World Wide Web address:** http://www.flowerbucket.com. **The Lowdown:** You've probably heard by now that the Flower Bucket sells long-stemmed roses for an amazingly cheap $9.99 a dozen, cash and carry. Their extra fancy bouquets are nothing to sneeze at either, starting at just $3.99 with the larger bunches usually selling for about $7.00. Fancier stems, like irises, were recently selling for $7.00 a bunch and super-healthy spider plants with plenty of offshoots were just $10.00.

ROSEXPRESS
804 West Washington Boulevard, Chicago IL 60607. 312/563-0060. * Sears Tower, 233 South Wacker Drive, Lower Level 1, Chicago IL 60606. 312/575-8660. **Toll-free phone:** 800/LONG-ROSE. **World Wide Web address:** http://www. rose-express.com. **The Lowdown:** If the name didn't give it away, this florist specializes in long-stemmed roses. Their philosophy is simply to "sell the highest quality flowers at the lowest possible price while providing the best customer service." They certainly make every effort to keep everyone happy too. A delivered box of long-stemmed roses averages $39.99 and is delivered by tuxedo-clad drivers, just to make the occasion more romantic. (Keep in mind that prices vary due to market fluctuations and certain holidays.) Even if you're a procrastinator, your lucky lady doesn't have to miss out, because ROSExpress offers same day delivery service Monday through Saturday for orders placed before 1:00 p.m. So if you're still wondering why you shouldn't order from the local florist down the street, consider the fact that ROSExpress actually fills orders directly with the flowers they have sent to them from Ecuador. They don't gather orders simply to hand off to potentially inept florists. These people want to see you and your loved one happy. And if you foresee yourself having to apologize or profess your love several times over the year, then you'll ultimately benefit from the Frequent Flower program that each new customer is

automatically enrolled in. After you've ordered 12 dozen roses, your next dozen is free. Oh, it also helps if your loved one lives within the Loop since delivery is free there.

SMITH & HAWKEN
1780 North Marcey Street, Chicago IL 60614. 312/266-1948.
World Wide Web address: http://www.smith-hawken.com.
The Lowdown: You should feel privileged with a visit to Smith & Hawken; mainly a catalog operation, this outlet is one of only two in the nation. Housed in an old gas pumping station, the Smith & Hawken outlet is just a patio's walk away from the main retail store. Here, you'll find discontinued merchandise from Smith & Hawken's nationwide network of stores at prices that are sure to make the flowers bloom. In addition to seeds and plants, Smith & Hawken carries a phenomenal selection of gifts and accessories for the avid and occasional gardener. Weeders, wellies, and watering cans are just a few of the gorgeous items you'll be able to find at a discount. Open Monday through Friday, 10:00 a.m. - 7:00 p.m.; Saturday and Sunday, 10:00 a.m. - 6:00 p.m.

Food

AFFY TAPPLE
7110 North Clark Street, Chicago IL 60626. 773/338-1100. **The Lowdown:** No, the name is not a mistake. If you don't know about Affy Tapple, you should! The company makes some of Chicago's most beloved confections including delicious taffy apples, chocolate covered frozen bananas, and a number of other chocolate concoctions. This location is their plant, where they house a discount factory store in the front. It's like one big dented can aisle of a grocery store; perfectly edible (and always delicious) items that have been returned are sold for a fraction of their retail price. Open Monday through Friday, 9:00 a.m. - 5:00 p.m.; Saturday, 8:00 a.m. - 12:00 p.m.; closed Sunday. *$Cash Only$*

BLOMMER'S CHOCOLATE FACTORY
600 West Kinzie Street, Chicago IL 60610. 312/492-1336. **The Lowdown:** Cooks who work with chocolate do their shopping here. They rave about how Blommer's chocolate melts better than any of the stuff you can get in the grocery store. It costs a heck of a lot less, too. What more could anyone ask for? Well, how about free chocolate? Samples of hard candy and chocolate chips are yours for the munching in the store, while pocket change will pick you up two pounds (that's right, two pounds) of cocoa powder; great for baking and for making homemade hot chocolate. A bag of Blommer's darker cocoa, made with beans imported from Sudan, is inexpensive as well. The store offers several kinds of chips: regular semi-sweet chips, butterscotch-flavored, and white chocolate. Ardent chocoholics can buy a 10 pound block of chocolate (dark, milk, or white) for right around $17.50. Go nuts! Speaking of which, the store has also created unusual gift sets of nuts and candies. How about a miniature chocolate golf caddy, with dyed white-chocolate coated golf balls? Stop in and see these truly cheap deals for yourself. Open Monday through Friday, 9:00 a.m. - 5:00 p.m.

BYBLOS 1
5212 North Clark Street, Chicago IL 60640. 773/271-1005. **The Lowdown:** One of several great bakeries in Andersonville, Byblos 1 is a combination bakery-grocery-deli selling many grains, spices, and nuts in bulk, which can save you bundles. Some of the great buys seen here were Aris olive oil, just $7.99 a gallon, and basmati rice for $1.29 a pound. Legumes and beans are also available in bulk. Go nuts with the roasted pistachios ($3.99 a pound) and almonds ($2.99 a pound). Byblos 1 also has a wall of fresh spices for sale, blowing away regular grocery store prices. For example, curry is only $2.99 a pound, about the same you'd pay for a tiny canister of the stuff at a grocery store. For baked goods, a package of Byblos-brand pita bread (regular or whole wheat) is $1.00; thyme bread is $3.00 for six pieces; and spinach pies are $4.00. Open Sunday, 9:00 a.m. - 2:00 p.m.; Monday through Saturday, 9:00 a.m. - 8:00 p.m.

GREAT HARVEST BREAD COMPANY

2126 Central Street, Evanston IL 60201. 847/866-8609. ◆ 1050 South Arlington Heights Road, Arlington Heights IL 60005. ◆ 847/590-1111. 192 West Gartner, Naperville IL 60540. 630/369-5115. ◆ 736 Lake Street, Oak Park IL 60301. 708/848-5700. **World Wide Web address:** http://www.greatharvest. com. **The Lowdown:** The philosophy at Great Harvest is sort of a five-step program: 1) Be loose and have fun. 2) Run fast to help customers. 3) Bake phenomenal bread. 4) Create strong, exciting bakeries. 5) Give generously to others. They've got it all down pat at Great Harvest Bread Company. Aside from one of the friendliest staffs in town, you'll find some of the area's best fresh-baked bread. There's an amazing variety of breads here; they're all made with only the freshest ingredients and they're all delicious.

NUTS ON CLARK

3830 North Clark Street, Chicago IL 60613. 773/549-6622. ◆ 222 South Riverside, Union Station Food Court, Chicago IL 60606. ◆ 318 West Adams Street, Chicago IL. 190 North State Street, Chicago IL. **World Wide Web address:** http://www. nutsonclark.com. **The Lowdown:** From the original store location (and corporate headquarters) on North Clark Street, Nuts on Clark has branched out into smaller locations around the city, established a substantial mail-order business, and is now operating in cyberspace. All this in 20 years! The vast selection here may drive you crazy, but you'd be nuts not to get your pistachios, almonds, and even chocolates and popcorn at Nuts on Clark. Buying all of their merchandise in bulk allows them to pass great savings along to their customers. Some of the goodies you can afford to squirrel away are Turkish pistachios for $9.99 a pound (if you want them unshelled it'll cost you $1.00 more), squash seeds for $3.99 a pound, and sweetened banana chips for $4.79. Macadamias are under $16.00 a pound, probably as cheap as you'll find; peanuts in a shell are priced at $2.99 a pound. Not all the candies are made on the premises, such as the wide selection of Jelly Belly flavors; but the store's volume purchasing allows them to sell these for only $5.99 a pound. Cholesterol-free candies, sugarless items, and carob-covered nuts and sweets are the focal point of the back room, where you'll also find a miniature shrine to the Cubs and autographed photos of Nutty fans from coach Mike Ditka to The Who's Roger Daltrey. Meanwhile, gift boxes for every occasion are a specialty here, so stop in or call to check out their wide selection of prices.

OAK PARK FARMERS MARKET

460 Lake Street, Oak Park IL 60301. 708/445-3340x2279. **World Wide Web address:** http://www.oprf.com/ farmersmarket. **The Lowdown:** Unfortunately, this listing can only be enjoyed five months out of the year. But buying fresh produce from the Oak Park Farmers Market is well worth the wait. In fact, there's much more than just produce here. Oak Park Farmers Market sells cheeses, vinegars, honeys, freshly-made donuts (definitely worth a taste), indoor and outdoor plants, and flowers as well. Plus, there's a whole lot of bluegrass

music and fun going on, making this 10 mile trip a true pleasure. For over 25 years, Oak Park Farmers Market has been serving up some of the city's freshest and most delicious locally-grown fruit to visitors from all over. Everything here is homemade and tasty, from the fresh juice and coffee to the variety of homemade cheeses. You can even pick up a T-shirt, apron, or tote bag (designed by local artists) to prove your visit. Special events make a trip to Oak Park Farmers Market a real family affair. Plus, the nearby Oak Park Visitors Center (see separate listing) offers plenty of tours and historical sites to help you make a day out of the journey. Oak Park Farmers Market is held every Saturday from June through October, 7:00 a.m. - 1:00 p.m. The market is held rain or shine and is located on the northwest corner of Elmwood and Lake Streets. For visit their Website.

RICCI & COMPANY
162-164 West Superior Street, Chicago IL 60610. 312/787-7660.
The Lowdown: Ricci & Company prides itself on being one of the oldest wholesale nut companies in the Midwest (they've been around for nearly 80 years), a mark of their success. Why anyone would want to buy nuts, candy, and chocolate in a grocery store and pay top dollar is beyond me. At Ricci & Company the prices are lower and the quality is higher. The nuts are roasted fresh daily, and they stock quite a variety. Whole cashews cost $5.35 a pound; compare that to the canned cashews sitting on the shelf of the local market. Jumbo blanched peanuts, raw or salted, are $2.20 a pound, and shelled pistachios go for $6.00 a pound. If candy better suits your taste buds, you can save a bundle by paying just $1.20 a pound for spice drops or $2.40 a pound for chocolate-covered raisins. Whatever your liking, and wherever you live (in the U.S.), Ricci & Company can provide you with a savory snack. Open Monday through Friday, 7:00 a.m. - 4:30 p.m.; Saturday, 7:00 a.m. - 11:30 a.m.

SARA LEE BAKERY OUTLET
6210 North Western Avenue, Chicago IL 60659. 773/973-6210.
♦ 7650 West Touhy Avenue, Chicago IL 60631. 773/763-4785.
♦ 4028 West 59th Street, Chicago IL 60629. 773/581-9408.
♦ 742 East 87th Street, Chicago IL 60619. 773/783-6585. **The Lowdown:** These outlets sell baked goods which have been replaced in supermarkets and convenience stores by fresher packages, even though they haven't yet reached their expiration dates. By shopping here, you can save as much as 50 percent off the supermarket prices on the full range of Sara Lee baked goods, pound cakes, chocolate cakes, pies, danish, cheesecakes, bagels, and croissants. In recent years, Sara Lee has branched out into other kinds of packaged foods too including deli meats and frozen dinners, some of which you may also find here. You can save even more by purchasing in bulk quantities. Open daily.

SCHMEISSING BAKERY
2679 North Lincoln Avenue, Chicago IL 60614. 773/525-3753.
The Lowdown: If you go to Schmeissing Bakery, be sure and try their butter cookies, which are heavenly, whether plain or chocolate-dipped. The dipped cookies are actually two cookies

separated by a filling, and they are all decorated with colored, shredded coconut. These go for $8.25 a pound, which translates to about 30-40 cookies if they're dipped, or double that if they're plain. Schmeissing Bakery's white butter-top bread is $1.69 a loaf, tortes start at $12.95, and layer cakes are priced at a reasonable $9.99 and up.

SUPERIOR NUT & CANDY CORPORATION

1111 West 40th Street, Chicago IL 60609. 773/254-7900. ♦ 4038 North Nashville Avenue, Chicago IL 60634. 773/282-3930. **The Lowdown:** Everything in this store's name is true. You can save lots of money by purchasing these fine nuts and candies out of bulk dispensers, with a wide variety to choose from. Fresh roasted in-the-shell peanuts, for example, are just $1.19 a pound; raw Brazil nuts go for $2.89 a pound. And an assortment of roasted mixed nuts (the good ones, without any peanuts) sells for $4.89 a pound. Jumbo cashews are a bit pricier, but then, that is always the case; at $5.99 a pound, they're still better here than at other places. Sometimes, Jumbo cashews go on sale for as low as $3.99 a pound. You can also find related items, like trail mix for $2.49 per pound, and Hawaiian Delight for the same price, a mix of dried fruits, peanuts, and macadamia nuts. Freshly ground natural peanut butter sells for $1.79 a pound. All of these nuts are roasted in cholesterol-free oil, in Superior's own factory. Lest your sweet tooth be ignored, there is a treasure trove of candies here, too. They bear such familiar names as Tootsie Roll and Mary Jane, just $1.99 a pound; a 5 pound bag of Gummi Bears for $8.95; and jelly beans, $1.29 a pound. Superior also carries a selection of sugar-free and salt-free candies at $4.99 per pound. Open Monday through Saturday.

SWEDISH BAKERY

5348 North Clark Street, Chicago IL 60640. 773/561-8919. **The Lowdown:** Up in Andersonville, this bakery invariably has a line running straight out the door. These folks don't seem to mind the wait; they take advantage of the free coffee to the right of the counter. You'll find that the Swedish Bakery is well worth the wait, given their unbeatable pastries and prices. Choices include egg twist bread, skradda kaka, a sweet rye bread, limpa, and kringles. Even the fanciest items on the list aren't too pricey. Open Monday through Thursday, 6:30 a.m. - 6:30 p.m.; Friday, 6:30 a.m. - 8:00 p.m.; Saturday, 6:30 a.m. - 5:00 p.m.; closed Sunday.

Furniture:
Home & Office

AFFORDABLE PORTABLES
2608 North Clark Street, Chicago IL 60614. 773/935-6160. **The Lowdown:** This family-run store has been around for over two decades, specializing mainly in futons, sofas, and contemporary furniture. Solid wood and veneer products are available. Though some of the furniture is made of particleboard, the finishes here are more realistic-looking than those in other inexpensive stores, and solid wood and veneer products are available. Factory seconds, mixed in among the first-quality items, will save you even more bucks. The store is equally crowded with tons of merchandise and lots of customers. Futon frames start as low as $70.00. Mr. C spotted a sofa-style wood futon frame with arms selling for $200.00. About 50 different hardwood styles were seen with a couple of metal frames mixed in. There were sofas priced at $399.00 and $499.00, about $100.00 less than retail. Other bargains included such items as desks for $99.00 and queen-size platform beds for $149.95. They also carry bookcases, television carts, tables, chairs, lamps, and Mexican-style rustic furniture. Open Sunday, 12:00 p.m. - 5:00 p.m.; Monday and Thursday, 10:30 a.m. - 8:00 p.m.; Tuesday, Wednesday, and Friday, 10:30 a.m. - 7:00 p.m.; Saturday, 10:30 a.m. - 6:00 p.m.

AMERICAN OFFICE FURNITURE
805 North Milwaukee Avenue, Chicago IL 60622. 312/666-6779. **Toll-free phone:** 800/300-6779. **World Wide Web address:** http://amof.com. **The Lowdown:** American Office Furniture's 10,000-square-foot showroom provides ample space to display their merchandise, not to mention their huge savings. With all this room, it's no wonder they have one of the largest selections of high-quality office furniture and accessories available. The savings are unbelievable. On a recent visit, I found an executive leather high back chair (part of the La-Z-Boy Voyager Series) priced at $625.00, 45 percent less than the manufacturer's list price. Similar savings were found off the list price of a National Arrowood Laminate 2100 Series full pedestal arch top desk; the price tag here read less than $800.00. It's savings like these that pop up all around the store. American Office Furniture is a haven worth a look for anyone starting up a new business, or for those who are simply looking to improve upon (the furnishings in) an existing one. Call for hours.

ARONSON FURNITURE, APPLIANCES, AND ELECTRONICS
3401 West 47th Street, Chicago IL 60632. 773/376-3400. ◆ 4630 South Ashland Avenue, Chicago IL 60609. 773/376-3401. ◆ 5657 West Belmont, Chicago IL 60634. 773/889-0312. ◆ 8530 South Cottage Grove, Chicago IL 60619. 773/873-8999. ◆ 2301 West 95th Street, Chicago IL 60643. 773/445-1888. ◆ 2750 West Grand Avenue, Chicago IL 60612. 773/645-1600. ◆ 1379 North

Milwaukee Avenue, Chicago IL 60622. 773/235-9000. ◆ 6122 North Clark Street, Chicago IL 60660. 773/381-0800. **The Lowdown:** Since 1940, Aronson Furniture has been offering major brand name furniture, appliances, and electronics for the home. Over the years, it has grown into one of Chicago's most popular retailers, Aronson hasn't lost sight of its own humble beginnings. This is the kind of place for shoppers who want to stretch their budget, but want good value for their money. The merchandise selection features the latest in high-style furniture, brand name appliances, and state of the art electronics. From a few selection pieces to a full room, Aronson delivers it all. Unlike many other retail chains, Aronson also offers appliances and electronics with brand names such as Frigidaire, Amana, Whirlpool, RCA, Zenith, among many others. Additionally, Aronson prides itself on its customer service and prompt delivery. Aronson is well-known for their special financing specials; one offer may be for two years of interest free financing while another may allow no payments for up to six months. Notable sales that should make you stand up and take notice include their Half Price Sale, Warehouse Sale, and No Credit Refused special. All stores are open seven days a week and guarantee a credit plan that meets the needs of you and your family. Still, no matter how big they get, Aronson Furniture sees the future of their store as innovative, high-style, quality furniture at affordable prices.

THE BOMBAY COMPANY

308 East Rand Road, Arlington Heights IL 60004. 847/259-3583. **World Wide Web address:** http://www.bombayco.com. **The Lowdown:** Chances are you've wandered by the window of The Bombay Company and eyeballed a number of items you thought were out of your monetary reach. With this clearance center, the attainability of these items is completely within your financial means. Discounts range anywhere between 30 and 60 percent off. That's right, the sleek and sophisticated furniture, accessories, and creative gifts that you'd find in the retail stores can be found here at a fraction of the price. Since The Bombay Company specializes in classic styles, much of the inventory may be past season, but it's never out of style. Open Sunday, 11:00 a.m. – 5:00 p.m.; Monday through Friday, 10:00 a.m. – 9:00 p.m.; Saturday, 10:00 a.m. – 6:00 p.m.

DIRECT OFFICE FURNITURE WAREHOUSE

5041 North Western Avenue, Chicago IL 60625. 773/271-3000. ◆ 7232 North Western Avenue, Chicago IL 60645. 773/465-3300. **World Wide Web address:** http://www.directofficefurniture. com. **The Lowdown:** This duo of warehouses has an incredible amount of office furniture, stacked into row after row, in several rooms, upstairs and down. The Ravenswood location sells a mix of new and used stock, either one of which can save you lots of cash; the Far North branch deals primarily in used merchandise. Among the bargains in new items, a recent sale featured a variety of products by Hon, one of the leading manufacturers in the business furniture business. Several types of filing cabinets were as much as 50 percent off their retail prices; like a four-drawer letter-size model (with a list price of $222.00) selling for $99.00. The legal-size version was reduced from $260.00 to $129.00. Ergonomic chairs – in a variety of styles – were on sale too. How about one with padded armrests and a pneumatic lift, marked down from $230.00 to $126.00. Basic models were as low as just $79.00. New executive desks start from $149.00 everyday, with many choices in the $250.00 - $750.00 range; still several hundred dollars below retail. Direct Office Furniture also sells lines like Sauder assemble-it-yourself furniture; some of these desks can be had for a mere $149.00. Computer tables begin at just $65.00 each, for a rolling metal stand model. In used furniture, at either location, you can find basic office chairs from $20.00, and upholstered models in the $50.00 - $75.00 range. Mr. C saw a handsome oak-laminate executive's credenza for $250.00, very slightly scuffed; other desks can be as cheap as $50.00, perfect for the startup office. And dozens of file cabinets start at right around $50.00. And we haven't even gotten to the basement yet. Down in this rather musty area, you'll find older, more banged-up pieces, some of which you can probably get for a song. Poke around through more desks, chairs, filing cabinets, and bookshelves and you may uncover a hidden treasure; Mr. C saw a four-foot wide drafting table, still in quite good shape, for $350.00 (but probably negotiable). There was even a big old schoolteacher's desk and a rusty set of gym lockers. Other pieces include folding banquet tables, conference tables, fireproof files and safes, stacking chairs, and lateral files, both new and used. Direct Office Furniture also has a limited selection of office accessories, such as bookends, letter trays, and the like. The 7232 Western location hosts public auctions on Tuesday evenings, where you can get real dirt-cheap deals. Open Monday through Saturday, 9:30 a.m. - 5:30 p.m.

EUROPEAN FURNITURE WAREHOUSE

2145 West Grand Avenue, Chicago IL 60612. 312/243-1955. **World Wide Web address:** http://www.eurofurniture.com. **The Lowdown:** Sometimes you have to go a bit out of your way to find something out of the ordinary. West of downtown, European Furniture Warehouse is a 70,000-square-foot treasure trove of modern, fancy furniture at fantastic savings. These living room and dining room pieces can be as much as 20 - 60 percent below retail prices. Why? Because this family operation makes and sells copies of trendsetting designs by Mies van der Rohe, Breuer, and others. A chaise lounge by Le Corbusier, made to sell elsewhere for $1,129.00, was seen here for $799.00 in leather or dappled ponyskin coverings. A Biedemeier chest with a marble top, normally priced over $1,500.00, cost just $995.00. A stack of Bauhaus-style Wassily chairs (in chrome and grey, tan, or black leather) was on sale for $329.00 each. The store offers an impressive variety of coffee tables, sectional sofas, dining sets, and more. Upstairs in a loft space, European Furniture Warehouse displays a collection of traditional English and French designs. A French country-style writing desk in burled walnut was a handsome find at $1,200.00, well below its list price of $2,000.00. The Warehouse also recently opened up the second floor of the building, with three new galleries for bargain-hunting connoisseurs: Old Plank Road Antiques, Big City Rugs, and Traditions Gallerie. In addition to stylish furniture, the owner evidently has a taste for sports cars. One side of the warehouse is stocked not with Le Corbusiers, but with Corvettes, lovingly (and noisily) being restored during Mr. C's visit. Somehow, these seem to complement each other perfectly. Open daily.

GENTLY USED OFFICE FURNITURE
1300 West North Avenue, Chicago IL 60622. 773/276-6200. **The Lowdown:** Gently Used Office sells both new and used office furniture and accessories, all at discount. "We cater to the entrepreneur," manager Steven Schwartz is proud of saying. "The kind of person who wants to set up an office quickly and cheaply." Indeed, whether that may be a corner of your apartment or a downtown suite, there's plenty here to check out. Mr. C saw an L-shaped executive's desk by Alma, for instance, which might have sold for $2,000.00 originally, on sale for just $500.00. It was in very good shape, and quite impressive-looking. Smaller desks, with retail prices over $1,000.00, often sell here for around $200.00. And chairs are priced at $5.00 and up. There are file cabinets in all sizes and shapes, from such top manufacturers as Steelcase; originally $500.00 - $1,500.00, they are in the $150.00 - $400.00 range here. The previous location of Gently Used Office Furniture featured a huge, dusty basement stacked with older items at even cheaper prices; not just furniture, but all kinds of rare and unusual office equipment. The current location doesn't have a basement, but there is still an area piled high with this corporate flotsam and jetsam. Gently Used Office Furniture also sells new furniture including everything from ergonomic chairs to conference tables and modular systems, all readily available at discount prices. They stand prepared to beat the prices of any competitors. Parking is free and easy to find, too. Open Monday through Friday, 10:00 a.m. - 6:00 p.m.; Saturday, 10:00 a.m. - 4:00 p.m.; closed Sunday.

HOME 1*2*3
222 West Kinzie Street, Chicago IL 60610-4419. 312/661-0124. **World Wide Web address:** http://www.home123furniture.com. **The Lowdown:** From a $9.00 brass magazine rack to $99.00 Italian beechwood dining chairs, you'll find a lot more than just sofas and loveseats here, and all are high-quality in classic and contemporary styles. The store is simple to find, located right across the street from the Merchandise Mart. They have a very eclectic mix of direct import furniture from Italy, Scandinavia, and Indonesia, at very low prices. A cherrywood Shaker-style coffeetable is just $109.00, and a big, comfy sofa upholstered in a soft burlap-like material was seen for $500.00. For elsewhere around the house, an Italian wood/glass dining table was $399.00; a six-drawer cherry dresser was $599.00; and six-foot tall halogen torch lamps were just $19.00. A recent special sale included a computer desk with built-in keyboard, printer stand, and bookcase for just $299.00 (list price $450.00). There's not enough room to display everything on the main floor, so check out the lower level room for more bargains. How do they manage

the savings? The Home 1*2*3 Store buys directly from manufacturers, and in many cases you have to do your own assembly. Since they buy direct, you can pick out your own fabric on upholstered items, too. More bonuses: free popcorn to munch on while shopping, and a sense of humor evident on the assembly ratings tags attached to each piece, ranging from Easy to Don't Make plans. Home 1*2*3 also has its own free parking lot nearby. Open Monday through Friday, 9:30 a.m. - 6:00 p.m.; Saturday, 11:00 a.m. - 6:00 p.m.; Sunday, 12:00 p.m. - 5:00 p.m.

HUFFORD FURNITURE

310 West Washington Street, Chicago IL 60606. 312/236-4191.
The Lowdown: Wow! What a place. If big name, traditional furniture for the home is your style, you can save yourself a lot of money by purchasing it here. Hufford has long been known only to the most inside of the insiders, but has more recently opened its doors to a wider audience, winning rave reviews in the process. Fancy brands like Sherrill, ernhardt, and many others can be bought in this huge warehouse in the Loop, at discounts of up to 40 percent below list price. Make no mistake: these pieces were expensive to begin with and, technically, they're still not cheap. But you can save hundreds, even thousands of dollars by shopping here, and this furniture will be heirloom material for generations to come. Wander around through dining room table and chair sets, hutches and cabinets, bedroom wardrobe units, chests and desks, cocktail tables for the living room, and all the rest, in real mahogany, cherry, walnut and other rich woods. And yes, many of the larger items are more than a thousand dollars below their retail prices. Open Monday and Thursday, 8:30 a.m. - 7:00 p.m.; Tuesday, Wednesday, and Friday, 8:30 a.m. - 5:30 p.m.; Saturday, 9:30 a.m. - 3:30 p.m.

INTERIORS ON CONSIGNMENT

1809 West Webster Avenue, Chicago IL 60614. 773/384-0769.
The Lowdown: The amazing thing about this store is the consistently high quality of its merchandise. Owners Ellen and Kenneth Kohn say that people often stroll in and scarcely notice that everything here is used, and it really does look like a designer showroom. That's because they are very selective about which items they'll take in; they personally visit the homes of the people who want to sell their furniture through this store. Items must be in excellent condition, and not everything makes the cut. Each piece is priced at one-third to one-half below the value of a comparable new version; and, in order to keep things moving, the price is further reduced by 15 percent after one month. After two months, additional discounts are available. The Kohns clearly know their stuff, because even as fussy as they are, this large store is packed with traditional and contemporary furniture, paintings, jewelry, and other estate items. Among the items Mr. C found during his visit was a Barcelona chair and ottoman set by Knoll, valued at $9,000.00 new; here, it was selling for $4,000.00. A European-style formal dining table, with eight matching leather chairs, was seen here for $3,000.00 and could easily cost almost twice as much. And don't worry, not

everything here sells in the thousands. A handsome antique wash-basin stand in solid oak was seen for $298.00; a bow-front mahogany chest with two sets of double doors was $260.00; and a butcher-block rolling cart, never used, was $159.00. There are also things like halogen lamps, table lamps, ceiling fixtures, mirrors, headboards, and much, much more. It's a beautiful shop just to browse. New items are added frequently; a bulletin board displays photos of incoming pieces that have been scouted and are soon to arrive... another smart touch by this well-run business.

KRAUSE'S CUSTOM CRAFTED FURNITURE
2111 North Clybourn Avenue, Chicago IL 60614. 773/935-3900.
The Lowdown: Take a seat. You'll have to wait a bit to get a sofa or chair from Krause's, but that's because everything here is made to order (it can take about a month for orders to arrive from Krause's factory in California). They offer a choice of about 1,000 different upholstery styles, including Ralph Lauren and Laura Ashley imitation fabrics. The frames have a lifetime guarantee, and you can even save a bit more when the store holds frequent promotional sales. Mr. C found a handsome leather sofa for $999.00, reduced from an original $1,349.00; fabric-upholstered sofas run from about $600.00, and chairs, about $349.00. Many other kinds of items are available here to finish outfitting any room, such as coffee tables and lamps. These are not factory-direct, though, and the prices show it.

MAR-JEN FURNITURE
1536 West Devon Avenue, Chicago IL 60660. 773/338-6636.
The Lowdown: At this Uptown store, you'll find a range of low- to mid-range priced furniture. You may see European-style sofa and loveseat sets, with a choice of fabric coverings, for as low as $399.00; a dinette table and two chairs for $79.00; or a solid butcher-block table and four chairs for $139.00. Modern-looking leather sofas start under $600.00; put a halogen torch lamp beside one for just $15.00, one of the lowest prices I've seen anywhere. Much of the furniture here is modern in style, with lots of glass tops and such, but there are plenty of traditional looks available as well. Upstairs, in a low-ceilinged loft space, Mar-Jen Furniture has its clearance area of leftovers and floor samples. Many of these are scuffed or even broken, but don't be surprised if you find a genuine treasure or two: Mr. C spotted a mirror-top end table reduced from $200.00 to $139.00. Mar-Jen Furniture offers free delivery to any part of the city, north or south. Free layaway plans are available, too. Open Sunday, 11:00 a.m. - 5:00 p.m., Monday and Thursday, 10:30 a.m. - 8:00 p.m.; Tuesday, Wednesday, and Friday, 10:30 a.m. - 7:00 p.m.

MIKE'S FURNITURE
1259 North Ashland Avenue, Chicago IL 60622. 773/276-0599.
World Wide Web address: http://www.usedappliance.com.
The Lowdown: There's not too many places in the city that can rightfully claim to have some of the best prices in town, Mike's Furniture is the exception. With an enormous supply of used furniture and appliances, Mike's Furniture can get their hands on

just about any size, style, or color appliance you are looking for. Where else but at a used furniture store could you find a complete full-size bed set for $99.00 or a three-piece living room set with sofa, loveseat, and chair for under $200.00? Mike's has furniture and appliances for just about every room in the house. Parents-to-be can expect to save big on lots of baby and juvenile furniture like a crib with mattress for $105.00 or a bunk bed set for $189.00. Four-piece bedroom sets with dresser, mirror, chest, and headboard start at $249.00. A complete day bed will complete the look of any guest room for just $169.00; throw in a night stand for $39.00 more. Wouldn't your living room look great once you spruce it up with a new set of end tables (three for $69.00) or a gorgeous new lamp ($35.00 for two)? If you've always wanted a study but didn't think you could afford the necessities, now's your chance; bookcases can be had for $85.00 apiece. A variety of stoves, from the 1940s onward, start at just $79.00 apiece; refrigerators in a variety of sizes – from the minuscule to the monstrous – are $95.00 and up. If you're a little apprehensive about buying used, you'll be happy to know that all products are guaranteed for at least 30 days. Just be sure to look at the merchandise with a discerning eye before you purchase. If you can live with a little scratch on the side of your refrigerator, you'll make out just fine! If you're really nervous, stick to the furniture and home furnishings and forget the appliances. Open Monday through Saturday, 7:30 a.m. - 6:00 p.m.; closed on Sunday.

SHELDON CORD PRODUCTS

2201 West Devon Avenue, Chicago IL 60659. 773/973-7070. **Toll-free phone:** 800/621-7999. **The Lowdown:** If you're looking for name brand furniture at wholesale prices (who isn't?), give Sheldon Cord Products a try. After 50 years in business, they certainly know what the customer wants. Stop by their 50,000-square-foot warehouse and showroom and find the furniture you're looking for at prices you can afford. For those who love high-quality leather products, Sheldon Cord Products has got beautiful, three-piece Italian leather sofa, loveseat, and chair sets for as low as $1,295.00. For the kitchen, you can pick up a five-piece dinette set (a table and four chairs) for as little as $100.00. A complete queen-size pillow and mattress set – with a 10-year warranty – will complete your bedroom to the tune of just $250.00. Been meaning to turn that spare room into a comfy guest room? Why not head on over to Sheldon Cord and pick up a futon (including mattress) for just $99.95? Don't forget to bring your truck; you can pick up your purchases instantly at the warehouse. Even if you live outside of Illinois, give them a call (toll-free) and see if you can't work out a deal. If you're just starting out and want some furniture that isn't going to empty your wallet, Sheldon Cord is the place to go. Open Sunday, 11:00 a.m. - 5:00 p.m.; Monday through Friday, 9:00 a.m. - 7:00 p.m.; Saturday, 9:00 a.m. - 6:00 p.m.

VALUE CITY FURNITURE

8310 South Cicero Avenue, Burbank IL 60459. 708/422-2900.
♦ 1550 Irving Park Road, Hanover Park, IL 60103. 630/483-7171.

World Wide Web address: http://www.vcf.com.
The Lowdown: If you're going to be dishing out the bucks for a new apartment or new house, you're probably not too keen about paying top dollar for new furniture. And maybe a little paranoia is causing you to avoid those second-hand furniture stores where you would be forced to sleep where another person has slept before. Well you don't have to feel trapped because Value City Furniture sells new furniture at huge savings. A queen-size Sea Island cottage bed sells for half of its original price. And how about a new Hilton sofa with reversible seat and back cushions for under $600.00. And to complete the home facelift, you can find a solid oak five-piece dinette, including four arrowback side chairs for just under $500.00. With savings of up to 50 percent, prices under $30.00 for bookcases, bed frames, and various other home furniture are not at all unusual here. Open Monday through Saturday, 10:00 a.m. - 9:00 p.m.; Sunday, 12:00 p.m. - 6:00 p.m.

Health & Beauty Supplies

AROMA WORKSHOP

2050 North Halsted Street, Chicago IL 60614. 773/871-1985. **World Wide Web address:** http://www.aromaworkshop.com. **The Lowdown:** If you're tired of paying big bucks for designer perfumes that just don't smell as good at home as they did in the store, try creating your own unique scent. If you don't feel like doing the work yourself, the experts here will help you piece together the scent that is right for you. And while prices are more than what you'd pay for some designer impostor, they're certainly worth it. Aroma Workshop also carries a whole bunch of great beauty supplies and accessories. Open Sunday, 11:00 a.m. - 5:00 p.m.; Monday through Thursday, 12:00 p.m. - 8:00 p.m.; Friday, 11:00 a.m. - 7:00 p.m.; Saturday, 10:00 a.m. - 6:00 p.m.

DEVON DISCOUNT

2454 West Devon Avenue, Chicago IL 60659. 773/743-1058. **The Lowdown:** Devon Discount is a wholesale/retail distributor offering great savings on the basic stuff you use everyday, from soap and toothpaste. The prices on these household items are good; where this place really stands out, though, is in its perfumes and personal care products. Vitabath gel, for example, (which usually costs up to $20.00 in fancier department stores) is about half the price here. Designer fragrances for both men and women are stocked in mass quantities: two long walls are lined with names like Gucci, Armani, Ralph Lauren, Paloma Picasso, and just about any other brand you can think of. All are sold at 25 - 50 percent below retail prices. Devon Discount offers you other ways to save even more, such as generic copies of famous fragrances. Also, if only the genuine article will do, they may have your brand in a bottle that's missing its box or cap; things like that can garner you discounts of up to 50 percent.

PERFUMANIA

7601 South Cicero Avenue, Chicago IL 06052. 773/581-5458. ✦ 6465 West Diversey Avenue, Chicago IL 60635. 773/237-7020. **E-mail address:** info@perfumania.com. **World Wide Web address:** http://www.perfumania.com. **The Lowdown:** Even if you do prefer to save a buck or two when you shop, you don't have to wreak of designer-impostor fragrances to show it. Perfumania sells discounted perfumes and colognes to those who just might want to keep up with the latest scented trend. Envy for Women by Gucci costs $20.99 for a one-ounce eau de toilette spray (retail: $42.50), while on the more expensive side, 273 for Women by Fred Hayman costs $99.99 for a one-ounce bottle of perfume (retail price: $215.00). Men, don't think that just because this store sells perfume and beauty products that they won't have something for you. A large collection of equally discounted colognes can be found here as well. A 2.5 ounce bottle of Cool Water cologne for men by Davidoff will run you $29.99 (compared to the $44.00 retail price). Everyone can find something useful in the bath and body section. The savings here are incredible! A Papaya Freeze Bath Gift Set by Jerome Privee is valued at $42.00, sells at Perfumania for only $13.99. Suddenly, a bubble bath sounds very appealing.

SALLY BEAUTY SUPPLY
839 North State Street, Chicago IL 60610. 312/266-1810. ◆ 6185 North Lincoln Avenue, Chicago IL 60659. 773/588-7021. ◆ 2727 North Clark Street, Chicago IL 60614. 773/477-6222. **World Wide Web address:** http://www.sallybeauty.com. **The Lowdown:** For those of you who would like to get the professional styling products and supplies they use on you at the salon, without spending a fortune, stop in to Sally Beauty Supply. They have everything including hair brushes and combs; skin products; shampoos and conditioners; and nail polish galore. Some locations even carry more high-end items like barber chairs and industrial sized hair dryers. You're guaranteed to get blown away by the prices.

SHERWYN'S HEALTH FOOD SHOP
645 West Diversey Parkway, Chicago IL 60614. 773/477-1934. **The Lowdown:** For the serious vegetarian, homeopathy enthusiast, food allergy sufferer or the just plain health-minded, this enormous store is a haven, carrying over 17,000 products. The crowded bicycle racks out front make it easy to spot the store from Clark Street. With so much to see, granola, grains, and spices in bulk; walls of vitamins and even over a dozen kinds of honey, you can spend hours and hours here. The staff is always happy to explain products and answer questions, especially in the homeopathy department. Vegetarian staples like Edensoy soy milk are always price-reduced. Sherwyn's busy juice bar serves up carrot juice, beet-carrot juice, and drinks made from mixed vegetables including spinach. Bulk foods are available pre-bagged or do-it-yourself. Buy as much as you like; stocking up here can keep you and your budget healthy. Delivery is available and parking is free with a $25.00 purchase. Open Monday through Friday, 10:00 a.m. - 8:00 p.m.; Saturday, 10:00 a.m. - 7:00 p.m.; Sunday, 10:00 a.m. - 6:00 p.m.

SUNFLOWER SEED HEALTH FOODS
5210 South Harper Court, Chicago IL 60615. 773/363-1600. **The Lowdown:** Located in Harper Court, Sunflower Seed Health Foods offers great prices on a variety of all-natural foods and beauty products. You can do your grocery shopping, pick up your vitamins, and nix a trip to the local beauty counter all in one fell swoop here. Even if you're new to the whole health-kick thing, the staff will be more than happy to help you out and let you know the best products to buy. All this and competitive prices? It's almost too good to be true.

Home Furnishings

ARTISTS' FRAME OUTLET

1915 North Clybourn Avenue, Chicago IL 60614. 312/248-7713. **The Lowdown:** Artists' Frame Service, one of the world's largest custom framing facilities, now has an outlet filled with picture moldings, ready-mades, and beautiful photo frames. Molding selections range from Italian gold leaf to natural hardwoods. This basement outlet also offers a large selection of over-runs, mis-cuts, and mistakes. You are sure to find something to fit your needs here. Next door, Artists' Frame Service can cut down your frames, help you select matting, and fit your art or photos. Best of all, everything is priced to allow savings of 40 to 80 percent off regular prices. **NOTE:** The store is in the basement of Jayson Garden and serves as their outlet too.

BED MART

3154 North Clark Street, Chicago IL 60657. 773/477-1701. ◆ 1747 North Sheffield Avenue, Chicago IL 60614. 312/335-3336. ◆ 5353 North Broadway, Chicago IL. 773/506-9696. ◆ 3945 North Cicero Avenue, Chicago IL. 773/427-0018. ◆ 8111 South Cicero Avenue, Chicago IL. 773/767-1440. **World Wide Web address:** http://www.bedmart.com. **The Lowdown:** Okay, so the name isn't the most exciting you've ever heard. But Bed Mart's high-volume business will help you get a top-quality mattress at the best available price, and that's something to jump up and down about (not on the mattresses, please). In fact, they claim that they will beat any other retailer's price on a particular model. Bed Mart carries only the best, like the world famous Simmons, Simmons Beautyrest, and BackCare brand names. They also have a large selection of futons, daybeds, headboards, and bunkbeds – they've even got a futon bunkbed! During a recent promotion, Bed Mart was offering an all-new Simmons Beautyrest queen set for just $399.00. What a deal! Twin mattresses start at just $44.00. You can even finance your purchase for six months (with zero percent interest). And at Bed Mart, delivery is QUICK! Open Monday through Friday, 10:30 a.m. - 8:30 p.m.; Saturday, 10:00 a.m. - 6:00 p.m.; Sunday, 11:00 a.m. - 5:00 p.m.

THE BED SHOP

2156 North Clybourn Avenue, Chicago IL 60614. 773/248-9600. **The Lowdown:** The Bed Shop offers great pricing on top-of-the-line bedding and then some. They offer the largest selection of Stearns & Foster luxury bedding in all of Chicagoland, and carry the entire line of Sealy Posturepedic mattresses, with twins starting as low as $45.00 and queens for as little as $279.00. In addition to mattresses, The Bed Shop carries a huge inventory of headboards, futons, daybeds, bunk beds, rollaways, and more. **Cheap Deal:** As a special incentive to *Mr. Cheap's Chicago* readers, just mention you read about them in this book and save an additional 10 percent.

THE BEDDING EXPERTS

1871 North Clybourn Avenue, Chicago IL 60614. 773/528-9000. ◆ 3145 North Halsted Street, Chicago IL 60657. 773/871-3636. ◆ 4851 North Western Avenue, Chicago IL 60625. 773/728-7121. ◆ 3101 North Central Avenue, Chicago IL 773/622-0155. ◆ 4445 North Pulaski Road, Chicago IL 60630. 773/604-8200. ◆ 5689 South Archer Avenue, Chicago IL 60683. 773/585-2300. ◆ 156 North Wabash Avenue, Chicago IL 60601. 312/553-9724. ◆ 1226 South Canal Street, Chicago IL 60607. 312/563-1653. **The Lowdown:** The Bedding Experts is one of the biggest mattress chains in all of Chicagoland. At their frequent sales, you may find Sealy twin-size mattresses and box springs selling for as little as $38.00 each; queen sets for $168.00; and kings for $273.00 a set. These prices may be up to 60 percent or more off retail. Bed frames are also a good deal here, like a metal frame daybed for $148.00, bunk beds from $199.00, and a queen or king-size black iron bed frame for $299.99 or $399.99, respectively. Because Bedding Experts is such a large company, they can promise delivery within 24 hours; and all advertised items are guaranteed to be in stock. They also have a 60-day price guarantee on every item in stock; if you find your mattress cheaper somewhere else within two months (with proof, of course), they'll refund you the difference. Call for specific location hours.

CHEF'S CATALOG

3009 North Clark Street, Chicago IL 60657. 773/327-5210. **World Wide Web address:** http://www.chefscatalog.com. **The Lowdown:** Since 1979, Chef's Catalog has been synonymous with high-end kitchen goods. They're the nation's leading catalog retailer of just such products. This retail location is no slouch when it comes to big name brands and enormous selection. They offer great prices on manufacturers like All-Clad, Henckels, and KitchenAid, and they won't be undersold. But just what kind of deals did I see on my visit? How about a nine-piece, professional, hard anodized cookware set by Calphalon – which retails for $420.00 – for just $289.99? A five-quart, stainless steel stockpot by Cuisinart was marked down to half-price. Must-have furnishings, like a John Boos butcher block cart, were marked down by as much as $180.00. Even if it's just the smaller appliances and kitchen utensils you need, you can find them here at a discount. Capresso coffee grinders (with an impressive 17 grind selections) were $25.00 off. KitchenAid mixers, which will cost you an arm and a leg no matter where you shop, were seen in a variety of colors and sizes for as little as $239.99. If you're a gourmand who's into having only the best, Chef's Catalog is a great place to start building the kitchen of your dreams for less. If you can't make it to the store itself, order yourself a catalog (call 800/884-CHEF) or visit their online store.

COST PLUS WORLD MARKET

1623 North Sheffield Avenue, Chicago IL 60614. 312/587-8037. **World Wide Web address:** http://www.costplus.com. **The Lowdown:** Cost Plus World Market started back in 1958 when a San Francisco businessman turned his love for traveling and purchasing unique items into a thriving retail operation. Since that time, Cost Plus World Market has grown to include 90 stores throughout the country. But just what should someone expect to find here? For the most part, Cost Plus World Market specializes in furniture and home furnishings. In keeping with the company's origination, Cost Plus buyers travel the world looking for unique objects to bring back to America. They go to distant villages and exotic bazaars, looking for that perfect treasure. That said, you should keep in mind that not everything in the store is cheap per se. But then again, picking up an Argentina coffee table for $199.00 is much cheaper than traveling down there yourself! Cost Plus World Market is a great place to pick up decorative items and general knickknacks for your home or as a gift. Some great bargains included a variety of runners from Shima, Sedona, and Laltan; some gorgeous scented cathedral candles; and a fantastic wooden wine rack, capable of holding more than 40 bottles. Cost Plus World Market has even got the wine to go along with that rack; the beverage department carries an enormous selection of beer and wine from around the world, all at very budget-friendly prices. They carry lots of food from around the world as well. The stock at Cost Plus World Market is continually changing, so there's always something new to see.

CRATE & BARREL OUTLET STORE
800 West North Avenue, Chicago IL 60622. 312/787-4775.
♦ 3763 North Lincoln Avenue, Chicago IL 60618. 773/244-1188.
♦ 1860 West Jefferson Avenue, Naperville IL 60540. 630/357-1155. **World Wide Web address:** http://www.crateandbarrel.com. **The Lowdown:** If you love shopping at Crate & Barrel, you'll really have fun visiting their outlet stores. This is where you can find the out-of-season products that have been sent from the regular retail outlets along with special purchases and closeouts that can only be found in the outlets. Although some of the products are manufacturers' seconds, they still have to meet the Crate & Barrel high standards to be sold here. Besides finding wonderful bargains in dinnerware, glassware, office accessories, and all the other Crate & Barrel goodies you've come to know and love, the outlet stores are the only places where you can buy the Marimekko fabrics which are used for displays in the Crate & Barrel stores. Best of all, you can buy these goods at just $6.95 a yard; they retail for $39.95 a yard. If you can make it to the Naperville location, you'll find lots of furniture too. Sure, some of them have obvious flaws, but many are first quality store samples and custom orders that couldn't find a home elsewhere. If you're craving all the excitement of a bargain-hunting excursion with the incessant need for some fashionable home furnishings, Crate & Barrel is your place! Call for specific location hours.

EXPOSITION CARPET COMPANY
5718 North Broadway Street, Chicago IL 60660. 773/784-5600. **The Lowdown:** Way up on Broadway, in that part of town known as Epic, is one of Mr. Cheap's favorite places in all of Chicago to buy a carpet, remnant, or area rug. Direct purchasing from over three dozen carpet manufacturers, along with

Exposition's super-high sales volume helps keep prices ultra low. Even so, the salespeople still manage to steal the show with their friendliness. Stores buy their carpets at Exposition, since commercial carpeting is only $4.95 a yard. Sculptured nylon carpeting starts at a mere $6.75 per square yard. Household broadloom, including designs by J.C. Stevens at $19.00 per square yard installed, are also super deals. Coronet carpeting, available in a whopping 150 colors, is only $20.00 per square yard. Area rugs are another scene-stealer here, with 3,500 to choose from. Find Chicagoland's largest variety of area rugs from a pure wool hand-woven Turkish rug, valued at about $2,100.00 selling for $699.00. Nine by 12-foot Oriental rugs are $800.00, about half of their listed retail prices, and Oriental runners, 27 inches wide, are only $4.00 per linear foot. Regular Oriental throw rugs are also half off retail (a 2' x 4' was only $10.00). There are thousands (yes, thousands!) of remnants in stock, which sometimes go on sale for 10 - 70 percent off their already cheap-as-heck prices. A 12' x 20' remnant, listed at $615.00, recently sold for $389.00; and a 12' x 16' remainder was only $105.00 since a couple of hardly-noticeable spots were made during installation of the original roll at a trade show. If perfect, it would sell for $210.00. Mr. C also saw some Berber remnants, like a 12' x 24' piece for $300.00, half of its original list price. Exposition, which has been around for twenty-five years, offers to meet or beat any competitor's price. They will also deliver purchases for a mere $20.00 locally. If that wasn't enough, all marked prices include padding and installation - what a deal! Open weekdays, 10:00 a.m. - 8:00 p.m.; Saturday, 10:00 a.m. - 5:00 p.m.; Sunday 12:00 p.m. - 5:00 p.m.

HELLER BROTHERS BEDDING

254-0700

2828 West 48th Place, Chicago IL 60632. 773/~~376-9520~~.
The Lowdown: You could lose some sleep trying to find this South Side factory, but once you get there, the money you'll save will bring you plenty of zzzzz's. When you think about buying factory direct, this is the kind of place you're picturing. Co-owner Larry Heller took Mr. C on a tour of the whole operation, showing how he and his brothers make their mattresses from start to finish; that's how proud and confident he is of the high quality here. Each mattress is made individually, almost entirely by hand, using only small machinery; cranking 'em out at high speed would not be the Heller Brothers' way. Yet, because you can order and purchase directly from this no-frills showroom, you save big over famous name brands at fancier stores. All of the cost goes into quality, says Larry. They make a wide range of bedding including custom orders for school dorms and hospitals. When Chicago local Oprah Winfrey bought herself an antique four-poster, she asked these fellas to design a mattress to fit its unique specifications. They also make the beds for the Chicago Fire Department, and you know those guys need some good sleep. At Heller Brothers, you have quite a choice of densities and firmness, from simple foam fillings to the strongest-gauge inner springs. All of the mattresses are fully warrantied; some for as long as 10 or 20 years. So, how much for these resplendent resting places? Mattresses made with inner

springs (not foam) start from just $49.00 in twin size. Good quality sets kick in at about $100.00 for each piece, at least half of what you'd pay for lesser-quality name brands. And you can get a Premium full-size set for about $200.00, with queen-size sets from $275.00. If you only need a mattress, you can have one for about 60 percent of the price per set. Delivery is available, though not free. Open Monday through Friday, 8:00 a.m. - 3:00 p.m.; Saturday, 8:00 a.m. - 11:00 a.m.

J & D WHIRLPOOL AND BATH OUTLET

2730 North Elston Avenue, Chicago IL 60647. 773/252-6886. **The Lowdown:** Here's another no-frills setting, for appliances which are anything but. If you've always wanted a Jacuzzi, but found them somewhat out of reach, try looking here. This store also sells just about everything for the bathroom but tile, not to mention kitchen cabinets and sinks as well. The selection here is not large; there may only be four or five of a particular item on hand, each one a different model. But then, new stuff arrives all the time. The stock comes directly from the manufacturers; these are items which may have a slight blemish and cannot be sold at full price, but are in perfect working order. J & D does these manufacturers a favor by selling them off at discount. For example, a hot tub by Aquatic, with a DuPont Lucite finish, was recently on sale for $1,500.00, marked down from a retail price of $2,200.00. Why? It had a slight scratch, evidently made at the factory. Honestly, you couldn't see it unless you knew exactly where to look. Another hot tub was reduced from $1,700.00 to $1,200.00; there were several of these, completely unmarred. They were simply discontinued models. One Kohler tub was marked down from an original $2,500.00 to a soothing $600.00. Second-quality sink tops were reduced from $80.00 to $50.00 each. J & D also specializes in maple and cherry wood kitchen cabinetry. They bring in name-brand kitchen cabinets, and sell them at truckload factory direct prices. Lots of landlords and contractors shop here, checking in frequently just to see what may have come in. Suffice it to say, with the hot tubs in particular, most items don't hang around here for long.

LUNA CARPET & BLINDS

4256 West Belmont, Chicago IL 60641. 773/202-LUNA. **World Wide Web address:** http://www.lunacarpet.com. **The Lowdown:** Whether you're preparing to sell your house or simply tidying it up, don't overlook the area that probably sees more dirt a day than anywhere else. If you replace that dingy seventies' green colored carpet with a fresher, modern style and color, you just might see some higher bids on your home. And if that's the direction you're heading in, then you'll likely want to save a few pennies wherever you can. Luna Carpet & Blinds sells brand name carpets in a variety of styles and colors at low prices. And don't think that this is one of those transparent guarantees that never actually follow through. The Luna Challenge $100.00 guarantee assures customers that Luna will beat any competitor's price on a comparable carpet, or they will give you $100.00. Not a bad deal. With over 40 years in business, they must be doing something right because they seem to know what people want. Take their Luna Shop At Home Service, for example. You don't even have to shop around town because a team of carpet and/or blind experts will come to your house armed with carpet samples in different colors, styles, and brands. Not only is this convenient, but these experts can help assess your situation and make suggestions on carpet or blind styles. You never know, maybe with a new carpet in your home, you'll think twice before tramping those dirty shoes across it.

MODERN HOME FURNISHINGS

3015 North Lincoln Avenue, Chicago IL 60657. 773/327-7877.
• 1361 North Wells Street, Chicago IL 60610. 312/587-8788.
The Lowdown: Sometimes, if you're shopping for furniture on a budget, you have to sacrifice style. Not so at Modern Home Furnishings, where they carry the latest in contemporary styles at affordable prices. Furniture includes bedroom, dining room, and family room furniture. They've also got a great selection of contemporary lamps and artwork. It's a one-stop shopping destination if you're planning on redecorating any room in your house.

NORTHWESTERN CUTLERY

810 West Lake Street, Chicago IL 60607. 312/421-3666. **World Wide Web address:** http://www.northwesterncutlery.com. **The Lowdown:** For professional chefs and regular old cooks alike, maintaining an impressive and high-quality cutlery collection can really put a damper on your finances. It is not unheard of to pay more than $100.00 or $200.00 for a single knife. That is never the case with Mr. Cheap! Northwestern Cutlery offers the best in cutlery brand names including Henckels, Wüsthof Trident, Schrade, and Swiss Army. Yet they offer them at prices that are easy to swallow (the prices... not the cutlery), and that makes all the difference. Deals during my visit included a six-piece block set by J.A. Henckels Five Star including a 3" parer, 5" utility, 8" carver, 8" chef's, 9" steel, vegetable peeler, and hardwood block for $229.99 (originally $362.00). Similar block sets by Global and Mundial were spotted for as low as $128.00 - $149.95 (retailing between $159.00 and $249.95). There are also plenty of savings to be had on open stock items, like a set of Wüsthof Grand Prix kitchen shears for $22.50, or Kyocera 3" paring knife for $46.95. While this family-run operation started out as a door-to-door knife sharpening business, they've progressed beyond just cutlery. Northwestern Cutlery offers a fantastic supply of cookware as well by the industry's top names like All Clad and Calphalon. From Calphalon, Mr. C spotted a seven-piece set from their Professional Hard Anodized set for $260.00; and an eight-piece set from the Professional Non-Stick II line for $299.95. Professionals will love the deals on brushed aluminum pots and pans set by All Clad, like a six-piece set for just $289.95. Because they carry discontinued merchandise as well, Northwestern Cutlery is great at keeping your well-worn set of pots complete. There are even tons of kitchen utensils – including spoons, forks, ladles, and skimmers – to be found for well under $10.00 apiece. Just $5.95 will get you your choice of a Calphalon slotted spoon, spatula,

pasta fork, flat whisk, or stir fry scoop. Plus, Northwestern Cutlery is famous for the extras they throw in; no matter what you're here to purchase, chances are there's some sort of bonus or promotion going on like free lifetime sharpening or bonus utensils thrown in with your purchase. These deals are really unbeatable! Open Monday through Friday, 7:00 a.m. - 5:00 p.m.; Saturday, 7:00 a.m. - 4:00 p.m.

OLYMPIC CARPET CENTER

2719 North California Avenue, Chicago IL 60647. 773/276-1212. **World Wide Web address:** http://www.rugandcarpet.com. **The Lowdown:** Just off of the Kennedy Expressway at California and Diversey, Olympic Carpet Center offers great prices on a variety of rugs and carpets. They stock over 3,000 updated and current designs of area rugs, hand-made and machine-made, from as low as $45.00 for a 5' x 8' and $75.00 for a 8' x 11'. Olympic Carpet Center has discount prices on broadloom too, well below retail prices. But, perhaps the biggest deal here is their remnant selection, so large they can't even fit it all in this store! You may find 9' x 12' remnants for as little as $39.00, or 12' x 12' remnants starting from $49.00. These prices are as much as 80 percent below original retail rates. They claim to stock some 40,000 square feet of remnants, which Mr. C calculates to be roughly the amount required to carpet Lake Michigan shore-to-shore, and still have enough left over to do most of Daley Plaza. Open Monday through Friday, 9:00 a.m. - 9:00 p.m.; Saturday, 9:00 a.m. - 7:00 p.m.; Sunday, 10:00 a.m. - 6:00 p.m. Free parking is available. For information on Olympic Carpet Center's professional carpet cleaning service, call 773/772-7401.

SAMPLES

35 East Monroe Street, Chicago IL 60603. 312/346-7713. **The Lowdown:** If you've just acquired some cooking skills but can't afford the equipment to tweak them, this store is a Godsend. Samples sells a variety of kitchenwares and other random goods. During my visit, stainless steel seemed to be the theme; I spotted a five cup fondue set for $14.95 and a 12-quart stockpot was just $12.95. Dish towels, in a variety of colors, were another great steal. High-quality frames that could easily fetch $20.00 or more elsewhere were priced between under $10.00. You just can't go wrong will the prices at Samples.

SHOW CARPET OUTLET

4319 South Archer Avenue, Chicago IL 60632. 773/927-1177. **The Lowdown:** Show Carpet Outlet has two huge showrooms filled with broadloom and rugs, all selling at 40 percent - 70 percent below retail prices. These are closeouts and overstocks from mills all around the country, in a great selection of colors, patterns, and textures. Among the brands you'll find here are Galaxy, Cabin Craft, and many others. All of them are treated with stain protection. Prices here are by the square foot, not the square yard, making comparisons tricky; but rest assured that these prices are good indeed. Mr. C noticed a medium-pile sculptured synthetic, for example, in a handsome burgundy color.

Its retail price was $3.39 per square foot, and it sells here for $2.39; it was on special sale that week, however, further reduced to $1.89 per foot. This carpeting was Scotchgarded, and carried a 10-year warranty. Another good buy was a machine-made 6' x 8' oriental rug seen with a retail price of $249.00, marked down to just $49.95. Some 9' x 12' styles, with list prices of up to $350.00, sell for a mere $89.95. Show Carpet Outlet also sells plenty of durable tight-weave commercial carpeting in broadloom and runners, some as little as $.99 per foot. And we haven't even gotten to the other room yet. That's where you'll find an incredible selection of remnants, over 4,000 of them, in a vast range of sizes and materials. Whether you want a little 2' x 5' bound rug for $8.50, all the way up to a 12' x 36' piece for $119.00, you'll find lots of choices here. Remnants in 4' x 6' and 6' x 9' sizes are priced from just $19.00 and up; 9' x 12' sizes start at $49.00. Any remnant in this size or larger will include foam padding free with your purchase. Also, any purchase of wall-to-wall carpeting includes free padding and installation into the bargain. This place is one of the best carpet stores in town. There's even a waiting area with a TV set, for reluctant tag-alongs. Show Carpet Outlet offers a delivery service, as well as financing and layaway. Open Monday through Friday, 10:30 a.m. - 7:30 p.m.; Saturday, 10:30 a.m. - 5:00 p.m.; Sunday, 12:00 p.m. - 5:00 p.m.

WAXMAN CANDLES
3044 North Lincoln Avenue, Chicago IL 60657. 773/929-3000. **World Wide Web address:** http://www.waxmancandles.com. **The Lowdown:** If you've got a question about candles, it's best to ask The Waxman. While candles are pretty much inexpensive anywhere you go, a candle from Waxman is always appreciated. Their self-proclaimed title as "The Coolest Candle Store on Earth" is one I agree with whole-heartedly. Waxman's layer candle ($7.50 - $32.00) offers up numerous scents, creating a pleasing mix as each layer is uncovered; Waxman's "drippies" candles ($4.25/pair) are a great decoration for any old bottles or containers; floaters ($1.95 - $2.95 each) come in a variety of shapes and sizes and are great in creating a romantic aura or for any poolside gathering. My favorite candles, however, are the "manipulationz" ($8.00 - $12.00/pair). These smokeless, dripless candles are created through the twists and pinches of the candle-making clan; they're truly artistic and within your budget. Waxman has been making candles since 1970, and it shows. This store has got candle making and burning down to a science. Open Monday through Saturday, 11:00 a.m. - 7:00 p.m. (Thursday until 8:00 p.m.); Sunday, 12:00 p.m. - 5:00 p.m.

Jewelry & Accessories

BIJOUTERIE INTERNATIONAL

645 West Grand Avenue, Chicago IL 60610. 312/733-5600. **The Lowdown:** At this hideaway on the western edge of downtown, you can buy jewelry below retail prices. They have one of the largest selections of rhinestone and crystal neckwear, earrings, and bracelets in Chicago. Almost all jewelry is 50 percent off. Sterling silver runs 40 - 50 percent below retail prices. If you are feeling creative, you can make your own jewelry with beads and findings from all over the world. Fred, the owner loves lending a hand in the design of jewelry and he's also handy with repairs. Closed Sunday.

CHICAGO HOSIERY COMPANY

601 West Roosevelt Road, Chicago IL 60607. 312/226-0055. **The Lowdown:** The name says it all: this is a great place to stock up on hosiery and undergarments. What the name doesn't tell you is that it's a great place to stock up on these things cheaply. Best of all, the bargains are available for the entire family, not just mom or dad! Open Sunday, 9:00 a.m. – 4:00 p.m.; Monday through Saturday, 9:00 a.m. – 5:00 p.m.

THE JEWELER'S CENTER

5 South Wabash Avenue, Chicago IL 60603. 312/853-2057. **World Wide Web address:** http://www.jewelerscenter.com. **The Lowdown:** Shop where the jewelers shop. If you're in the market for some high-quality jewelry and are willing to shop around, The Jeweler's Center in the downtown Maller's Building is a great place to start. Since 1921, The Jeweler's Center has housed the Midwest's largest concentration of wholesale and retail jewelers. With 13 floors of shops, it's difficult to imagine that you wouldn't find something that you love. And, with more than 185 stores, it's hard to believe you wouldn't find something within your price range. Whether you're looking for gold, pearls, or gemstones they've got what you need. Note to would-be-husbands: if you're thinking of asking that special lady to be your wife, but you're not sure you can afford the perfect diamond, The Jeweler's Center is a godsend. Stop on by and see what they have to offer. It's hard to miss the enormous Art Deco building. Open Monday through Saturday, 9:00 a.m. - 5:00 p.m.; closed Sunday and all major holidays. Also, for the month before Christmas, stores within The Jeweler's Center maintain individual hours. Give your favorite store a buzz to see when they're open.

SILVER ON OAK

104 East Oak Street, Chicago IL 60611. 312/266-2211. **The Lowdown:** It's the Gold Coast, Chicago's ritziest neighborhood. For many years, this store (formerly Great Lakes Jewelry) has been selling silver jewelry of all types and sizes. Wander around and take a look at the exotic belts and buckles,

including silver buckles in the shapes of turtles, alligators, frogs, and all sorts of other creatures. Also, the store stocks pearls in all sizes and colors – all at discount prices; and hundreds of earrings, necklaces, and bracelets starting around $19.00. Just recently, the store has begun selling designer sunglasses with brand names like Dior, Versace, Fendi, and Gucci – all at a 50 percent discount. Open Monday through Saturday, 11:00 a.m. - 6:00 p.m.

STATE AND COMPANY

9 North Wabash Avenue, First Floor, Chicago IL 60602. 312/795-9200. **Toll-free phone:** 800/765-3989. **E-mail address:** sales@stateandcompany.com. **World Wide Web address:** http://www.stateandcompany.com. **The Lowdown:** For more than 40 years, State & Company has been treating regular customers like you to wholesale prices on their fabulous selection of diamonds. Though they're in the heart of Jewelers Row – a very prestigious place to be – State and Company does not charge the outlandish prices you'll see elsewhere in the area. And with over 500 engagement settings in stock, all tastes and styles have been well accounted for. Mr. C spotted diamond earrings for as little as $140.00 a pair; try finding savings like that somewhere else in this town! The philosophy is simple: offer the best possible prices on all the merchandise offered. If only all jewelry stores were so logical. Open Monday through Saturday, 9:00 a.m. - 6:00 p.m.

STUDIO V ART DECO

672 North Dearborn Street, Chicago IL 60610. 312/440-1937. **E-mail address:** studiov@enteract.com. **World Wide Web address:** http://www.studiovchicago.com. **The Lowdown:** Looking for some costume jewelry or funky frames as a simple gift for a guy or a gal? Studio V offers a fun assortment of both new and vintage items, and owner Jack Garber specializes in doing business with those people who are looking for a "something old, something new" wedding gift. Vintage silver lockets start around $20.00, and marcasite jewelry, pins, earrings, and necklaces range in price from $18.00 - $140.00. Mr. Garber makes a point of stocking lots of sterling silver, bakelite, and estate jewelry in his huge display cases. Vintage compacts – including those made of mother-of-pearl – are big sellers, as are new and used perfume bottles and business card cases. For men, there are hundreds of cufflinks in stock, as well as tin toys, money clips, flasks, and posters. The funky picture frames I mentioned before start at a very reasonable $12.00. Drop in today and see what kind of gifts you can pick up. Open Monday through Saturday, 12:00 p.m. - 6:00 p.m.

WABASH DIAMOND COMPANY

2 North Wabash Avenue, Chicago IL 60602. 312/251-9900. **E-mail address:** sales@wabashdiamond.com. **World Wide Web address:** http://www.wabashdiamond.com. **The Lowdown:** Wabash Diamond Company is one of a number of similar stores along Jewelers Row. One major difference is that this store offers unbeatable wholesale prices to the public. They specialize in

engagement rings and loose diamonds and, because the shop is on premises, they can also custom design jewelry. **Cheap Deal:** Mention that you saw the company in *Mr. Cheap's Chicago*, and the nice folks at Wabash Diamond Company are prepared to offer you a free ring cleaning and inspection.

WABASH JEWELERS MALL

21 North Wabash Avenue, Chicago IL 60602. 312/263-1757. **World Wide Web address:** http://www.wabashjewelersmall. com. **The Lowdown:** The Wabash Jewelers Mall consists of 23 separate vendors, all at one address. As you walk in the door, you see row upon row of glass counters, each with a different merchant selling his or her own stock. The advantage for them is lower overhead costs; the advantage for you is bargain prices. Competition amongst the dealers, as you may guess, can be stiff, though they claim it's all friendly enough, but, depending on what you're looking for, you may be able to do some very convenient comparison shopping and come away with a sweet deal. Prices can be as much as 50 percent below retail value; many are near wholesale price, plus sales tax. And with so many mini-shops, just about every kind of item is represented: diamonds, colored gemstones, pearl, watches and watch repair, estate jewelry, and more. Open Monday through Friday, 10 a.m. - 5:30 p.m. (Thursdays until 6:30 p.m.); Saturday, 10:00 a.m. - 5.00 p.m.

Liquor & Beverages

BINNY'S BEVERAGE DEPOT

213 West Grand Avenue, Chicago IL 60610. 312/332-0012. **The Lowdown:** Binny's Beverage Depot touts itself as the world's largest discount liquor store, and they're not kidding. Once you find the entrance from the street (down a couple steps and around the corner), this River North store can save you plenty on everything from soda to champagne. They even hold occasional large-scale wine-tasting sessions. Binny's Beverage Depot imports wines from France and Italy, and also stocks many wines from less snooty (and therefore, less expensive) countries like Spain and Australia. These countries produce wines which are considered comparable to many of the fancier vineyards in taste, but each bottle costs several dollars less in price. But wine isn't the only thing you'll find great prices on; liquor and beer prices are also dramatically reduced. Binny's has free parking too (just steer clear of the shipping trucks). Open Sunday, 11:00 a.m. - 5:00 p.m.; Monday through Saturday, 7:30 a.m. - 8:00 p.m.

CASEY'S LIQUORS

1444 West Chicago Avenue, Chicago IL 60622. 312/243-2850. **Toll-free phone:** 800/213-BEER. **E-mail address:** beerstore@ aol.com. **The Lowdown:** While this west-of-town store has good deals on all kinds of liquor, Casey's is particularly renowned for good deals on all kinds of beer. Whether your taste runs to great domestic microbrews like Sierra Nevada Pale Ale (just $6.99 for a six-pack of bottles), or good old Budweiser (24 cans for $11.99), you'll find excellent prices here. Kegs start as low as $59.95 for Bud, Miller, and Old Style. Casey's Liquors also offers great deals on some of the world's finest cigars, and they'll ship *anything anywhere*.

COFFEE & TEA EXCHANGE

3311 North Broadway Avenue, Chicago IL 60657. 773/528-2241. ♦ 833 West Armitage Avenue, Chicago IL 60614. 773/929-6730. **The Lowdown:** With all the coffee craze going on in Chicago, it's a wonder there aren't more places like this; places where you can buy fresh gourmet beans at reasonable prices. After all, even if you do have a Starbucks on your corner (at this point, who doesn't?), you still need something to get you up and out of the house, right? At the Broadway location, Coffee & Tea Exchange roasts its own coffee beans in dozens of flavors. These same beans sit out at both stores, in huge bins, ready to be scooped up for you by the busy clerks. The crowds are understandable, considering that most bean varieties are just $6.00 - $7.00 per pound. Coffee & Tea Exchange always features weekly specials at incredible prices: One "Coffee of the Week" is always available for just $4.99 a pound. Look for the "Coffee of the Week" to span the spectrum of roasts, from your basic French roast to a unique three-bean blend. Then there's the "Flavor of the Week" for $5.49 a pound. Of course, you can also try out the goods before you make a purchase. Grab yourself a cup of fresh-brewed coffee and mosey on over to the natural wood counter. Even by the cup, the Coffee & Tea Exchange will afford you some great savings. A single cup of the house blend is $.87; a double espresso is just $1.25; and you can get a whole mocha steamer for $1.80. They offer similar prices on cappuccino, flavored coffees, and iced coffees as well. As the name would suggest, Coffee & Tea Exchange also sells a myriad selection of loose teas, these start at just $.69 per ounce, with exotic flavors and all kinds of Green, English, and Oriental brews. Call for specific location hours.

GOLD STANDARD/CHALET WINE SHOPS
40 East Delaware Street, Chicago IL 60611. 312/787-8555.
♦ 405 West Armitage Avenue, Chicago IL 60614. 312/266-7155.
♦ 1531 East 53rd Street, Chicago IL 60615. 773/324-5000.
The Lowdown: Gold Standard/Chalet Wine Shops remain one of the best kept secrets in Chicago. They are stocked with wines from all over the world including Spain, France, South Africa, and South America, all at outstanding values. The beer and spirits department offers unusual choices and the specialty foods and cheeses won't disappoint. But there's more: olive oils, vinegars, cookies, crackers, and specialty chocolates are just a few of the fine foods you'll find here. Gold Standard/Chalet is the perfect place to find gifts for the gourmet cook in your life. Call for specific location hours.

INTELLIGENTSIA COFFEE ROASTERS
3123 North Broadway, Chicago IL 60657. 773/348-8058. **World Wide Web address:** http://www.intelligentsiacoffee.com.
The Lowdown: If Seattle is a Starbucks town, Chicago just might be an Intelligentsia type place. Like the often imitated Emerald City coffee giant, Intelligentsia Coffee Roasters couples a lovable mix of good coffee with a bit of friendly academia. While the number of Starbucks outlets certainly outweighs the number of Intelligentsia spots (there's only one), you'll notice that – all around town – some of the city's most elegant and popular restaurants are brewing Intelligentsia beans. You can serve these same great beans up at your place too! While there are a number of roasts that go over the limit of what one might consider "cheap," there are plenty of pounds to be purchased for under $10.00. Plus, when you buy your beans in the store, you can take advantage of their "Roasters Special" as well as enjoy a complimentary cup of coffee while they prepare your order. French, Italian, Viennese, Turkish, Cajun, and Intelligentsia House are just a few of the blends you can pick up for less than $9.50 a pound. Intelligentsia also hand blends a variety of loose teas at prices that are just as easy on the pocket. Green, herbal, Chinese, Indian, and oolong teas start at $1.65 for an eighth of a pound. If you can't make it to the store (retail or virtual), Intelligentsia also accepts phone orders at 888/945-9786. Open Sunday, 7:00 a.m. - 10:00 p.m.; Monday through Thursday, 6:00 a.m. - 10:00 p.m.; Friday, 6:00 a.m. - 11:00 p.m.; Saturday, 7:00 a.m. - 11:00 p.m.

SAM'S WINE & SPIRITS

1720 North Marcey Street, Chicago IL 60614. 312/664-4394. **E-mail address:** sams@samswine.com. **World Wide Web address:** http://www.sams-wine.com. **The Lowdown:** This large, well-stocked, full-service liquor store rambles on and on; every section is bulging with cases of wine, beer, liquor, champagne, cordials, and soda. Each week brings special sales on many items, to which you are alerted by electronic message boards that hang overhead. The sales clerks are kept very busy, squeezing through the aisles crowded with displays and customers (at least, this was the case on a weekend visit by Mr. C). Still, they are super-friendly and will stop amidst all the craziness the moment you ask for help. Mr. C uncorked several good deals on champagnes including a bottle of Bollinger's Special Cuvee for just $22.00, and a 1985 vintage bottle of Dom Perignon for $69.00. There are rows upon rows of wines to choose from. You can find good prices in all varieties, but for dependable and inexpensive options, try some of the lesser-known wine producers. A bottle of Chilean Caliterra Sauvignon Blanc sells for just $3.99, marked down from $5.50. Sam's Wine & Spirits seems to carry every beer, especially those from American microbreweries. A recent sale featured a six-pack of Australia's Snakebite beer for $2.99, or $10.99 for a case. In the liquor section, Mr. C noted Bushmills Irish Whiskey at $19.99 for a 1.75 liter bottle; and a one-liter bottle of Tanqueray gin for $15.75. Wine tasting sessions are another fun (and cheap) feature at Sam's Wine & Spirits. These take place every Saturday. If you've always wanted to be considered a wine connoisseur, Sam's also sponsors lectures by renowned wine experts. For more information call, visit their Website, or stop in to get on their mailing list. Open Sunday, 11:00 a.m. - 6:00 p.m.; Monday through Saturday, 8:00 a.m. - 9:00 p.m.

TEN REN TEA & GINSENG COMPANY OF CHICAGO

2247 South Wentworth Avenue, Chicago IL 60616. 312/842-1171. **The Lowdown:** If you enjoy not only great teas, but the entire culture surrounding tea, you should pay a visit to Ten Ren Tea & Ginseng Company. They grow their own tea in Asia and import it directly here, where you can select from a bewildering array of teas, both loose and in bags. The friendly folks here will be happy to explain what each variety is like. And to experience the full effect of a typical tea ceremony, make an appointment for the owner to conduct one at the small wooden table in the front, or if it's not too crowded, he may be willing to give a quick demonstration without an appointment. There is no charge to participate. But make no mistake, there will be some hefty price tags on some of these teas. Ten Wu Supreme, a type of oolong tea, can be exotically-priced at close to $200.00 per pound. Still, the majority of these teas are reasonably priced under $10.00. A basic box of Orange Spice and Hibiscus Spice sells for $2.35; dozens of other varieties sell for between $2.00 and $5.00 a box – including lemon, oolong, jasmine, plum, and ginger. Each kind of tea sold is touted for various health benefits, which they have carefully researched. For example, one kind of tea may combat the common cold; another, the Dieter's Tea, is made for those looking to lose some weight. The staff will be happy to explain these benefits to you; whether or not you believe them is another matter. While you're there, don't forget to check out their wide variety of teapots in different colors and styles.

TREASURE ISLAND

3460 North Broadway, Chicago IL 60657. 312/327-3880. ◆ 1639 North Wells Street, Chicago IL 60614. 312/642-1105. ◆ 75 West Elm Street, Chicago IL 60610. 312/440-1144. ◆ 680 North Lake Shore Drive, Chicago IL 60611. 312/664-0400. ◆ 2121 North Clybourn Avenue, Chicago IL 60614. 312/880-8880. **The Lowdown:** Treasure Island is a paradise for beverage bargains. You can afford to celebrate when Moet & Chandon champagne is only $32.99 for the 750ml bottle. Absolut vodka is only $15.79 for the same size, and a liter of J&B is just $21.99. Beer drinkers will appreciate the prices on quality brands like Samuel Adams, only $5.99 for a six-pack. Wines, like Beringer White Zinfandel at $6.49 a bottle, and Sutter Home Chenin Blanc for just $4.99, are just some of the treasures you may find here. Call for specific location hours.

WINE DISCOUNT CENTER

1826 North Elston Avenue, Chicago IL 60622. 773/489-3454. **The Lowdown:** For years, people have been flocking to this Elston Avenue shop for unbeatable values on fine wines. With an eye for high quality in every price range, store manager Jim Buckley and his staff taste as many as 200 wines per month to cull out the 50 - 70 best to offer to customers. His prices are nearly always a few dollars less than other stores – about 10 - 20 percent below chain retail stores which cannot offer nearly the same selection, and certainly not the wine knowledge or service. Wine prices range from as little as $4.00 to $300.00 or more, with outstanding values in each price categor, and Buckley will gladly meet or beat anyone else's advertised price. Wine Discount Center uses its small store to advantage by focusing its selection on quality wines; because the sales staff has tasted each wine, they are adept at suggesting foods to go with every one. You can try a few of them out yourself when you stop by for a complimentary wine tasting each Saturday afternoon. Wine Discount Center features wines from all the major wine-producing regions of the world – France, Spain, Italy, Germany, Portugal, Chile, Argentina, Australia, and New Zealand. Of course, many of the best producers from California, Washington, and Oregon are available. The store offers a free monthly mailing to customers, announcing the latest arrivals; call or stop in to get on the mailing list. Open Sunday, 12:00 p.m. - 5:00 p.m.; Monday through Friday, 10:00 a.m. - 7:00 p.m.; Saturday, 9:00 a.m. - 5:00 p.m.

Luggage

EMPORIUM LUGGAGE
128 North LaSalle Street, Chicago IL 60602. 312/372-2110. ♦ 12 South Wabash Avenue, Chicago IL 60603. 312/201-0845.
The Lowdown: This premier luggage retailer has been in the Loop since 1985, and in the luggage business since 1947. They sell an excellent variety of luggage, briefcases, computer cases, palm pilot cases, leather agendas, leather notepad covers, travel accessories, and fine writing instruments. They carry lots of major brand names like Hartmann, Samsonite, Andiamo, Briggs and Riley, Filofax, Waterman, and Bosca. Emporium Luggage offers some of the luggage world's most competitive everyday prices, along with a frequent selection of sale items that make the discounts even better. There's always a fantastic supply of genuine leather briefcases on hand, with prices starting as low as $99.99. Mr. C spotted some great buys on carry-on luggage, like a 20-inch bag with in-line skate wheels and a retractable handle just $59.99. For the fashion-conscious who crave a dose of style and pizzazz, Emporium Luggage offers a spectacular array of Kenneth Cole briefcases for both men and women. But, let's not forget about vacation travel: Emporium Luggage offers a super assortment of duffel bags – in lots of sizes and colors – starting at just $24.99 apiece. The service is friendly, helpful, and professional and the atmosphere – though set in a bustling business and shopping district – is quite relaxed. Call for specific location hours.

FLITE LUGGAGE & REPAIR
309 West Chicago Avenue, Chicago IL 60610. 312/664-2142.
The Lowdown: At Flite, they say that "lower overhead means lower prices." Based on the prices that I've seen, they must be telling the truth. Whatever you could possibly need for travel or business, they have it: suitcases, business cases, purses. Best of all, this isn't a store full of no-name, cheapie leather. Flite has got top name brands like Dooney & Bourke, Delsey, Tumi, Samsonite, and Travelpro. They've also got a repair center on-site, so you can rest assured that your luggage will be well tended to. Flite Luggage is also the only luggage retailer to offer the Travel Safe Warranty: you will be guaranteed five years of free repair on any Travel Safe product you purchase. All you need to do is bring the damaged product back to the store and Flite will do the rest. If you live in the Homewood IL area, you should know that Flite Luggage operates another store there. Elke's Luggage (18046 Martin Avenue, Homewood IL 60430. 708/798-1800) offers the same great pricing and Travel Safe Warranty as their Windy City counterpart. Stop in either location and get your trip started right. Call for specific locatin hours.

IRV'S LUGGAGE WAREHOUSE
820 West North Avenue, Chicago IL 60622. 312/787-4787. **Toll-free phone:** 888/300-IRVS. **E-mail address:** Irv@Irvs.com.

World Wide Web address: http://www.Irvs.com.
The Lowdown: When planning an already costly vacation, the last expense you need is luggage. This is where Irv's Luggage Warehouse can help you out. They offer name-brand, quality luggage, business cases, and travel accessories at deeply discounted prices. In fact, if you find the same luggage for a lower price within 30 days of purchasing it from Irv's, they will refund you the difference plus an additional ten percent of the difference. Some of their hottest deals include a Briggs & Riley 28-inch vertical pullman for just $269.49 (listed at $625.00) and an Andiamo carry-on garment bag for $426.00 (listed at $710.00. A Kenneth Cole 22" carry-on is listed at $270.00, but costs only $119.99 at Irv's. They have all the biggest names in luggage, like Hartmann, Boyt, Travelpro, and Samsonite. Plus, they have luggage and backpacks to suit the adventuresome traveler as well.

KAEHLER TRAVEL WORKS
900 North Michigan Avenue, 5th Floor, Chicago IL 60611. 312/951-8106. ◆ Water Tower Place, 6th Floor, Chicago IL 60611. 312/951-7989. ◆ 2070 North Clybourn, Chicago IL. 773/296-9908. ◆ Clark Street & Monroe Street, Chicago IL. 312/960-5680. **World Wide Web address:** http://www.ktworks.com. **The Lowdown:** Though their locations are usually situated within pricey environs, Kaehler Travel Works offers some hefty savings on the best names in luggage and travel necessities. Brand names include Tumi, Dakota Metro, Briggs & Riley, and Kenneth Cole. On Mr. C's visit, every item in Atlantic's Professional Series was at least 50 percent off. Now I don't know about you, but paying $169.99 for a $400.00 carry-on suiter sounds like a good idea to me! Call for specific location hours.

THAT'S OUR BAG
200 North Michigan Avenue, Chicago IL 60601. 312/984-3510. **The Lowdown:** That's Our Bag offers tremendous savings on a variety of accessories. Whether the bag you're looking for is for work or play, That's Our Bag has got plenty to choose from. Look through the many different styles and colors of wallets and purses, or try one of their backpacks on for size. For work, they've got plenty of briefcases and computer bags for both men and women. For the savvy traveler, check out the prices that That's Our Bag offers on some great luggage pieces by the likes of Samsonite and Kenneth Cole. If you know what you want and are just shopping around for the best price, That's Our Bag is definitely a place to do some comparison shopping. Call for hours.

Musical Instruments

CHICAGO BAND & ORCHESTRA COMPANY
THE CHICAGO PERCUSSION CENTER
333 South State Street, Chicago IL 60604.
312/341-0102. **E-mail address:** cbo@bandandorch.com.
World Wide Web address: http://www.bandandorch.com.
The Lowdown: Unless you're playing the kazoo, you will likely find that musical instruments can cost a hefty sum no matter where you buy them. Chicago Band & Orchestra Company and The Chicago Percussion Center are considered to be the city's "complete band and orchestra super-store." They carry over 12,000 items, with particular emphasis on saxophone and percussion instruments. You can choose from both new and used instruments. A used, vintage-looking Olds Super Bb Trumpet was recently priced at $495.00, and a used Selmer Signet Soloist wood clarinet (in good condition) could be bought for just $480.00. Open Monday through Friday, 10:00 a.m. - 6:00 p.m.; Saturday, 10:00 a.m. - 4:00 p.m.

CHICAGO MUSIC EXCHANGE
3270 North Clark Street, Chicago IL 60657. 773/477-0830.
World Wide Web address: http://www.chicagomusicexchange. com. **The Lowdown:** Chicago Music Exchange knows guitars... and they've got a huge inventory of new, used, and vintage guitars to prove it. Brand names include Fender, Gibson, Gretsch, and Rickenbacker and prices start as low as $400.00. Of course, if you're looking to buy only top-of-the-line equipment, you should expect to pay; a vintage Gretsch Silver Jet caught Mr. C's eye for its looks but quickly made its way off my wish list at $5,500.00. Still, there are plenty of guitars that are high in quality and low in price. New items are arriving all the time, so it might pay to keep checking back in.

THE ELECTRIC KEYBOARD
816 Dempster Street, Evanston IL 60202. 847/866-6966. **World Wide Web address:** http://www.electrickeyboard.com.
The Lowdown: Just make sure you've thought of a way to get your goodies home, as you'll have to travel to Evanston to get The Electric Keyboard's discounts. The Electric Keyboard carries a selection of used (yes, you guessed it) electric keyboards. Since 1990, they have been a premiere source for discounts for Chicagoland's electronic musicians. Equipment and accessories are a good mix of new and used merchandise. In addition to instruments, The Electric Keyboard also carries a discounted supply of books and software. New merchandise is arriving all the time, so it pays to stop in (in person or virtually) pretty often.

GAND MUSIC AND SOUND
780 Frontage Road, Northfield IL 60093. 847/446-GAND. **E-mail address:** website@gand.com. **World Wide Web address:**

http://www.gand.com. **The Lowdown:** While I try and keep this book centered within Chicago, sometimes it pays to take a journey outside the city. Especially in the case of instrument purchasing; buying a new keyboard, guitar, etc. can be a very costly investment. And, with any big money purchase, I like to give you an idea of all the great places (including the surrounding areas) where you might find the styles and prices you had your heart set on. With more than 200 brand name keyboards, digital pianos, guitars, amps, and recording devices in stock, it's hard to imagine that Gand wouldn't have what you are looking for. Brand names like Akai, Amek, Bose, Crown, DBX, Ensoniq, Fender, Kurzweil, Lexicon, Martin, Taylor, and Yamaha help to fill the many musical departments with the highest quality instruments and accessories for less. Open Sunday, 12:00 p.m. - 5:00 p.m.; Monday through Friday, 12:00 p.m. - 8:00 p.m.; Saturday, 11:00 a.m. - 6:00 p.m.

KURT SAPHIR PIANOS
123 Green Bay Road, Wilmette IL 60091. 847/256-5225. **The Lowdown:** A store that has stayed in the same family for seven generations, Kurt Saphir restores old pianos, many of which come to the store through estate sales and the like. Roger Ebert bought his piano here; Mr. C adds his own thumbs-up. Saphir also sells brand-new models, in the middle- to upper-end price range. Mason & Hamlin, Bosendorfer, Charles Waltor, and Knabe are the predominant brands carried here. If you're shopping for value and quality, be sure to check them out.

MUSIC HOUSE, INC.
2925 West Devon Avenue, Chicago IL 60659. 773/761-3770. **E-mail address:** mhinc@musichouseinc.com. **World Wide Web address:** http://www.musichouseinc.com. **The Lowdown:** It's hard to find a better street for bargain shopping than Devon, and this tiny store has great prices on violins, guitars, and other band instruments. Because they're used, they're marked way down from original prices; but everything is in good condition. The selection varies, depending on what owner Richard Trumbo can find. Music House also offers lessons; they are dedicated to fostering musical talent in kids and even offer free lessons each Saturday. Throughout the year, Music House classes perform small concerts around the city. Call for more information on lessons, events, and hours.

MUSICIAN'S NETWORK
5505 North Clark Street, Chicago IL 60640. 773/728-2929. **The Lowdown:** Located in Andersonville, this music shop can save you plenty on lots of new and used equipment. If your in the market for a vintage instrument, put Musician's Network at the top of your list of places to stop by. I found a used Rickenbacker 3000 series bass (with case) for $350.00; vintage Marshall heads for under $600.00; and a new Ampeg B-15 amplifier for under $1000.00. The store has a high rate of turnover, mostly on its more inexpensive trade-ins, so the selection varies widely from week to week.

THE SOUND POST

3640 West Dempster, Skokie IL 60076. 847/679-6070. ♦ 25 West Calendar, LaGrange IL 60525. 708/352-3338. **World Wide Web address:** http://www.soundpostmusic.com. **The Lowdown:** It's easy to see why this local chain of music equipment stores is so popular; an extremely knowledgeable staff and fantastic prices are just the beginning. The Sound Post offers expert advice and top of the line musical equipment at reasonable prices. Each store carries a good selection of excellent-condition used equipment as well, allowing musicians on a budget to go up a step in quality. Even musicians just starting out should feel good about shopping here. The Sound Post even offers music lessons! Still, one of the most comforting things about shopping here is that the salespeople are not here to move equipment out the door; they're here to make sure that you are happy with your purchase months and even years after you leave the store. All employees have been well-trained by big name manufacturers; most are even musicians themselves. Couple that with some of the best prices in town and you've got a store that is worth the drive outside of town. Open Sunday, 12:00 p.m. - 4:00 p.m.; Monday through Thursday, 11:30 a.m. - 8:00 p.m.; Friday, 11:30 a.m. - 6:00 p.m.; Saturday, 10:00 a.m. - 5:00 p.m.

ZZOUNDS PIPER'S ALLEY

230 North Avenue, Chicago IL 60614. 312/280-4664. **World Wide Web address:** http://www.zzounds.com. **The Lowdown:** ZZounds Piper's Alley offers some of the biggest names in musical instruments, with one of the largest selections around, all at the lowest prices you can find from an authorized dealer. They have a large and interesting collection of unusual and hard-to-find world instruments. They only carry new merchandise at Zzounds and they promise to meet or beat the lowest advertised price from any other authorized dealer. A Washburn XB400 Bantam bass guitar was seen for almost half its original price. ZZounds rotates their stock often, so if you don't find what you're looking for today, try again next week or next month. Free parking is offered at the indoor lot next to the store. Open Sunday, 12:00 p.m. - 5:00 p.m.; Monday through Saturday, 12:00 p.m. - 8:00 p.m.

Outlet Malls

GURNEE MILLS MALL
6170 West Grand Avenue, Gurnee IL 60031. 847/263-7500. **Toll-free phone:** 800/YES-SHOP. **E-mail address:** gurnee@millscorp.com. **World Wide Web address:** http://www.gurneemillsmall.com. **The Lowdown:** Located about 40 miles outside of Chicago, it will take you less than an hour to reach this bargain shopping paradise. No matter what you're looking for, Gurnee Mills Mall is guaranteed to have it at a great price. If you're looking for luggage, two separate Bentley's Luggage outlets and a Samsonite store are sure to have something great. If accessories are your bag, Claire's Boutique, The Icing, and Sunglass World should be right up your alley. Want to refurbish your home entertainment facilities? Bose Speakers, Panasonic/Technics, Radio Shack, and Sam Goody will definitely come in handy. For the newlyweds who don't quite have it all, The Bedding Experts, Corning Revere, Sunbeam/Oster, and Tiffany Lamp are sure to help out. If you're here for purely selfish fashion reasons (translation: clothes shopping), you'll probably never want to shop anywhere else. From A - Z, Gurnee Mills Mall has got all your favorite clothing stores: Abercrombie & Fitch, Ann Taylor, Athlete's Foot, Bugle Boy, The Children's Place, Dockers, Florsheim, Gap, Guess?, Levi's, Nautica, Nine West, Oshkosh B'gosh, Pacific Sunwear, Polo, Track 'n Trail, Van Heusen, and Wilson's Leather are just a few of the more than 200 stores. Visit their Website to find out about this week's Hot Buys, where stores list even further weekly or monthly discounts. Open Sunday, 11:00 a.m. - 6:00 p.m.; Monday through Saturday, 10:00 a.m. - 9:00 p.m.

THE ORIGINAL OUTLET MALL
7700 120th Avenue, Kenosha WI 53142. 414/857-7961. **The Lowdown:** If you're willing to take the trip to Kenosha, Wisconsin, The Original Outlet Mall will definitely yield a bargain or two. Just about an hour outside of Chicago, The Original Outlet Mall houses nearly 100 discount and outlet stores from some very recognizable and some not-so-recognizable names. Still, if it's bargains you're after, you should have no problem finding them here. A free parking lot will save you even more money. Open Sunday, 11:00 a.m. - 6:00 p.m.; Saturday, 10:00 a.m. - 6:00 p.m.; Monday through Friday, 10:00 a.m. - 9:00 p.m.

PRIME OUTLETS AT HUNTLEY
11800 Factory Shops Boulevard, Huntley IL 60142. **Toll-free phone:** 888/545-7222. **World Wide Web address:** http://www.primeoutlets.com. **The Lowdown:** Just 50 miles west of Chicago sits this mall with more than 55 brand name outlets. Like all the malls in the Prime Outlets family, you'll find only the first names in fashion. Men will appreciate savings on clothing by Britches, Bugle Boy, S&K Menswear, and Van Heusen Direct. Women will love trying on clothing from the stores they

love most like Casual Corner, Designer Connection, and Petite Sophisticate. Other popular stores include American Outpost, The Gap, and Levi's for clothing; Bass and Nine West for shoes; Samsonite for accessories; and Mikasa, Pfaltzgraff, and Sunbeam/Oster for home goods. Open Sunday, 11:00 a.m. - 6:00 p.m.; Monday through Saturday, 10:00 a.m. - 9:00 p.m. In January and February, Prime Outlets at Huntley closes at 7:00 p.m. from Monday through Thursday.

PRIME OUTLETS AT KENOSHA

11211 120th Avenue, Suite 19A, Pleasant Prairie WI 53158. 262/857-2101. **World Wide Web address:** http://www. primeoutlets.com. **The Lowdown:** It seems that, in the Midwest, Kenosha is the king of outlet shopping. Prime Outlets at Kenosha upholds this title with more than 65 brand name shops. They've got all your favorites including Andrew Marc, Brooks Brothers, Columbia Sportswear, Donna Karan, Fila, Gap Outlet, J. Crew, Liz Claiborne, Mikasa, Polo/Ralph Lauren, Nike Factory Outlet, Noritake, Tommy Hilfiger Company Store, and Versace. More than just clothing, Prime Outlets at Kenosha offers a wide range of items from stores like Chicago Cutlery and Black & Decker to Rug Decor and Vornado. This is an especially great place to get some holiday shopping done. Just be warned that, as Mr. C is not the only one who thinks this is a great place, it can tend to get crowded – especially during the holiday season. Open Sunday, 11:00 a.m. - 6:00 p.m.; Monday through Saturday, 10:00 a.m. - 9:00 p.m. During January and February, the mall closes at 6:00 p.m. Monday through Thursday.

PRIME OUTLETS AT MICHIGAN CITY

601 Wabash Street, Michigan City IN 46360. 219/879-6506. **World Wide Web address:** http://www.primeoutlets.com. **The Lowdown:** While there aren't too many outlet malls in Chicago, there are plenty within a reasonable driving distance. Only an hour from downtown Chicago, Prime Outlets at Michigan City offers significant discounts on some top designer labels. Among the more than 120 stores, you'll find significant discounts on brand name clothing for the entire family, shoes, handbags, luggage, jewelry, cosmetics, fragrances, housewares, furnishings, gifts, and specialty items. Outlets for Guess?, Ellen Tracy, ESPRIT, J. Crew, Gap, Levi's, Eddie Bauer, and Tommy Hilfiger are just a few of the places you can fashion your family. Men can look like a million bucks at work with a quick trip to Brooks Brothers; while women can choose the always-trendy fashions at DKNY. Ralph Lauren packs a one-two punch with a dressier Polo/Ralph Lauren outlet along with a more casual Polo Jeans outpost. Your kids will look fantastic in clothing by Oilily with goodies from Toy Liquidators. Accessorize yourself with trips to Cosmetics Company, Perfumania, Easy Spirit, Rockport, Timberland, and Coach. Housewares have never looked so good (or cheap) at places like Chef's Outlet, Lenox, Oneida, Waterford Wedgwood, and Crate & Barrel. Open Sunday, 10:00 a.m. - 6:00 p.m.; Monday through Saturday, 9:00 a.m. - 8:00 p.m. In January and February, the mall is only open until 6:00 p.m. Monday through Saturday.

Party Supplies

CARD AND PARTY WAREHOUSE
4216 West Belmont Avenue, Chicago IL 60641.
773/736-4900. ◆ 1880 West Fullerton Avenue,
Chicago IL 60614. 773/342-1500. ◆ 6253 North McCormick
Boulevard, Chicago IL 60659. 773/478-6200.
The Lowdown: It looks more like a festival in here than a
warehouse, with balloons, streamers, and bright colors splashed
all around. What makes this place even brighter is that these
decorative items are all being sold at prices of up to 70 percent
below retail. You can save 25 - 50 percent on packs of
invitations, and 50 percent off all greeting cards. The clearance
section even has cards priced at just $.25 apiece. Some
additional bargains have included a complete set of plastic
utensils for eight people for just $.63; a pack of 50 plastic
drinking cups for $3.00; mylar balloons, with prints for every
conceivable occasion, priced at three for $5.00; and six of those
little exploding champagne bottle party favors for $1.00. If you
want to decorate a complete theme party from floor to ceiling,
whether for children or grownups, this is a great place to look
and save. Open daily. Call for specific location hours.

FACTORY CARD OUTLET
5123 South Pulaski Road, Chicago IL 60632. 773/585-7733.
◆ 2585 North Elston Avenue, Chicago IL 60647. 773/486-0948.
◆ 8045 South Cicero Avenue, Chicago IL 60652. 773/582-7787.
The Lowdown: This chain takes the superstore approach to the
greeting cards and party supplies market. At Factory Card Outlet,
all holiday and greeting cards are priced at $.39 each. Period.
And they don't just have a few, yellowing leftovers from last
Arbor Day; it's a huge, current selection. Obviously, high-volume
business allows them to make up the difference elsewhere. What
else do they sell here? Everything you need to invite people to a
party, decorate it, and serve them food and drink. And it's all
sold at 30 - 70 percent below retail prices. Whether you want to
go simple, with color-coordinated plates and napkins, or go all
out with 10-inch tapered candles in a palette of colors, 80-foot
rolls of streamers, paper or plastic tablecloths, and helium
balloons, you'll find what you need here at a significant discount.
Seasonal supplies, of course, are a specialty, and they are
available well in advance of major holidays. Do people make fun
of you for doing your Christmas shopping in July? Come in here
and you'll be among friends (you'll also be amid bargains on
cards, wrapping paper, and so on). When its back to school time,
keep Factory Card Outlet in mind, as they offer tremendous
savings on some great school supplies.

FANTASY HEADQUARTERS
4065 North Milwaukee Avenue, Chicago IL 60641. 773/777-0222.
Toll-free phone: 800/USA-WIGS. **E-mail address:**
info@fantasycostumes.com. **World Wide Web address:**
http://www.fantasycostumes.com. **The Lowdown:** No, you

won't find lots of matching pastel party cups and plates, but you will find a wide variety of themed party decorations and attire, including basics like balloons, streamers, and toy prizes. Fantasy Headquarters is a city block long store with over one million items in stock. You may find people shopping here for an upcoming theatrical performance, TV filming, corporate sales meeting, rock concert, masquerade ball, or (of course) a Halloween party. They rent and sell costumes, accessories, masks, makeup, hats, wigs, and hairpieces. The hats start at just $1.09; masks at $.99; wigs at $9.99; and complete costumes at $29.99. Whether you're shopping for dress-up ideas or for an actual costume, Fantasy Headquarters has plenty of options. Open Sunday, 11:00 a.m. - 5:00 p.m.; Monday through Friday, 9:30 a.m. - 8:00 p.m.; Saturday, 9:30 a.m. - 6:00 p.m.

JEANNIE'S LET'S CELEBRATE
3950 North Harlem Avenue, Chicago IL 60634. 773/625-0233.
The Lowdown: When it's time to celebrate – no matter what the occasion – it's time to head to Jeannie's Let's Celebrate. You'll find fantastic deals on all the paper and party supplies you could possibly imagine. Everyday, you'll find such great deals as 50 percent off all greeting cards, 20 percent off custom invitations, and balloon bouquets from just $3.99. Plus, Jeannie's Let's Celebrate offers discounted centerpieces and party favors for all occasions. Just picking a party theme is hard enough; Jeannie's Let's Celebrate makes the ordeal of party-throwing that much easier a task (and oh-so-easy on your pocket).

PARTY CITY
1755 West Fullerton Avenue, Chicago IL 60614. 773/525-0399.
World Wide Web address: http://www.partycity.com.
The Lowdown: Party City doesn't kid around when they call themselves *the* discount party super store. With more than 20,000 items in stock, they carry one of the nation's largest supplies of party needs – all under one roof (or, in this case, two)! From the beginning preparations to the final execution, they have the supplies you'll for creating a fantastic shindig. Start out with the invitations. Even when personalized you'll still be saving 30 percent off prices you'd pay elsewhere. You can create a theme and stick to it when purchasing your balloons and decorations. And if you're handling the food by yourself, they've got plenty of catering supplies and tableware at everyday low prices. Open Sunday, 10:30 a.m. - 6:00 p.m.; Monday through Saturday, 9:30 a.m. - 9:00 p.m.

PARTY FAVORS PLUS
3938 West Touhy Avenue, Lincolnwood IL 60645. 847/933-1970.
E-mail address: Info@partyfavorsplus.com. **World Wide Web address:** http://www.partyfavorsplus.com. **The Lowdown:** Okay, so maybe it's cheating a little, but if you don't have the means to make it to this suburban store, the Party Favors Plus Website offers the same great deals. Party Favors Plus offers a variety of party favors and more (hence the "Plus"). For even the most elegant of occasions, Party Favors Plus has got the goodies to make it all come together. Birthday parties, weddings, baby

and bridal showers are just a few of the events they specialize in. Party Favors Plus has also got a wonderful supply of decorations for specific holiday events, like Christmas. Best of all, if you're willing to purchase your favors and decorations a bit in advance, the savings can be out of this world (we're talking up to 75 percent here)! What's more, virtually everything in stock is customizable, making the occasion that much more special. For the wedding of your dreams they've got gorgeous ring pillows for as little as $49.95 and beautiful cake tops for the same price (trust me, it'll save you a few bucks if you don't order it from the caterer); make it a sweet 16 to remember with some gorgeous party favors for as little as $2.75 apiece; welcome that new baby with a fantastic ceramic bootie centerpiece (in pink or blue) for just $15.95. Even if you're not sure where to start, Party Favors Plus can provide you with some great ideas. Open Sunday, 11:00 a.m. - 4:00 p.m.; Monday and Thursday, 10:00 a.m. - 8:00 p.m.; Tuesday, Wednesday, and Friday, 10:00 a.m. - 6:00 p.m.; Saturday, 10:00 a.m. - 5:00 p.m.

Pets & Supplies

ANIMAL WELFARE LEAGUE
10305 Southwest Highway, Chicago Ridge IL 60415. 708/636-8586. ◆ 6224 South Wabash Avenue, Chicago IL 60637. 773/667-0088. **World Wide Web address:** http://www.animalwelfareleague.com. **The Lowdown:** Though they *do* have a location in Chicago, it is the Chicago Ridge location that offers pet adoption services. Founded in 1935, Chicago's Animal Welfare League ensures the love and care of abused or neglected pets and provides low-cost medical attention to pet-loving families on a limited income. Because more than just cats and dogs are left at shelters everyday, just about any animal you can imagine is available for adoption here. Hamsters, rabbits, guinea pigs, iguanas, turtles, and birds are just a few of the animals looking for a home. And, while it's true that you'll be saving a significant amount of money by adopting than if you purchased these animals at a pet store or from a breeder, you'll also be making the difference in the life of an animal in need. Adoption fees vary with each animal: Dogs are $75.00, cats are $30.00, ferrets are $60.00, female rabbits are $25.00, male rabbits are $20.00, guinea pigs are $10.00. If you have access to the Internet, you can even look at pictures of available pets by visiting their Website (listed above) or The Pet Shelter Website at http://www.petshelter.com. Adoption hours are daily, 11:00 a.m. - 5:00 p.m. (until 7:30 p.m. on Tuesday and Thursday).

THE ANTI-CRUELTY SOCIETY
510 North LaSalle Street, Chicago IL 60610. 312/644-8338. **E-mail address:** info@anticruelty.org. **World Wide Web address:** http://www.anticruelty.org. **The Lowdown:** For more than a century, The Anti-Cruelty Society has been promoting happy pet/owner relationships. Since they recognize that most animals are left at a shelter for reasons that could have been prevented, they are dedicated to teaching and ensuring that people and their pets know and love one another. If you're looking to adopt a pet, they ask that you and every member of your household come in and interact with the animals beforehand. Since they know the history of many of the animals, they can help to find the right pet for you and your family. If you are ready to adopt, you must come prepared with a photo I.D. (proving that you are 18 years or older) and a copy of your current lease or your landlord's name and phone number. Just $55.00 later (pending Society approval, of course), you could be the proud parent of a new pet! And just what does this $55.00 pay for? The adoption fee includes a series of shots and vaccines, heartworm and leukemia test, spaying/neutering, collar and tag, leash or carrier, and 15-day free post-adoption pet care. If you're bringing home Fido for the first time, they'll also throw in some obedience classes to make the ordeal less stressful. But pet adoption is not the only reason The Anti-Cruelty Society is listed in this book. Whether you adopted your pet at The Anti-Cruelty Society or not, they've got plenty of services that can save you

some money. In addition to the general Introduction to Obedience class that is included in dog adoption fees, ACS offers a six-week puppy training class ($65.00) and an eight-week beginner class for dogs that are older than six months ($85.00 if you adopted your pet at ACS, $100.00 for the general public). The Anti-Cruelty Society offers a number of inexpensive veterinary services, like a $25.00 spay/neuter clinic and a free mobile vaccination van. In addition, The Society hosts a number of special events throughout the year, like fundraisers and animal book author presentations. Call or visit their Website for information on any of ACS's services or to get a list of upcoming events. Open for adoptions daily, 12:00 p.m. - 5:00 p.m. Office is open Monday through Friday, 8:30 a.m. - 4:30 p.m.

FELINES INC.
P.O. Box 60616, Chicago IL 60660. 773/465-4132. **World Wide Web address:** http://www.felinesinc.org. **The Lowdown:** Felines Inc. is one of the many Chicagoland shelters dedicated to finding loving homes for homeless, unwanted, or abused cats and kittens. Because Felines Inc. is a no-kill shelter, some of the animals that come here will remain here for the rest of their lives. On average, there are about 200 felines living in the shelter at any given time. Now, it's up to you to pick one (okay, maybe two) to bring home. All cats have been spayed or neutered (unless it's a kitten), dewormed, and vaccinated. Before stopping by to browse the lot of potential purring pals, it is necessary to call for a telephone screening interview and set up a time to come in. Adoption fees are $40.00 for adults and $55.00 for kittens ($25.00 of this fee will be refunded once your pet has been spayed or neutered). To help with the cost of pet care, Felines Inc. also offers a variety of low-cost veterinary services. And if you feel the need to bring more than just one home (come on, cats need friends too), they'll give you an additional discount on fees. Only cash or check payments are accepted. Call now to schedule an appointment.

GREATER CHICAGO FERRET ASSOCIATION
P.O. Box 7093, Westchester IL 60154-7093. 708/442-8650. **World Wide Web address:** http://www.gcfa.com. **The Lowdown:** While it is well-known that there are plenty of city shelters overrun with cats and dogs, it is a little known fact that the number of ferrets who are brought to shelters is rapidly increasing. Unfortunately, conflicting policies and the lack of proper knowledge about ferrets prevents many high-profile shelters and societies from taking these little guys in. Fortunately, in 1987, the G.C.F.A. was established for just this purpose. From its humble beginnings in the basement of one of the founding members, G.C.F.A. has grown into a full-service organization that works worldwide to ensure their mission of a population that is more educated and aware of the needs of ferrets. Since its founding, close to 3,000 ferrets have called G.C.F.A. home for a little while; at any given time it is likely that there are more than 100 ferrets in the shelter. For those who want to become ferret owners, G.C.F.A. offers an inexpensive and strategic adoption plan. Since very few people are educated

as to the needs of these animals, a G.C.F.A. member will speak with you and answer any questions to determine your capability. Adoption requirements include that the animal be taken into your own home, that you are at least 18 years of age, that you are willing to learn about the care of these animals and ask questions, that you are willing and able to accept this animal into your family. Their mission is simple: G.C.F.A. seeks to place ferrets into the hands and homes of ferret-friendly individuals. Adopted ferrets will be spayed or neutered and will have received many of their necessary shots and vaccinations. Adoption fees are $70.00 if the animal is under one year, $55.00 is the animal is one to three years old, and $40.00 if the animal is more than three years old. Even if you don't have the time and energy to devote to becoming a ferret owner, you can certainly learn all about them. Six times a year, G.C.F.A. holds meetings with guest speakers; and, each Fall, they hold their annual ferret show which attracts ferrets and their owners from all over the country. Call or visit their Website for further information or to set up an appointment to speak with an adoption counselor. Please be aware that, as ferrets can be easily startled, households with members under the age of five are not usually a good match.

THE HARMONY HOUSE FOR CATS
773/463-6667. **The Lowdown:** Founded in the early 1970s, The Harmony House for Cats is like a homeless shelter for felines. In this cageless, no-kill shelter for cats, there are more than 120 cats running around at any given time, and they're all waiting for you to take them home. While many of the animals arrive in an abused and/or neglected state, The Harmony House for Cats staff works hard to love and care for these animals and restore their trust in humans. Once their faith has been restored, it is you who will benefit from this friend for life. The entire adoption process takes about one hour. You should come equipped with a driver's license or picture I.D., all members of the cat's new household, and a copy of your current telephone bill with your current address if you are not listed in the phone book. Just think: The more animals that get adopted, the more space that opens up for other cats in need. Please call before stopping by The Harmony House for Cats. Open Friday, 4:00 p.m. - 8:00 p.m.; Saturday, Sunday, and Monday, 12:00 p.m. - 4:00 p.m.

NAPERVILLE HUMANE SOCIETY
1620 West Diehl Road, Naperville IL 60563. 630/420-8393. **E-mail address:** nhs@ntsource.com. **World Wide Web address:** http://www.chicagobiznet.com/nhshumane. **The Lowdown:** Dedicated to providing loving homes for unwanted dogs and cats, Naperville Humane Society takes their pet adoption process seriously. To ensure that pets are being placed in the best home possible, NHS has a simple list of rules that must be followed: First, adoptive pet parents must be at least 21 years of age and be able to prove so with picture identification; second, parents must fill out a questionnaire to be reviewed by the NHS adoption board; third, NHS asks that all members living under the roof stop by and get acquainted with their new pet, ensuring that pet and family are a great match; finally – but

most importantly – adoptive parents agree to have their new pet spayed or neutered. In creating the perfect pet/family match, NHS also prefers to place animals that are six months old or older in homes with small children. Because kittens and puppies can often act like babies themselves, adopting an older pet makes it a much easier adjustment. NHS's Website will even let you browse through the pictures and profiles of many of their pets that are currently up for adoption. While NHS is listed in this book because it is an inexpensive way to adopt a new pet, it is also listed because of the important service they are providing. NHS (along with other local humane societies and animal shelters) are helping to make the world a much more loving and friendly place for cats and dogs, and that is definitely a goal that Mr. C supports 100 percent! Open Monday, 5:00 p.m. - 8:00 p.m.; Wednesday through Friday, 1:00 p.m. - 6:00 p.m.; Saturday and Sunday, 12:00 p.m. - 4:00 p.m.

PETCO
2000 North Clybourn Avenue, Chicago IL 60614. 773/665-1368.
♦ 2046 North Halsted Street, Chicago IL 69657. 773/935-7547.
♦ 3118 North Ashland Avenue, Chicago IL 60657. 773/935-7388.
♦ 4072 North Milwaukee Avenue, Chicago IL 60641. 773/777-7387. ♦ 4614 Harlem Avenue, Harwood Heights IL. 708/867-7700. **World Wide Web address:** http://www.petco.com.
The Lowdown: In addition to being one of the nation's only pet-friendly places of business (that's right, you and Spot can browse the aisles right alongside each other), PETCO offers some of the area's best prices on all sorts of pet supplies. Inside, you'll find food, toys, and everything else imaginable for your cat, dog, rabbit, guinea pig, snake, iguana, fish, etc. (the list goes on and on). Whomever your pet of choice, chances are PETCO has got something for him/her on their shopping list. Plus, most stores offer a select group of live animal departments such as aquatics, birds, reptiles, and small companions (mice and hamsters, for example). PETCO also works in conjunction with many local and national animal shelters to find loving homes for animals in need. Many stores set aside a living area for animals awaiting adoption; they will also provide you with the names of several local shelters where you can find more pets; plus, they often set up a donation area where – even if you can't take a pet home – you can make sure to contribute to the cause. In keeping with their low prices on pet products, PETCO also offers a number of on-the-premises, low-cost pet services such as grooming and a wellness clinic. Grab a pamphlet when you drop in and find out about all their upcoming events; and remember, these are all activities that you and your pet can do together! Call for specific location hours.

TREE HOUSE ANIMAL FOUNDATION
1212 West Carmen Avenue, Chicago IL 60640-2999. 773/784-5488. **World Wide Web address:** http://www. treehouseanimals.org. **The Lowdown:** Since 1971 Tree House Animal Foundation has provided sick, injured, and abused cats with a safe and cageless home. Because Tree House is a no-kill shelter, animals are invited to stay for as long as they need. Because many of the pets are overlooked due to handicaps or

illnesses, Tree House ensures a safe environment for these special felines for the duration of their lives. The adoption process at Tree House can take up to two hours, so be sure you set aside enough time to pick out the perfect pet. You will need two forms of identification (one asserting that you are 18 years or older), and a copy of your most recent phone bill if your number is unlisted. The adoption fee of $55.00 includes all necessary shots and vaccinations, spay or neuter of your animal, deworming, and a 30-day health guarantee. If you already have a cat, Tree House can still offer you services such as a free behavioral advice hotline and a pet food pantry to help low-income pet owners feed their furry little friends. When you buy toys for kitty from the Tree House store, you are also helping to provide financial support to such a worthwhile organization. Tree House's 12-inch crawly critter is filled with organically-grown catnip and is sure to provide your cat with hours of entertainment for just $3.95; doggie throw toys can be had for as little as $5.95 apiece; and individually-sewn cat pillows are sure to keep your cat (and wallet) comfortable at $16.95. For more information, call or visit their Website. Adoption hours are Sunday, 12:00 p.m. - 5:00 p.m.; Wednesday through Friday, 12:00 p.m. - 4:00 p.m.; Saturday, 10:00 a.m. - 5:00 p.m.; closed Monday and Tuesday.

WEST SUBURBAN HUMANE SOCIETY

1901 West Ogden Avenue, Downers Grove IL 60515. 630/960-9600. **World Wide Web address:** http://www.wshs-dg.org. **The Lowdown:** West Suburban Humane Society is a volunteer-based animal shelter dedicated to improving the lives of unwanted cats and dogs. If you're searching for that perfect pet, look no further than West Suburban Humane Society. The rules of adoption are simple: First, you fill out the adoption questionnaire to be reviewed by one of the Society's volunteers (forms can be downloaded from their Website to make the process even quicker); next, you and your family can meet all the available pets and choose the one that is right for you. The cost for adopting a pet ($75.00) is more than reasonable. If you're taking home a kitten or cat, this fee includes several shots and vaccines, spay/neutering, I.D. tag and collar, a carrier, and a free vet exam. If you're taking home a puppy or dog, your $75.00 will go towards vaccines and shots, I.D. tag and collar, a leash, and a free vet exam. Because the folks at West Suburban Humane Society care about their animals, they are happy to offer lots of advice before and after the adoption process is complete. They are concerned about your happiness as much as your pet's, and they'll work hard to find you a perfect match. Before you visit, you can even cruise the Society's Website, where you'll be introduced to many of the pets that are currently available for adoption. It's a great way to get the adoption procedure started. Adopting a pet from a humane society is a great for the wallet and the heartstrings. Open Monday through Friday (except Wednesday), 11:00 a.m. - 2:00 p.m. and 7:00 p.m. - 9:00 p.m.; Saturday and Sunday, 11:00 a.m. - 3:00 p.m.; closed Wednesday.

Sewing & Fabrics

AYLA'S ORIGINALS
1511 Sherman Avenue, Evanston IL 60201. 847/328-4040. **E-mail address:** ayla@aylasoriginals.com. **World Wide Web address:** http://www.aylasoriginals.com. **The Lowdown:** In Africa, beads are associated with affluence and social rank; in America, that may not necessarily ring true, though Ayla's Originals has a way of making you feel aristocratically noble. With thousands of beads to choose from in a wide range of prices, you can create ornate jewelry for a fraction of what it costs to buy it ready-made. They sell rare beads and collectibles, bead strands, delicas and seed beads, individual beads, and books about beading. Individual polymer beads in a variety of shapes, sizes, designs, and colors can cost as little as $.60 each. For about $1.00 or so, you can buy a tube of Japanese seeds to string on a necklace. Ayla's Originals has some genuine, high-quality beads and one of the widest selections of African trade beads in Chicago. Open Sunday, 12:30 p.m. - 4:00 p.m.; Monday through Friday, 10:00 a.m. - 6:00 p.m.; Saturday, 10:00 a.m. - 5:00 p.m.

CARAVAN BEADS
3361 North Lincoln Avenue, Chicago IL 60657. 773/248-9555. **E-mail address:** caravan@ripco.com. **World Wide Web address:** http://www.caravanchicago.com. **The Lowdown:** Anyone shopping at Caravan Beads better have an inkling as to what they are looking for; because with over 600,000 beads to choose from, you're not likely to make any quick decisions otherwise. This North Side store sells beads native to an array of different countries. You'll find the Midwest's largest selection of Japanese seed beads and all of the Delica colors. They also carry Czech and Indian glass beads, as well as semi-precious, bone, horn, and crystals. If, once you get home, you realize that you don't know what to do with your purchases, consider taking a Caravan beading class. Classes start at $15.00 and cover such areas as wireworking, beginner earrings, stringing techniques, glass beadmaking, and netted bracelet making. For a list of classes or for more information, call, drop in, or visit their Website. Open Sunday, 11:00 a.m. - 5:00 p.m.; Monday, Tuesday, and Friday, 11:00 a.m. - 7:00 p.m.; Thursday, 11:00 a.m. - 8:00 p.m.; Saturday, 11:00 a.m. - 6:00 p.m.; closed Wednesday.

CHICAGO FABRIC SALES COMPANY
72 East Adams Street, Chicago IL 60603. 312/427-1528. **The Lowdown:** With a back room full of low-priced bins with lace, trimmings, fabric scraps, remnants, and craft kits, you're bound to find something of interest at Chicago Fabric Sales. The store offers everything the aspiring and/or established designer or seamstress needs. From designer remnants, buttons, and buckles to brocades and tapestry, there's nothing they don't have. Whether your project is elegant or casual, they've got the

materials to suit your needs: velvet, wool, linen, silk, fur, patent leather, and rubber are just a few of the many finds. Frequent specials make the prices even more budget-friendly.

FISHMAN'S FABRICS

1101 South Desplaines Street, Chicago IL 60607. 312/922-7250.
The Lowdown: Since 1903, Fishman's Fabrics has been offering the largest selection of textiles and trimmings at some of the best prices in town. Luckily, they don't reserve the savings for just retail entities; you can cash in on them too! Fishman's three floors are jam packed with savings on fabrics of all sorts including silk, wool, linen, and cotton. For many local interior decorators, Fishman's is always a first stop; remnants of the same merchandise that can be found at the Merchandise Mart (often selling for $100.00 or more per yard) can be purchased here for as little as $9.95. Free parking is an added bonus. Open Sunday, 9:30 a.m. – 5:00 p.m.; Monday through Friday, 9:30 a.m. – 5:00 p.m.

LOOMCRAFT HOME DECORATING FABRICS

640 North LaSalle Street, Chicago IL 60610. 312/587-0055.
The Lowdown: Buying closeouts and seconds in big lots allows this chain to cut prices. Their selection consists of home decorating fabric for upholstery and drapes. The store is neatly organized by color and pattern, which saves time, though it can be a bit dizzying. Their remnant table is super-cheap, though there may not be enough of one pattern for a full project. Fortunately, prices in the rest of the store are very reassuring. First quality floral prints, similar to Laura Ashley designs, were seen for $12.99 a yard, with a retail value of up to $32.00 elsewhere. $12.99 - $19.99 a yard for cotton prints; $19.99 a yard for velvets; and $16.99 - $36.99 a yard for chenilles and other upholstery fabrics are prices you'd typically find at Loomcraft. Frequent sales offer additional discounts of as much as 20 - 70 percent. Call to find out when the next sale is happening. If you see something you like, buy it right away, as Loomcraft can't guarantee what stock they will ever get in again.

SINGER FACTORY OUTLET

4914 West Irving Park Road, Chicago IL 60641. 773/545-6834.
• 3906 North Harlem, Chicago IL 60634. 773/625-1515.
The Lowdown: In Chicago, it pays to go to the biggest name in sewing machines... and one that we all associate with high quality. Chicago's Singer Factory Outlet offers fantastic savings on new and used machines, cabinets, and other sewing furniture. All products, even the used ones, are guaranteed lowest prices, from 20 - 50 percent off the manufacturer's list price. Now that's something to sing about. If you do choose to buy here, you'll really reap the benefits. For those who may have the desire but not the skills, Singer Factory Outlet offers free lessons by professional instructors. The outlet also repairs and trades all makes and models, in addition to offering free estimates. Open Sunday, 12:00 p.m. - 5:00 p.m.; Monday through Saturday, 10:00 a.m. - 5:00 p.m. (until 8:00 p.m. on Monday and Thursday).

TEXTILE ARTS CENTRE
RECYCLE SALE ROOM

916 West Diversey Parkway, Chicago IL 60614. 773/929-5655.
World Wide Web address: http://collaboratory.acns.nwu.edu/
textilearts. **The Lowdown:** Nowhere else in Chicago will you find
a group more dedicated to the sewing and textile arts industry
than at the Textile Arts Centre. This non-profit organization hosts
all sorts of knitting, weaving, crocheting, and other crafty
classes. For the shopper in you, they have the Recycle Sale
Room, which is a virtual sewing paradise for the thrifty and
creative. A shopping bag full of upholstery fabric samples goes
for $5.00. And what if you had the chance to find that sewing
pattern you saw years ago in a magazine, but haven't seen
since? Here, vintage arts and crafts magazines and patterns are
priced at just $.25 each. If you can find a purpose for a pound of
yarn, you should surely spend the $4.00 it will cost you. They
also sell buttons, weaving looms, and other sewing supplies.
Open Wednesday through Friday, 12:00 p.m. - 6:00 p.m.;
Saturday and Sunday, 12:00 p.m. - 4:30 p.m. As weekend hours
are subject to change, make sure you call to confirm that the
Recycle Sale Room is open.

TROY CORPORATION

2701 North Normandy Avenue, Chicago IL 60707. 773/804-9600.
Toll-free phone: 800/888-2400. **World Wide Web address:**
http://www.troy-corp.com. **The Lowdown:** This wholesale fabric
warehouse does dabble in the retail business, so it just might be
worth a glance if you're picking up that sewing project you
haven't worked on in years. Generally, they sell fabric remnants
to the public. That doesn't mean they'll only sell you a foot of one
pattern that can only be used as a dust rag. In fact, Troy
Corporation sells first quality remnants and full pieces of 15
yards or more in length that any Martha Stewart wannabe could
find plenty of uses for. If your next project is a pair of pants for
the fall, you'll find corduroy solids that sell for $2.70 per 50
yards. Perhaps a new pair of flannel pajamas is what you're
thinking about. Flannel patterns go for $1.80 per 50 yards. In the
pound goods section, you can find some great bargains for
smaller projects by grabbing a blend of slightly irregular, short
length cotton prints for just $3.20 per pound (about $1.00 per
yard). Open Monday through Friday, 8:30 a.m. - 4:30 p.m.

VOGUE FABRICS

Water Tower Place, 835 North Michigan Avenue, Chicago IL
60611. 312/787-2521. • 623 West Roosevelt Road, Chicago IL
60607. 312/829-2505. **World Wide Web address:**
http://www.myvoguefabrics.com. **The Lowdown:** Whether
you're a big-name fashion designer or a parent looking for just
the right print for your child's Halloween costume, you will
certainly find what you're looking for at Vogue Fabrics. The store
is dubbed "America's Premier Fabric Store", and it lives up to its
reputation. They stock about a million yards of fabric in
thousands of different prints. Prices start at just $1.00 per yard.
If you're thinking about making yourself a new silk dress, take
comfort in how much you will save by shopping here; silks start

at just $1.99 a yard, and most range from $5.99 to $9.99 per yard. Or, if you are more interested in trendy name brands, consider Vogue Fabric's well-known designer collection with names like Donna Karan and Calvin Klein. Most designer fabrics sell for below wholesale prices here. It really doesn't matter what you're creating because this store has it all, from delicate lace to soft Polar and Nordic fleece fabric. The beauty of this fabric store is that you don't have to sacrifice service for price. They can match or find sample swatches of fabrics to suit your needs, while retaining the low prices. The Michigan Avenue location is open Sunday, 12:00 p.m. - 6:00 p.m.; Monday through Friday, 10:00 a.m. - 7:00 p.m.; Saturday, 10:00 a.m. - 6:00 p.m. The Roosevelt Road store's hours of operation are Sunday 12:00 p.m. - 5:00 p.m.; Monday through Saturday, 9:30 a.m. - 6:00 p.m. (until 8:00 p.m. on Thursday).

Shoes & Sneakers

ADAMS FACTORY SHOE OUTLET

3655 West Irving Park Road, Chicago IL 60618. 773/539-4120. **The Lowdown:** Here at the Adams Factory Shoe Outlet, you can save from 10 - 60 percent off retail on all kinds of shoes for men, women, and children. Adams sells factory overstocks, samples, slight irregulars, and closeouts in styles from casual to dress shoes, work shoes to athletics. They also sell accessories, like hosiery and handbags. The store aims to carry only American-made products. They actually have a unique pricing system here. If a price ends in and "8" ($49.98 for example), then the shoe is first-quality. If the price ends in a "9" (such as $49.99), the shoe is slightly irregular. If the price ends in a "0" (like $49.90), the shoe is a closeout, overrun, or sample. Shoes are cleaned and repaired, if necessary, before they are put on display; and irregular shoes are clearly labeled as such. There is also a good selection of specialty shoes. Women's therapeutic shoes, which would normally cost you anywhere between $115.00 and $170.00, sell here for $44.99 - $89.99. Men's therapeutic shoes, which can cost as much as $200.00 or more, sell here for $59.99 - $99.99. For those who need a special size, Adams carries men's shoes from sizes 5 - 18; women's shoes from sizes 1 1/2 - 14; and narrows and wides. They even carry wide-width shoes for kids, a size that can be difficult to find in even the priciest of children's boutiques. Adams serves free coffee and tea in the store, plus lollipops for the kids. And here's something you seldom see anymore: full service including sizing. Open Monday through Saturday, 9:00 a.m. - 6:00 p.m.; Sunday, 10:00 a.m. - 4:30 p.m.

ALAMO SHOES

5319 North Clark Street, Chicago IL 60640. 773/784-8936. **E-mail address:** alamo@alamoshoes.com. **World Wide Web address:** http://www.alamoshoes.com. **The Lowdown:** The selection at Alamo Shoes is more than impressive, with boxes and boxes of shoes for children, men, and women. You will find all sorts of names and styles for work and play. Alamo carries specialty widths and sizes too. Men's shoes run up to a size 18 and women can search out the perfect fit for that narrow foot! Men can choose from such names Timberland, Birkenstock, Clarks, Rockport, Kenneth Cole, and Ecco while women will debate over Munro, Easy Spirit, Nine West, and Steve Madden. Athletic shoes include Adidas, Reiker, Nike, and New Balance. Kids can also get great shoes by Teva, Converse, Stride Rite, and Keds and can even take some free balloons home with them. You can even park free right across the street. Open Sunday, 10:00 a.m. - 6:00 p.m.; Monday through Friday, 9:00 a.m. - 8:00 p.m.; Saturday, 9:00 a.m. - 6:00 p.m.

ALTMAN'S SHOES & BOOTS FOR MEN

120 West Monroe Street, Chicago IL 60603. 312/332-0667. **The Lowdown:** Since 1932, Altman's Shoes & Boots has been

offering men great discounts on top name brand footwear. Unlike other discount stores – where you have to have extremely small or large feet to find anything – Altman's Shoes & Boots for Men carries a wide range of shoes for feet of all sizes (5 - 20, AAAA - EEEE). From casual to dressy, they carry an entire range of styles. You can't go wrong with names like Alden, Bass, Birkenstock, Bostonian, Cole Haan, Dr. Marten, Ecco, New Balance, Rockport, Timberland, and others. Open Monday through Friday, 8:30 a.m. - 6:00 p.m.; Saturday, 8:30 a.m. - 4:30 p.m.

ARROWSMITH SHOES

109 South State Street, Chicago IL 60603. 312/782-4546. **The Lowdown:** From the nondescript storefront outside, you might not expect to see such a colorful array of shoes upon entering, but there it is! Arrowsmith offers men a large selection of shoes at discount prices. Whether your style is casual, business, outdoorsy, or Western, Arrowsmith has got the shoe to fit.

DSW SHOE WAREHOUSE

3131 North Clark Street, Chicago IL 60657. 773/975-7182.
◆ 2155 West 22nd Street, Oakbrook IL 60521. 630/571-9313.
◆ 202 Orland Park Place, Orland Park IL 60462. 708/460-3168.
◆ Woodfield Promenade Shopping Center, 901 Perimeter Drive, Schaumburg IL 60173. 847/240-1594. ◆ 9426 Skokie Boulevard, Skokie IL 60077. 847/674-2772. **World Wide Web address:** http://www.dswshoe.com. **The Lowdown:** True to the "warehouse" in its name, the store is a self-serve haven of shoes, shoes, shoes. Choose from top name brands for men and women, all at prices that are 20 - 50 percent below what you'd find at the local department store. Whether its shoes for work or sneakers for play, DSW has got it. With such tremendous everyday values, just one trip is sure to make a regular customer out of you! Call for specific location hours.

GOODY TWO SHOES

3366 North Clark Street, Chicago IL 60657. 773/935-8742. **The Lowdown:** For the shoe-loving woman, Goody Two Shoes is heaven on earth. Here you will find stylish brand name shoes at affordable prices. Stroll the aisles of boxes at your own pace and help yourself to anything you see in your size. The sales staff will not pester you unless you ask them to. Goody Two Shoes also offers accessories like bracelets and purses which are perfect for coordinating with the new kicks you will surely be purchasing. Open Tuesday through Friday, 12:00 p.m. - 7:00 p.m.; Saturday, 11:00 a.m. - 7:00 p.m.; Sunday 12:00 p.m. - 6:00 p.m.

LOOP FOOTWEAR

142 South Wabash Street, Chicago IL 60603. 312/368-5010. **The Lowdown:** This store sells urban casual, dress shoes, and Western footwear at very competitive prices, with terrific sales to boot! What's more, promotional shoes by Giorgio Brutini, Stacy Adams, and Marco Vicci are always sold on a two-for-one sale price.

LORI'S DESIGNER SHOES

824 West Armitage Avenue, Chicago IL 60614. 773/281-5655. **World Wide Web address:** http://www.lorisdesignershoes.com. **The Lowdown:** They call themselves "The Sole of Chicago" and it's easy to see why: With prices like these, I'd be surprised to find anyone in the city who hasn't bought a pair of shoes from Lori's. While many of the stores listed in this chapter offer deals on past season leftovers, Lori's discounts overstocks of current styles. The discounts may not be as deep as at other places listed in this chapter, but let's not forget that we're dealing with current styles here. With prices up to 30 percent below retail, you can do quite well at Lori's. Styles range from casual sneakers to strappy evening sandals and everything in between. For the most casual of looks, try a pair of fuzzy pink slippers by Steve Madden for $24.00; for a dressier style by Steve Madden, try his modernized, chunky-heeled loafer for $66.00. Other brand names spotted included Charles David, Via Spiga, Joan and David, Adrienne Vittadini, Kenneth Cole, and Vic Matie. The bride-to-be should be thrilled to find tons of shoes by Dyeable and Unlisted, as well as a range of wedding day accessories, like a white beaded handbag by Pantera for $38.00. Lori's carries a wide range of accessories like socks, hosiery, handbags, and jewelry. Don't be surprised to find names like Hue, Calvin Klein, Giorgio Armani, Joan & David, and Anne Klein among the bargains. Mr. C spotted some great jewelry boxes by Binny for $18.00, along with some animal print CD holders for $38.00. Lori's is a great place to do some budget-friendly shopping for your oh-so-stylish friends. While, from the rather trendy look of the place, you might expect a number of well-dressed salespeople to hover over you offering cappuccinos and whatever else you're little hearts desire, don't forget that this is still a discount store; service is strictly self-serve. Salespeople are certainly around to answer questions, but you'll be finding your own shoes and sizes. As word has gotten out on this store, the crowds have grown; there's always a ton of people buzzing about. If you find a style you like and your size, it's a good idea to jump on it; shoes don't last long out on the floor here. It's a good thing there are new shipments arriving all the time. Open Sunday, 12:00 p.m. - 5:00 p.m.; Monday through Thursday, 11:00 a.m. - 7:00 p.m.; Friday, 11:00 a.m. - 6:00 p.m.; Saturday, 10:00 a.m. - 6:00 p.m.

SHOE CARNIVAL

201 Commons Drive, Chicago Ridge IL 60415. 708/422-1303. • Cermak Plaza, 7001-B West Cermak Road, Berwyn IL 60402. 708/795-4771. **World Wide Web address:** http://www. shoecarnival.com. **The Lowdown:** With more than 140 locations throughout the country, Shoe Carnival is quickly becoming a favorite spot for those who love to shop for brand name shoes, while saving money! Unlike many other discount chains, where merchandise is just put on the floor, Shoe Carnival is arranged into category and size. Shoes for the whole family can be found here, and found easily with directional and category signs. All merchandise is placed on the floor, so there's no waiting around for a salesperson or finding out (after all that waiting), that the

only color left in your size is hot pink. Each week brings a new sales promotion, like 30 percent discounts on all women's and children's boots.

SHU SHOES
1127 North State Street, Chicago IL 60610. 312/787-7223.
The Lowdown: You just got a great deal on a new outfit, but haven't got a shoe to wear. What to do? Head on over to Shu Shoes, where today's latest styles of women's shoes can be found at prices that are usually at least $10.00 off retail. On Mr. C's visit, there was a back wall offering an additional 50 percent off the already-low prices. A pair of David Aaron loafers I had admired just a few days previously at Bloomingdale's for $90.00 were a mere $45.00 here. Shu Shoes carries the hottest names including Steve Madden, Via Spiga, and Kenneth Cole.

Sporting Goods

CHICAGO TENNIS & GOLF COMPANY
1880 West Fullerton, Chicago IL 60614.
773/489-2999. **Toll-free phone:**
800/246-4006. **E-mail address:** custservice@chicagotennisgolf.
com. **World Wide Web address:** http://www.chicagotennisgolf.
com. **The Lowdown:** For the best prices on golf and tennis
equipment, look no further than Chicago Tennis & Golf Company.
Here you will find one of the largest selections of this type of
merchandise in the metro area. Everything from apparel to
footwear and accessories are available at discount prices. Recent
sales included men's Dexter golf shoes reduced from $140.99 to
$44.99; Prince Synergy tennis racquets priced at $64.99; and
Izzo golf bags for $99.99. Open Monday through Friday, 10:00
a.m. - 7:00 p.m.; Saturday, 10:00 a.m. - 6:00 p.m.; Sunday,
12:00 p.m. - 5:00 p.m.

KOZY'S CYCLERY AND FITNESS
601 South LaSalle Street, Chicago IL 60605. 312/360-0020.
✦ 3712 North Halsted Street, Chicago IL 60613. 773/281-2263.
✦ 1451 West Webster, Chicago IL 60614. 773/528-2700.
The Lowdown: Mr. Kozy is an adamant believer in customer
service. Shopping at any of his locations is truly a pleasant
experience, with knowledgeable, athletic sales associates who
can tell you all about the products. They're not nosy at Kozy's,
though. If you want to just poke around, they'll let you. Bicycles
at Kozy's consist mainly of brand names, including well-known
ones like Schwinn, Trek, Cannondale, Specialized, and Gary
Fisher. Kozy's regularly has these name brands on sale starting
at $199.99. They also have 175 models on display, with 35 - 40
models always on sale. Kozy's has an excellent selection of
accessories as well, with prices that are quite competitive. A
Kryptonite Kryptolock, for example, is about $30.00. Kozy's also
provides 30-day price protection, for the skeptics out there.

NEVADA BOB'S GOLF
60 East Lake Street, Chicago IL 60601. 312/726-4653.
World Wide Web address: http://www.nevadabobs.com.
The Lowdown: As a widely-recognized national chain, Nevada
Bob's carries a huge selection of golf clubs, sets, accessories, and
apparel, all at good prices. At prices like these, you can manage
to hit the green more than once a season; plus, with the
enormous selection, you can get the whole family in on the fun.
New to the sport? Pick up a Pro Select, seven-piece men's starter
set for under $130.00; women will enjoy the same brand's 10-
piece graphite set for about $100.00 more. Even the kids can get
in on the action: a junior NXT set was spotted at an
unbelievably-low price. But wait a minute, don't forget the
accessories. Nevada Bob's stocks a huge inventory of bags, carts,
and everything else golf, like a Wilson Carry Smart bag for men
or women; or a folding, steel cart by Bentley. Last but not least,
you'll need golf balls... lots of golf balls. If you don't mind a little

discoloration or other visual imperfection, you can pick up a 12-pack of Dunlop closeout balls (they've been measured to endure perfect compression and shape) for about $10.00. Call for hours.

PLAY IT AGAIN SPORTS

2101 West Irving Park Road, Chicago IL 60618. 773/463-9900. **World Wide Web address:** http://www.playitagainchicago.com. **The Lowdown:** Play It Again Sports is the perfect store for the novice athlete in a number of different sports. If you're an experienced in-line skater and can master the half-pipe by now, then you may prefer to buy your skates from a specialized dealer. But, if you're just starting out, and want a pair that can withstand your falls while you decide if you were meant to roll or walk, then this store will no doubt have what you're looking for. They carry new and used equipment for hockey, in-line skating, snowboarding, golf, skiing, baseball, and plenty of other sports. What if you're interested in purchasing some larger exercise equipment, such as a treadmill or exercise bike, but are unwilling to commit to the hefty price tag? The used equipment at Play It Again Sports is often nearly identical to the new equipment, and the prices here are lower and more affordable than most retail sporting goods stores. Unless you have the makings of the next great Olympian (and, rightfully, can and will pay full price for top-of-the-line equipment), it just makes sense to shop here. Call for hours.

RECYCLE BIKE SHOP

1465 South Michigan Avenue, Chicago IL 60605. 312/987-1080. **The Lowdown:** Recycle Bike Shop sells both new and used bicycles, with used bikes starting as low as $50.00. They carry a good range of brand names, including GT and Diamondback. All used bikes are fully reconditioned; they do their own repairs in the shop. Recycle Bike Shop may be a bit out of your way, but the folks here say that the cheap rent means low prices, so it will be worth your trip. Open Monday through Friday, 10:00 a.m. - 6:00 p.m.; Saturday and Sunday, 12:00 p.m. - 4:00 p.m.

SKATESHACK

4655 Old Tavern Road, Lisle IL 60532. 630/416-3945. ◆ 6116 South Cass Avenue, Westmont IL 60559. 630/241-1111. **World Wide Web address:** http://www.skateshack.com. **The Lowdown:** While both locations of Skateshack are a bit out of the city, they offer a great selection and guaranteed low prices for skating enthusiasts. Skateshack carries Illinois' largest selection of skateboards and accessories by names like A-Team, Element, and Zoo York. Decks, in a variety of styles and sizes, are priced about 10 percent below retail, with wheels, trucks, and hardware offering the same discount amounts. Inline skates by K2, Rollerblade, and Roces are sold for up to 40 percent below retail. Mr. C spotted a pair of Rollerblade Roadhouse skates, originally $329.95, for $199.95. For those who prefer the challenge of a snow-filled landscape, Skateshack offers a great collection of snowboards. Expect to see savings of $20.00 - $40.00 on boards from K2, Gnu, and Ride. To complete the look, Skateshack also sells lots of clothing and accessories. Hats, pants, shorts, T-shirts, sweatshirts are just a few of the items you'll find here along with shoes by Vans, Axion, DC, and Emerica at savings of up to 10 percent. Skateshack's commitment to customer service makes it a treat to shop here; if you find a lower price anywhere within two weeks of your purchase, Skateshack will issue you a credit in the amount of the difference. It's perks like that that make a trip outside of the city worthwhile. Open Sunday, 12:00 p.m. - 4:00 p.m.; Monday through Friday, 12:00 p.m. - 8:00 p.m.; Saturday, 10:00 a.m. - 5:00 p.m.

SPORTMART
3134 North Clark Street, Chicago IL 60657. 773/871-8500.
♦ 6420 West Fullerton Avenue, Elmwood Park IL 60707. 773/804-0044. **World Wide Web address:** http://www.sportmart.com.
The Lowdown: Sportmart is your basic, all-American, all-around sports center, with competitive prices every day on equipment and clothing for just about any athletic endeavor. From baseball, football, and basketball to running and hiking, there are plenty of choices to meet your every need. Clothing and gear are a big part of the store, with things like NFL and NBA replica jerseys by Champion for adults and kids, not to mention caps for seemingly every single professional and college team ever to play. Save on shoes from Reebok, Nike, Asics, Converse, and more. Reebok aerobic shoes for women were recently seen for just under $30.00. Lots of shoes for kids, too, as low as $20.00. Wilson Hammer System tennis racquets start at $29.00, while Ektelon racquetball weapons begin as low as $23.00. For hikers, there are full lines of backpacks from Eastpak, Jansport, and High Sierra, like the popular Jansport styles with leather bottoms. Nike small duffel bags were reduced to half their price. Open daily.

UNIVERSAL BOWLING & AWARDS STORES
619 South Wabash Avenue, Chicago IL 60605. 312/922-5255.
♦ 1926 South Mannheim Road, Westchester IL 60154. 708/562-3431. **World Wide Web address:** http://www.universal-bowling.com. **The Lowdown:** Not too big and not too fancy, Universal primarily sells bowling balls and shoes at discount, but also offers a few golf clubs. Bowling balls by Columbia and Brunswick, some of them discontinued, are almost always available at greatly discounted prices. Men's Brunswick X-Cell shoes were under $60.00 on a recent visit, available in sizes 7-13. Women's shoes by Dexter, in the Raquel style, were under $40.00. Close-outs on men's and women's golf clubs, mostly by Universal, were bargains. Open Monday through Saturday, 8:30 a.m. - 5:30 p.m. (Saturday, 8:30 a.m. - 2:00 p.m. in the summer).

Stationery, Office, & Art Supplies

THE ART STORE

1574 North Kingsbury Street, Chicago IL 60622. 312/573-0110. **World Wide Web address:** http://www.artstore.com. **The Lowdown:** Everyday discounts from 20 to 50 percent off list prices are just one of the reasons why this store is so popular. Even without these deep discounts, those looking for art supplies might still come in just for the helpful staff. More than salespeople, The Art Store staff is like a team of problem-solvers, ready with a quick and insightful answer to all your art questions and needs. With over 30,000 items to choose from, there's probably nothing they don't have in stock. Oil and acrylic paints by Winsor Newton, Gamblin, Liquitex, and Golden; artist brushes by Robert Simmons and Grumbacher; drawing and decorative papers from Canson and Fabriano; and ergonomically-sound and pneumatic chairs from Alvin and Mayline are just a small sampling of the products you'll find at The Art Store. They even have their own brand of oil, acrylic, and tempera paints, excellent pre-stretched canvas, gesso and artists brushes that are guaranteed to be the best value for your money. Whether you draw, paint, sculpt, or are involved in digital media, The Art Store can fill your needs.

FLETCH'S ART SUPPLY OUTLET

786 East Rand Road, Arlington Heights IL 60005. 847/392-7000. **Toll-free phone:** 800/CLOSE-OUTS. **The Lowdown:** It might be worth your while to travel a bit out of the city for prices like these. At Fletch's Art Supply Outlet, discounts of 50 percent and more are the norm. Whatever your art supply need, Fletch's has got it for less. They offer lots of closeout products by Shiva and Liquitex, like quick-dry oils in a whole palette full of colors for just $.99 each (listed at $3.50). You can pick up a two ounce tube of acrylic paint for anywhere between $1.98 - $4.80; or a half ounce tube of professional watercolors at 60 percent below retail. Fletch's carries a full line of other artist accessories, like brushes for as little as $1.95 and stretched canvasses for as low as $2.37. Whether you paint professionally or for your own enjoyment, Fletch's Art Supply Outlet can keep your art supply costs completely within reason.

GENESIS ARTISTS VILLAGE

2417 North Western Avenue, Chicago IL 60647. 773/292-2992. **World Wide Web address:** http://www.artsupply.com. **The Lowdown:** Genesis Artists Village is like a little community where starving artists can unite. They offer some of the city's best prices on some of the most sought-after art and drafting supplies. At any given time, you'll find hundreds of clearance items that are reduced even further from the already low, low prices. Some of the deals that I saw included a 50-sheet pad of newsprint paper for $.99, hard bound sketch books for as little as

$4.48, an artist's knife for $1.29, and an array of oil colors and acrylics for $1.29 apiece. They continue their communal feeling by offering lots of great classes and workshops that are educational and affordable. For as little as $5.00 you can be taught the basics of studio art by a professional artist. If you're just starting out on your artistic journey, the helpful and knowledgeable staff will be more than happy to assist you in finding the perfect products. Open Monday through Friday, 9:00 a.m. - 9:00 p.m.; Saturday and Sunday, 10:00 a.m. - 6:00 p.m.

PAPER SOURCE
232 West Chicago Avenue, Chicago IL 60610. 312/337-0798.
The Lowdown: If you're looking for some different gifts and ideas for your creative self, try this River North store. All of the papers sold here are handsome indeed, and can make an elegant and inexpensive gift idea. But it was the rubber stamps on the second floor which attracted Mr. C's eye for the offbeat. For about $5.00, you can buy rubber stamps of everything from elaborate initials to pictures of celebrities to constellations and more. Paper Source can also supply you with the ink pads in a variety of colors. This can be a good place to look for unusual party, shower or wedding invitations; save some cash and impress your friends by making your own. Open Monday through Friday, 10:00 a.m. - 7:00 p.m.; Saturday, 10:00 a.m. - 5:00 p.m.; Sunday, 12:00 p.m. - 5:00 p.m.

PEARL ART & CRAFT SUPPLIES
225 West Chicago Avenue, Chicago IL 60610. 312/915-0200.
World Wide Web address: http://www.pearlpaint.com.
The Lowdown: Pearl is a sort of art supply department store, now nearing its seventieth year. They offer a complete line of paints, paper, portfolios, easels, canvas, tools, tables, lamps, chairs, storage systems, computer desks, and pretty much everything for the studio or office. Among the many sale items recently spotted (Pearl's everyday prices are great, but there are always special promotions for even better deals) included an HP-B Pro-Pak airbrush kit, listed at $185.00, selling here for $100.00; a Gagne 16" x 18" lightbox reduced from $170.00 to $75.00; a 60-piece Rembrandt soft pastel set, half-price at $70.00; a Rover portable office storage system, marked down from $295.00 to $140.00; and the comprehensive *Artist's Handbook*, with information on the latest techniques and technologies, reduced from a cover price of $30.00 to $19.99. Pearl offers lots of package deals too, so grab a flyer when you come in the front door. Drop in for yourself and see what kind of deals you can find!

Thrift Stores

AMERICAN SCIENCE AND SURPLUS
5316 North Milwaukee Avenue, Chicago IL 60630. 773/763-0313. **E-mail address:** info@sciplus.com. **World Wide Web address:** http://www.sciplus.com. **The Lowdown:** Located in Gladstone Corner Shopping Center, American Science and Surplus is not your typical thrift store. You may or may not find hand-me-down bell-bottoms or oldies records here, but you will certainly find something that interests or fascinates you. They carry tons of neat stuff that could be handy for science projects, theatrical productions, party favors, or homemade Halloween costumes. Among a random assortment of items, they carry motors, hospital gowns, CD cases, wire, springs, beakers, and military surplus. How's that for variety? As for collectible toys, the Sewer Urchin, a four-inch plastic man that bobs in and out of water when it is filled with baking soda, goes for $2.25 for three (and that's including the plastic pod that each toy comes in). Should you find that you suddenly need, say, an ice shaver, American Science and Surplus stocks enough industrial, military, and educational gadgets to suit your needs.

THE ARK THRIFT SHOP
1302 North Milwaukee Avenue, Chicago IL 60662. 773/862-5011.
♦ 3345 North Lincoln Avenue, Chicago IL 60657. 773/248-1117.
♦ 1505 West Chicago Avenue, Chicago IL 60622. 312/733-3314.
The Lowdown: Perhaps the ultimate in Chicago thrift stores when it comes to selection, The Ark Thrift Shop sells donated clothing and furniture at some of the lowest prices you'll see anywhere. Lots of designer goodies are hidden among the dozens of racks and shelves in these warehouse-sized stores. And you'll feel good knowing that all the proceeds go to charities providing medical care to the needy. In addition to clothing, The Ark Thrift Shop carries a good selection of household items and furniture. Many of the recliners and sofas should be categorized as dorm room, frat house, or first apartment variety, like a $28.00 velour recliner, or an easy chair (in a lovely shade of chartreuse) for $18.00. Other household goodies seen were a five-setting china set including plates, saucers, tea cups, and bowls, along with a sugar bowl and creamer. They carry lots of cheap vases too, some for under $1.00. The Ark Thrift Shop also carries wide selections of other useful items such as luggage; there were about three dozen different suitcases to choose from when Mr. C visited the Lincoln Avenue store. In the overwhelmingly vast clothing department, Mr. C spotted an incredible buy: a pair of ladies' Ferragamo shoes, with nary a scuff, for $2.00. Much of the selection is rather worn out, but you never know when you may come across such a find. The store adheres to a one-price minimum policy on its clothing: for example, all suits start at $5.00, and all ladies' dresses start at just $2.50. Some of the better-quality items included a man's grey Botany 500 suit, a woman's London Fog trench coat, and a man's Scottish Tussah

silk jacket by Arthur Dickson. Lots of toys, like a $25.00 wide-handlebar Schwinn bicycle, are crammed into the stores, too. Be wary of the appliances though since most look like they may be able to qualify as antiques instead. All stores are closed on Saturday; call for specific location hours.

CHICAGO ARMY-NAVY SURPLUS COMPANY
605 West Ogden Avenue, Downers Grove IL. 630/969-1786. **World Wide Web address:** http://www.chiarmy.com. **The Lowdown:** We all know what kinds of things an Army-Navy surplus store sells, Mr. C is just here to tell you where they are. Operating both a retail store and an online business, Chicago Army-Navy Surplus Company offers some very good prices on heavy-duty, military goods like clothing, footwear, and gloves. If it fits your style, you can pick up a very cool (and a very warm) arctic parka or flight jacket for as little as $125.00 and T-shirts for as little as $6.00. They also carry such field essentials as pocket knives; a must for anyone who likes to spend their time in the great outdoors. Again, shopping Army-Navy stores is not for everyone; but if the style fits you, the price is definitely right!

CHICAGO'S RECYCLE SHOP
5308 North Clark Street, Chicago IL 60640. 773/878-8525. **The Lowdown:** What can you expect to find at Chicago's Recycle Shop? The sky's the limit... and then some. There's really no rhyme or reason to what is sold here, but it's a whole lot of fun to pile through! Chicago's Recycle Shop is like an everyday flea market; there are plenty of antiques, collectibles, and treasures to uncover. For decades, they have been famous among the theater crowd for props and period looks. If you're into vintage goodies, this place has got clothing and furniture from just about every era and niche of society. Open Monday through Saturday, 9:00 a.m. - 6:00 p.m.; closed Sunday.

CHILDREN'S WHITE ELEPHANT SHOP
2380 North Lincoln Avenue, Chicago IL 60614-3394. 773/281-3747. **The Lowdown:** Located in Chicago's trendy Lincoln Park area, White Elephant is one of Children's Memorial Hospital's oldest fundraising activities. Merchandise ranges from vintage to contemporary designer clothing at a fraction of the original cost. A large selection of costume jewelry, shoes, and other accessories start at a mere $1.00. The furniture offered ranges from the raggy to the stately, and has something for every taste and budget. Household goods such as dishes, pots and pans, and other bric-a-brac are always on hand and can be had for a song (almost). The items you want to keep a close eye on are the electronics; though the store does test them and sell them "as is," they cannot guarantee them. For those of you who are a whiz with a toolbox, these might be an especially good deal; for the rest of us, check these items out carefully. Weekends can be very busy, due to an influx of students from the adjacent DePaul University campus, so it might be better to visit during the week. Parking can be tough, but the store is easily accessible via several public transport routes. Open Monday through Saturday, 10:00 a.m. - 5:00 p.m.; Sunday, 11:00 a.m. - 4:00 p.m.

DESIGNER RESALE OF CHICAGO
658 North Dearborn Street, Chicago IL 60610. 312/587-3312.
• 124B Skokie Road, Wilmette IL 60091. 847/920-1565.
The Lowdown: If you shop on the Magnificent Mile, your wallet may be feeling the strain of high-priced retail stores. So instead of sacrificing quality for price, try shopping at Designer Resale of Chicago just four blocks away. This consignment shop carries all the same names as the fancier Magnificent Mile stores, but at a fraction of the cost. One of the great and unique things about this shop is that they date all their clothing as soon as it passes through the doors. That way, you'll know whether it's a hot new item or if it's been sitting around waiting for you to take it home. Like a department store, Designer Resale of Chicago stocks items that are completely in-season. And, as the name suggests, much of the clothing is top of the line. See, it is possible to dress yourself in brand names like Chanel and Armani and still be able to afford dinner at night. Both locations are open Monday through Saturday, 11:00 a.m. - 6:00 p.m.; Sunday, 12:00 p.m. - 5:00 p.m.

THE OUTLET STORE
5402 North Elston Avenue, Chicago IL 60630. 773/685-5770.
The Lowdown: And just what kind of outlet store is this place anyway? It's an outlet for every widget ever known to man, that's what. Thingamajigs abound in this store crammed with everything at prices up to 90 percent off. Open Monday through Friday, 9:00 a.m. - 5:00 p.m. (until 8:00 p.m. on Wednesdays); Saturday, 10:00 a.m. - 5:00 p.m.

THE RIGHT PLACE
5219 North Clark Street, Chicago IL 60640. 773/561-7757.
The Lowdown: One of Andersonville's many resale shops, The Right Place has a decent assortment of clothing, furniture, and thrift shop bric-a-brac. Some items found were a 10x12-foot Oriental rug, and a handsome cream-colored dresser in fine condition. Among the clothing finds was a woman's three-piece linen suit, skirt, top, and blazer. The Right Place carries plenty of children's clothing too, not to mention a good selection of popular toys and games, many in their original boxes.

VILLAGE DISCOUNT OUTLET
2855 North Halsted Street, Chicago IL. • 3301 West Lawrence Avenue, Chicago IL. • 12914 Western Avenue, Blue Island IL 60406. • 4635 North Elston Avenue, Chicago IL. • 2043 West Roscoe Street, Chicago IL. • 4898 North Clark Street, Chicago IL. • 6419 South Kedzie Avenue, Chicago IL. • 4020 West 26th Street, Chicago IL. • 2515 Chicago Road, Chicago IL. • 2514 West 47th Street, Chicago IL. • 7443 South Racine Avenue, Chicago IL. **The Lowdown:** This isn't an outlet at all, really, but a chain of thrift stores run by the Salvation Army. Some of these stores are in converted warehouses and are worth venturing into for aisle after aisle of men's, women's, and children's clothing at rock-bottom prices. Some of the goodies found here included men's silk ties, Izod boys' rugby shirts, and girls' suede Minnetonka moccasins0. While clothes shopping, you may come

upon some cute toys for the kids, like a stuffed rabbit for a quarter. **NOTE:** For information about other store locations, please call the central office at 708/388-4772.

ENTERTAINMENT

Art Galleries

ATLAS GALLERIES
535 North Michigan Avenue, Chicago IL 60611. 312/329-9330. ◆ 900 North Michigan Avenue, Level 6, Chicago IL 60611. 312/649-0999. 800/545-2929. **Toll-free phone:** 800/423-7635. **World Wide Web address:** http://www. atlasgalleries.com. **The Lowdown:** This pair of Gold Coast art galleries, which first opened in 1967, displays everything from Rembrandt to up-and-coming artists in a variety of media. They feature original oils, etchings, watercolors, sculpture, graphic art, and museum-quality prints. With the likes of Renoir, Whistler, and Maimon, this is no lightweight collection. The 535 North Michigan location is open Sunday, 11:00 a.m. - 5:00 p.m.; Monday through Friday, 10:00 a.m. - 9:00 p.m.; Saturday, 10:00 a.m. - 6:00 p.m. The 900 North Michigan Avenue location is open Sunday, 12:00 p.m. - 6:00 p.m.; Monday through Thursday, 10:00 a.m. - 7:00 p.m.; Friday, 10:00 a.m. - 8:00 p.m.; Saturday, 10:00 a.m. - 6:00 p.m.

CATHERINE EDELMAN GALLERY
300 West Superior Street, Chicago IL 60610. 312/266-2350. **World Wide Web address:** http://www.edelmangallery.com. **The Lowdown:** The year was 1987 when a newly graduated art student with an entrepreneurial spirit decided to open up her own art gallery. Since that time, the Catherine Edelman Gallery has become one of the Midwest's most widely-recognized photographic art galleries. Such renowned artists as Annie Leibovitz, Herb Ritts, and Michael Kenna have all had shows here. What's especially great about this gallery is that, as Ms. Edelman was once herself a working photographer, she offers great opportunities to up-and-comers who are without gallery support. Open Tuesday through Saturday, 10:00 a.m. - 5:30 p.m.

ILLINOIS ART GALLERY
100 West Randolph Street, #2-100, Chicago IL 60601. 312/814-5322. **World Wide Web address:** http://www.museum. state.il.us. **The Lowdown:** Located on the second floor of the James R. Thompson Center, this small but serious gallery shows work by Illinois artists, both historic and contemporary. Operated by the Illinois State Museum, their offerings span all media including paintings, sculpture, photography, and even film and video. Richard Hunt, Gertrude Abercrombie, Roger Brown, Margaret Wharton, and Carl Wirsum are just a few of the famous Illinois artists who have had work shown there. Several times a year, the gallery also hosts panel discussions with artists; specific lectures for school groups can even be arranged in advance. The atrium of this massive building, a work of art in itself, functions as a second gallery space. In fact, the center has its own permanent collection, comprised of winners from statewide competitions in painting, photography, ceramics and

glass, printmaking, drawing, and sculpture. On display throughout the atrium, these pieces are part of the largest single collection of contemporary Illinois artwork. Open Monday through Friday, 9:00 a.m. - 5:00 p.m.

insideART
1651 West North Avenue, Chicago IL 60622. 773/772-4416. **World Wide Web address:** http://homepage.interaccess. com/~jentes/index.htm. **The Lowdown:** Now here's a place that could easily fit into the Shopping chapter as well. Their mission statement alone will let you know why I like them; they're "dedicated to helping people find, enjoy, and buy contemporary art they like and can afford." Sounds like a winning proposal to me. Aside from fostering the public's appreciation of art through affordable sales of talented up-and-comers, insideART offers great exhibitions. Monthly exhibitions show the works of emerging artists in the Chicago area. The public is invited to come and browse these innovative works in a truly relaxed and unpretentious atmosphere. insideART also offers a number of fantastic art tours. Geared toward groups of five to 100 people, insideART takes a completely interactive approach to the art gallery tour. Participants are asked to take a journey across the city and meet the artists and other creative folk behind the scenes. If you don't come out of there with a new wall hanging, you'll surely emerge a much more enlightened art lover. Call to get on the mailing list, for upcoming events, and for current gallery hours.

INTUIT: THE CENTER FOR INTUITIVE AND OUTSIDER ART
756 North Milwaukee Avenue, Chicago IL 60622. 312/243-9088. **E-mail address:** intuit@art.org. **World Wide Web address:** http://outsider.art.org. **The Lowdown:** The name of this gallery refers to a group of artists around 1945 who felt like outsiders in relation to the New York art community. The focus here is on works produced by untrained artists of all kinds. As you can imagine, this gallery lends itself to some pretty unusual exhibits. Recent events have included collections of vintage hand puppets and E2K, a celebration of the 65th birthday of Elvis Presley. Open Wednesday through Saturday, 12:00 p.m. - 5:00 p.m. and by appointment.

PERIMETER GALLERY
210 West Superior Street, Chicago IL 60610. 312/266-9473. **The Lowdown:** The Perimeter Gallery exhibits contemporary art by established artists. With offerings ranging from the abstract to representational, the Perimeter Gallery knows no boundaries. The Perimeter features paintings, drawings, prints, and sculpture. Showings have included paintings by Joseph Piccillo, sculpture by John McQueen, and ceramics by Toshiko Takaezu. Open Tuesday through Saturday, 10:30 a.m. - 5:30 p.m.

STUDIO ONDAS
1529 North Wells Street, Chicago IL 60610-1307. 312/664-9220. **World Wide Web address:** http://www.affordable-art.com. **The Lowdown:** Artists Kathleen Patrick and Joseph Catanzaro

opened this Old Town gallery as a place to display and sell their art. Yet, while it is listed in the Art Gallery chapter, Studio Ondas is unique in that it could just as easily have made the cut for the Home Furnishings section of this book. If simply browsing through a series of paintings isn't enough, Studio Ondas makes it possible for you to go one step further and become an art collector. The philosophy here is that everyone, not just the well heeled, should be able to add a great piece of professional artwork to his or her collection. Works include lots of contemporary work, abstracts, landscapes, and more; many have a distinctly Chicago feel to them (for example, several works are visually inspired by the sounds of Chicago jazz and blues). See something you like? Prices start at a mere $200.00. You can even pick up a signed limited edition print for just $39.00. Open daily, 12:00 p.m. - 9:00 p.m.

THE WEST SIDE GALLERY DISTRICT
The Lowdown: Art lovers who find themselves on Chicago's west side on the first Friday of any given month are in luck. First Friday Art Walks will allow you to explore the many different offerings of The West Side Gallery District, an affiliation of more than 15 galleries. Participating establishments include: idao Gallery, 1616 North Damen Avenue, Chicago IL 60647. 773/235-4724; Morlen Sinoway Atelier Furniture-Art-Design, 2035 West Wabansia Avenue, Chicago IL 60647. 773/235-4779; Eclectic Junction for Art, 1630 North Damen Avenue, Chicago IL 60647. 773/342-7865; Gallery 1633, 1633 North Damen Avenue, Chicago IL 60647. 773/384-4441; and The Stolen Buick Studio, 1303 West Chicago Avenue, Chicago IL. 773/226-5902. For more information, you can call the idao Gallery at 773/235-4724. First Friday Art Walks are offered the first Friday of every month (obviously), from 6:00 p.m. - 9:00 p.m. So put on your walking shoes and get ready to inundate yourself with culture!

WOOD STREET GALLERY & SCULPTURE GARDEN
1239 North Wood Street, Chicago IL 60622. 773/227-3306.
The Lowdown: Wood Street Gallery & Sculpture Garden is a unique place in the Wicker Park area. The gallery has five separate areas where up to four different artists can show their works simultaneously. A large sculpture garden, with meandering paths, ponds, and stone seating can be enjoyed year-round. It was created so that people could learn to appreciate the contrast of contemporary sculpture in a garden setting. Every year during the holidays, the gallery has a group show entitled "Small Packages" where over 50 artists display work that is 12 inches or under. It is the perfect opportunity to pick up a unique gift for someone who may be difficult to shop for. The gallery also often hosts free public lectures by its artists. Open Tuesday through Friday, 11:00 a.m. - 5:30 p.m.; Saturday, 10:00 a.m. - 5:00 p.m.

Arts & Cultural Centers

ALLIANCE FRANÇAISE DE CHICAGO
810 North Dearborn, Chicago IL 60610. 312/337-1070. **World Wide Web address:** http://www.afchicago.com. **The Lowdown:** If you've always longed to parlez vous français, now is your chance. Alliance Francaise de Chicago offers French enthusiasts the chance to learn more about the culture, from the language to the customs. They offer a number of different classes during the day, evening, and night and teach the language for all purposes: general interest, travel, business, etc. A complete French library will help to accelerate your learning, and introduce you to some classics you may never have read before. If you don't have time for a full class, there are plenty of lectures and workshops given throughout the year that should easily quench your knowledge thirst. Full classes are $175.00 for members and $205.00 for non-members. If you're thinking of taking more than one class, becoming an Alliance Francaise de Chicago member is a great idea as it will save you money in the long run. Memberships can be purchased for as little as $55.00. On Saturdays, Alliance Francaise de Chicago even offers classes for children ages four - 12. But language isn't the only thing they're teaching here: the French are well-known for their taste in food and wine. As a tribute to this, the Alliance offers courses on French wines and cooking demonstrations. They even run an enormously popular French film series with which you can immerse yourself even further into the French culture. For a listing of classes and upcoming events, call or visit their Website.

AMERICAN INDIAN CENTER
1630 West Wilson Avenue, Chicago IL 60640. 773/275-5871. **E-mail address:** aic@mcs.net. **World Wide Web address:** http://www.mcs.net/~aic. **The Lowdown:** The American Indian Center is a Chicago gathering place for people of all tribes living in and around the city. The American Indian Center was formed in 1953 when, in response to the Indian Relocation Act, the city saw a deluge of Native American people migrate to Chicago. Since then, the Center has changed from a place of safety and community to a cultural center for both Indians and non-Indian alike. School groups are welcome to come in and hear traditional stories and music, become craftsmen for the day, and learn more about the Native American culture. Weekly bingo, arts and crafts fairs, and bimonthly flea markets are just some of the other events that take place here. Call or visit their Website to find out about the latest happenings.

BALZEKAS MUSEUM OF LITHUANIAN CULTURE
6500 South Pulaski Road, Chicago IL 60629. 773/582-6500. **The Lowdown:** The Balzekas Museum of Lithuanian Culture is not your typical ethnic museum that merely highlights the history

and presence of a particular culture. Aside from the country of Lithuania itself, this museum boasts the largest Lithuanian resources in the world. In many ways, it is an interactive museum; since much of the information contained here is records, artifacts, and collections, people often use these resources to trace Lithuanian family history. In fact, if you believe you might have some Lithuanian roots to trace, come to the museum armed with questions for the on-staff genealogist. They also set up a Lithuanian Pioneer Project to gather information on those who emigrated to the U.S. before World War I. The museum houses the permanent exhibit, *Lithuania Through the Ages*, as well as several art galleries, photo archives, an audio and visual hall, and a children's museum of immigrant history. Other museum interactive offerings include Lithuanian language classes, art classes, children's ballet classes, and folk art workshops. Rates are $4.00 for adults, $3.00 for students and seniors, and $1.00 for children. They're open daily, 10:00 a.m. - 4:00 p.m., so no excuses. **$Cash Only$**

CHICAGO CULTURAL CENTER
78 East Washington Street, Chicago IL 60602. 312/744-6630. **World Wide Web address:** http://www.cityofchicago.org/Tour/CulturalCenter/. **The Lowdown:** What a wonderful, civilized offering; this is the kind of facility that makes a city great. Looking to see a movie or hear a concert on a limited budget? Need a quiet place to cool your jets after a day of downtown shopping? New to town and in need of helpful information to get around? Stop into the Chicago Cultural Center, where you can find all this and more... for free. Run by the city's Department of Cultural Affairs, the Chicago Cultural Center is committed to making lively and enriching entertainment accessible to the public. They present nearly 1,000 free events annually in the building's many galleries, concert halls, and studios. During one month alone, you may have had the chance to take in an exhibit of antique bicycles; a reading of works by Bernard Shaw; performances of music and dance; cooking demonstrations; cabaret performances of gospel, opera, jazz, classical, improvisational, or world music; and a young people's concert. They also sponsor Chicago SummerDance, a festival of dance lessons; art exhibits at local galleries; guided tours of historic landmarks; and Chicago Neighborhood Tours (there is a charge for CNT). Before, after, or during these events, relax in the Randolph Cafe on the main level. Enjoy one of the cabaret performances scheduled every weekday at 1:00 p.m. and on Thursdays at 6:30 p.m. Open Monday through Wednesday, 10:00 a.m. - 7:00 p.m.; Thursday, 10:00 a.m. - 9:00 p.m.; Friday, 10:00 a.m. -6:00 p.m.; Saturday, 10:00 a.m. - 5:00 p.m.; Sunday, 11:00 a.m. - 5:00 p.m. For more information about arts events here, call 312/ FINE-ART (346-3278).

DAVID ADLER CULTURAL CENTER
1700 North Milwaukee Avenue, Libertyville IL 60048. 847/367-0707. **The Lowdown:** Well, this one's quite a ways out of town, but there's so much going on here that I just had to throw it in. Three Fridays a month, the David Adler Cultural Center presents

an open jam session. Admission is free, but donations are suggested (and greatly appreciated). Musicians from around the area come to sing and play folk music. On the second and fourth Saturday of each month, DACC presents a folk and ethnic concert series. These feature local talent, with the occasional national artist mixed in. Tickets are just $10.00 for the general public and $8.00 for members. The music begins at 8:00 p.m. DACC holds true to its claim of being a center of culture; throughout the year they offer various classes and workshops that will help you explore the business and aesthetics of the performing arts. Call for more information on upcoming events.

EVANSTON ART CENTER

2603 Sheridan Road, Evanston IL 60201. 847/475-5300. **World Wide Web address:** http://www.evanstonartcenter.org. **The Lowdown:** Established in 1929, Evanston Art Center is one of Chicago's oldest community art centers. They encourage you to "awaken your senses and challenge your mind," and they do a great job of ensuring that you'll have the resources to do just that. The center showcases a number of changing exhibits from both emerging and established artists. They also offer guided tours of the galleries (with a professional on hand to let you know what it is you're seeing) and several lectures throughout the year. Almost as beautiful as the art that you'll see here is the mansion that houses it all. Built in 1926, the Harley Clark mansion has long been home to the Evanston Art Center. Evanston Art Center offers over 100 classes and workshops for both children and adults. Classes are usually priced between $100.00 and $300.00, which is quite a deal if you check out the prices at a local college. Call or visit their Website to learn about upcoming classes and admission requirements. Admission to the center is a suggested donation of $3.00. Open Sunday, 2:00 p.m. - 5:00 p.m.; Monday through Thursday, 10:00 a.m. - 4:00 p.m. and 7:00 p.m. - 10:00 p.m.; Friday and Saturday, 10:00 a.m. - 4:00 p.m. The gallery is closed the fourth Thursday night of every month.

FERMILAB CULTURAL EVENTS

Wilson Hall, Kirk Road & Pine Street, Batavia IL 60510-0500. 630/840-ARTS. **E-mail address:** audweb@fnal.gov. **World Wide Web address:** http://www.fnal.gov. **The Lowdown:** The Fermi National Accelerator Laboratory, site of the highest energy particle accelerator in the world, may seem like an unlikely place to go for the performing arts. Nevertheless, this laboratory plays host to fantastic art, music, film, and lecture series, all at great prices. The Fermilab Art Gallery, on the second floor of Wilson Hall, offers a variety of ever-changing art exhibits and is open Monday through Friday, 9:00 a.m. - 5:00 p.m. The Fermilab Art Series offers a variety of musical, dance, and theater performances including blues and folk legends as Koko Taylor and Arlo Guthrie. Tickets are generally priced between $15.00 and $22.00. Throughout the year, Fermilab hosts a number of public lectures on a variety of topics, running the gamut from physics and science to history and music. Tickets are generally $5.00. For lots of family entertainment, drive the 35 miles out of

Chicago for the Fermilab Friday night film series. From recent favorites to obscure classics, the Fermilab film series offers a varied calendar of film screenings. From horror classics by the likes of Alfred Hitchcock and James Whale, to foreign films by Akira Kurosawa and Roberto Benigni, to independent features by Hal Hartley and John Sayles, all types of film fans are bound to find something to their liking. Tickets are $4.00 for adults and $1.00 for children under 12. All scheduled events take place in Wilson Hall's Ramsey Auditorium and begin at 8:00 p.m. For even better discounts, order tickets for three or more Art Series events and get 10 percent off your purchase. For the most up-to-date schedule, call or visit their Website.

GOETHE-INSTITUT CHICAGO

150 North Michigan Avenue, Suite 200, Chicago IL 60601. 312/263-0472. **World Wide Web address:** http://www. goethe.de/uk/chi. **The Lowdown:** The Goethe-Institut Chicago, in cooperation with other cultural and educational institutions, presents cultural programs intended to foster a cultural exchange of ideas and inform the American public of current social and artistic issues in Germany. The language department of the Goethe-Institut offers information for German teachers and professors on language and culture, conducts workshops, and provides didactic materials for German instructors. They even offer language instruction by native German speakers on the premises. The Goethe-Institut's information center/library offers more than 8,000 books (in German and English), and an extensive video and audio tape collection, slides, periodicals and newspapers, and an expanding software and CD collection. Library hours are Wednesday and Friday, 12:00 p.m. - 5:30 p.m.; Thursday, 3:00 p.m. - 8:00 p.m.; Saturday, 11:00 a.m. - 3:00 p.m. To find out about current cultural, language department, or library events, call the office during business hours (Monday through Thursday, 9:00 a.m. - 5:30 p.m.; Friday, 9:00 a.m. - 4:00 p.m.) or visit their Website.

HAROLD WASHINGTON LIBRARY CENTER

400 South State Street, Chicago IL 60605. 312/747-4300. **The Lowdown:** Mr. Cheap has always said that the library is a great place to look for fun and inexpensive activities. Working in tandem with the Chicago Cultural Center (see separate listing), the Washington Library Center presents a full slate of movies, music, dance, art exhibits, and children's activities, all for free. Find everything from the practical, like a lecture on how to repair bad credit, to the whimsical, such as poetry readings by local authors. In their spacious auditorium, you can enjoy events such as classical concerts performed on their Steinway grand, and films during the Midweek Matinee movie series. The auditorium also offers dance performances, children's theater, and even opera. In their other venues around the building, there are art exhibits, career workshops, and a permanent exhibit on the tenure of the library's namesake, Mayor Harold Washington. You can take a free public tour of this large, beautiful building; group tours can be arranged by calling 312/747-4136. All programs here are free of charge, though some programs may require

advance reservations. Open Monday, 9:00 a.m. - 7:00 p.m.; Tuesday and Thursday, 11:00 a.m. - 7:00 p.m.; Wednesday, Friday, and Saturday, 9:00 a.m. - 5:00 p.m.; Sunday, 1:00 p.m. - 5:00 p.m.

HELLENIC MUSEUM & CULTURAL CENTER
168 North Michigan Avenue, Chicago IL 60601. 312/726-1234. **E-mail address:** Hellenicmu@aol.com. **The Lowdown:** Regardless of your heritage, the Hellenic Museum & Cultural Center is a great place to visit when you're looking for an inexpensive way to pass time. The museum will shed some light on the life, history, and influence of Greeks in America. You'll find pottery, tapestries, embroidery, and paintings from as far back as the Byzantine era. Collections and exhibits rotate throughout the year, so there's always something new to see. Because the Hellenic Museum is also a cultural center, they don't just offer you some impersonal artifacts behind a glass case. They incorporate music, lecture, dance, and art demonstration programs for the public. They are part of The Field Museum's Cultural Connections events and offer summer programs for children. For more information on upcoming events and programs, call or write the museum. Museum admission is a suggested donation of $4.00. Open Monday through Friday, 10:00 a.m. - 4:00 p.m.; closed Saturday and Sunday.

HOTHOUSE
31 East Balbo Drive, Chicago IL 60605. 312/362-9707. **World Wide Web address:** http://www.hothouse.net. **The Lowdown:** Anything and everything is possible at HotHouse. This nonprofit cultural center is dedicated to providing its patrons with the most entertaining and diverse of offerings. On any given evening, you can witness some of Chicago's best art performances. For the most part, performances are live music; but poetry, lectures, theater, and dance often sneak their way into the schedule as well. Admissions vary, depending on the event. Call or visit their Website to hear about what's coming up this month.

IRISH AMERICAN HERITAGE CENTER
4626 North Knox Avenue, Chicago IL 60630. 773/282-7035. **World Wide Web address:** http://irishamhc.com. **The Lowdown:** If you've ever wondered what the heck Erin Go Braugh means, the significance of the Claddagh ring, or whether or not Guinness actually does taste better in Ireland, this is place to find out. In the Irish American Heritage Center's library, you can browse through such Irish treasures as *The Book of Lindisfarne* or the premiere editions of Francis O'Neill's music books. The center's museum – which was opened in 1991 by the President of Ireland, Mrs. Mary Robinson – houses a phenomenal collection of Bellique China, art work, and textiles. A set of maps highlights the contributions of the Irish culture for a time period of more than 600 years. Yet, while all this educational stuff can be interesting, let's face it – you're here for some fun! Friday night is movie night at the Irish American Heritage Center. Every week at 7:30 p.m., watch on as the center presents current hits, treasured classics, and documentaries that focus on the history

and culture of the Irish (everywhere from Dublin to Hell's Kitchen). Throughout the year, you can also catch art exhibits, fashion shows, plays, concerts, and many other fun activities. Each week, the center offers a variety of classes that will teach you everything from needlework to Irish set dancing to the Gaelic language. The cost depends on the event, but many are well below $10.00 if not free, and all are well worth the money. Additionally, live Irish music can be heard every Friday and Saturday night in their Fifth Province Pub. There is no cover charge and great pub food is available. If you live in the area and like what you hear so far, you should consider becoming a member of The Claddagh Group. The Claddagh Group is a community of adults (anyone between the ages of 21 and 45) that partake in a host of educational, cultural, and (especially) social events together: pub crawls, dinner parties, and bike rides are just the beginning. There are no fees to join the group, but you do pay your way for all events. It's a great way to meet some friends and/or just get out of the house. Call or visit their Website for more information and to learn about upcoming events.

KAPUT KAPOT

717 West Armitage Avenue, Chicago IL 60614. 312/867-1792. **The Lowdown:** If you've ever wondered what it feels like to truly be an artist and create something beautiful, here's your chance. Kaput Kapot is a design-your-own-pottery studio. Most of the legwork has been done for you; the shelves are stocked with a plethora of pottery (in all shapes and sizes); all you have to do is pick a pot and a few of your favorite colors. Then it's time to go to town! The on-site staff will be more than happy to throw a few pointers your way if you're having trouble. You can decorate some dinnerware for Dad, a mug for Mom, a teapot for teacher, or a food bowl for Fido. Or you can just be selfish and create a masterpiece for your own pottery collection. Once you've finished the artistry, the nice people at Kaput Kapot will hold on to your creation for firing and glazing. In just a few days, you can come back to pick it up! Budding artists will appreciate the chance for their art to receive worldwide exhibition; each month, Kaput Kapot picks a Kapiece of the month. The winning creation is featured for an entire month on their Website. What's best is that – as you pick the pot – you also pick the price. Pots range in price from $1.50 - $70.00 (plus painting fees of $6.00 per hour). Weekly specials make the fun even cheaper. Bring in two plain white rolls of paper towels on a Tuesday and you'll receive one hour of free painting; on Thursday nights, between 7:00 p.m. - 9:00 p.m., you're invited to kick back and relax with a little television and half-price painting fees. Like your own living room, food and drink (including alcohol) are always welcome! Reservations are not required, but they are suggested. So, whether you're looking to do a little redecorating, create an unusual gift for someone special, or just have a lot of fun, Kaput Kapot is the answer. Open Tuesday through Thursday, 12:00 p.m. - 9:00 p.m.; Friday through Sunday, 12:00 p.m. - 6:00 p.m.; closed Monday.

MEXICAN FINE ARTS CENTER MUSEUM

1852 West 19th Street, Chicago IL 60608. 312/738-1503. **E-mail address:** mfacm@wwa.com. **World Wide Web address:** http://www.mfacmchicago.org. **The Lowdown:** Located in the South Side neighborhood of Pilsen, the heart of Chicago's Mexican population, the Mexican Fine Arts Center Museum represents nothing less than the entire spectrum of Mexican art and culture. It's the largest institution of its type in the United States, with exhibits ranging from the traditional to the avant-garde. Four major exhibitions take place each year in the main gallery. One showcases contemporary art; another folk art; a third, art from some of the 56 indigenous peoples of Mexico; the fourth exhibit is the annual Day of the Dead show. The Mexican Fine Arts Center Museum's west wing gallery shows work from its permanent collection. In their courtyard gallery, you can see work by today's emerging artists, as well as by students in the museum's children's art education programs. Admission is free to all ages, all the time. Open Tuesday through Sunday, 10:00 a.m. - 5:00 p.m.

NORTH LAKESIDE CULTURAL CENTER

6219 North Sheridan Avenue, Chicago IL 60660. 773/743-4477. **The Lowdown:** Housed in an old mansion on Lake Michigan near the Loyola University campus, North Lakeside Cultural Center presents a wide variety of inexpensive music and theater performances. Their regular Sunday Afternoon at the Mansion series can offer anything from classical piano to Gershwin. The Theater at the Mansion series features productions by the much-respected Equity Library Theatre company, and is one of the top-rated writing workshops in the city. Tickets to concerts are just $5.00 at the door and $3.00 for members and senior citizens. The Center also has an art gallery, with exhibits that change monthly. Call for a schedule of upcoming events.

UNDER THE PICASSO

50 West Washington Street, Chicago IL. 312/744-1742. **E-mail address:** culture@ci.chi.il.us. **World Wide Web address:** http://www.ci.chi.il.us/Tourism/Picasso. **The Lowdown:** Every weekday at 12:00 p.m., in front of the Daley Civic Center, the Chicago Department of Cultural Affairs brightens up the downtown lunch hour with free arts performances on the plaza in front of Picasso's famous sculpture. These events may consist of anything from a celebration of Jamaican Independence Day, full of music and colorful dance, to standup comedy or ballet. In the summer, there are even open-air farmers markets. Inside the building lobby itself, a small but serviceable art gallery offers more free culture, such as works from the Chicago Print and Drawing Fair. To find out what's scheduled for this week, call 312/346-3278 for a recorded message.

Bars & Nightclubs

THE CUBBY BEAR

1059 West Addison Street, Chicago IL 60613. 773/327-1662. **The Lowdown:** Since 1953, residents and visitors to the Wrigleyville area have looked to one place for hours of great fun, dining, and entertainment before and after a Cubs game: The Cubby Bear. Located directly across from Wrigley Field, The Cubby Bear is one of the most obvious (read: crowded) spots to drop in for a bite to eat or a drink when you've got tickets to a game. But baseball season isn't the only time to visit The Cubby Bear; they offer live music several nights a week and an open jam session every Wednesday. As an added bonus, stop by for the jam session and you can enjoy $.10 wings and $.25 beers. Is it still 1953 in here? You would think so with those prices! Even if you're not here in time for the specials, The Cubby Bear's kitchen serves up a well-priced menu of traditional American favorites (chicken tenders, potato skins, salads, soups, and ribs) every day from 11:00 a.m. - 1:00 a.m. On Sunday they offer an all-you-can-eat brunch buffet for just $7.50 per person. The price includes an all-access pass to the omelette and carving stations, along with plenty of waffles, French toast, biscuits and gravy to go around and around again. Open Sunday through Friday, 11:00 a.m. - 2:00 a.m.; Saturday, 11:00 a.m. - 3:00 a.m. When The Cubs are playing, The Cubby Bear opens its doors at 10:00 a.m. But keep in mind, the specials are not valid during the home games.

DRAGON ROOM

809 West Evergreen Avenue, Chicago IL 60622. 312/751-2900. **The Lowdown:** After a hard day at the office, people often head off to the nearest bar to have a drink; Dragon Room offers these people the unique opportunity to try something a bit different. With a full bar selection, you're more than welcome to order your favorite drink, but why not melt into the Asian-styled surroundings and opt for some warm sake and an Ebi roll instead? Dragon Room is the city's (and probably one of the nation's) only combination nightclub and sushi bar. And they do both well. This sushi isn't straight from a box to your plate, there's lots of prep time that go into making it some of the best sushi in the city. They know what they're doing, and the lines of people waiting to grab a bite themselves only prove that. But let's not forget about the nightclub half of Dragon Room. Since its opening, Dragon Room has attracted some of the biggest celebs in the world of music, sports, and every other arena you could imagine. Don't look too hard for your favorite stars though, chances are they're being pampered in the fantastic VIP room that lives upstairs, where you and I can only long to be! Back on Earth, Dragon Room caters to an artistic, sophisticated crowd. The majority of patrons are under the age of 30 and are all looking to have a good time in an unpretentious setting such as this one. Join the party of music and dance when Dragon Room lets 2 DJs duke it out for your attention, spinning the best and

latest dance beats. If you need a minute to recuperate from elegance overload, there are a number of plush sofas aligning the lower level that long to be lounged in. And get this for amenities, there is a full bar in the women's bathroom. For all those guys who have ever wondered why it takes women so long to go to the bathroom and why they have to go in pairs, maybe this answers the question. The best thing about nightclubs, from a Cheapster point of view, is that you can really be the one to determine how much you spend. Once you pay the cover charge, the rest is up to you. At Dragon Room, just make sure you bring enough for some sushi! Call or visit their Website for a listing of upcoming events. Open Wednesday through Sunday, 10:00 p.m. - 4:00 a.m. (until 5:00 a.m. on Saturday).

EMPTY BOTTLE
1035 North Western Avenue, Chicago IL 60622. 773/276-3600. **E-mail address:** info@emptybottle.com. **World Wide Web address:** http://www.emptybottle.com. **The Lowdown:** Empty Bottle has long been considered one of the city's most popular and unpretentious nightspots. It has long been their philosophy that down-to-earth people and down-to-earth prices are the ingredients for a successful bar; add to that a fantastic lineup of live musical performances and you've got Empty Bottle. Virtually every night of the week, Empty Bottle offers a sampling of some of the industry's most talented performers. But whether it's rock, pop, or jazz that's playing, you can bet the music will be experimental: mainstream just isn't in the vocabulary here, and it's a good thing! Ticket prices range from about $5.00 - $10.00 on any given night. Best of all, the food and drink prices here are unbelievably cheap: $1.00 bottles of beer can often be found at Empty Bottle (and at prices like that, I'm sure there are plenty of empty bottles actually lying around). Plus, the food is anything but typical. Forget the wings and nachos you'll find at so many other drinking establishments and instead opt for a plate of baba ganoush with pita; skewered tandoori chicken with yogurt and mint chutney; or roasted bell peppers with kalamata olives and feta cheese. Pasta entrees include orechiette with broccoli, pine nuts, raisins, and garlic-chili oil; penne with eggplant, zucchini, bell pepper, tomato, and feta cheese; and fettucine alfredo with chicken, spinach, and mushrooms. They also carry a good selection of burgers and sandwiches, with nothing on the menu costing more than $7.00. They even offer a great weekend brunch so that, technically, you could spend the majority of your weekend here. Now that's what I call relaxing! Open Sunday, 12:00 p.m. - 2:00 a.m.; Monday through Wednesday, 4:00 p.m. - 2:00 a.m.; Thursday and Friday, 3:00 p.m. - 2:00 a.m.

GAMEWORKS
601 North Martingdale Road, Suite 115, Schaumburg IL 60173. 847/330-9675. **World Wide Web address:** http://www.gameworks.com. **The Lowdown:** While it seems that GameWorks might be more at home in the chapter for children's activities, GameWorks is a great adult getaway. Steven Spielberg helped to design this place, so you can only imagine the childlike creativity that went into building it. Two levels of fun offer well

over 150 games. Live musical acts even grace the stage once a week, making it a true night life experience. A full bar menu offers up plenty of bottled and draft beers, an impressive wine list, any cocktail you can imagine, and lots of specialty margaritas and martinis. Many of these beverages are even available in half-yard glasses that become a great souvenir when you're done consuming. The GameWorks Grill offers a wide assortment of appetizers, sandwiches, pizzas, and entrees for a quick and satisfying meal. While you're welcome to bring the kids during the day, you must be of legal drinking age to enter the facility after 10:00 p.m. Throughout the week, GameWorks hosts a variety of special promotions that make a stop here even more affordable: Punch Out For Lunch is their weekday lunch special (11:00 a.m. - 2:00 p.m.) where $12.00 will get food, drink, and 30 minutes of play time; become a "$5 Scholar" on Thursdays (7:00 p.m. - close) when a single $5.00 bill will get you a $10.00 play card, a pitcher of beer, or a select menu item. Money-saving promotions like these are running all the time; give them a call or visit their Website for more information. Open Sunday through Thursday, 10:00 a.m. – 1:00 a.m.; Friday and Saturday, 11:00 a.m. – 2:00 a.m.

HIDDEN COVE
5338 North Lincoln Avenue, Chicago IL 60625. 773/275-3955.
The Lowdown: If you like a little excitement with your cocktail, Hidden Cove is the place to find it. It's the site of many local and national trivia competitions; so, if you find yourself yelling at the television set and becoming enraged at contestants who don't know the answer during *Jeopardy*, you can show off your wide-ranging base of useless knowledge here. Think you've got the makings of the next (but much cooler) Frank Sinatra? Hidden Cove offers karaoke every night at 8:00 p.m. so you can sing your heart out! There's plenty of typical bar entertainment here as well, like pool tables, satellite television, and darts. But it's not every bar in Chicago that has a team in the Windy City Darters Association. Free parking outside makes the trip that even more economical. Open Sunday through Friday, 11:00 a.m. - 4:00 a.m.; Saturday, 11:00 a.m. - 5:00 a.m.

HOUSE OF BEER
16 West Division Street, Chicago IL 60610. 312/642-2344.
The Lowdown: With a menu comprised of more than 100 beers and a plethora of sports-yielding television sets, House of Beer is all about the serious sports fan. House of Beer is also *About Last Night*; yes, I *am* referring to that mid-1980s romantic comedy starring Rob Lowe and Demi Moore. If you've seen the movie, you probably remember Mother Malone's, the fictitious bar where the not-always-so-happy couple met. House of Beer was used for many of those scenes. If you're in the mood for a competitive game of foosball, they've got your table ready and waiting. You can also showcase your hand-to-eye coordination with a game of air hockey. With so many beers to choose from and a variety of drink specials throughout the week, House of Beer will keep your wallet as happy as your taste buds. Open Sunday, 11:00 a.m. -

4:00 a.m.; Monday through Thursday, 4:00 p.m. - 4:00 a.m.; Friday, 1:00 p.m. - 4:00 a.m.; Saturday, 11:00 a.m. - 5:00 a.m.

JOE'S SPORTS BAR
940 West Weed Street, Chicago IL 60622. 312/337-3486. **World Wide Web address:** http://www.joesbar.com. **The Lowdown:** If you're looking to relax with a great night of sports-watching, follow the crowd to Joe's. Housed in an old warehouse, Joe's Sports Bar offer four rooms of entertainment. Tons of televisions (both big and small), video games, and pool tables are only the beginning of the fun you can have. In the warmer months, the outside beer garden at Joe's offers a refreshing option to a smoke-filled bar. Stop by after 10:00 p.m. on a Wednesday, Friday, or Saturday night when Joe's offers live music. While I'd love to tell you what kind of musicians play here, Joe's sets no limits; all genres are covered. They even clear out the tables near the stage area, so you should feel free to get your groove on! Joe's Sports Bar charges a cover only on show nights, and it's usually $7.00 or less. It's always a good deal. Even better are the food and drink specials: Wednesday nights, bask in the glory of $1.00 Bud and Bud Light bottles and $1.00 well drinks; Thursday nights offer 25-ounces of Sam Adams for $4.00, 25-ounces of Bud for $3.50, and half-price pizzas. If there's a big game on, you better get there early as lines can be pretty long. Why not get there early and grab a bite to eat before the game starts? Joe's offers a great menu of all your pub favorites. Late night hours make Joe's Sports Bar a great option any time of night (or morning, for that matter). Open Sunday, 11:00 a.m. - 12:30 a.m.; Monday through Friday, 5:00 p.m. - 4:00 a.m.; Saturday, 11:00 a.m. - 4:00 a.m.

JOHN BARLEYCORN MEMORIAL PUB
658 West Belden Avenue (at North Lincoln Avenue), Chicago IL 60614. 773/348-8899. **World Wide Web address:** http://www.johnbarleycorn.com. **The Lowdown:** In an area so steeped in charm, it only makes sense that John Barleycorn would situate himself here. The building itself – built in 1890 – reeks of old world tradition and quaintness. The pub boasts the location's original cast molding and hand-tooled tin ceilings. The best part about the place is that – since the time that John Dillinger was a regular – prices haven't increased too drastically. With one of Lincoln Park's largest draft beer selections, you can bet you'll find a deal on ale almost every night of the week. On Wednesday, you can join in the $6.95 all-you-can-eat fish and chips buffet and wash it all down with a $2.00 glass of Sam Adams. On Thursday, show your Irish and/or your Cheapster roots by indulging in $2.00 pints of Guinness and $2.00 black and tans. When you get the teensiest bit hungry, John Barleycorn is there to serve you in the food department as well. The large menu consists of appetizers (onion loaf, nachos, potato skins, breaded calamari); soups (New England clam chowder, French onion); salads (Greek, Caesar); and sandwiches (Philly cheesesteak, Louisiana chicken). John Barleycorn Memorial Pub also offers a number of inexpensive pasta dishes and is well-known throughout town for their delicious burgers. They even

offer a good selection of brunch items after 9:00 a.m. on Saturday and Sunday. See! Whether you're here to eat or drink (or both), John Barleycorn Memorial Pub is a great place to do it cheaply. Open Sunday, 9:00 a.m. - close; Monday through Friday, 3:00 p.m. - 2:00 a.m.; Saturday, 9:00 a.m. - 3:00 a.m.

LIQUID

1997 North Clybourn Avenue (at Racine Avenue), Chicago IL 60614. 773/528-3400. **E-mail address:** liquidswings@msn.com. **The Lowdown:** After entering Liquid, dubbed "The Original House of Swing," you'll swear that you've gone back a few decades. For those who can't swing dance, this is the place to learn how to jump and jive. Free beginner swing dance lessons are offered on Wednesday and Thursday and start at 8:00 p.m. Friday. Saturday and Sunday, Liquid switches over to a Latin groove of salsa, merengue, tango, cumba, mariachi, and Latin rock. Free beginner Latin dance lessons start at 9:00 p.m. on Saturday and Sunday. Valet parking, a full dinner menu, and private party accommodations are also available. The cover charge varies, but generally ranges from $6.00 - $12.00.

THE MAP ROOM

1949 North Hoyne, Chicago IL. 773/252-7636. **E-mail address:** info@maproom.com. **World Wide Web address:** http://www.maproom.com. **The Lowdown:** Okay, so The Map Room could probably be listed in a variety of different chapters. The Map Room bills itself as "The Travelers Tavern", but don't be fooled by the name. Sure, for the weary traveler The Map Room is a great place to relax and unwind. But it is also a place many regulars feel comfortable frequenting. Coffee drinks (regular, latte, cappuccino, espresso) are one specialty here. Grab yourself a cup of the usual and find a spot to sit and peruse the *Trib* or leisurely flip through one of the many travel books on the shelf. Of course, there is more to The Map Room than meets the eye. This is also a great place to listen to live music every Friday and Saturday night. A variety of musical tastes are represented from rock to reggae. And best of all, there is never a cover. Shows start at 9:30 p.m. on Fridays and 10:00 p.m. on Saturdays. But wait, there's more. Beer and wine are another specialty at The Map Room. On Monday nights, Chicago brews are only $3.00; and on Wednesdays, imports are the same low price per bottle. For those who want to get a taste of culture, why not register for the Beer or Wine School. Learn how to become a master beer brewer or a wine connoisseur. Call or check their Website for further details.

MORSELAND MUSIC ROOM

1218 West Morse Avenue, Chicago IL 60626. 773/764-6401. **E-mail address:** music@morseland.com. **World Wide Web address:** http://www.morseland.com. **The Lowdown:** There's always something to see and hear at Morseland Music Room. As the name suggests, live music is the main attraction here. Most nights, you're likely to find a local band onstage, playing anything from jazz to rock. On Sunday night, comedy is the name of the game at Morseland. You can laugh your way right to the bar and pick up a $1.50 Rolling Rock bottle! Tuesday is open mike night. From 8:00 p.m. - 10:00 p.m., you can listen to the poetry, music, and other oratories given by the performers who choose to take the stage. Besides low admission, Morseland Music Room offers a number of money-saving perks: regular drink specials include $2.50 Guinness drafts on Wednesday and $2.50 selected microbrew drafts on Thursday. Included in the cover charge is your invitation to gorge yourself on the Morseland grub buffet. For those nights when there's no cover charge, a single buffet serving is just $1.00 while a bottomless plate will cost you $3.00. Staples include mac and cheese, hot buttered noodles, spicy chicken with rice, and – the house specialty – Brendon's "meat and potatoes." If you're not willing to wash it all down with the drink special, you can choose from the more than 50 beers they offer. Hang out upstairs and relax with a game of pool or Ping-Pong. Open Sunday, 8:00 p.m. - 2:00 a.m.; Tuesday through Friday, 8:00 p.m. - 2:00 a.m.; Saturday, 8:00 p.m. - 3:00 a.m.; closed Monday.

PARTYBUS

312/266-7330. **E-mail address:** partybus@chicagomotorcoach. com. **World Wide Web address:** http://www. chicagomotorcoach.com/partybus2.htm. **The Lowdown:** What would it be worth to spend the night bouncing from club to club with no cover charges to pay, lines to wait in, taxi to call, or car to drive home? Does $35.00 sound reasonable? It does to me! Partybus takes off every Thursday, Friday, and Saturday night at 9:00 p.m. and will take you and a busload of your new friends to four of the city's most happening nightspots. For solo travelers looking to explore the night life or groups of people who just want to party and not have to worry about minor details like "getting in," Partybus is an excellent alternative. It's also a great chance to meet some like-minded individuals and some new friends. Call or visit their Website for more information. Reservations are required, so be sure to call ahead.

PLAZA TAVERN

70 West Monroe Street (at Dearborn Street), Chicago IL 60603. 312/977-1940. **The Lowdown:** Okay, so you might not be able to afford dinner at Plaza Tavern, but you can still indulge in all the luxury even if you're on a budget. All you need to do is stop by their oyster bar for Happy Hour on Monday through Friday, from 4:00 p.m. - 7:00 p.m. You'll be treated to some really fantastic drink and food specials, each for $1.99. Drop in on a Monday and get a Bud Light, walk in on a Wednesday and you can get a mini martini, and Thursdays thrill with a Stoli cocktail. Every night of the week offers up a different drink special. The food menu includes (again, everything is an unbelievable $1.99) popcorn and peel and eat shrimp, chicken tenders, jalapeño poppers, spicy chicken wings, and oyster shooters. If you're having so much fun that you don't want to leave, you can enjoy live jazz while sipping on a cocktail in the Fountain Room Lounge. You'll be breathing in the same air of sophistication at a much less expensive price. It's deals like these that will make you want to kick up your heels!

Children's Activities

BRONZEVILLE CHILDREN'S MUSEUM
Evergreen Plaza, 96th Street and Western Avenue, Evergreen Park IL. 708/636-9504. **The Lowdown:** This is the nation's first and only children's museum dedicated to African-American culture. The museum is named for the area where African-Americans first settled in Chicago and Bronzeville has since bloomed into a retail and cultural mecca. Past exhibits have included, a look at the life of George Washington Carver and How Blacks Built the West. On a recent visit, Amazing Dinosaurs was the main exhibit. Admission is $3.00 for adults and $2.00 for children. Open Tuesday through Saturday, 10:00 a.m. - 5:00 p.m.

BUILD-A-BEAR WORKSHOP
Woodfield Shopping Center, Schaumburg IL 60173. 847/517-4155. ◆ Oakbrook Center, Oak Brook IL 60523. 630/928-0497. **World Wide Web address:** http://www.buildabear.com. **The Lowdown:** Here's one place where you can nix a trip to the toy store altogether. Build-A-Bear Workshop lets kids do just that: make their own teddy bears and other stuffed animals. Kids can choose all the different ingredients that will make up their new friend. As kids are especially sensitive to different kinds of materials and textiles (yes, the silky-smooth feel of their baby blanket is the reason they take it off to college and beyond with them), this is a great way for them to pick out the perfect toy. Depending on how elaborate your child wants to get (or how creative you allow them to be), prices can range anywhere from $10.00 - $25.00, with outfits and accessories ranging from $3.00 - $15.00. Call for specific hours.

CHICAGO CHILDREN'S MUSEUM
Navy Pier, 700 East Grand Avenue, Chicago IL. 312/527-1000. **World Wide Web address:** http://www.chichildrensmuseum. org. **The Lowdown:** Travel to the Sahara and unearth dinosaur bones. Test the principles of aerodynamics with your own designs. Go on-air to report the news. Create one-of-a-kind paintings and sculptures. These are just a few of the hands-on activities you can enjoy at Chicago Children's Museum. With a diverse selection of interactive permanent and traveling exhibitions, workshops, and programs, children and adults alike have fun while learning. Admission is $6.50 per person, $5.50 for seniors. Members and children under one year are free. Open Tuesday through Sunday, 10:00 a.m. - 5:00 p.m.; Mondays from Memorial Day through Labor Day, most school holidays, and on Thursday evenings for Free Family Night, 5:00 p.m. - 8:00 p.m.

DISNEYQUEST
55 East Ohio Street, Chicago IL 60611. 312/222-1300. **The Lowdown:** So that trip to Orlando turned into a trip to Chicago and the kids are disappointed? No problem, just take them to DisneyQuest, a sort of virtual theme park. Design and

ride your own virtual roller coaster with the help of Bill Nye, or enjoy the fun of Aladdin's Magic Carpet Ride, Hercules in the Underworld, Invasion! and ExtraTERRORestrial Encounter, Buzz Lightyear's Astroblaster, and much more. Kids can enjoy all five floors of fun for just $16.00 for two - three hours, or $26.00 for an all-day pass (which allows for re-entry). There's even a retail store and two restaurants on the premises, so there are plenty of other options for parents who don't feel like joining in. For even better savings, you can pick up an annual pass for just $79.00. Open Sunday, 10:00 a.m. – 10:00 p.m.; Monday through Wednesday, 11:00 a.m. – 7:00 p.m.; Thursday and Friday, 11:00 a.m. – 12:00 a.m.; Saturday, 10:00 a.m. – 12:00 a.m.

DuPAGE CHILDREN'S MUSEUM

1777 South Blanchard Road, Wheaton IL 60187. 630/260-9960. **World Wide Web address:** http://www.dcmrats.org. **The Lowdown:** It's not often that you hear kids actually asking to go to the museum. Of course, this is not your typical kid-unfriendly art museum, nor an advanced science-oriented one that would not suit a toddler. The DuPage Children's Museum has enough exhibits to attract even the youngest and rowdiest bunch. They have an AirWorks For Kids exhibit in which kids can create air mazes, make air rockets, float objects, and conduct all sorts of air movement experiments. And, of course, where else would you allow kids to play with saws and hammers? At the museum, kids can construct their own creations with wood and nails. It's a chance for your little ones to show off their own creativity and craftsmanship. Among other fun distractions, the museum also has a waterworks, magnet, and kid-netic motion area. Even the tiniest tots will have fun in the young explorers area. The best part about this museum (at least for the paying adult) is the admission price. Just $4.50 per person covers a full day of amusements. Open Tuesday through Saturday, 9:30 a.m. - 5:00 p.m. (Wednesday until 8:00 p.m.); Sunday, 12:00 p.m. - 5:00 p.m.; Monday, 9:00 a.m. - 12:00 p.m. (members only). **NOTE:** At the time this book went to print, DuPage Children's Museum was in the process of moving their facilities to 301 North Washington Street in Naperville IL. If you are planning a visit sometime after the year 2001, it is a good idea to give them a call and verify their location.

ECHO

67 East Adams Street, Chicago IL 60604. 312/294-3000. **World Wide Web address:** http://echo.chicagosymphony.org. **The Lowdown:** Combining their love for music with their love for children, the Chicago Symphony Orchestra has created ECHO, a hands on music museum. Kids are invited to learn about how music is made and how it is performed. They'll even get the opportunity to play an instrument of their own and hear how it sounds when recorded. More than teaching the aesthetic value of music, ECHO teaches kids and their families how music is used in the context of different cultures. The museum's A-Musing Room is broken down into five separate areas housing a number of different activities. After you've visited all five areas, ECHO pieces together the music created by each child and presents it

on their Orchestra Wall. ECHO's Music Lab, which is available to groups by appointment only, further enlightens children through a series of games. As group tours are often scheduled, it is a good idea to try and make a reservation beforehand. Admission to the A-Musing Room is $2.50 for children under 17 and senior citizens, and $5.50 for adults. Admission to both the A-Musing Room and Music Labs is $5.00 for children under 17 and seniors, and $11.00 for adults. Open Sunday, 11:00 a.m. - 5:00 p.m.; Tuesday through Saturday, 10:00 a.m. - 5:00 p.m.; closed Monday.

HEALTH WORLD

1301 South Grove Avenue, Barrington IL 60010. 847/842-9100. **World Wide Web address:** http://www.jfkhealthworld.org. **The Lowdown:** Without preaching in a classroom, this nonprofit health education museum accomplishes the same goal of bringing awareness of a healthy lifestyle to children. Health World has six main interactive exhibits. The Living Gadget area is devoted to human anatomy and includes a flex test, a height and weight area, and a jumping height area. In the Health Village area, children can sample a day in the emergency room, doctor's office, or dentist's office. The Us 'N Stuff area may be a possible alternative to having a formal chat with kids about how their bodies react to things they do, like smoking and drinking. Teach children about street safety, emergency situations, and common house hazards in the Safety Challenge area. The Life Trek area is a human development section that traces all aspects from birth to old age. The last exhibit, the Oak Forest area, shows the importance of caring for the environment by allowing kids to explore the indoor forest area. Health World also has a discovery spaces section, an auditorium, several classrooms, and a library resource center. Admission is $5.00 per person; children under two and members are free. Open Monday through Thursday, 10:00 a.m. - 3:00 p.m.; Friday, 10:00 a.m. - 8:00 p.m.; Saturday and Sunday, 10:00 a.m. - 3:00 p.m.

KIDDIELAND AMUSEMENT PARK

8400 West North Avenue, Melrose Park IL 60160. 708/343-8003. **World Wide Web address:** http://www.kiddieland.com. **The Lowdown:** Can't make it down to Disney World on your budget? Spend the day at Kiddieland instead and think of the money you will save on airfare and admission fees. With a name like Kiddieland, you know this is one place your kids will like. Besides, if they're under 36 inches tall, they're admitted free with a paying adult. To save even more money, you can enter the park after 5:00 p.m. and save $3.00 off the regular admission price. All the basics are here, with a ferris wheel, water slides, an arcade, plenty other games and rides, plus newer attractions for kids of all ages. General admission is $17.50 for adults; $14.50 for kids ages three - five; $10.50 for seniors. Prices include unlimited self-serve softdrinks, rides, and parking. Hours vary through the season. Open seven days a week during the summer; weekends and evenings during the spring and fall; closed during the winter.

KIDS ON THE FLY

5200 North Bessie Coleman Drive, Chicago IL 60605. **The Lowdown:** Here's one activity you'll want to save for your arrival and/or departure from Chicago. If you're flying into O'Hare, Kids on the Fly offers parents a relaxing moment in the midst of all the craziness of travel. Designed in a joint effort between Chicago Department of Aviation and the Chicago Children's Museum, Kids on the Fly is located on the departure level of the airport's Terminal 2. It's a great, free exhibit that will be sure to psyche your kids up for the flight home. A number of displays – including a two-story airplane that kids can actually play on, an air traffic control tower, and a baggage check – are perched right next to a number of benches where parents can rest and keep an eye on their kids. It's a great idea and a great cheap thing to do. Best of all, it's open early and closed late so, no matter how long your flight delay, the little ones will be entertained. For more information, call the Chicago Children's Museum at 312/527-1000. Open daily, 7:00 a.m. - 12:00 a.m.

KOHL CHILDREN'S MUSEUM

165 Green Bay Road, Wilmette IL 60091. 847/256-6056. **The Lowdown:** Kohl Children's Museum is a nonprofit educational institution for children, parents, and educators whose mission is to foster learning through interactive, multi-sensory exhibits and programs. Ongoing permanent exhibits include All Aboard!, a lively exhibit about trains and public transportation; Jewel-Osco, a child-sized grocery store; People, an interactive exhibit celebrating diversity through play; H_2O, a dynamic water environment; Grandma's Attic; Cozy Corner; StarMax Technology Center; and the Construction Zone. The museum also offers daily discoveries, hands-on workshops, parties, and more. Admission is $5.00 for adults and children. Members and children under 1 year are always free.

LAMBS FARM

I-94 & Route 176, Libertyville IL 60048. 847/362-6774. **The Lowdown:** Lambs Farm started out as a pet store and has grown to become much more. What is most unique about the farm is that it is also a home to many disabled adults who live and work here. There's lots to do and see for children of all ages. The younger kids will like the petting zoo, where they can get up close and personal with sheep, goats, chickens, and llamas. Older kids may be more interested in the 18-hole miniature golf course and the snack bar. Nevertheless, there will be something to keep everyone amused. Admission and parking are free but additional activities will cost extra. Keep in mind that all proceeds help to support and sustain the farm and its workers. Open daily, 10:00 a.m. - 5:00 p.m.

LIFELINE THEATRE

6912 North Glenwood Avenue, Chicago IL 60626. 773/761-4477. **World Wide Web address:** http://www.lifelinetheatre.com. **The Lowdown:** The KidSeries at Chicago's Lifeline Theatre combines the best in children's literature and stories with the excitement of live theater. Started in 1983 by a group of five

Northwestern graduates, Lifeline Theatre is dedicated to providing high-quality theater at an affordable price. With a particular interest in exposing children to theater, they offer a number of low-cost performance options. In addition to regular performances, they offer an in-school residency program and offer pay-what-you-can performances for families who might not otherwise be able to afford a ticket. KidSeries productions have included works by some of the world's most beloved children's authors including Roald Dahl, Rudyard Kipling, and E. B. White. Works presented have included *Mrs. Piggle-Wiggle*, *Mike Mulligan and His Steam Shovel*, *The Cricket in Times Square*, *James and the Giant Peach*, *Stuart Little*, *Just So Stories*, and *The Rescuers*. If you purchase tickets to a KidSeries performance in advance, the cost is just $7.00 per person. If you're paying at the door on the day of the show, you can pay what you wish if there are tickets available. Just remember, Lifeline Theatre is providing an enormously generous service to the theater-going community; you should "wish'"to pay them accordingly. While the "C" in Mr. C definitely stands for cheap, it certainly doesn't stand for *cheapskate*. KidSeries performances take place on Saturday and Sunday. Call or visit their Website for specific times. If you want to put the kids to bed early, you should also be aware of Lifeline's Main Stage productions. They have presented such great works as *Pride and Prejudice*, *Jane Eyre*, *Dracula*, and *The Overcoat*. They even attempt to bring the child out in adult theater-goers by presenting the stories you loved as children: *The Lion, the Witch and the Wardrobe* and *A Wrinkle in Time* are two such productions. Main Stage tickets are $18.50 for adults, $15.00 for students and seniors, and $12.00 for groups of 12 or more. Preview shows and rush tickets are also available (rush tickets can be purchased one half hour before the show) for $10.00 each.

MAGIC TREE BOOK STORE
141 North Oak Park Avenue, Oak Park IL 60301. 708/848-0770.
The Lowdown: This full-service specialty store offers much more than kiddie-oriented books, videos, clothes, and toys. Every Tuesday at 10:00 a.m., Magic Tree Book Store offers a magical storytelling session that is sure to enchant your little one. Call to hear about other upcoming events. Open Sunday, 12:00 p.m. - 4:00 p.m.; Monday, Thursday and Friday, 10:00 a.m. - 8:00 p.m.; Tuesday and Wednesday, 10:00 a.m. - 6:00 p.m.; Saturday, 9:30 a.m. - 5:30 p.m.

RACING RAPIDS ACTION PARK
880 East Main Street, East Dundee IL 60118. 847/426-5525.
World Wide Web address: http://www.santasvillageil.com.
The Lowdown: When it heats up during the summer, a trip to Racing Rapids Action Park in East Dundee might just be the solution to help you cool down. They've got water slides, go carts, and bumper boats that are sure to please just about everyone in your group. Among other rides, the Twister Tube Slide will chute you and your tube down with 4,000 gallons of water per minute. If thrill-seeking speed is not your idea of fun, you may enjoy the Lazy River Tube Ride which will allow you to

follow the slower current. Admission is all-inclusive: $12.95 will cover unlimited access to rides and shows all day, parking, and access to the picnic area. Children under two are always admitted free. If you're thinking of visiting nearby Santa's Village (see separate listing) as well, you can get an extra special deal if you visit both in one day: On Monday and Tuesday, a combination admission to both parks is just $22.95 while Wednesday through Sunday and holidays offer a dual pass for $25.95. It's an entertaining (not to mention exhausting) way to spend the day. If you can visit their Website, you just might be able to find some additional savings: they frequently offer a cyber coupon that will afford you an even better discount. Racing Rapids Action Park is open from early June through early September. Call ahead for hours (usually 11:00 a.m. - 6:00 p.m.).

SANTA'S VILLAGE
601 Dundee Avenue, Dundee IL 60118. 847/426-6753. **World Wide Web address:** http://www.santasvillageil.com. **The Lowdown:** Even if it isn't Christmas time, Santa's Village is open and happy to have you and your kids. You won't see the big guy making a list and checking it twice, but you can be sure that he's watching! For $18.95 per person (Wednesday through Sunday), your family can be out of the house and roaming around Santa's Village for the day. If you choose to go on a Monday or Tuesday, it will only cost you $15.95 per person (children under two are always free). Whatever day you choose, this place is surely grand enough to entertain even the most distracted child. Santa's Village is made up of Three Worlds. Santa's World features the original frozen North Pole and the Balloon Race Ride. You'll also find a number of rides including Dracor the Dragon, and some games of skill here. The second part of Santa's Village is called Old McDonald's Farm and has, you guessed it, farm animals. Here, it's okay for the kids to wallow with the pigs. They'll be able to pet all types of animals, from rabbits to llamas. The more adventurous will enjoy a stop at Coney Island. Complete with the 63-foot high Typhoon roller coaster, this is the place for thrill-seekers. You'll also have the chance to ride the Great Wheel, the Galleon Pirate Ship, the Yo-Yo, and the Dodge 'Em Bumper Cars, among other rides. Since you'll probably want to make a day out of this excursion, my cheap advice is to pack a lunch. There's a picnic area in the park that will provide you with a bit of serenity and some extra money in your pocket. And if you intend to make the most of your day, you can pay $22.95 on a Monday or Tuesday or $25.95 on Wednesday through Sunday (and holidays) to gain admission to both Santa's Village and Racing Rapids Action Park (see separate listing). If you have Internet access, be sure and check out their Website, where you can occasionally find coupons for even further savings. Oddly enough, Santa's Village is *NOT* open around Christmas time, but rather from May through September.

College Performing Arts

DePaul UNIVERSITY

60 East Balbo Drive, Chicago IL 60605. 312/922-1999. **World Wide Web address:** http://theatreschool.depaul.edu. **The Lowdown:** The Theatre School at DePaul University provides a great opportunity for adults and children to enjoy the arts. The Showcase series presents about five productions each season, with tickets priced between $6.00 and $12.00. Each of these includes a night (usually the second Wednesday of the run) when DePaul students can get two-for-one tickets. Discounts are also available for seniors, alumni, and DePaul employees; subscription rates are available, too. The Theatre School also offers Chicago Playworks. Founded in 1925 as the Goodman Children's Theatre, Chicago Playworks is a series of shows geared towards families and young children. Performances have included *Snow White*, an adaptation of *The Miracle Worker*, and *Peter Pan*. Ticket prices are only $7.00 and group rates are available. They also have a New Directors series, which features free productions directed by M.F.A graduate students. The number of these shows varies with the number of M.F.A. candidates each year. All DePaul University Theatre School productions are held in the Merle Reskin Theatre (formerly the Blackstone – for you theater aficionados), at the address shown above. The exception is the New Directors Series productions, which are held at smaller theatres in Chicago, most recently at the Athenaeum Stage Three, 2936 North Southport Avenue.

LOYOLA UNIVERSITY THEATRE DEPARTMENT

6525 North Sheridan Road, Chicago IL 60626. 773/508-3830. **World Wide Web address:** http://www.luc.edu/depts/theatre. **The Lowdown:** Each academic year, Loyola University's Theatre Department sponsors some eight performances, four large mainstage productions, and four smaller studio works. The mainstage shows are cast with Loyola students, with world-renowned directors and some of Chicago's top designers designing the productions. Productions include such famed plays and musicals as *The Crucible*, *A Little Night Music*, and *Romeo and Juliet*. Mainstage tickets can be purchased for about $10.00 per person, or $2.00 with a student ID. Tickets for Loyola's studio performances can be had for about $5.00 apiece. For added savings, you could consider purchasing a series ticket, where you can see all four mainstage productions for $30.00. Call the Theatre Department box office for a schedule of upcoming performances. But that's not all Loyola has to offer in the way of entertainment: The Playwright's Center, a professional theatre company dedicated to the development of new theater works and the fostering of emerging playwrights, is also housed in the Loyola University Theatre Department. A series of Monday night stage readings happens monthly, and is free to the public. In case you're wondering just how good these playwrights are, I'll let you in on a little secret: David Mamet got his start here. But wait, that's not all. Loyola's Music Department also sponsors student performances, and they're all free! The various music groups and styles include a gospel choir, a symphony orchestra, jazz bands, and more. You can give the Music Department a jingle at 773/508-8300 to find out the where and when. While you're here, don't forget to take a stroll through the D'Arcy Fine Arts Museum, which brings the work of professional artists to campus. If you don't find the canvas landscapes all that titillating, you can gaze at the real thing too: The school boasts an all-glass wall that overlooks Lake Michigan.

NORTHEASTERN ILLINOIS UNIVERSITY
5500 North St. Louis Avenue, Chicago IL 60625. 773/583-4050x3042. **World Wide Web address:** http://www.neiu. edu/~music. **The Lowdown:** The Music Department at Northeastern Illinois University offers a number of diverse musical performances throughout the year, at a variety of venues and prices. Admission is always a lot less than if you were going to a professional performance, but that doesn't mean that these students aren't professionals. Attending a college event helps you see the performers of tomorrow at their finest. The Music Department ensembles include such diverse musical stylings as a concert band, guitar ensemble, jazz band, opera workshop, string orchestra, and the University chorus. To hear about upcoming events, call or visit their Website.

NORTHERN ILLINOIS UNIVERSITY
School of Music, DeKalb IL 60115. 815/753-1551. **World Wide Web address:** http://www.vpa.niu.edu/music. **The Lowdown:** With close to 400 students in their music department, one thing you can count on at Northern Illinois University is diversity. Students stage performances throughout the year, many times with no admission fee. Even when an admission is charged, the fee is nominal at best. Percussion, trumpet, violin, and bassoon recitals are just a few of the events I stumbled across, and all were free of charge. They also house a number of ensembles with such diverse styles as a campus string orchestra, a marching band, a steel band, and an opera workshop. Kick back and watch as these stars of tomorrow fine tune their instruments while you look on. Call or visit their Website for a listing of upcoming events.

NORTHWESTERN UNIVERSITY
Pick-Staiger Concert Hall, 1977 South Campus Drive, Evanston IL 60208. 847/491-5441. **The Lowdown:** Music lovers of all ages will find a trek (just barely) into the suburbs to the Northwestern University's Pick-Staiger Concert Hall well worth the trip. Pick-Staiger Concert Hall is the scene of more than 160 concerts each year, with most ticket prices falling within the $2.50 and $20.00 range. These performances include everything from the University Symphony Orchestra to a Jazz Night featuring the Jazz Lab Band and the Jazz Ensemble. Northwestern University's School of Music also presents several concerts throughout the

year, featuring international guest artists; tickets for these performances are still reasonably priced at $13.00 - $20.00 apiece. Guests have included guitarist Pepe Romero, violinist Pinchas Zukerman, the Scottish Chamber Orchestra, the Zimbabwe Mbira Leaders Ensemble, drummer Max Roach, world-renowned cellist Yo-Yo Ma, and others. To hear a recording of the current week's offerings call 847/467-PICK. For the younger set, Pick-Staiger offers Kids' Fare, a series of Saturday morning programs giving children the chance to experience the arts first-hand. Whether singing and dancing to popular Cole Porter songs, or stepping in formation with the Northwestern Wildcat Marching Band, little ones won't have a chance to get fidgety at these shows. Admission is just $2.00 - $4.00. As if all that weren't enough, Northwestern's Theatre and Interpretation Center offers drama, dance, and stuff that defies simple description, at reasonable prices. Performances have included such troupes as the Ballet Gran Folklorico de Mexico. Tickets to these events generally range from $12.00 - $15.00. Then, there is the N.U.D.E. Showcase (No, it's not what you're thinking!): This stands for Northwestern University Dance Ensemble, and admission to their live, onstage acts is only $5.00. And finally, they have Performance Hours, an eclectic blend of drama and experimentation, which are free and open to the public.

SHERWOOD CONSERVATORY OF MUSIC
1312 South Michigan Avenue, Chicago IL 60605. 312/427-6267. **The Lowdown:** Since student musicians look for any opportunity to play in front of an audience, you can often see their first-quality performances without paying top-quality prices. At the Sherwood Conservatory, in fact, you can enjoy such performances for free. Sherwood presents both student and faculty performances. In addition, the conservatory has open houses every quarter; these events feature all kinds of ensembles performing live, and they're free and open to the public. Call to get on the mailing list.

UNIVERSITY OF CHICAGO DEPARTMENT OF MUSIC
1010 East 59th Street, Chicago IL 60637. 773/702-8484. **E-mail address:** music@uchicago.edu. **World Wide Web address:** http://music.uchicago.edu. **The Lowdown:** Each year, the University of Chicago Department of Music offers more than 90 delightful musical performances by its 11 diverse ensembles, all of them for little or no money. Ensembles range from an *a cappella* choir to a jazz ensemble, and from a wind ensemble to chamber music. The 100-piece University Symphony Orchestra is widely known for its imaginative productions of unusual works, as well as for performances of major symphonic repertoire. General admission is just $6.00, $4.00 for students, and $10.00 for reserved seating. Special events like the annual Gilbert and Sullivan production of Handel's *Messiah* are just a little bit more. Want a real bargain? Check out the free weekly chamber music concerts presented every Thursday during the school year at 12:15 p.m. in Fulton Recital Hall. You won't pay a dime! Complementing the Department of Music's student/community groups are two professional ensembles: the Department's award-

winning Artists-in-Residence, the Pacifica String Quartet, and the University's own Contemporary Chamber Players, a pillar of new music in Chicago. Both ensembles offer tickets for incredibly low prices: $5.00 - $15.00. For more information on upcoming events, call 773/702-8069 or visit their Website.

UNIVERSITY OF CHICAGO'S UNIVERSITY THEATER

5706 South University Avenue, Chicago IL 60637. 773/702-3414. **The Lowdown:** University of Chicago's University Theater provides top-notch dramatic performances at affordable prices. Admission to these fine productions is only $5.00 - $8.00. University Theater has two kinds of performances: Mainstage and Studio. Mainstage productions are the group's big shows; they run the gamut from Shakespeare to modern works, dramas to musicals. Presentations include the improvisational comedy revue Off-Off-Campus. Studio productions are smaller, simpler shows that focus on the acting challenges at hand. This is where you'll have the chance to see student-written work, experimental shows, and one-act plays. Call the box office directly for show schedules and advance ticket sales at 773/702-7300.

Comedy Clubs

COMEDY COMEDY
3000 Warrenville Road, Lisle IL 60532. 630/226-9700. **World Wide Web address:** http://www.comedycomedylive.com. **The Lowdown:** Formerly known as The Funny Bone, Comedy Comedy has changed its name and location, but not the high quality of its laughs. Since its founding in 1986, Comedy Comedy has presented some of the best names in stand-up comedy including Brett Butler, Richard Jeni, Bill Maher, Jeff Foxworthy, Drew Carey, and – everyone's favorite Partridge kid – Danny Bonaduce! What's especially great about their new location in Lisle is that it's in the Radisson Hotel. Being located within a hotel, Comedy Comedy can now offer you even better savings when you combine dinner in the hotel with your comedy dessert. They've even got some great accommodation deals where you can come for the Comedy Comedy show, and stay for the night, all at great savings. You'll have to call the hotel for further details, but believe me, they're well worth it. If you're looking to get out of the house for the night, an evening of laughs is the perfect recipe. Show times are Friday and Saturday, 8:00 p.m. and 10:30 p.m.

COMEDYSPORTZ
3209 North Halsted, Chicago IL 60614. 773/549-8080. **The Lowdown:** ComedySportz offers the very latest trend in improvisational comedy – the sports format. This is where two teams of comedians compete for points through improvised scenes and songs based on audience suggestions. If you have ever watched Drew Carey and friends on *Who's Line Is It Anyway?*, you get the idea. Violations may include anything from misusing imaginary doors to plain old bad acting. Who wins at the end of the night? It's different every time. Tickets are $15.00. But here's an extra tip for all you loyal devotees: This is one of the few comedy shows where tickets actually turn up at the Hot Tix booths. Stop by the day of the performance and you can get tickets for half-price, if available. Face-offs are Friday and Saturday at 8:00 p.m. and 10:30 p.m.

IMPROVOLYMPIC
3541 North Clark Street, Chicago IL 60657. 773/880-0199. **E-mail address:** improv@enteract.com. **World Wide Web address:** http://www.improvolymp.com. **The Lowdown:** Right across from Wrigley Field, ImprovOlympic is Chicago's home to long-form improvisational comedy and some of the best-known names in the business. Co-run by a former Second City director, it is unsurprising that ImprovOlympic has begotten the careers of several Second City and *Saturday Night Live* alumni (that seems to be the comedic career path around these parts) including Chris Farley, Mike Myers, and Tim Meadows. The Andys Dick and Richter are also one-time ImprovOlympians. Two floors offer two distinct styles of improvisational comedy: downstairs, The

Cabaret is home to The Harold performances, where long-form improv is an art-form. Tickets for Harold performances are $9.50 each, and performances take place Wednesday and Thursday at 8:00 p.m.; Friday and Saturday at 8:00 p.m. & 10:30 p.m.; and Sunday at 8:00 p.m. The show at 8:00 p.m. on Wednesday is a free performance. The Cabaret also hosts the ImprovOlympic's Cagematch, where the fate of two competing teams is decided by audience vote. Cagematch takes place Friday at 12:00 a.m. and tickets are free. If you're looking for a little interactive fun, join in the improv games (for free) at the 12:00 a.m. show on Saturday; audience participation is mandatory (though individual participation is optional). The Del Close Theater, which is located upstairs, hosts a number of theatrical performances based on improvisation. Call or visit their Website for a list of upcoming shows and ticket prices.

JAKO'S

4300 North Lincoln Avenue, Chicago IL 60625. 773/478-4110. **The Lowdown:** This neighborhood sports bar and restaurant serves up laughs for a suggested contribution of just $5.00. Munch on a burger and fries or pizza while watching some of the city's most practiced comedians – many of who are with The Second City or The Annoyance Theater – polish up their acts. It's a great, low-key place to catch a bite to eat and a few laughs. Call to find out when these laugh-riots take the stage. Open Sunday through Friday, 4:00 p.m. - 2:00 a.m.; Saturday, 4:00 p.m. - 3:00 a.m.

THE MONKEY BAR

1157 West Wrightwood Avenue (at Racine Avenue), Chicago IL 60614. 773/935-3760. **The Lowdown:** Every Wednesday night, between 9:00 p.m. and 12:00 a.m., The Monkey Bar hosts an open mike for comedians. While the term "comedian" should be used loosely in the case of some of these performers, it can still be funny just watching them struggle up there. But rest assured, there are plenty of comedy professionals (translation: comedians who get paying gigs in well-respected clubs) who come to The Monkey Bar to test out their new material on an unsuspecting audience. As The Monkey Bar is a neighborhood establishment, finding a place to sit and enjoy the show shouldn't be too hard. They also offer some great beer specials, a jukebox full of good music, a pool table, and darts to boot. The fact that there is no cover means you'll be laughing your way to the bank; and you can rest easy knowing you haven't fallen prey to exorbitant admissions or drink minimums. Open daily at 6:00 p.m.

THE PLAYGROUND IMPROV THEATRE

3341 North Lincoln Avenue, Chicago IL 60657. 773/871-3793. **World Wide Web address:** http://www.the-playground.com. **The Lowdown:** With 13 member ensembles, this nonprofit organization is completely dedicated to advancing comedic improvisation as an art form. Shows at The Playground are experimental; they allow their member players to fool around with the rules of improv and, in the process, create a truly unique experience. In addition to providing laughs, The

Playground players provide community outreach programs to get the community involved in their mission. What makes The Playground such a great place to see a show is that, with so many member ensembles, the repertoire is always-changing. While all the ensembles may be united in the fact that they know what is funny, they're also different insofar as their particular senses of humor go. With names such a Blind Snipers, Cinco de Bob, and Homey Loves Chachi, you can be sure you're in for a riotous good time. And with ticket prices in the $5.00 - $7.00 range, you can come back as often as you like. Call or visit their Website for a listing of upcoming shows.

THE SECOND CITY
1616 North Wells Street, Chicago IL 60614. 312/664-4032. **World Wide Web address:** http://www.secondcity.com. **The Lowdown:** In the early 1950s, a group of politically-aware students from the University of Chicago decided to start up a theater where they could call the shots and let their comedic minds wander. Since that time, The Second City (originally called The Compass Players) has become synonymous with comedic talent. Alumni of The Second City have gone on to make legendary names for themselves in movies, television, and just plain comedy. The list reads like an encyclopedia of who's who in the world of comedy: Alan Alda, John Candy, Jerry Stiller, George Wendt, Shelley Long, Paul Mazursky, and Catherine O'Hara are just a few of the people who got their start here. And as far as those members of The Second City who have gone on to perform on Saturday Night Live, well just who hasn't't? Dan Aykroyd, Bill Murray, Gilda Radner, Chris Farley, Mike Myers, and Tim Meadows are all alumni too! Now, I bet you're wondering how much such a stellar group of actors, directors, and writer might charge for a glimpse of their brilliance? Tickets are just $6.00 - $15.00 apiece. In addition to the main stage, there is also The Second City e.t.c., just a few steps away (see separate listing). The Second City, in conjunction with several area restaurants, will also help to lessen the planning of your evening by offering great discounts when you buy a dinner and show package. The meals range from casual to fine dining, and will cost you anywhere between $16.00 and $33.00 per person. Great food, great fun, and the chance to be one of the premier witnesses to some of today's most highly-regarded comic acting. What more could one ask for in an evening? For more information on upcoming shows or prices, give them a call or visit their Website.

THE SECOND CITY E.T.C.
1608 North Wells Street, Chicago IL 60614. 312/642-8189. **World Wide Web address:** http://www.secondcity.com. **The Lowdown:** If you want to know the history of The Second City, read the preceding listing; if you want to get high-quality laughs at a low-cost price, read on. The Second City e.t.c. is like the trial period before progressing to The Second City main stage. Performances at The Second City e.t.c. are intended to help the players work out the glitches (while entertaining the audience, of course) before moving to the main stage just a few doors away. Comedy revues here are just as hysterical as the

shows at The Second City, and you'll be able to take part in the shaping of a production. Ticket prices are generally $15.00 each. Call or visit their Website for a listing of upcoming events.

ZANIES COMEDY CLUB

1548 North Wells Street, Chicago IL 60610. 312/337-4027. **The Lowdown:** While Chicago, in general, is well-known for fostering some of today's top comedic talent (a good number of sitcom stars started here), Zanies has long been considered one of the city's top comedy clubs. Since their opening in the late 1970s, they have boosted the careers of several then-unknowns like Jerry Seinfeld and Jay Leno. So, while the prices here aren't the cheapest in town (they're not the most expensive either), I think it's only fair so say that this kind of comedic caliber justifies shelling out a couple of extra bucks. Tickets are generally $15.00 - $16.00 and there is a two-drink minimum. Shows take place Tuesday through Thursday at 8:30 p.m.; Friday at 8:30 p.m. and 10:30 p.m.; Saturday at 7:00 p.m., 9:00 p.m., and 11:15 p.m.; Sunday at 8:30 p.m.

Dance Theater

ACADEMY OF MOVEMENT AND MUSIC

605 Lake Street, Oak Park IL 60302. 708/848-2329. **The Lowdown:** Many of the Academy of Movement and Music's concerts will take you into the suburbs, but the money you'll save will make it worth the trip. Performed by Academy of Movement and Music's company-in-residence, MOMENTA, they focus on reconstructing historical American modern dance, particularly the work of choreographer Doris Humphrey. Tickets start at only $10.00 for adults, and about $8.00 for students and seniors. A city performance is likely to run you a few dollars more, around $12.00. For the best deals, try making it to one of the matinee performances; tickets start at just $5.00. Call for a listing of upcoming events.

THE ANATOMICAL THEATER

1148 North Milwaukee Avenue, Suite 3-D, Chicago IL 60622. 773/227-7358. **The Lowdown:** When one thinks of The Anatomical Theater, the term "cutting-edge" comes immediately to mind. Since its inception, The Anatomical Theater has awakened social awareness and an appreciation for choreography in its audiences. Through their interweaving of all types of media and incorporation of social themes, The Anatomical Theater is a lesson in current affairs as much as it is a pleasure for the eyes. In addition to their performances, they offer a number of workshops, lectures, and classes that will let you interact with the performers. Since they perform their unique brand of dance/theatre all around the world, Chicago-based performances can be sporadic. Call for more information on event dates and ticket prices. **Cheap Deal:** Mention that you read about The Anatomical Theater in *Mr. Cheap's Chicago* and you'll be entitled to a special discount.

CHICAGO MOVING COMPANY

3035 North Hoyne Avenue, Chicago IL 60618. 773/880-5402. **The Lowdown:** Founded in 1972, Chicago Moving Company has long been known for its premiere modern dance performances. While you should be able to catch them near your home town at some point (they tour *everywhere*), a Chicago performance is highly recommended. Performances are most often held at The Athenaeum Theatre (2936 North Southport Avenue) and The Harold Washington Library (400 South State Street). Ticket prices rarely reach much above $15.00. If you're feeling really inspired by the performances, the Chicago Moving Company also offers beginning and intermediate dance classes in its home studio, a beautiful turn-of-the-century park fieldhouse. Classes are just $10.00 each. Call for more information on classes or upcoming performances.

DANCE CENTER OF COLUMBIA COLLEGE

1306 South Michigan Avenue, Chicago IL 60605. 312/344-8300. **World Wide Web address:** http://www.colum.edu.

The Lowdown: As one of America's largest centers for contemporary dance, Dance Center of Columbia College has been known to host a number of extremely talented professional national and international dance troupes. Admission is generally $20.00 (though they do host a number of free events as well). Call or visit their Website for more information.

HUBBARD STREET DANCE
1147 West Jackson Boulevard, Chicago IL 60607. 312/850-9744. **World Wide Web address:** http://www.hubbardstreetdance. com. **The Lowdown:** It's no wonder that even the late Fred Astaire was impressed with Hubbard Street Dance troupe; they're truly a talented group. Hubbard Street Dance combines elements of jazz, modern ballet, and theatre dance to create a truly unique dance theater experience. And it's an experience that is being sought out all around the world. Based in Chicago, the members of Hubbard Street Dance spend much of their time traveling the world and showing off their dance steps. But it's when they're home in Chicago that these artists truly shine. Throughout the year, Hubbard Street Dance performs at venues all around the city. Tickets range from the cheap ($15.00) to the still affordable ($45.00). Whatever the cost, it's always a worthwhile ticket. Call or visit their Website to find out about of upcoming area performances.

THE JOFFREY BALLET
70 East Lake Street, Suite 1300, Chicago IL 60601. 312/739-0120. **E-mail address:** information@joffrey.com. **World Wide Web address:** http://www.joffrey.com. **The Lowdown:** There's probably not much I can say about The Joffrey Ballet that you don't already know. Since its founding in 1956, The Joffrey Ballet has carried on as one of the world's most recognizable names in dance theater. The Joffrey Ballet has found its way to just about every corner of the world; they have performed in each of the 50 United States and have reached audiences in too many countries to mention. Still, through it all, they have remained focused in their determination to make such artistry available to everyone. That said, the only thing I can tell you about The Joffrey Ballet that you may not have already known is that tickets can be quite affordable. You can catch a performance for as little as $20.00 - $30.00. And I'm not talking the high-altitude seats here; I'm saying that $30.00 can easily snatch you a seat in the orchestra pit. Since they *do* travel the world, it's a good idea to get on their mailing list so you can find out – well in advance – when they'll be back in the Windy City. Call or visit their Website to find out when and where The Joffrey Ballet will be next.

LINKS HALL
3435 North Sheffield Avenue, Second Floor, Chicago IL 60657. 773/281-0824. **E-mail address:** linkshall@mindspring.com. **The Lowdown:** What you'll get at Links Hall is world-class live art in an intimate neighborhood space. The presenting season, which usually starts in December with the Winter Solstice percussion concert by Michael Zerang and Hamid Drake, ends in August with the annual Chance Dance Festival. In the months

between, there are plenty of great dance and performance art presentations. Part of the National Performance Network, Links Hall has presented well-known visiting artists including Simone Forti and Patrick Scully. Tickets range from $5.00 - $10.00. Call for more information on upcoming events.

MUNTU DANCE THEATRE OF CHICAGO
6800 South Wentworth Avenue, #3E96, Chicago IL 60621. 773/602-1135. **E-mail address:** muntudance@aol.com. **World Wide Web address:** http://www.muntu.com. **The Lowdown:** More than a dance company, Muntu Dance Theatre takes aspects of ancient African and African-American dance, music, and culture and blends them into a theatrical, dance-based performance. Throughout the world, critics and audiences can't get enough of the rhythmic sounds and pulsating dance moves of Muntu. The company name, taken from the Bantu language, translates to "the essence of humanity"; that's exactly what Muntu's performances are all about, uniting the audience in culture, spirit, and "the essence of humanity." Most local performances take place at The Athenaeum Theatre (2936 North Southport Avenue) and Kennedy King College (6800 South Wentworth Avenue). Ticket prices vary, but generally range between $15.00 and $20.00. Call or visit their Website to find out about upcoming performances and ticket prices.

RIVER NORTH CHICAGO DANCE COMPANY
1016 North Dearborn Street, Chicago IL 60610. 312/944-2888. **E-mail address:** rivnodance@aol.com. **The Lowdown:** For more than a decade, River North Chicago Dance Company's performances have been characterized by show-stopping style and a well-earned reputation for highly theatrical and engaging contemporary dance. This professional national touring company has established itself as a vital and influential force in Chicago's cultural community, recognized by *Chicago Sun-Times* as a company with a "sheer passion for dance [that] can only be the product of years of hard work and a clear artistic vision." Always welcomed with open arms, River North Chicago Dance performances are quick to sell out, so it's a good idea to buy your tickets early. Ticket prices change with each venue, but admission is generally around $20.00.

Festivals

CHICAGO BLUES FESTIVAL

312/744-3370. **World Wide Web address:** http://www.ci.chi.il.us. **The Lowdown:** Chicago calls itself "The Blues Capital of the World." It's considered one of the true birthplaces of this uniquely American music. For three days each June, on just as many stages, you can find out why this is no empty claim. Festival-goers in past years have heard the likes of Junior Wells, Lonnie Brooks, Elvin Bishop, and Staple Sisters. Visit the City of Chicago Website for more information on when and where the next festival is taking place.

CHICAGO GOSPEL FESTIVAL

312/744-3370. **World Wide Web address:** http://www.ci.chi.il.us. **The Lowdown:** Somewhere in between the Jazz and Blues Festivals, the joyous sounds of gospel also fill the air every year for a two-day festival, usually held in July. A parade of national stars and local choruses take the stage in these free concerts. Performers have included Al Green, The Chicago Mass Choir, Otis Clay, and Andre Crouch. Visit the City of Chicago Website for information on this year's festival.

CHICAGO HUMANITIES FESTIVAL

312/661-1028x20. **E-mail address:** chf@chfestival.org. **World Wide Web address:** http://www.chfestival.org. **The Lowdown:** Each November, Chicago becomes a cultural mecca for two weekends. During these two weekends, writers, artists, musicians, scholars, and political figures flock to the city to celebrate the Chicago Humanities Festival. Each year, a common theme is chosen as a central issue for programs surrounding the weekends' events. One year, the festival's He/She theme delved into male and female similarities, differences, and relationships. Each of the festival's presentations, dramatic performances, film screenings, lectures, exhibitions, and readings is focused on this central idea. In the past, performers and presenters have included Peter O'Toole, Stevie Wonder, Arthur Miller, Sir Ranulph Fiennes, and Toni Morrison. The beauty of this particular festival (besides the obvious cultural offerings) is its dependability. The Chicago Humanities Festival is an annual event and, since its inception in 1990, tickets prices have not been raised from the original $3.00 admission. Throughout the year, the Festival sponsors a number of public programs that are often free. To find out about upcoming events, give them a call or visit their Website.

CHICAGO INTERNATIONAL FILM FESTIVAL

312/425-9400. **E-mail address:** filmfest@wwa.com. **World Wide Web address:** http://www.chicago.ddbn.com/filmfest. **The Lowdown:** Started in 1964, the Chicago International Film Festival is North America's oldest competitive film festival. For more than two weeks each October, the city of Chicago comes together to screen and honor some of the world's most impressive displays of filmmaking. Screenings include features, shorts, documentaries, and student films. Part of what makes this festival so prestigious is its International Feature Film Jury, which consists of 10 accomplished film professionals from around the world; Chicago International Film Festival is also the only U.S. festival chosen to host the FIPRESCI award, presented by the esteemed International Film Critics Association – an accomplishment in itself! What's more, at a majority of the screenings, the audience is invited to interact with the directors and/or actors as they introduce and follow up their films with a question-and-answer session. And believe me, we're not taking little-known nobodies here: The Chicago Film Festival is hailed as one of the world's most noteworthy and, therefore, draws an impressive crowd from the filmmaking community. Past directors and actors who have appeared include Geoffrey Rush, Spike Lee, Billy Bob Thornton, Morgan Freeman, Anouk Aimee, Jacqueline Bisset, Ethan Hawke, Janet McTeer, and Christopher Lee. Another part of the festival is the Lifetime Achievement Tribute, dedicated to honoring filmmakers and actors who have undeniably changed, altered, and affected the history of film: François Truffaut, Howard Hawks, Oliver Stone, Al Pacino, Jodie Foster, John Travolta, Lauren Bacall, and Michael Douglas are just a few of the recipients. But just what does it cost for a regular Joe or Jane like you – someone who is definitely not Martin Scorsese – to get into a host of events like these? Surprisingly, ticket prices are pretty much the same (if not cheaper) than a regular movie theater. Single ticket prices are just $9.00 for non-members and $7.50 for members. Screen a movie before 5:00 p.m. on a weekday or weekend and pay just $4.00 or $5.00, respectively. If you're looking for a more glamorous experience for your money, you can attend one of the festival's special presentations for $11.00 ($9.00 for members), partake in the opening night festivities for $15.00 ($12.50 for members), or be part of the awards ceremony (which includes the award presentations, cocktails, and dancing) for $25.00 ($20.00 non-members). A great way to save even more money (if you're planning on seeing a few of the featured films) is to buy one of the festival's ticket packages: A $90.00 Pass-Port will allow you admission to 16 screenings; while the $275.00 Tour-The-Fest Pass will let you in on the fun of 50 different screenings. For die-hard film buffs, don't forget that funding for events like these can often be difficult to get and, as it is such a vast undertaking, volunteers are always needed. If you'd like to volunteer, give them a call or e-mail the festival. I'll see you in October!

CHICAGO JAZZ FESTIVAL

312/744-3370. **World Wide Web address:** http://www.ci.chi. il.us. **The Lowdown:** Chicago has an international reputation for jazz; for over 15 years, this festival has been a testament to that fact. The fact that this festival is run by the Jazz Institute of Chicago lets you know that this celebration is definitely worthwhile. Four days of jazz headliners in mid-September make the approach of winter a little more bearable. Artists who've been heard here include Charlie Haden & The Liberation Music

Orchestra, Count Basie Orchestra, Dr. John, and Sir Roland Hanna. The Chicago Jazz Festival also aims to keep the kids entertained (and enlightened) with a children's stage, showcasing the various ethnic influences that have affected the music. Visit the City of Chicago Website to find out when this year's festival is taking place.

CHICAGO UNDERGROUND FILM FESTIVAL

3109 North Western Avenue, Chicago IL 60618. 773/866-8660. **E-mail address:** info@cuff.org. **World Wide Web address:** http://www.cuff.org. **The Lowdown:** Since its inauguration in 1994, the Chicago Underground Film Festival has grown into one of the world's largest subversive film fests. Programming the latest in underground features, shorts, and documentaries, Chicago Underground Film Festival has locally and internationally premiered some of the genre's best and most important works. CUFF provides a fantastic experience for lovers and makers of the avant-garde alike; a forum to view and talk about the work. Each year, the film festival also pays tribute to a stand-out in the world of underground film. Honorees have included such luminaries as "The Pope of Trash" John Waters and *Sweet Sweetback Baadasssss* Melvin Van Peebles. The festival takes place for one week in August, and screenings take place at The Village Theater (see separate listing). Individual tickets are $6.00 apiece and can be purchased in advance through Ticketmaster (though you will pay additional fees), or through The Village Theater box office on the day of the show. For those who would like to attend more than one event, there are three festival pass options. For $75.00 you can gain an all-access pass to all of the festival screenings, parties, and events; for $25.00 you can gain admission to any five screenings of your choice (making the cost just $5.00 per movie); and for $15.00 you can help to kick off the festival with a ticket to the opening night film and festivities. For those who love cinema but are tired of the mainstream boredom, Chicago Underground Film Festival is the perfect opportunity to see how truly daring and entertaining a diversion from commercialism can be.

GRANT PARK MUSIC FESTIVAL

312/742-GPMF. **World Wide Web address:** http://www. grantparkmusicfestival.com. **The Lowdown:** For 10 weeks each summer, you and yours can enjoy music under the stars in Chicago's Grant Park. Presented at The Petrillo Music Shell (at the corner of Columbus and Jackson Drives), Grant Park is a delightful setting for a variety of free concerts and performances. Green trees laced with delicate lights – the skyline looming above them – are your backdrop for classical music featuring the Grant Park Symphony Orchestra. The festival, the country's only remaining free series of its kind, also presents the Dance at Dusk series on Monday evenings at 7:00 p.m. The Dance at Dusk series features such troupes as Ballet Chicago and the Joseph Holmes Chicago Dance Theatre. In addition, there are performances of ethnic dance in Hispanic and African styles. The schedule begins in mid-June and continues through the end of August. There are plenty of folding chairs – set up like any auditorium – or you can bring a blanket, relax on the lawn, stretch out, and have a picnic. Shows take place on afternoons and evenings, weekdays and weekends; call for a current schedule. **NOTE:** In 2001, the Grant Park Music Festival plans to move to a new pavilion in the now under-construction Millennium Park. Call for more information.

THE MAGNIFICENT MILE LIGHTS FESTIVAL

North Michigan Avenue: From Oak Street to the Chicago River, Chicago IL. 312/642-3570. **World Wide Web address:** http://www.themagnificentmile.com. **The Lowdown:** It doesn't have to be summertime for you to enjoy a festival. The Magnificent Mile Lights Festival proves that, even amidst those notorious Chicago winters, there is lots of fun to be had in the city. Each year, as the holiday season approaches, businesses along the Magnificent Mile send out their season's greetings by lighting up the entire street. But the sparkling white lights are not the only treasures to behold; walk along the streets lined with holiday-decorated windows, or take in one of the Disney-produced shows. The festival lasts an entire weekend in late November (usually the weekend right before Thanksgiving). For more information, call or visit their Website.

PRINTERS ROW BOOK FAIR

312/987-9896. **E-mail address:** prbookfair@aol.com. **World Wide Web address:** http://www.printersrowbookfair.org. **The Lowdown:** If you love books, you shouldn't miss the Printers Row Book Fair. Each June, this historic neighborhood just south of the Loop hosts the country's third largest book fair. Festivities include writers and poets reading from their work, author signings, musical performances, lively panel discussions, and storytelling for children. Artists demonstrate the crafts of papermaking, hand marbling, calligraphy, and binding. And there are plenty of booksellers and publishers selling their new, used, and antiquarian goods. For nearly a decade, this fair has attracted some of the most celebrated names in publishing, including Sara Paretsky, Susan Sontag, Studs Terkel, and Kurt Vonnegut. All Book Fair events are free and open to the public. Call or visit their Website for more information.

SKOKIE FESTIVAL OF CULTURES

847/933-4355. **World Wide Web address:** http://www.skokieculturefest.org. **The Lowdown:** Just about 20 minutes outside of the city, the Skokie Festival of Cultures will bring you around the world in one weekend. Held annually in May, Skokie Festival of Cultures offers an abundance of entertainment options to all who attend. Learn about an entirely new culture, or teach your kids about their own. Assyrian, Chinese, Finnish, Hellenic, Pakistani, Thai, and Turkish are just a few of the cultures that are represented each year. Learn more about the Bahá'í faith, view some traditional Indian art, or test your knowledge of American state capitals. There's plenty to see, do, and eat... and I do suggest you do all three! A great merchandise bazaar will let you browse through the different cultural goods. But don't think all this fun is reserved for the grown-ups; Skokie Festival of

Cultures offers a number of children's activities that will enlighten as well as entertain. There's also enough storytelling and interactive fun to make them want to come back the next day. For more information on this year's dates, call or visit their Website.

TASTE OF CHICAGO
The Lowdown: For 10 days each summer, Grant Park becomes religious ground for gastronomes from all over. The annual Taste of Chicago offers visitors the chance to taste the variety of food that makes the Windy City the city of choice for many lovers of fine food. More than 70 restaurants from all over bring samples of their cooking for the days of food and frolic. Tickets to enjoy can be purchased singly or in books for use at all of the food vendors. The cost for a book of 10 tickets is just $6.00. Use them wisely, for this event is a true culinary safari. In addition to the food, Taste of Chicago offers three stages of entertainment and special events. Don't be surprised if you hear some top recording artists, or watch on as professionals perform the latest dance steps. The Chicago Country Music Festival even jumps in in the midst of the festivities to add some Western spice to all that food.

WINTERBREAK CHICAGO
312/744-3370. **Toll-free phone:** 800/2-CONNECT. **World Wide Web address:** http://www.enjoyillinois.com/winterbreak. **The Lowdown:** Chicago just might be one step ahead when it comes to taking care of their residents. To put an end to those wintertime blues, WinterBreak Chicago entertains residents and tourists alike from January 1 through March 31 each year. Each weekend offers a different cultural theme. One weekend might become a Chicago Blues Weekend, while another might offer a little "March Madness." Some cultural highlights in the past have included swing night, a Norman Rockwell exhibit, an Alvin Ailey American Dance Theater, and the Illinois PGA Golf Expo. Even the hotels join in the celebration; by offering discounted rates of course. For more information and to order your free brochure and value pass ("value" being the key word), call or visit their Website.

WORLD MUSIC FESTIVAL
312/742-1938. **The Lowdown:** Chicago's World Music Festival features more than 10 days of traditional and contemporary music from countries and cultures from all around the world. In the past, international groups from as many as 25 countries have taken to the stage. If an event is not free (most are), tickets are generally under $10.00 apiece.

Movies

BENSENVILLE THEATRE

9 South Center Street, Bensenville IL 60106. 630/860-7774. **The Lowdown:** This two-theater movie house shows second-run movies for just $1.50 at all times. If you missed a particular movie last time around, this is a great place to see it today (while saving more than a few bucks in the process). *$Cash Only$*

BREMEN THEATRE

6813 159th Street, Tinley Park IL 60477. 708/429-1010. **The Lowdown:** This second-run theater, at the Brementowne Mall, has six screens ready to serve up some cinema. Tickets are just $1.75 at all times. And if that weren't cheap enough for you, tickets are just $1.00 all day on Tuesday. Call for a listing of today's scheduled movies.

BREW & VIEW AT THE VIC THEATRE

3145 North Sheffield Avenue, Chicago IL 60657. 312/618-8439. **World Wide Web address:** http://www.brewview.com. **The Lowdown:** Brew & View is a whole new experience in the world of second-run cinema. Another old movie palace that's been given a modern twist, Brew & View combines the best aspects of renting videos at home with the experience of going out to the movies. Here, you see hit films that have just left the mainstream houses, on the big screen, but you sit at tables, eat pizza, and drink beer as you watch. And that's for a double feature, folks; anybody remember those? On Thursdays, beer and soda costs only $.50 (plus a $2.00 cup charge). On Thursdays, Fridays and Saturdays, they add a midnight movie to the regular 8:00 p.m. and 10:00 p.m. starts. Three movies, one price. Add it all up; did you ever think you could go out to dinner and a couple of movies for under $10.00? Such a deal! Brew & View changes its lineup almost every week. They also frequently interrupt the movie schedule for live rock concerts (not as cheap), so call or check the newspapers for information. General admission is $4.00. You must be at least 18 years old to enter and a valid I.D. is required. Doors open 30 minutes before each movie.

CHICAGO FILMMAKERS

5243 North Clark Street, Chicago IL 60640. 773/293-1447. **The Lowdown:** Chicago Filmmakers screens the kind of films, shorts, documentaries, and experimental works that may not even reach most art houses. The films seen here are among the newest and gutsiest being made in the city and from around the world. Many are short works gathered under one title to form some sort of theme. Themed screenings have been presented under such titles as *With No Apologies*, *Bodies in Crisis*, and *Cultivated Fear: Encountering Violence in the U.S.* Chicago Filmmakers also presents locally-made music videos. Screenings are usually held once or twice a week (unless there's a festival) and admission is just $6.00. For an even better bargain, regular moviegoers should think about becoming a member. For just $25.00, one of your membership perks will be $3.00 admission to all screenings. What's more, you'll get four free tickets to regular Chicago Filmmakers events. It's true... membership does have its privileges. Call for more information on becoming a member or for an upcoming calendar of events.

CLASSIC CINEMAS OGDEN 6

1227 East Ogden Avenue, Naperville IL 60563. 630/357-5050. **World Wide Web address:** http://www.classiccinemas.com. **The Lowdown:** Located in the Ogden Mall, this discount theater is a popular spot for bargain-loving cinephiles. Sure, the movies are in their second-run, but with amazingly low admission prices and free soda and popcorn refills, it almost pays to wait and see a movie here. Admission is $1.50 at all times.

DAVIS THEATRE

4614 North Lincoln Avenue, Chicago IL 60625. 773/784-0894. **The Lowdown:** Neither a strictly first-run theater nor a strictly second-run, the Davis Theatre is unique in that is combines the two and offers all day discounts. Every day, two of the Davis Theatre's four auditoriums will show new films (often an independent or an art house movie) at the cost of $4.00 before 6:00 p.m. and $6.00 thereafter. Senior citizens are $4.00 at all times. The Davis Theatre's other two auditoriums show second-run for just $1.50 for the first showing, and $2.50 thereafter. The Davis Theatre also offers some great double features at a discount. Call to find out what's playing.

ELK GROVE THEATRE

1050 Town Center, Elk Grove IL 60007. 847/228-6707. **World Wide Web address:** http://www.classiccinemas.com. **The Lowdown:** This second-run moviehouse has six theaters, all equipped with the latest in Dolby Surround Sound technology. Admission is just $1.75 at all times and, what's more, the theater has the one amenity that we all crave when we go to the movies: lots of legroom. The Elk Grove Theatre even has a number of loveseats installed in each of the auditoriums, affording for a comfortable as well as cheap cinematic experience. If the price of food and drinks at movies nowadays really gets you in an uproar, the Elk Grove Theatre has one more thing you should know about: free soda and popcorn refills!

FACETS CINÉMATHÈQUE

1517 West Fullerton Avenue, Chicago IL 60614. 773/281-4114. **World Wide Web address:** http://www.facets.org. **The Lowdown:** Facets Cinémathèque, operated by Facets Multi-Media, is the textbook definition of an art house. Facets screens an ever-changing lineup of foreign films, silents, and the kind of on-the-edge flicks that win awards at Cannes, but don't show up at your local megaplex. In fact, one of the cinema's two screens is solely dedicated to showing experimental films and documentaries that were intended just for video. Other offerings have included rediscovered silents like 1929's *Diary of a Lost Girl*; early works by Pedro Almodovar, the famed Spanish director who gave us the classic *Women on the Edge of a Nervous Breakdown*; and the annual Blacklight Film Festival, featuring works by local and national black filmmakers. Facets sometimes works in conjunction with other local and national film, historic, and ethnic organizations to bring thematic film series and director retrospectives. Marcello Mastroianni is just one film icon who has been honored. Facets Cinémathèque is also home to the Chicago International Children's Film Festival which, they will tell you, has been adorably deemed "Cannes for Kids." If you're a real (non-mainstream) film buff, consider becoming a Facets member. Membership fees start as low as $35.00, and will entitle you to discounted screenings and rentals. Yes, Facets does rent films as well (even if you're not a member). In fact, they have a rental catalog of well over 16,000 titles. These same lost classics and hard-to-find movies are also available for purchase through the Facets Website and their mail order catalog, which lists about 30,000 titles (again, you don't have to be a member to purchase films either). Call or visit their Website to get on their mailing list and/or receive a free catalog. *$Cash Only$*

THE FILM CENTER, SCHOOL OF THE ART INSTITUTE

Corner of State Street & Randolph Street, Chicago IL 60603. 312/443-3733. **World Wide Web address:** http://www.artic. edu/saic/art/flmcntr. **The Lowdown:** You are not likely to see that latest multimillion-dollar-special-effects-filled blockbuster at the Film Center, but you will get the opportunity to see films that cannot be seen and will not be shown anywhere else in Chicago. Hailed by critics as "the single best source of quality film in Chicago," The Film Center has continued to uphold this reputation since 1972. Each month, The Film Center features world, historic, and thematic cinema that may focus on the work of a particular director, or the contemporary work of a particular country. In addition to this, you'll also be able to see long-standing annual series such as the Festival of Films from Iran, Black Harvest Film and Video Festival, and the Hong Kong Film Festival. As part of its regular programming, The Film Center has also given locals the chance to meet such international stars as Kenneth Branaugh, Jackie Chan, Derek Jacobi, and Chow Yun-Fat. Two free 15-week lecture series each year only add to the unique nature of The Film Center and its educational components. The Film Center also houses vast archives of every director who has ever made a film, as well as a collection of over 10,000 stills. Admission to all films is just $7.00. For an even better deal, if you fork over $35.00 for a membership, you'll be entitled to an admission price of just $3.00. More expensive memberships ($50.00 - $75.00) yield additional free passes, free classes, and sneak previews of major motion pictures. For more information, visit their Website or call the 24-hour hotline at 312/443-3737.

HIGHLAND PARK THEATRE

445 Central Avenue, Highland Park IL 60035. 847/432-3300. **The Lowdown:** Fans of the independent and other hard-to-find

movies will particularly like this theater, as these films are usually well-represented. Four screens present a diverse mix of second-run movies, all at prices that can't be beat. Catch one of the theater's daily bargain matinees (before 6:00 p.m.) and pay just $3.50. All movies after 6:00 p.m. are just $5.00 per person. Even if this theater is a bit out of the way, these are some deals that are hard to pass up. *$Cash Only$*

LAKE THEATRE
1022 Lake Street, Oak Park IL 60301. 708/848-9088. **World Wide Web address:** http://www.classiccinemas.com. **The Lowdown:** Housed in an old Art Deco treasure of a building, the Lake Theatre offers seven theaters, completely equipped with Dolby Digital Surround Sound. Daily matinees (all shows before 6:00 p.m.) will afford you great savings at just $4.50 per ticket. Catch a show after 5:00 p.m., and the ticket jumps to a still reasonable $7.50. Senior citizens and children are welcome to a $4.50 admission price at all times. As is the case with all Classic Cinemas theaters, refills on soda and popcorn are always free. Lake Theatre also presents a number of special events, like a free monthly film discussion series. If you're one of those people who likes to discuss the film you've just seen with other moviegoers, this is your chance to do so. Call or visit their Website for a list of upcoming events.

LOEWS CINEPLEX PIPER'S ALLEY THEATER
1608 West North Wells Street, Chicago IL. 312/642-7500. **The Lowdown:** Okay, so here's the scenario: you've got a few hours to kill before catching a show at The Second City (see separate listing). You could walk around and check out some of the great restaurants and shopping mentioned elsewhere in this book, but why not relax those tired dogs and catch a flick? Loews Piper's Alley's four screens show the latest and best in independent cinema. On Mr. C's last visit, the latest films from Neil Jordan and Pedro Almodovar were playing. Get the picture? Though, as one wanders through the long hallway to their designated theater, you wonder if they've always shown independents. They've left many of their old movie posters up: while Tim Burton's *Edward Scissorhands* seems to fit the current Piper's Alley mold, I'm not so sure that *Back to the Future II* does. As for the theaters, they are clean and comfy. Free soda refills are just one of the ways in which you'll save money; drop in for a movie before 6:00 p.m. and tickets are just $5.50 apiece.

LOGAN CINEMA
2646 North Milwaukee Avenue, Chicago IL 60647. 773/252-0627. **The Lowdown:** All four screens of the Logan Cinema show second-run features at a bargain price of just $3.00 all the time. Tickets go on sale 15 minutes before the movie starts. You can't go wrong with that kind of savings. *$Cash Only$*

NAVY PIER IMAX THEATRE
700 East Grand Avenue, Chicago IL 60611. 312/595-0090. **The Lowdown:** Sure, you've been to the movies! But have you ever been to an IMAX movie? The Navy Pier IMAX Theatre houses

a six-story screen; that's an entire 60-feet high and 80-feet wide. It's undoubtedly the largest screen in Chicago. Yet, it's not only the size that's impressive: Navy Pier IMAX utilizes some of the world's most advanced 3-D technologies. The headsets employ a liquid crystal technology that makes the viewer feel one with the screen. IMAX sound is another feature where the word enormous comes to mind. The auditorium is replete with speakers big and small, and even houses one subwoofer that – alone – weighs more than 3,000 pounds. Screenings range from nature films like *The Living Sea*, to literary and visual journeys with *Mark Twain's America*, to rock and roll at its finest with *The Rolling Stones at The Max*. Tickets are $8.75 for adults, $7.00 for senior citizens, and $5.50 for children.

PARK FOREST THEATRE
340 Main Street, Park Forest IL 60466. 708/503-0707. **World Wide Web address:** http://www.classiccinemas.com. **The Lowdown:** This second-run moviehouse offers more than five movie choices for just $1.75 per person at all times. Plus, refills on soda and popcorn are always free. As part of the Classic Cinemas group of movie theaters, they also play host to a variety of special events, like a film and discussion series. For more information on these special events, call or visit their Website.

PORTAGE THEATRE
4050 North Milwaukee Avenue, Chicago IL 60641. 773/202-8000. **The Lowdown:** The Portage Theater is a second-run movie theater that offers true bargains. Admission is $1.75 all day Tuesday through Sunday; and just $1.00 all day Monday. *$Cash Only$*

THREE PENNY
2424 North Lincoln Avenue, Chicago IL 60614. 773/935-5744. **The Lowdown:** The Golden Age of Hollywood meets the indie-centric world of today at Three Penny cinema. Since its opening in the 1920s, Three Penny has witnessed the ever-changing styles, tastes, and stars of Hollywood. This first-run cinema has two theaters that feature mostly art-house and independent films. Admission is $7.00 for adults, and $4.50 for students and seniors. For a better bargain, they offer matinees on weekends for $4.50. And for those of you who go to the movies for the full experience, you'll appreciate the $1.00 popcorn and drink refills. Children under six are not allowed into the theater at any time. *$Cash Only$*

TIVOLI THEATRE
5021 Highland Avenue, Downers Grove IL 60515. 630/968-0219. **World Wide Web address:** http://www.classiccinemas.com. **The Lowdown:** Built in 1928, the Tivoli Theatre was one of the first theaters east of the Rocky Mountains to be designed for sound movies. Luckily for you, the devoted moviegoer, many other theaters have caught on to the trend. Still, there aren't too many theaters in the Chicago area that can boast such things as bargain admission at all times, free refills on all sizes of popcorn and soft drinks, and seating for more than 1,000 people. Such

enormous capacity makes Tivoli Theatre the venue of choice for several local performance groups like the Midwest Ballet Theatre. The theatre has undergone careful renovations so that it retains all its original historic charm. On the second Monday of each month, the Tivoli Theatre also welcomes the After Hours Film Society to sit and enjoy one of many classic or art house films. All films are in their second run. Admission is $1.75 at all times.

VILLAGE NORTH THEATER
6746 North Sheridan Road, Chicago IL 60626. 773/764-9100.
The Lowdown: Though night time prices can get a little steep for Mr. C's tastes, the Village North Theater does offer some great ways to save throughout the day – to those who qualify, of course. Catch any of the theater's bargain matinee flicks (movies showing before 6:00 p.m.) and pay just $4.75. Better still, children, college students, and senior citizens always pay only $4.75 per ticket. They couldn't have picked a better spot to offer student discounts – Loyola University is just a few steps away!

THE VILLAGE THEATER
1548 North Clark Street, Chicago IL 60610. 312/642-2403.
The Lowdown: The Village Theater maintains its claim as "Chicago's only bargain art theater." It is a first-run movie theater that offers special midnight shows on Friday and Saturday nights. For a real bargain, catch a movie anytime on a Tuesday when the Village Theater has a $4.00 ticket price. General admission is $6.50; senior citizens, students with valid IDs, and children under 12 are $4.00; bargain matinees before 6:00 p.m. are $4.00. Open daily.

YORK THEATRE
150 North York Road, Elmhurst IL 60126. 630/834-0675.
World Wide Web address: http://www.classiccinemas.com.
The Lowdown: A trip to the York Theatre is like a trip back in time to the Golden Age of cinema. Built in 1924, the York has long held a tradition of showing great movies to an appreciative audience. The theatre's original Spanish-style decor has been carefully restored, preserving the entire proscenium. Yet, it wasn't until this long-loved treasure was acquired by Classic Cinemas that it became known as one of the premier bargain cinemas. All five screens offer first-run films and Dolby Digital surround sound. The York also offers free refills on all sizes of soft drinks and popcorn. All shows before 6:00 p.m. are just $4.00 per person; after 6:00 p.m., tickets rise to a still very reasonable $6.50 for adults and $4.75 for seniors, students, and children. Call or visit their Website to find out what's playing. While you're there, don't forget to take a minute to drop by the American Movie Palace Museum (see separate listing); it's housed just upstairs.

Museums

ADLER PLANETARIUM & ASTRONOMY MUSEUM
1300 South Lake Shore Drive, Chicago IL 60605. 312/922-STAR. **World Wide Web address:** http://www.adlerplanetarium.org. **The Lowdown:** Adler Planetarium has long been considered the Midwest's leading museum for astronomy and space exploration. Journey through new exhibits in the refurbished 1930s planetarium and explore the Sky Pavilion, a 60,000 square foot addition to the original planetarium. Experience two new sky shows: "Millennium Mysteries" in the Sky Theater and "Blueprint for the Red Planet" in the StarRider Theater, one of the world's first interactive virtual environment theaters. Admission is $5.00 for adults, $4.00 for seniors and children (4-17), children three and under are free. StarRider and Sky Theater tickets are $5.00 per person for all ages. Open Monday through Thursday, 9:00 a.m. - 5:00 p.m.; Friday, 9:00 a.m. - 9:00 p.m.; Saturday and Sunday, 9:00 a.m. - 6:00 p.m.

AMERICAN MOVIE PALACE MUSEUM
152 North York Road, Second Floor, Elmhurst IL 60126-2806. 630/782-1800. **World Wide Web address:** http://www.historictheatres.org. **The Lowdown:** Founded in 1969, the Theatre Historical Society of America is the only group of its kind: a national organization whose main goal is to record and preserve the architectural, cultural, and social histories of more than 8,000 theatres nationwide. One of the main ways in which they educate the public is through the American Movie Palace Museum, located upstairs from the historic York Theatre (see separate listing). But just what do you showcase in such a museum? The American Movie Palace Museum features such interesting pieces as movie posters, programs, and photographs; the museum even houses a large scale model of Chicago's Avalon Theatre, complete with working fountains and flying doves. If you think a group tour would be the perfect thing to suit your upcoming event, call and see if arrangements can be made. Admission is free, though donations are always welcome. If you're doing research on the movie palaces of days gone by, the American Theatre Architecture Archive may be just the place to uncover your thesis. Fees may apply and you must schedule an appointment, so call ahead or visit their Website for more information. Both the museum and the archives are open Monday through Friday, 9:00 a.m. - 4:00 p.m. with occasional weekend and evening hours.

THE ART INSTITUTE OF CHICAGO
111 South Michigan Avenue, Chicago IL 60603. 312/443-3600. **World Wide Web address:** http://www.artic.edu. **The Lowdown:** The Art Institute of Chicago houses one of the world's finest collections of paintings, sculpture, photography, decorative arts, architecture, and more from all over the world.

Among the more than 225,000 art objects, the museum's permanent collection boasts such masterpieces as Georges Seurat's famous *A Sunday on La Grande Jatte* and Grant Wood's, *American Gothic*. The museum also holds lectures by renowned artists, art historians, and curators every Tuesday evening at 6:00 p.m. Free gallery tours are given every day at 2:00 p.m.; walks through selected galleries take place Tuesday and Friday at 12:15 p.m.; and free Voices readings are given every Thursday at 12:15 p.m. The museum also sponsors frequent demonstrations, workshops, storytelling, and other special activities. Call or visit their Website to learn about upcoming events. Admission is a suggested donation of $8.00 for adults; $5.00 for students, seniors, and children; and free to members and children under five. For an even better bargain, visit the museum on a Tuesday, when the admission fee is waived all day. Open Monday through Friday, 10:30 a.m. - 4:30 p.m. (until 8:00 p.m. on Tuesday); Saturday, 10:00 a.m. - 5:00 p.m.; Sunday, 10:00 a.m. - 5:00 p.m.

THE CHICAGO ATHENAEUM AT SCHAUMBURG
190 South Roselle Road, Schaumburg IL 60193. 847/895-3950. **World Wide Web address:** http://www.chi-athenaeum.org. **The Lowdown:** The only independent museum of art, architecture, and design in the country, the stated mission of this museum is to educate the public on the importance of Good Design. The Chicago Athenaeum sponsors a variety of programs including gallery walks, special performances and events, and competitions. One recent exhibit highlighted the contributions of women and African Americans to the field of architecture and design. Admission is $3.00 for adults, $2.00 for seniors and students.

CHICAGO HISTORICAL SOCIETY
Clark Street at North Avenue, Chicago IL 60614-6099. 312/642-4600. **World Wide Web address:** http://www.chicagohistory.org. **The Lowdown:** From the drama of the early frontier days to the tragedy of the Great Chicago Fire, and the rebuilding that followed, the story of Chicago is an exciting and unique one indeed. The Chicago Historical Society reconstructs the city's development by combining artifacts, photos, and paintings with hands-on displays. Suddenly, you realize history wasn't all that long ago, and it's still unfolding. This is another great place where you can have fun, learn a lot, and not empty your wallet in doing so. Admission is a suggested donation of $5.00 for adults, $3.00 for students and seniors, $1.00 for children under 12, and free to members and children under six. On Monday, the admission fee is waived for all. Open Sunday, 12:00 p.m. - 5:00 p.m.; Monday through Saturday, 9:30 a.m. - 4:30 p.m.

THE CUNEO MUSEUM AND GARDENS
1350 North Milwaukee Avenue, Vernon Hills IL 60061. 847/362-3042. **E-mail address:** cuneo@lake-online.com. **World Wide Web address:** http://www.lake-online.com/cuneo. **The Lowdown:** For those readers who don't know, John Cuneo

was a prominent businessman during the early part of the 20th century. He purchased this mansion in 1937 and it remained a private home until 1990. Tour the mansion to get a glimpse of life in the lap of luxury. The Venetian-influenced architecture and magnificent decor will take your breath away. Beyond this glorious structure, are 75 sprawling acres which comprise lakes, gardens, fountains, and a private 9-hole golf course. Mansion tours are $10.00 for adults, $9.00 for seniors, and $5.00 for children 12 and under as well as students. Tickets to view the grounds are $5.00 per car. Open Tuesday through Saturday, 10:00 a.m. - 5:00 p.m. Please call ahead or check the Website for specific tour schedules.

THE DAVID AND ALFRED SMART MUSEUM OF ART

University of Chicago, 5550 South Greenwood Avenue, Chicago IL 60637. 773/702-0200. **E-mail address:** smart-museum@uchicago.edu. **World Wide Web address:** http://smartmuseum.uchicago.edu. **The Lowdown:** Really, no price would seem too high for the chance to view over 7,000 works of art spanning over 5,000 years. But admission to the David and Alfred Smart Museum of Art is free, making its collection truly priceless. The museum, named for the founders of *Esquire* magazine, was designed by renowned architect Edward Larrabee Barnes. It contains precious works in a number of media, from ancient Greek vases, with a rare example by Euphronios, to furniture by Frank Lloyd Wright; not to mention sculptures by Degas, Matisse, Moore, and Rodin; photographs by Walker Evans; watercolors by Grosz, Heckel, and Nolde; and collections of ancient Chinese bronzes and modern Japanese ceramics. The museum presents special exhibits, like the German Print Portfolio 1890-1930: Serials for a Private Sphere and Art of the Persian Courts. Free lunchtime tours of the special exhibits are offered, as well as regular tours of the permanent collection. They also host free symposia, such as "Russia: The Land, the People" and "Sigmund Freud and Art." And there are children's programs like Valentine's Day Fun and Games, in which children are supplied with ribbons, papers, and markers to create their own artistic valentines. While the kids are busy being creative, adults are invited on a special tour of the collection. The theme? Love, of course. Call or stop in for a listing of upcoming events. Open Tuesday, Wednesday, and Friday, 10:00 a.m. - 4:00 p.m.; Thursday, 10:00 a.m. - 9:00 p.m.; Saturday and Sunday, 12:00 p.m. - 6:00 p.m.

DuSABLE MUSEUM

740 East 56th Place (between 57th & Cottage Grove Avenue in Washington Park), Chicago IL 60637-2495. 773/947-0600. **World Wide Web address:** http://www.dusablemuseum.org. **The Lowdown:** Named after Chicago's first non-Native American permanent citizen, a black Haitian named Jean Baptiste Pointe DuSable, this museum is dedicated to preserving the culture and heritage of the African American population. The museum houses a number of permanent and temporary exhibits that explore the experiences and contributions of African Americans to the history of our nation. The DuSable Museum also helps to enlighten and

increase awareness of the important role of African American culture through a number of entertaining and educational programs. The museum hosts a number of jazz and blues concerts, featuring fantastic up-and-comers and renown local artists. Tickets generally run $10.00 - $15.00. The museum also hosts an extraordinary cinema series, showcasing the works of the greatest black actors, directors, and writers. The DuSable Museum takes an especially keen interest in providing programs for kids. Storytelling and musical performances are just a few of the things that take place throughout the year, all free with admission. The Children's Penny Cinema is another great way to teach your children about history. For just a penny (yes, those bronze-colored circles you never know what to do with), kids can enjoy the museum's annual summer film festival. Works by such artistic trailblazers as Melvin Van Peebles and Ernest J. Gaines are always on the menu here; and kids will learn about issues like slavery, segregation, and the importance of preserving one's cultural and family heritage. Adults are welcome at the Saturday Afternoon at the Movies Series, with or without children. Museum admission is $3.00 for adults, $2.00 for students and seniors, $1.00 for children under 13, and free to children under 6. Sundays are free to everyone. Open Sunday and holidays, 12:00 p.m. - 5:00 p.m.; Monday through Saturday, 10:00 a.m. - 5:00 p.m.

THE FIELD MUSEUM

1400 South Lake Shore Drive, Chicago IL 60605. 312/922-9410. **World Wide Web address:** http://www.fmnh.org. **The Lowdown:** Looking for big fun? Drop by the Field Museum to visit Sue, the largest and most complete T. Rex skeleton ever found. With more than nine acres of exhibits and over 19 million artifacts and specimens from around the world, there is bound to be something for everyone. Whether you want to explore ancient Egypt, travel the Pacific, or experience life in a Pawnee earth lodge, you can do it here. Got a big school project? Get a jump on it at the Webber Resource Center, where you can browse through maps, books, artifacts, and videotapes. The Resource Center staff is available to answer any questions. Regular admission is $7.00; $4.00 for children under 11, students, and senior citizens; free to museum members, teachers, and military personnel with I.D. The Field Museum is free to all on Wednesday. Open daily, 9:00 a.m. - 5:00 p.m.

GLESSNER HOUSE MUSEUM

1800 South Prairie Avenue, Chicago IL 60616. 312/326-1480. **E-mail address:** info@glessnerhouse.org. **World Wide Web address:** http://glessnerhouse.org. **The Lowdown:** Yet another bit of architecture worth seeing. The Glessner House Museum (completed in 1877) is the work of Henry Hobson Richardson. Richardson has been credited as an influence to another famed architect, Frank Lloyd Wright. This is a national historic landmark that showcases decorative arts, specifically the English arts and crafts movement. If you are interested, you better book quickly. Tours are first come, first served, and are limited to seven people. Tours last approximately one hour and are offered

Wednesday through Sunday at 1:00 p.m., 2:00 p.m., and 3:00 p.m. Admission is $7.00 for adults, $6.00 for students and seniors, children ages five - 12 are $4.00. Wednesdays are free to everyone.

INTERNATIONAL MUSEUM OF SURGICAL SCIENCE

1524 North Lake Shore Drive, Chicago IL 60610. 312/642-6502. **E-mail address:** info@imss.org. **World Wide Web address:** http://www.imss.org. **The Lowdown:** Odd but informative, the IMSS was touted as the "Best Off Beat Museum" by *Chicago* magazine. Housed inside an old mansion, the museum showcases a collection that spans over 4,000 years of surgical history. More than 7,000 artifacts from around the world are on display, from surgical instruments to skulls. The suggested donation is $5.00 for adults and $3.00 for students and seniors. Open Tuesday through Saturday, 10:00 a.m. - 4:00 p.m.

JOHN G. SHEDD AQUARIUM

1200 South Lake Shore Drive, Chicago IL 60605. 312/939-2438. **World Wide Web address:** http://www.sheddnet.org. **The Lowdown:** The aquarium itself is home to some six thousand aquatic animals from every one of the seven seas. You can observe such exotic creatures as electric eels, sea anemones, and piranhas. The aquarium also houses the Caribbean Reef exhibit, a 90,000-gallon tank filled with sea turtles, sharks, moray eels, and more. If you're there at the right time, you may even get to see a diver hand-feed these animals while talking with visitors through a dive mask microphone. Regular admission to the Aquarium and the Oceanarium is $11.00 ($9.00 for children and seniors) and you should purchase these tickets in advance. Children under two are free at all times for all exhibits. While Mr. C doesn't like to look a gift seahorse in the mouth, it is important to point out that free admission on Mondays isn't exactly free. The Oceanarium, a re-creation of a Pacific Northwest coastline complete with beluga whales, white-sided dolphins, sea otters, and harbor seals doing their thing in a natural environment, is always an additional $6.00 ($5.00 for children under 12 and senior citizens). But the usual aquarium admission is waived (or is that waved?) on Mondays, so you can see the aquarium for free and have a whale of a time. The aquarium also runs a number of special programs throughout the year including scientific courses and hands-on workshops. Call the education department or visit their Website for more information.

LIZZADRO MUSEUM OF LAPIDARY ART

220 Cottage Hill Road, Elmhurst IL 60126. 630/833-1616. **The Lowdown:** People of all ages enjoy this unique museum dedicated exclusively to the beauty of stone carving and the mysteries of earth science. The museum features a large collection of Chinese jade and other hard stone carvings from around the world. Other displays include animal dioramas, mineral specimens, gemstones, and geological phenomena. The Lizzadro Museum holds educational programs on select Saturdays, and videos every Sunday at 3:00 p.m. Admission is

$3.00 for adults, $2.00 for senior citizens, and $1.00 for students. Free parking is available. And for a real bargain, visit the Lizzadro Museum on a Friday when admission is free. Open Tuesday through Saturday, 10:00 a.m. - 5:00 p.m.; Sunday, 1:00 p.m. - 5:00 p.m.

MUSEUM OF BROADCAST COMMUNICATIONS

Chicago Cultural Center, 78 East Washington Street, Chicago IL 60602-4801. 312/629-6000. **World Wide Web address:** http://www.mbcnet.org. **The Lowdown:** Lights! Camera! Action! Learn about the history of radio, television, and the famous personalities that made them work. Housed in the Chicago Cultural Center (see separate listing), this museum takes you behind the scenes of broadcasting from the time of its inception to the present day. An exhibit of Edgar Bergen's famous trio (Charlie McCarthy, Effie Klinker, and Mortimer Snerd) and showings of award-winning commercials only scratch the surface of the fun to be had. Exhibits on subjects like the Nixon/Kennedy debate illustrate the impact that television has on our lives and perceptions. Get a feel for the high-stress world of television news by sitting behind the anchor desk of your own newscast. Along with their permanent collections, the museum creates special exhibits that explore not only the entertainment aspect of television and radio, but the social impact as well. One exhibition, "My Little Margie to Murphy Brown: Images of Women in TV", included an exhibit and panel discussions exploring the dichotomous roles of women as contented housewives and workplace superheroines. Admission is free. For even more fun, head on up to the second floor archives room where, for a $2.00 per booth admission fee, you can view and listen to over 70,000 hours of radio and television programs, television commercials, and nightly newscasts from the past 12 years. Open Sunday, 12:00 p.m. - 5:00 p.m.; Monday through Saturday, 10:00 a.m. - 4:30 p.m.

MUSEUM OF CONTEMPORARY ART

220 East Chicago Avenue, Chicago IL 60611-2604. 312/280-2660. **World Wide Web address:** http://www.mcachicago.org. **The Lowdown:** Known for its challenging and controversial exhibitions including photography by Robert Mapplethorpe, the MCA prides itself on showing a provocative mix of contemporary art. The MCA exhibits an equal mix of works by established artists and experimental up-and-comers. Exhibitions have included photographs by Emmet Gowin, paintings by Libby Wadsworth, and early handpainted pop art by Roy Lichtenstein and Andy Warhol. In addition to art exhibits, MCA presents a series of lectures and other educational programs as well as First Fridays. At each First Fridays, visitors can unwind after work and enjoy an eclectic and intriguing mix of cultural happenings, ranging from live music and performance art to experimental films and hands-on art stations. First Fridays are held on the first Friday of each month. Tickets, which include museum admission and live entertainment, are $12.00 ($6.00 for MCA members) and are available at the event. Hors d'oeuvres and a cash bar are available. Guests must be 21 years or older. Admission prices are

$7.00 for adults, $4.50 for students and seniors, and free for children 12 and under. Admission is free to everyone all day on Tuesdays. Open Tuesday, 10:00 a.m. - 8:00 p.m.; Wednesday through Sunday, 10:00 a.m. - 5:00 p.m. Closed Mondays.

THE MUSEUM OF CONTEMPORARY PHOTOGRAPHY
Columbia College Chicago, 600 South Michigan Avenue, Chicago IL 60605. 312/663-5554. **The Lowdown:** Shutterbugs and admirers alike would be crazy not to snap a peek at the treasures hidden in The Museum of Contemporary Photography. Various exhibitions of contemporary photographs and photographically related images in a variety of styles have gained this museum an international reputation. Artists often lecture on their work, and group tours can be arranged by appointment. Admission is free. Open Monday through Friday, 10:00 a.m. - 5:00 p.m. (Thursday until 8:00 p.m.); Saturday, 12:00 p.m. - 5:00 p.m.; closed Sunday.

MUSEUM OF HOLOGRAPHY
1134 West Washington Boulevard, Chicago IL 60607. 312/226-1007. **E-mail address:** hologram@flash.net. **World Wide Web address:** http://www.museumofholography.com. **The Lowdown:** When you think of holography, you just might think of the cool double image effect you can see on stickers. But the technology that goes in to making that effect, and ultimately that dumbfounded reaction on people, is impressive. The Museum of Holography (the only one of its kind in the U.S.) gives an overview of the use of lasers in holography and how it is used in science, business, and specifically art. The museum is home to an impressive collection of 200 holograms. Founded in 1976, the museum houses not only an exhibit area, but a School of Holography that has taught several thousand students. Its research center has been in the forefront of experimentation and development in computer generated holography, natural color holography, and photoresist holography. Admission is $3.00 for adults; $2.50 for students. Open Wednesday through Sunday, 12:30 p.m. - 5:00 p.m.

MUSEUM OF SCIENCE AND INDUSTRY
57th Street at South Lake Shore Drive, Chicago IL 60637. 773/684-1414. **E-mail address:** msi@msichicago.org. **World Wide Web address:** http://www.msichicago.org. **The Lowdown:** This massive building opened as part of the great Columbian Exposition of 1893, and it's the only remaining structure from that historic event. Offering literally hundred of exhibits on science and technology and their industrial applications, the museum is big on visitor participation. Find out what lip balm, running shoes, and plastic cups have in common in Petroleum Planet. Transform yourself into a hydrocarbon molecule and follow petroleum on its journey from crude oil to products we use everyday. Experience a miniature fairyland in Colleen Moore's Fairy Castle, which contains over 1,000 tiny treasures. One of the MSI's biggest attractions is the Omnimax Theater, part of the adjoining Henry Crown Space Center. The Omnimax is a five-story, domed, wraparound, 350-seat theater

which boasts one of the largest sound systems in the world. It takes you to distant lands, under the sea, and to the outer reaches of the universe. The Henry Crown Space Center, of course, is where you can see the actual Apollo 8 spacecraft and find out what it's like to be on the Space Shuttle or even on another planet! Admission to the museum is $7.00 for adults, $6.00 for senior citizens, $3.50 for children three to 11; and free to children under three. Admission is free to everyone on Thursdays. The Omnimax has a separate admission fee: Omni tickets are $8.00 for adults, $7.00 for seniors, $6.00 for children three to 11; and free to kids under three when seated on an adult's lap. Open Monday through Friday, 9:30 a.m. - 4:00 p.m.; Saturday and Sunday, 9:30 a.m. - 5:30 p.m. During the summer, most holidays, and spring break, the museum is open 9:30 a.m. - 5:30 p.m. daily.

NATIONAL VIETNAM VETERANS ART MUSEUM

1801 South Indiana Avenue, Chicago IL 60616. 312/326-0270. **E-mail address:** nvvamart@cs.com. **World Wide Web address:** http://www.nvvam.org. **The Lowdown:** Featuring more than 700 works by the soldiers who were there, the National Vietnam Veterans Art Museum offers a unique perspective of the Vietnam War. If you weren't involved in Vietnam (or weren't yet born), this museum will give you the unique opportunity to get inside the heads of the people who were actually there. You'll find art in all forms, including paintings, drawings, sculpture, poetry, and photography. What is so amazing about this collection of art is that it unites 115 artists (some former enemy soldiers) from North and South Vietnam, Cambodia, Thailand, Australia, and America. Don't expect to find a biased twist to this museum nor a happy ending. A crash course in history and reality is what you'll find, and what history buffs and artists alike will appreciate. Admission is $5.00 for adults, $4.00 for students and seniors. Open Sunday, 12:00 p.m. – 5:00 p.m.; Tuesday through Friday, 11:00 a.m. – 6:00 p.m.; Saturday, 10:00 a.m. – 5:00 p.m.; closed Monday.

THE NEWBERRY LIBRARY

60 West Walton Street, Chicago IL 60610. 773/943-9090. **World Wide Web address:** http://www.newberry.org. **The Lowdown:** Bibliophiles who like to browse through used book shops in search of some rare treasures will love The Newberry Library, an independent research library. It is chock full of rare collections, including 1.5 million printed titles; 5 million manuscript pages and 300,000 historic maps dating back to the Middle Ages. Most people flock to this library for its genealogical resources or its art exhibits. In many ways, it is more like a museum than library. Among the extensive Western European history, literature, and research collection, you'll find some of Thomas Jefferson's letters, as well as George Washington's journal publication of an Ohio territory expedition. Throughout the year, the library presents lectures, musical concerts, dramatic performances, and symposia. The Newberry Library does differ from most museums in one aspect, though: free admission. They also offer free tours on Thursdays at 3:00 p.m. and Saturdays at 10:30 a.m. Open

Tuesday through Thursday, 10:00 a.m. - 6:00 p.m.; Friday and Saturday, 9:00 a.m. - 5:00 p.m. The exhibit gallery is open Monday, Friday, and Saturday, 8:15 a.m. - 5:30 p.m.; Tuesday through Thursday, 8:15 a.m. – 7:30 p.m.; closed Sunday.

PEGGY NOTEBAERT NATURE MUSEUM
2430 North Cannon Drive, Chicago IL 60614. 773/755-5100. **World Wide Web address:** http://www.chias.org. **The Lowdown:** The Peggy Notebaert Nature Museum is an exciting, hands-on place to explore the worlds of science and nature. The museum's exhibits are designed to provoke questions and elicit surprise, triggering conversations that transform observers into active participants. Permanent exhibitions include the Judy Istock Butterfly Haven, where visitors can stroll through a 2,700 square-foot glass atrium that's alive with butterfly species native to Illinois and North America. Another exciting exhibit is Ameritech Environmental Central, where groups of participants use the latest data provided by the Environmental Central Website and group discussions facilitated by the staff to sort out a solution to some of today's large-scale environmental problems. For the little ones, there's the Children's Gallery, where kids ages three to eight can learn about the geological environments they inhabit. Admission is $6.00 for adults, $4.00 for students and seniors, and $3.00 for children. Open daily, 10:00 a.m. - 5:00 p.m. in the winter (until 8:00 p.m. on Wednesday); 10:00 a.m. - 6:00 p.m. in the summer (until 8:00 p.m. on Wednesday).

ORIENTAL INSTITUTE MUSEUM
1155 East 58th Street, Chicago IL 60637. 773/702-9521. **The Lowdown:** On the campus of the University of Chicago, this museum has one of the world's foremost collections of artifacts from the ancient lands of Nubia, Persia, Egypt, Mesopotamia, Assyria, and other places in what we now call the Middle East. Measure yourself next to a seventeen-foot-tall red quartzite statue of King Tut, from Thebes in the year 1330 B.C. See how modern-day language experts decipher ancient hieroglyphic writing, step by step. Gaze upon gigantic ceremonial objects and delicate handcrafted jewelry. The museum also offers a number of special programs to shed more light on these artifacts. On Sunday at 2:00 p.m., short films are shown on specific subjects, again followed by a gallery tour. Free admission. Open Tuesday through Saturday, 10:00 a.m. - 4:00 p.m. (Wednesday evening until 8:30 p.m.); Sunday, 12:00 p.m. - 4:00 p.m.

PEACE MUSEUM
314 West Institute Place, Chicago IL 60607. 312/440-1860. **World Wide Web address:** http://www.peacemuseum.org. **The Lowdown:** The Peace Museum preserves the art and artifacts of peace movements and other political struggles, much of which is done by local grassroots organizations. The museum presents four exhibitions per year that illustrate the history and culture of peacemakers worldwide. Visitors can browse the museum's library and shop in the museum store after viewing the exhibitions. Admission is $3.50 for adults; $2.00 for seniors,

students with a valid ID, and children; free to museum members. Open Tuesday through Saturday, 11:00 a.m. - 5:00 p.m.

THE POLISH MUSEUM OF AMERICA
984 North Milwaukee Avenue, Chicago IL 60622. 773/384-3352. **E-mail address:** pma@prcua.org. **World Wide Web address:** http://www.prcua.org/pma. **The Lowdown:** Chicago's Polish Museum of America is among the oldest and largest ethnic museums in the United States. Its location, south of what is now called Polish Village, is in the heart of the first Polish neighborhood in Chicago. The museum mostly exhibits works by Polish and Polish-American artists; paintings, sculpture, drawings, lithographs, and more. Military leaders Pulaski and Kosciuszko, scientists Copernicus and Sklodowska-Curie, and musicians Paderewski and Chopin all have their place in the Polish Museum. The museum library contains 60,000 volumes, 250 periodicals, and a number of records, discs, and videocassettes. Open daily, 11:00 a.m. - 4:00 p.m. (though it's always a good idea to call ahead and verify hours first). Admission is a suggested donation of $2.00 for adults, $1.00 for students and seniors, free to members.

THE SMITH MUSEUM OF STAINED GLASS WINDOWS
Navy Pier, 400 East Grand Avenue, Chicago IL 60611. 312/595-5024. **World Wide Web address:** http://www.navypier.com. **The Lowdown:** As one of the newest visitor attractions to hit Navy Pier, The Smith Museum is unique in that it is actually the first museum of its kind in the United States. If you don't know a thing about the significance and style of stained glass windows, bring a notebook and prepare to learn! The museum is actually arranged by artistic theme: Victorian, Prairie, Modern, and Contemporary. What's best about the museum is that while you'll be receiving a lesson in stained glass, you'll also learn more about the Windy City itself. The great majority of windows on display were installed somewhere in the Chicago area and can be useful in tracking the city's urban revolution. You'll see windows by Louis Comfort Tiffany and John LaFarge as well as windows created in the likeness of Dr. Martin Luther King, Jr. and Michael Jordan. Admission to the museum is free. Call ahead for hours.

SPERTUS INSTITUTE OF JEWISH STUDIES
618 South Michigan Avenue, Chicago IL 60605. 312/322-1747. **E-mail address:** sijs@spertus.edu. **World Wide Web address:** http://www.spertus.edu. **The Lowdown:** The Spertus Institute covers 3,500 years of Jewish history with over 3,000 works in its main galleries. In addition, it houses the Zell Holocaust Memorial and sponsors special exhibits on Judaic themes. Some exhibits have included The Nazi Olympics, Berlin 1936 and The Spertus Prize (for Jewish ceremonial designs). The Spertus also offers many activities for children. The Rosenbaum Artifact Center at Spertus Museum has a hands-on exhibit designed to allow children to explore the ancient Near East using the same techniques as real archaeologists. Admission is $5.00; $3.00 for children, students, and senior citizens; free on Friday; maximum family admission is $10.00. Open Sunday through Wednesday,

10:00 a.m. - 5:00 p.m.; Thursday, 10:00 a.m. - 8:00 p.m.; Friday, 10:00 a.m. - 3:00 p.m.; closed Saturday.

SWEDISH AMERICAN MUSEUM
5211 North Clark Street, Chicago IL 60640. 773/728-8111. **World Wide Web address:** http://www.samac.org. **The Lowdown:** For a real bargain, you can see a variety of Scandanavian art from paintings to sculpture to lithographs for just $4.00. And kids get in for just $2.00. At the Swedish American Museum, you can experience the immigration to Chicago through a brand new permanent exhibit. The museum also sponsors a number of related cultural events including theater, jazz, folk music, and dancing. Call for information on their current schedule. Open Tuesday through Friday, 10:00 a.m. - 4:00 p.m.; Saturday and Sunday, 10:00 a.m. - 3:00 p.m.

TERRA MUSEUM OF AMERICAN ART
664 North Michigan Avenue, Chicago IL 60611. 312/664-3939. **World Wide Web address:** http://www.terramuseum.com. **The Lowdown:** The Terra Museum of American Art houses a permanent collection of notable works by Winslow Homer, Mary Cassatt, John Singer Sargent, Arthur Dove, James Abbott McNeill Whistler, and many others. The museum hosts a variety of exhibitions that explore issues in American art. Admission is $7.00 for adults; $3.50 for seniors; free to students with valid IDs, children under 12, members, educators, U.S. veterans; free on Tuesday and the first Sunday of each month. Open Tuesday, 10:00 a.m. - 8:00 p.m.; Wednesday through Saturday, 10:00 a.m. - 6:00 p.m.; Sunday, 12:00 p.m. - 5:00 p.m.

TRAILSIDE MUSEUM
738 Thatcher Avenue, River Forest IL 60305. 708/366-6530. **The Lowdown:** This fantastic wooded area offers some of the city's most beautiful hiking trails, as well as the chance to kick back and bask in the beauty of nature. Throughout the year, Trailside Museum offers a number of educational programs that teach about the environment and what we can do to preserve it. Trailside Museum is also home to Cook County's Wildlife Rehabilitation Center; much of their time is dedicated to helping sick and abandoned animals. Admission is free. Open Friday through Wednesday, 10:00 a.m. - 4:00 p.m.; closed Thursday.

UKRAINIAN INSTITUTE OF MODERN ART
2320 West Chicago Avenue, Chicago IL 60622. 773/227-5522. **E-mail address:** uima@netzero.com. **World Wide Web address:** http://www.brama.com/uima. **The Lowdown:** Another of Chicago's many small but proud ethnic museums, the Ukrainian Institute of Modern Art existed here even before there was such a museum in Ukraine. The permanent collection is a cultural gem, containing over 100 pieces by artists who share a Ukrainian heritage, from paintings and crafts to wood sculpture. The main exhibit hall has some six curated shows a year, while concerts, lectures, and other programs round out the institute's offerings. Open Wednesday, Thursday, Saturday, and Sunday, 12:00 p.m. - 4:00 p.m.

Music: Classical

CHICAGO A CAPPELLA

2936 North Southport Avenue, Suite 210, Chicago IL 60657. 773/755-1628. **Toll-free phone:** 800/SING-WOW. **E-mail address:** singwow@aol.com. **The Lowdown:** This group of musicians brings the not-so-traditional art of *a cappella* singing to the stage. Chicago *a cappella* is one of fewer than 50 fully-professional vocal ensembles in the United States. Their repertoire spans the Renaissance music of the 15th and 16th centuries, as well as modern music of the last few decades. Consisting of nine solo voices, Chicago *a cappella* has received praise for their recordings, live broadcasts, and energetic performances. The beauty of this group is that, while other classical music ensembles cash in on their stereotypical affluent audience, Chicago *a capella* keeps admission prices to a minimum. Tickets are $20.00 for adults, $15.00 for seniors, and $10.00 for students. The concerts are held in the Three Arts Club of Chicago (see separate listing), First Congregational Church in Evanston, and Unity Temple in Oak Park.

CHICAGO STRING ENSEMBLE

91 Brandon Road, Northfield IL. 312/332-0567. **World Wide Web address:** http://homepage.interaccess.com/NCSE. **The Lowdown:** The Chicago String Ensemble is a 22-member group that has been together for almost 20 seasons, enjoying great critical acclaim during that time. The ensemble's repertoire includes selections from 18th, 19th, and 20th century composers. Concerts frequently add guest soloists of one sort or another, including singers. One of the half-dozen concerts they do each season is a showcase of work by Chicago-based composers. The most expensive tickets to these performances are $25.00; Mr. C doesn't find this to be overpriced, especially since the CSE is the only professional string orchestra in the Midwest. What's even better is that you can get lesser-priced tickets for just $20.00 (seniors pay $18.00 and students get the best deal of all, tickets for $13.00). Performances take place several times per season at Newberry Library, 60 West Walton Street, Chicago. Call them for information about their schedule and about money-saving subscriptions.

CHICAGO SYMPHONY ORCHESTRA

220 South Michigan Avenue, Chicago IL 60604. 312/294-3000. **Toll-free phone:** 800/223-7114. **World Wide Web address:** http://www.chicagosymphony.org. **The Lowdown:** If you think you'd have to mortgage your home to pay for an evening at Orchestra Hall, think again. While the best box seats in the house can go up to $175.00 per ticket (yikes!), there are alternatives. First, it is worth noting that not every seat in the hall is so outrageously priced. While many tickets are $60.00 and higher,

there are several sections in the $20.00 - $40.00 range and even some for under $15.00, depending on the concert. Option number two: students and senior citizens can take advantage of rush tickets. These tickets are available after 5:00 p.m. on the day of a performance (after 12:00 p.m. on matinee days) and are priced at just $12.50. Remember, you must have valid identification to obtain discounted tickets. It's best to call Symphony Center before trekking down there: they'll let you know whether or not discount tickets are available. Also, the Chicago Symphony Orchestra has a number of special programs with ticket prices that won't break your budget. Sundays at Orchestra Hall in the Ballroom are early evening performances priced at only $17.00 per ticket. Often, the audience is invited to enjoy light refreshments and conversation with the musicians after the performance. For a pleasurable mixture of music and art, try Sundays at The Art Institute in Fullerton Hall. This series consists of five concerts, each of which includes members of the Chicago Symphony Orchestra, exploring connections between music and the fine arts. The $19.00 ticket price includes admission to the Art Institute of Chicago, a slide presentation and lecture, full-length concert in the museum, and a self-guided tour of selected galleries. Back at Orchestra Hall, the Chicago Symphony Orchestra also presents the Kraft Family Matinee Series which provides a great opportunity to introduce children to the joys of classical music. Ticket prices range from $9.00 - $21.00; box seats can be had for $40.00 apiece. These concerts take place on Saturdays at 11:00 a.m. and 12:30 p.m. But wait, we're not finished yet! If all that isn't enough, how about free open rehearsals and performances by the Civic Orchestra of Chicago, the training orchestra of the Chicago Symphony? There are generally six programs per season, and they include a pre-concert lecture. One phone call can get you a free schedule of all Symphony Center events with times and ticket prices. And you thought you had to be rich to enjoy the symphony?

CHICAGO YOUTH SYMPHONY ORCHESTRA

410 South Michigan Avenue, Chicago IL 60605. 312/939-2207. **E-mail address:** cyso@cyso.org. **World Wide Web address:** http://www.cyso.org. **The Lowdown:** Don't be fooled by this group of young musicians; they're not your average high school band. The Chicago Youth Symphony Orchestra consists of three orchestras, a chamber music program, and a summer residency at Grant Park Music Festival. These talented students have won state awards, as well as national and international recognition for musicianship and a repertoire of orchestral music that rivals that of any professional symphony. If you choose to attend one of their performances at Symphony Center's Orchestra Hall, admission can run between $8.00 for the cheapest seats and $32.00 for dress circle seating. They even offer a free music series – the Orpheus Young Artists series – one Tuesday each month at 12:15 p.m. at the Harold Washington Library.

CIVIC ORCHESTRA OF CHICAGO

220 South Michigan Avenue, Chicago IL 60604. 312/294-3420. **World Wide Web address:** http://www.chicagosymphony.org.

The Lowdown: As the training orchestra for the Chicago Symphony Orchestra, The Civic Orchestra of Chicago recruits from among the world's best young orchestral players. Throughout the year, they present full orchestra, chamber orchestra, and chamber ensemble concerts at Symphony Center and other local venues at no charge to the public. The *Chicago Tribune* calls the orchestra "prodigiously gifted" and they even made their way to Carnegie Hall in March of 2000. Here's your chance to see, hear, and enjoy some of the world's future maestros. For tickets and information on upcoming events, drop by the Symphony Center box office, visit their Website, or call PhoneCharge at 312/294-3000.

CUBE CONTEMPORARY MUSIC ENSEMBLE
600 South Dearborn Street, Suite 2016, Chicago IL 60605. 312/554-1133. **E-mail address:** cube@cubeensemble.com. **World Wide Web address:** http://www.cubeensemble.com. **The Lowdown:** CUBE Contemporary Music Ensemble combines world music with performance and visual arts to create one of the city's most unique chamber music experiences. Since 1992, CUBE has presented audiences with a variety of imaginative performances that combine the beautiful sounds of the woodwind, piano, and percussion instruments with visually-stimulating dance, performance art, and sculptures. The result is a series of highly-anticipated concerts that are given at venues throughout the city. The best way to enjoy CUBE is to attend all four of their yearly performances. Buying a subscription will entitle you to a savings of 15 percent, with tickets to the entire lineup costing just $60.00 per person (that's $15.00 per show). Students and senior citizens get even better deals with a four-show subscription costing just $32.00 per person. If purchasing tickets individually, prices range from $10.00 - $18.00. CUBE makes a night of chamber music a pleasure for the auditory and visual senses alike.

GEJA'S CAFE
340 West Armitage Avenue, Chicago IL 60614. 773/281-9101. **World Wide Web address:** http://www.gejascafe.com. **The Lowdown:** Okay, so it's not opening night at Orchestra Hall, but this restaurant is a great place to go for live classical and flamenco guitar, presented every night of the week. The specialty of the house is fondue (cheese, meat, seafood, or chocolate) as a snack, meal, or dessert. Two people can share to keep the tab reasonable. Geja also has a good wine list. Plus, there's never a cover charge or a drink minimum, so feel free to stroll on in, enjoy the music, and tap your feet all night long.

LYRIC OPERA OF CHICAGO
20 North Wacker Drive, Chicago IL 60606. 312/332-2244. **World Wide Web address:** http://www.lyricopera.com. **The Lowdown:** As one of the most respected opera companies in the world, Lyric Opera of Chicago has hosted some of the world's most famous singers, directors, conductors, and designers. June Anderson, Rockwell Blake, Vladimir Chernov, Samuel Ramey, Placido Domingo, Ann Murray, and Luciano

Pavarotti have all performed with Lyric Opera of Chicago; Marek Janowski and Sir John Pritchard have both conducted; Robert Altman, Jon Dexter, and Harold Prince have all had stints as stage directors; and John Conklin and David Hockney have both been production designers here. Okay, so I've given you the big build-up, now what will it cost you for an evening of high-brow, in-demand entertainment? Surprisingly little, if you're willing to let the best seat in the house go to the guy or gal who can afford it! On the weekend, there are a variety of first and second balcony seats that can be had for anywhere between $36.00 and $66.00. What's even better is that if you go to a weekday performance (Monday through Thursday), the choice of affordable seating even includes the main floor with prices ranging from $29.00 - $59.00. Sounds easy enough, right? Not quite. Due to the high number of subscription tickets, tickets to the performances can be rather hard to come by. Buy them early if you can. If not, don't worry, Mr. C has come through for you once again! The old adage "if you can't beat 'em, join 'em" seems particularly pertinent here. If you're having trouble beating the throngs of opera fans to the phone for tickets, why not become a member of a Lyric Opera of Chicago Chapter? For a $50.00 contribution plus $15.00 in dues you'll become part of a group of true opera lovers. As always, membership has its privileges: like two free admissions to a designated working rehearsal; two admissions to a season preview concert; lots of educational, volunteer, and social gatherings; an invite to participate in OPERATHON, where you'll get the chance to meet celebrated opera stars; an invitation to the annual luncheon; a free subscription to the *Chapter Notes* newsletter; and a 10 percent discount at Chicago area Borders Books & Music stores. For more information, call 312/332-2244x5656. Another great opportunity for opera lovers in the area is to become a volunteer in the education department of Lyric Opera of Chicago. Upon completion of training, volunteers will work in many different aspects of the behind-the-scenes educational efforts. They may help in giving lectures at various local establishments, give backstage tours of the Civic Opera House, or work with elementary schools in the area to enlighten youngsters. For more information on volunteer opportunities, call 312/332-2244x5912. The regular performance season runs from September to March.

THE UNIVERSITY OF CHICAGO PRESENTS

1010 East 59th Street, Chicago IL 60637. 773/702-8068. **The Lowdown:** For nearly a century, The University of Chicago Presents has been host to what the *Chicago Sun-Times* calls "one of the area's most sophisticated line-ups." The Chamber Music Series, The Howard Mayer Brown International Early Music Series, and the Regents Park Discovery Concert have a tradition of presenting the world's most distinguished classical musicians. The concerts take place at the University of Chicago's Mandel Hall, Chicago's finest chamber music venue, and in the historic Rockefeller Memorial Chapel. Subscriptions are available each year with various subscriber benefits. Single tickets are just $25.00 for the general public and $10.00 for students. For more information on upcoming events, give them a call.

Music: Folk, Rock, & Pop

ABBEY PUB
3420 West Grace Street, Chicago IL 60618. 773/478-4408. **World Wide Web address:** http://www. abbeypub.com. **The Lowdown:** In addition to being a fine restaurant, the Abbey Pub serves up healthy portions of music, sports, and – of course – pints. Music performances encompass everything from traditional Celtic fiddles to country music and rock. The place really fills up, so be sure to get there early. On Sunday, 8:00 p.m. marks the beginning of their Irish music jam; on Monday, the Abbey Pub offers traditional barn dancing lessons for $5.00; Tuesday is a night for open mike performances; Wednesday night offers some great bluegrass; Thursday is set aside for Irish concerts; and Friday and Saturday nights offer up various live acts. While the Abbey Pub is well known throughout the city as one of the biggest and best Irish pubs, the food is also worth mentioning. Drop in on a Saturday or Sunday morning and enjoy their menu of traditional Irish fare. Open daily, 9:00 a.m. - 2:00 a.m.

CHICAGO BRAUHAUS
4732 North Lincoln Avenue, Chicago IL 60625. 773/784-4444. **The Lowdown:** Can't afford a trip to Bavaria? Take a trip to the next bext thing... the Chicago Brauhaus. You can hear lively German-American music here Wednesday through Monday with no cover charge and no drink minimum. Of course, you'd be missing out on an essential part of the scene if you come here and don't try their old-world brew. On Saturdays and Sundays, the fun starts at 1:00 p.m. with lively accordion music. Then at 6:00 p.m., the five-piece house band takes over for the evening. Oom-pah all you like; lederhosen optional. The Brauhaus, of course, serves up traditional German and American dinners including wiener schnitzel, bratwurst and the like. Prices are fairly moderate, and reservations are recommended. Open Sunday through Friday, 11:00 a.m. - 2:00 a.m.; Saturday, 11:00 a.m. - 3:00 a.m.

CHICAGO MUSIC MART AT DePAUL CENTER
333 South State Street, Chicago IL 60604. 312/362-6700. **The Lowdown:** If an afternoon spot of live music is what you're craving, Chicago Music Mart's "Tunes at Noon" should be right up your alley. Performances take place Monday through Saturday at 12:00 p.m. sharp. Musical styles range from classical to jazz to rock. Chicago Music Mart appreciates all genres. Drop by or give them a call to find out about this month's schedule. Best of all, all performances are free and open to the public.

MARTYRS'
3855 North Lincoln Avenue, Chicago IL 60613. 773/404-9494. **World Wide Web address:** http://martyrslive.com.

The Lowdown: Is it possible for a cool club to offer great live music at an affordable price? What about a cool club that offers great live music that – if not free – could cost you as little as $2.00? It's all possible at Martyrs', a fantastic Lincoln Park club open six nights a week. On Monday nights, you can count on some live Irish music; you can also count on a crowd any night that the Dark Star Orchestra – a Grateful Dead tribute band – is booked to play. Still, you can expect the musical genre to change (sometimes drastically) from night to night, so there's always something new to see. The kitchen at Martyrs' serves up a variety of good food that just might surprise you. When was the last time you ordered a plate of hummus at a bar? Both food and drink prices are completely within reason, and the intimate atmosphere makes the entire experience even more pleasing. On weekend mornings, from 10:00 a.m. - 3:00 p.m., Martyrs' serves a great brunch that includes such things as shrimp cakes and eggs, a smoked salmon plate, and banana walnut pancakes. But can one place do so many different things well? The proof is in one visit to Martyrs'. Open Monday through Friday, 5:00 p.m. - 2:00 a.m.; Saturday, 5:00 p.m. - 3:00 a.m.

METRO

3730 North Clark Street, Chicago IL 60613. 773/549-0203. **World Wide Web address:** http://www.metrochicago.com. **The Lowdown:** Just one block from Wrigley Field, Metro is one of Chicago's most popular live rock venues, and it's easy to see why. The club attracts some fantastic local and national talent, and has been known to spawn the careers of several well-known acts. Do the names Smashing Pumpkins or Ministry sound familiar? And it's not uncommon for famous bands like The Black Crowes to put on a surprise show. Well after hitting the big time, venerable singers like James Brown and Bob Dylan have played Metro. Since it's opening in 1982, Metro has put on more than 5,000 shows. It's the club's intimate setting that makes it such a great place to catch a show; you'll feel like you're watching a (really good) garage band at your best friend's house party. Word to the sensitive: it seems that Metro is one of the few places left in the city (and probably the country) that allows smoking. Consider yourself warned that the smell of cigarette smoke will definitely be following you home. The seating has been removed from the main floor, so if you like to mosh, stand up front and they'll be sure to oblige you (though, if James Brown were playing, I'm not sure how appropriate it would be to mosh). For those less inclined to get wild, the second balcony does offer some sedentary options. There's live music almost every night. Metro plays host to a number of local and national acts. There's a full bar selection, but the presence or absence of a wristband on your arm will be the deciding factor of whether or not you're allowed to drink. While tickets to see a well-known performer can rise up to about $20.00 (still not a bad deal), ticket prices are usually in the $5.00 - $8.00 range. With a seating capacity of 1,100, you should have no problem nabbing a ticket or two. The fact that Metro has its own box office will allow you to save money on the usual Ticketmaster service fees. The box office (a.k.a. The Clubhouse) is located at 3728 North Clark

Street and is open Sunday, 12:00 p.m. - 6:00 p.m.; Monday through Thursday, 12:00 p.m. - 8:00 p.m.; Friday, 12:00 p.m. - 10:00 p.m. Tickets at the box office are always cash only. Early shows (starting from 6:30 p.m. - 7:00 p.m.) are open to all ages; late shows (starting at 9:00 p.m. or later) are for people 18 or over. Wander downstairs at Metro and you'll find their patron nightclub, SmartBar. Playing lots of dance music and designating Sunday "Soul Night," you're bound to bump into more than one area college student. But remember, SmartBar is always a 21+ gig. For a list of upcoming events, call or visit their Website. To keep abreast of the latest happenings, join the Metro mailing list. *$Cash Only$*

OLD TOWN SCHOOL OF FOLK MUSIC
CHICAGO FOLK CENTER

4544 North Lincoln Avenue, Chicago IL 60625. 773/728-6000.
♦ Old Town School of Folk Music, Children's Center, 909 West Armitage Avenue, Chicago IL 60614. **World Wide Web address:** http://www.oldtownschool.org. **The Lowdown:** In this particular school, folk music is the core curriculum, and it attracts over 3,000 students a week and 30,000 concert-goers annually. Every Friday night (except holidays and during the summer), the Old Town School of Folk Music hosts an informal gathering of students, teachers, local musicians, and folk enthusiasts. The evening begins at 6:30 p.m. with a song circle. Admission is free, and everyone is welcome to join in the singing. At 8:30 p.m. the more formal part of the evening gets underway with featured guests. These are usually established regional groups, preceded by a warm-up act of local musicians or students. There's a $3.00 - $5.00 cover charge for the second half. What a bargain! Sunday afternoons feature their Showcase Series of new talent, as well as a Children's Concert Series; tickets for these shows are usually priced at $8.00. Call for a brochure that details all of these, plus other concerts and class offerings.

SCHUBAS TAVERN & HARMONY GRILL

3159 North Southport Avenue, Chicago IL 60657. 773/525-2508. **World Wide Web address:** http://www.schubas.com. **The Lowdown:** The 100-year old neo-Gothic building that houses Schubas Tavern makes a handsome diversion from the typical Chicagoland bar. Following a 1988 refurbishing, the interior of Schubas Tavern was restyled to its original, turn-of-the-century grandeur. With high tin ceilings and a gorgeous mahogany bar, Schubas Tavern is as much a place to admire visually as it is anything else. Every night of the week, from 10:00 p.m. - 2:00 a.m., Schubas offers a great menu of live music from a variety of genres. From jazz and blues to rock and pop, there's no doubt that they're always serving up something exciting. Depending on when you go, tickets generally range in price from $4.00 - $12.00. For a listing of upcoming shows, call or visit their Website. And if the music doesn't have you singing, the food at the adjacent Harmony Grill certainly will. Seven days a week, they serve up lunch and dinner to a restaurant full of happy recipients. They offer you old-time pub favorites like a number of starters (wings, chicken fingers, French fries); salads

(Caesar, mixed greens, Cobb); sandwiches (burgers, grilled chicken, reuben); and entrees (meatloaf, macaroni and cheese, fried chicken). On the weekends, Harmony Grill serves up a delicious country breakfast too. So whether you're hungry for food or thirsting for live music, this is a great place to stop by.

TWO WAY STREET COFFEE HOUSE
1047 Curtiss Street, Downers Grove IL 60515. 630/969-9720. **World Wide Web address:** http://www.twowaystreet.org. **The Lowdown:** Since 1970, Two Way Street Coffeehouse has been serving up a bit more than just coffee. In fact, the name is a bit misleading as the venue is actually located within a church. Every Friday night, they play host to an exciting and fun folk concert. Many of these performances combine music with storytelling. Since you won't be able to resist the offerings while you listen, they offer a great spread of coffee, tea, cider, hot chocolate, soda, and snacks. Two Way Street Coffeehouse is also open on the first and third Saturday of each month at 2:00 p.m. for a fantastically fun singaround. The cost of the Friday night concert is a suggested donation of $3.00. Doors open at 7:30 p.m. and performances start at 8:45 p.m., which gives you just enough time to kick back and enjoy the relaxed and casual atmosphere.

THE WILD HARE   *yes!!*
3530 North Clark Street, Chicago IL 60657. 773/327-4273. **The Lowdown:** If you've got something to celebrate, why not do it at The Wild Hare? Originally called The Wild Hare and Singing Armadillo Frog Sanctuary, the truncated version of this club still delivers some of the city's best reggae music. The hordes of local Jamaicans who populate the club on any given night are the proof. The Wild Hare couples a relaxed, friendly setting with the peaceful vibes of great reggae, aptly dubbing themselves "the reggae capital of America." Of course, like Graceland with Elvis, the walls of The Wild Hare are adorned with pictures of "the king" of reggae, Bob Marley. As it is he who has inspired many, if not all of the performers, such an abundant tribute seems only right. The Wild Hare's tremendous sound system is a perfect complement to the fantastic acts that take the stage here. You won't be able to stop dancing! If and when you hit the bar, don't forget where you are: order up some of the house specialty, rum punch, or a bottle of Red Stripe. Trust me, it'll make the night much more authentic. For the most part, the cover charge will run you anywhere between $5.00 - $8.00; though on nights of better-known reggae acts like Shabba Ranks, that price can rise to $15.00 - $20.00. Cheapsters will want to know that the best times to visit The Wild Hare are Monday, Tuesday, or any night before 9:00 p.m., when there's no cover charge at all. The music gets started around 9:30 p.m. Open Sunday through Friday, 7:00 p.m. - 2:00 a.m.; Saturday, 7:00 p.m. - 3:00 a.m. *$Cash Only$*

Music: Jazz & Blues

ANDY'S

11 East Hubbard Street, Chicago IL 60611. 312/642-6805. **The Lowdown:** Andy's is a well-known spot amongst jazz aficionados the world over. The casual, unpretentious atmosphere attracts a talented breed of musicians as well as an appreciative audience. Because they keep their prices in check, Andy's should also be attracting any true cheapsters like yourself. There's barely a quiet moment in this hidden little spot; shows start up at 12:00 p.m. (on weekdays) and continue throughout the evening. The musical focus here is on swing and bebop. For the most part, musical acts revive their performances weekly, making this a place full of regulars. The best time to visit may be for their weekday lunch, when no cover and a decent menu full of salads and sandwiches (along with a few entrees) will make for quite a pleasing meal. The second and third shows start up around 5:00 p.m. and 9:00 p.m. respectively. While they do entail a cover charge, it is usually never any more than $7.00. The drinks and food are both reasonably priced, making Andy's one of the best deals in this city full of jazz opportunities. Open Sunday, 7:00 p.m. - 12:30 a.m.; Monday through Friday, 12:00 p.m. - 2:30 a.m.; Saturday, 6:00 p.m. - 1:30 a.m.

BLUE CHICAGO

736 North Clark Street, Chicago IL 60610. 312/642-6261. ◆ 536 North Clark Street, Chicago IL 60610. 312/661-0100. **E-mail address:** blues@bluechicago.com. **World Wide Web address:** http://www.bluechicago.com. **The Lowdown:** As two of the most respected blues clubs in Chicago, Blue Chicago is not all about charging ridiculous admissions for mediocre entertainment. A single cover charge of $5.00 - $7.00 is all you need to pay to gain access to both of these clubs. Every night, they present some of the city's finest blues entertainers and you can be there to witness the magic. Plus, while your ears are being treated to the music, you'll eyes will be treated to the wonderful artwork of John Carrol Doyle that lines the walls. Right next door to one of the clubs (at 534 North Clark Street), Blue Chicago operates the Blue Chicago store where you'll find lots of unique and reasonably-priced apparel, artwork, and CDs. They even host an all-ages blues night every Saturday at 8:00 p.m. (no smoking or alcohol permitted). To find out who's playing at either club this month, call or visit their Website. The 736 North Clark location is closed on Sunday and the 536 Clark Street location is closed on Monday. Both are open Tuesday through Saturday.

B.L.U.E.S.

2519 North Halsted Street, Chicago IL 60614. 773/525-8371. **The Lowdown:** This nothing-fancy-just-hard-hitting-music club has been around for more than 20 years. It rocks well into the night, seven nights a week, showcasing great howlers from the national circuit. Son Seals, Otis Rush, Billy Branch, and Chubby Carrier and the Bayou Swamp Band are just some of the many stars who play the club regularly, with cover charges usually right around $9.00. This friendly spot is just the place to relax and soak in some local culture after a tiring day of sightseeing. Music starts up around 9:00 p.m. every night. For an up-to-date listing of who's playing, call 773/528-1012. Open daily, 8:00 p.m. - 2:00 a.m.

BUDDY GUY'S LEGENDS

754 South Wabash Street, Chicago IL 60605. 312/427-0333. **The Lowdown:** In this town, Buddy Guy is a legend. The rest of the country is finally discovering this, too. Equally worthy is his music club, where you can enjoy live blues and a buffet every Friday (5:00 p.m. - 8:00 p.m.) for free. It's their After Work special, serving up chicken wings, fries, and other nibbles along with the music. It's not the most generous buffet ever seen, but you can make one good pass and have a nice snack, and hey, it's all free! While that is one fine deal, the weeknight cost won't leave you crying the blues either. Cover charges for Sunday through Wednesday are only $4.00, and Thursdays are $5.00. Not bad for national stars like Ronnie Earl, Duke Robillard, Maria Muldaur, and Otis Rush. Weekends get more expensive, around $10.00 - $12.00, depending on the musicians. If you're inclined to stick around, there are pool tables and a full menu of burgers and sandwiches. Open Sunday, 6:00 p.m. - 2:00 a.m.; Monday through Thursday, 5:00 p.m. - 2:00 a.m.; Friday, 4:00 p.m. - 2:00 a.m.; Saturday, 5:00 p.m. - 3:00 a.m. *$Cash Only$*

CHECKERBOARD LOUNGE

423 East 43rd Street, Chicago IL 60653. 773/624-3240. **The Lowdown:** When it comes to the history of blues in Chicago, the Checkerboard Lounge is one place that any true fan knows about. While the neighborhood is a little rundown (abandoned buildings surround the club), one moment inside and the atmosphere lightens. The club's tiny stage has held the weight of some of the blues world's heaviest talents: Muddy Waters, Little Milton, B.B. King, Junior Wells, and Koko Taylor are just a few of the names I'll use to impress you. Still, not everyone who has appeared on the Checkerboard stage can be considered a blues icon: The Rolling Stones and Led Zeppelin are just two examples. Just a quick glance at one of the picture-covered walls will surely tell you a story or two, and the waitstaff will do the same. Much different from its downtown challengers, the club's South Side neighborhood makes for a relaxing, de-yuppified blues experience. While the cover can sometimes reach up to $20.00 when someone big is playing (still, with the names I've already mentioned, that's not too shabby a price), prices are usually around $5.00. There's $3.00 parking right across the street and $8.00 valet service. The live music starts after 9:30 p.m.; before that, there's a fantastic mix of blues on the Checkerboard jukebox. Open Sunday through Friday, 11:00 a.m. - 2:00 a.m.; Saturday, 11:00 a.m. - 3:00 a.m. *$Cash Only$*

FITZGERALD'S

6615 Roosevelt Road, Berwyn IL 60402. 708/788-2118. **World Wide Web address:** http://www.fitzgeraldsnightclub.com. **The Lowdown:** This club is best known for live jazz and blues, but that's not all there is to see here. This is a club steeped in history: Los Lobos, Robert Cray, and Stevie Ray Vaughn have all played here. Lonnie Mack and Koko Taylor both made live recordings here. FitzGerald's has also been the scene, quite literally, for a few big movies, including *The Color of Money*. Remember when Elisabeth Shue sang the blues in *Adventures in Babysitting*? She did it at FitzGerald's. Or, in *A League of Their Own*, when Madonna and her cohorts tore up the rug at a local roadhouse? You guessed it. Throughout the week they offer various musical genres including jazz in all its incarnations: big band, vintage, hot, and swing. You also shouldn't be surprised to see a number of rock, bluegrass, or folk acts take the stage. It's really a melting pot for all styles of music and all types of people. So, stop in. Who knows? You may end up seeing the next great act, or being in the next big movie... without breaking the bank. Tickets start at just $4.00 a show and rarely cost more than $15.00 apiece. To hear about upcoming events, call or visit their Website.

THE GREEN MILL LOUNGE

4802 North Broadway, Chicago IL 60640. 773/878-5552. **The Lowdown:** Walking into this Uptown club, once owned by Al Capone, feels like a trip back to that earlier time. The Green Mill has been carefully restored to speakeasy glory with ornate bas-relief pictures set into the walls, lounge lighting, high-backed upholstered booths... and of course, the sounds of a sultry saxophone or a brassy big band fill the room. Amazingly enough, the prices for this entertainment seem to be from a bygone era, too. There's live jazz seven nights a week, and the cover charges range from $2.00 - $7.00 for music starting around 9:00 p.m. (8:00 p.m. on Saturdays, 11:00 p.m. on Sundays). Ah, but any die-hard jazz fan is just waking up at that hour. Make your way to the club at 12:00 a.m. on Fridays and Saturdays, when the second group hits the stage, and admission is only $2.00. Better yet, by 1:30 or 2:00 a.m., the Green Mill All-Stars take over. From then, until they knock off just before dawn, there is no cover charge at all. If that wasn't enough, every Sunday evening from 7:00 p.m. - 10:00 p.m., a mere $5.00 will afford you entry to the Uptown Poetry Slam. Yes folks, the beatniks battle it out in the ring, or rather, on the stage. Traveling by car or cab, instead of public transit, is advisable in this part of town late at night.

JAZZ SHOWCASE

59 West Grand Avenue (between Clark & Dearborn Streets), Chicago IL 60610. 312/670-BIRD. **World Wide Web address:** http://www.jazz-showcase.com. **The Lowdown:** Opened in 1947, Jazz Showcase is the world's second oldest jazz club. "What's the oldest?" you may ask... it's New York City's Village Vanguard. But that's not important right now! Located in the River North area of Chicago, Jazz Showcase's prime location makes it a great spot for an after-dinner drink for those who've

been toiling away in the Loop all day, as well as those shopping along the Magnificent Mile. The acoustics have been carefully-designed to give you the best (and least painful) listening experience. In keeping with Mr. C's simple living philosophy, they don't impose any minimum drink requirements on you either. The only favor that they do ask is that you refrain from talking too loudly during a set. Here at Jazz Showcase, it's all about the music. More specifically, it's all about JAZZ! Jazz Showcase is one of the only clubs that books national jazz acts on a full-time basis. Cover varies, but is usually between $15.00 and $20.00. While the cover charge is usually for only one set, employees of the Jazz Showcase will be happy to let you hang on for the second show, provided there's not a huge line to get in. If you've got the kids, they offer a Sunday matinee show too where tickets are discounted for students, seniors, and musicians; kids under 12 are allowed in for free. If you're looking for an even further bargain, opt for one of Jazz Showcase's dinner packages. For just $35.00 per person, you can enjoy dinner right across the street at Maggiano's Little Italy (see separate listing) and then drop on in and sit down at your reserved Jazz Showcase table. For more information or to make reservations, you must call Maggiano's Little Italy (312/644-7700). Showtimes are Sunday at 4:00 p.m., 8:00 p.m., and 10:00 p.m.; Tuesday through Thursday at 8:00 p.m. and 10:00 p.m.; Friday & Saturday at 9:00 p.m. and 11:00 p.m.

JOE'S BE-BOP CAFE & JAZZ EMPORIUM
Navy Pier, 700 East Grand Avenue, Chicago IL 60611. 312/595-JAZZ. **World Wide Web address:** http://www.joesbebop.com. **The Lowdown:** From the same folks that brought you the venerable Jazz Showcase (see separate listing) comes Joe's Be-Bop Cafe & Jazz Emporium. Located on Navy Pier, Joe's offers live jazz in a gorgeous setting. Seven nights a week they offer live jazz with no cover and no drink minimums. Add to that the fact that they've got a fantastic menu of Southern-style cuisine, and you've got your entire night covered. Choose from a menu of barbecued goodies and other Southern delights like jambalaya and crawfish etouffee. Joe's also offers a good selection of appetizers, soups and salads, sandwiches, and desserts to either accompany your meal or serve as an ersatz meal in itself. Joe's also keeps an impressive selection of wine and beer, and it's all reasonably-priced too. Each Sunday from 10:30 a.m. - 2:30 p.m., Joe's Be-Bop Cafe has what they deem a Gigantic Jazz Brunch. If anything is gigantic about it, it's got to be the Bloody Mary bar. Concoct your own libation from a choice of more than 140 items. Ingredients range from six different Bloody Mary blends to meats such as pepperoni and pulled pork. What an experience! Plus (if you don't turn your drink into something edible), they've got a great spread of brunch foods like biscuits and gravy, baked cheese grits, made-to-order omelettes, and carved meats. For a real visual treat, try the outdoor seating at Joe's; it overlooks the activity of Navy Pier and the gorgeous architecture of the city itself from across Lake Michigan. The restaurant is open Sunday, 11:30 a.m. - 10:00 p.m.; Monday through Thursday, 11:00 a.m. - 11:00 p.m.; Friday and

Saturday, 11:00 a.m. - 12:00 a.m. If you're here for the music, performances take place Sunday, 10:30 a.m. - 2:30 p.m. & 6:00 p.m. - 10:00 p.m.; Monday through Thursday, 6:00 p.m. - 10:00 p.m.; Friday and Saturday, 7:00 p.m. - 10:00 p.m.

KINGSTON MINES CHICAGO BLUES CENTER

2548 North Halsted Street, Chicago IL. 773/477-4646. **World Wide Web address:** http://www.kingston-mines.com. **The Lowdown:** First and foremost, let's establish the fact that this is a blues club. And not just any old blues club; Kingston Mines Chicago Blues Center is one of the oldest (over 30 years) and largest blues clubs in Chicago. Here, you'll experience such renowned artists as Magic Slim, Billy Branch, John Primer, and Charlie Love. Seven nights a week, two bands play on two stages. But what's on the menu besides great music? How about lots of great food? Mushrooms, zucchini wedges, okra, and onion rings – they're all here, they're all deep-fried for your delight, and they're all just $4.25 a plate. And what would a night of down-home eating be without a plate of wings? Purchased in quantities of 10 ($6.00), 20 ($11.50), and 30 ($16.50). For dinner, try a half or full slab of New Orleans-style BBQ ribs ($8.75 - $13.75). In keeping with the Louisiana feel, you can also try a plate of fried catfish for $7.25. But not everything is bad for your diet: grilled chicken salad and a garden burger are just two of the healthier options. The club opens at 8:00 p.m., with music starting around 9:30 p.m. Cover charge is $9.00 (Sunday through Wednesday), $10.00 (Thursday), and $12.00 (Friday and Saturday). Call or visit their Website to find out who's playing.

ROSA'S LOUNGE

3420 West Armitage Street, Chicago IL 60647. 773/342-0452. **World Wide Web address:** http://www.rosaslounge.com. **The Lowdown:** Often touted as Chicago's friendliest blues club, there's no doubt in this writer's mind that it is also one of the best. Since 1984, Rosa's Lounge has been providing music-lovers with an authentic and quality blues experience. Performers like The Kinsey Report, Sugar Blue, Billy Branch, and house band Melvin Taylor & The Slack Band don't slack when it comes to providing top-notch entertainment. In addition to nights at the club, Rosa's Lounge gives classes on several Blues-related topics to anyone who's interested. They also host a series of Blues Cruises when the weather turns warm where, for $35.00, you can enjoy a night of gorgeous scenery, food, dancing, and – of course – music! You'll have to give them a call for info on these special events. In the meantime, make sure to hit the club by 10:00 p.m., when the music really gets cranking. Rosa's Lounge is Chicago blues at its most authentic and best. Tickets are generally $5.00 - $10.00. Open Tuesday through Friday, 8:00 p.m. - 2:00 a.m.; Saturday, 8:00 p.m. - 3:00 a.m.

| Outdoors |

BROOKFIELD ZOO
First Avenue & 31st Street, Brookfield IL 60513-0719. 708/485-0263. **World Wide Web address:** http://www.brookfieldzoo.org.
The Lowdown: This is a 216-acre zoo known throughout the world for its innovative naturalistic, multi-species exhibits and its international role in animal breeding and conservation. With more than 2,700 animals, you'll see more than just lions and tigers and bears (oh my!). You'll see dolphins in the Seven Seas Panorama, giraffes, zebras, antelope, and African wild dogs in Habitat Africa!; gorillas, orangutans, and monkeys in Tropic World; and North American river otters, alligators, and a variety of bird species in The Swamp. Admission is $7.00 for adults; $3.50 for children 3 - 11 and seniors 65 and over; free to children 2 and under and to zoo members. From October through March on Tuesdays and Thursdays, admission to the zoo is free. Brookfield Zoo charges separately for Dolphin presentations, Children's Zoo admission, and Motor Safari tram rides. Parking is $4.00 for cars and $8.00 for buses. Brookfield Zoo is open daily, from 10:00 a.m. - 5:00 p.m. with extended summer hours of 9:00 a.m. - 6:00 p.m.

CALDWELL WOODS
6200 West Devon Avenue, Chicago IL 60659. 312/742-6200. **Toll-free phone:** 800/870-6200. **World Wide Web address:** http://www.chicagoparkdistrict.com. **The Lowdown:** This Far North park offers great opportunities for outdoor fun all year round. In the warm weather, cool down with a test-drive of the Caldwell Woods water slide. In the winter (late November to early March), ice skating is what's on the menu. Free skating is offered Monday through Thursday, 3:00 p.m. - 7:30 p.m.; Friday, 3:00 p.m. - 5:00 p.m.; Saturday and Sunday, 12:30 p.m. - 3:30 p.m. Don't fret if you've lost your skates, they'll be happy to rent you a pair (provided they have your size on-hand) for just $3.00 per person. Caldwell Woods also offers open hockey games Tuesday and Thursday starting at 8:00 p.m. Cost to join in a game is $5.00 and you MUST wear a helmet! Throughout the year, there are lots of other events that take place here, like a haunted walk through the woods at Halloween-time, but you'll have to call for more information. A free parking lot only adds to the money-saving fun. Call for hours as they can change with the weather.

CHICAGO BOTANIC GARDEN
1000 Lake Cook Road, Glencoe IL 60022. 847/835-5440. **World Wide Web address:** http://www.chicago-botanic.org. **The Lowdown:** From the Japanese Garden to the traditional English Walled Garden, enjoy the beauty of nature in spring, summer, fall, or winter at the Chicago Botanic Garden. You can take a narrated tram ride and get fascinating information about the horticulture around you, or use the self-guided tour maps to

enjoy this exceptional beauty on your own. You can also walk through the educational greenhouses, a living catalogue of plants from around the world, ranging from the most common house plants to the truly exotic flora. Special exhibits and family activities also take place year-round. For an aesthetically-pleasing dining experience, pack your own lunch and eat at one of the garden's designated picnic spots. Admission is free. If you're driving, the parking fee is $7.00 per car ($5.00 for seniors on Tuesdays). Open every day (except Christmas), 8:00 a.m. until sunset.

FRIENDS OF THE CHICAGO RIVER

407 South Dearborn Street, Suite 1580, Chicago IL 60605. 312/939-0490. **World Wide Web address:** http://www. chicagoriver.org. **The Lowdown:** Every summer, this nonprofit group sponsors canoe tours and a series of walking tours along the river. As you stroll along its banks, a trained docent will explain the river's fascinating development, discussing important contemporary issues as well. Eight different tours rotate weekly; each begins at 10:00 a.m. and lasts until about noon. Comfortable shoes are strongly recommended! Each tour meets in a different location; call for a schedule of upcoming tours. In addition to their great walking tours, the Friends of the Chicago River sponsor monthly canoe trips each summer at very reasonable prices. The registration fee for each trip is $25.00 for nonmembers, plus an additional $25.00 for the rental of a canoe and supplies. If this is something you think you'd like to do more often, consider becoming a member; this knocks both fees down to $15.00 each. In fact, when you sign up for any trip, you can become a member for a mere $5.00. Since an individual membership is normally $25.00, this amounts to a significant savings. Rates do tend to increase annually, but you should always be able to get a deal along these lines. Canoe trips are usually on Sundays and begin about 9:00 a.m. and last until around 4:00 p.m. Bring a brown bag lunch! Pre-registration is required. The season runs from May through October, with about six canoe trips a year.

GARFIELD PARK CONSERVATORY

300 North Central Park Avenue, Chicago IL 60624. 312/746-5100. **World Wide Web address:** http://www. chicagoparkdistrict.com. **The Lowdown:** Here at the Garfield Park Conservatory you can see 5,000 species of plants valued at around 2 million dollars. The good news is that you don't have to spend anywhere near this much to see them; in fact, admission is free. The conservatory's six houses contain almost every type of plant imaginable, from the most exotic Bird of Paradise to more common varieties. Guides will show you around and trained personnel will answer your questions on house plants and gardening. You can even call them and they will answer your horticultural questions over the phone. Throughout the year, they present several flower and plant shows that feature plants grown at the conservatory. Call for exact show dates and more information.

GRANT PARK

331 East Randolph Street, Chicago IL 60602. 312/742-7529.
World   Wide   Web   address: http://www.
chicagoparkdistrict.com. **The Lowdown:** Okay, so you've heard
about all the activities that take place here, but what about the
park itself? Grant Park offers a number of entertainment options
year-round. From the sporting action of Daley Bicentennial Plaza
(see separate listing), to The Petrillo Music Shell, this 220-acre
land mass serves as an outdoor cultural center in the midst of
the city. Grant Park comprises the area from Roosevelt Road to
Randolph Street and Michigan Avenue to Lake Michigan. In
addition to its gorgeous lakefront view, Grant Park offers lots of
beautiful horticulture. Within the park you'll find the country's
largest remaining stand of elm trees as well as a pair of
symmetrical rose gardens. Buckingham Fountain, which can be
found at the park's entrance, is one of the city's most frequently
photographed landmarks. There's plenty of picnic tables and
even a children's area to while away the hours with your family.
For leisurely folk who are looking for more of an intellectual
challenge, there are several chess tables set up throughout the
park. Hutchinson Arvey Field, which is located on the Roosevelt
Road side of the park, is home to an abundance of adult softball
leagues and several kid's day camps. Six lighted tennis courts
are free and open to public use. If all of this seems just a bit too
overwhelming, they'll be happy to provide you with a free map
that will allow you to take a self-guided tour of the park, paying
particular attention to the trees and landscape Open daily, 7:00
a.m. - 11:00 p.m.

LINCOLN PARK CONSERVATORY

2391 North Stockton Drive, Chicago IL 60614. 312/742-7736.
The Lowdown: If you have a love for all things green, then you
simply must take a walk through the Lincoln Park Conservatory.
It's completely free and located near the Lincoln Park Zoo (see
separate listing). As you wind your way around inside the
glassed-in conservatory, you'll pass through its palm house, fern
house, orchid room, and special exhibit room, each one a
distinctly different, balmy habitat. The conservatory has outside
gardens as well. They hold five major shows a year (call for
specific dates). In October they show chrysanthemums, and from
December into early January, their holiday show features
poinsettias and other plants of the season. Azaleas and camellias
take center stage in February, and the Spring Show in March and
April features lilies and other blooms of spring. Open daily from
9:00 a.m. - 5:00 p.m., you can spend a whole day here, or just
an hour at lunchtime.

LINCOLN PARK ZOO

2200 North Cannon Drive, Chicago IL 60614. 312/742-2000.
The Lowdown: Lincoln Park Zoo is perhaps one of the best in-
city zoos anywhere. The zoo houses more than 1,000 birds,
animals, and reptiles from all over the world, all hanging out in
carefully reproduced versions of their natural habitats. Highlights
include one of the world's largest collections of apes, a couple of
polar bears enjoying a dip in their very own 266,000-gallon pool,

and a bird house with a free-flight aviary. You'll have to duck your head as exotic and colorful birds zip past you! Lincoln Park also is home to the Pritzker Children's Zoo, where kids can study animals in an intimate setting; and the Farm-in-the-Zoo, a real working farm where you can observe cow and goat milking, horse grooming, butter churning, and more. The zoo also hosts summer camps which give children a hands-on opportunity to be with animals, visit behind-the-scenes, go on field excursions, make crafts and more. Camp fees can get pretty steep, but considerable savings are available to zoo members. Call for more information. Open daily, 9:00 a.m. - 5:00 p.m. If you arrive by car, parking will cost you $7.00.

MIDWAY PLAISANCE
59th Street & Woodlawn Avenue, Chicago IL 60637. **World Wide Web address:** http://www.chicagoparkdistrict.com.
The Lowdown: Built for the 1893 World's Columbian Exposition, the original intention of Midway Plaisance was to create an easy route between Jackson and Washington Parks. Yet, as the site of the world's first Ferris Wheel, this little throughway continues to attract tourists every day. This 80-acre park was designed by Frederick Law Olmsted, the same guy who brought us a little place in New York City known as Central Park. What remains from the olden days (albeit not the 1800s) is The Fountain of Time. Built in 1922 by Lorado Taft and Howard Van Doren, The Fountain of Time is one of Chicago's most photographed landmarks. The Hyde Park location will also allow you to take a great (self-guided) tour of the famous University of Chicago architecture. In the winter, Midway Plaisance is also the place for free skating. The park's rink offers free skating Monday through Thursday, 3:00 p.m. - 7:30 p.m.; Friday, 3:00 p.m. - 5:00 p.m.; Saturday and Sunday, 12:30 p.m. - 3:30 p.m. Skate rentals will cost you an extra $3.00 for adults, $2.00 for kids. Still, at any time of year, Midway Plaisance is a great place to relax and get some fresh air. **NOTE:** At the time of this writing, Midway Plaisance was in the process of developing a year-round skating spot in conjunction with the University of Chicago. The rink would allow for ice skating in the winter and in-line skating in the summer. Visit their Website for more information.

THE MORTON ARBORETUM
4100 Illinois Route 53, Lisle IL 60532-1293. 630/719-2465. **World Wide Web address:** http://www.mortonarb.org.
The Lowdown: About 25 miles west of downtown Chicago, The Morton Arboretum is a 1,700-acre nonprofit outdoor museum with more than 3,600 kinds of trees, shrubs, and other plants displayed in woodlands, wetlands, gardens, and a restored native prairie. Established in 1922 by Joy Morton, founder of the Chicago-based Morton Salt Company, the Arboretum's mission is to collect and study trees, shrubs, and other plants from around the world. They then display these plants in naturally beautiful landscapes for people to study and enjoy, and to learn about how they can grow plants in ways that enhance the environment. In addition to encouraging the planting and conservation of trees and other plants for a greener, healthier, and more beautiful

world, The Morton Arboretum offers an extensive array of year-round educational opportunities for kids and adults alike. The summer explorers' program for kids is just one of the ways in which The Morton Arboretum succeeds in fulfilling its mission. Families can enjoy the arboretum's year-round beauty by driving its 11 miles of roads or hiking its extensive pathways. The Morton Arboretum also conducts special events throughout its changing seasons including a Fall Color Festival, Buds 'n Blossoms in the spring, a large Arbor Day celebration, and the magical Twilight Tree Walk and winter wonderland Yuletide Celebration. Admission is $7.00 per car for non-members. Open daily (365 days a year), 7:00 a.m. - 7:00 p.m. Daylight Savings Time (until 5:00 p.m. Central Standard Time).

NAVY PIER
600 East Grand Avenue, Chicago IL 60611. 312/595-PIER. **Toll-free phone:** 800/595-PIER. **World Wide Web address:** http://www.navypier.com. **The Lowdown:** As Chicago's premiere tourist attraction, what kind of visitor would you be if you didn't visit? Originally opened in 1916, Navy Pier was designed as a shipping and recreation facility and has since been used as a military training center and a campus to the University of Illinois. The Pier fell into disuse throughout much of the 1970s and 1980s, but was redesigned into the state's most visited entertainment attraction. The revitalized Pier features more than 50 acres of shops, restaurants, parks, tour and dinner cruise boats, and entertainment attractions. Besides being home to the Chicago Children's Museum and the IMAX Theater (see separate listings), Navy Pier offers visitors a variety of top-quality dining, shopping, and entertainment options. The 50,000-square-foot Family Pavilion (housing the two just-mentioned attractions) is chock full of fun. Plenty of shops will provide you with hours of happy browsing alone, regardless of whether you make a purchase: learn a trick or two at Magic Masters, take a trip to Hollywood with a stop in at Giant Screen, and make the rest of your friends jealous when you purchase some souvenirs at Oh Yes Chicago. The Navy Pier food court offers a number of quick and cheap dining options (read: fast food with a twist) like America's Dog, King Wah Express, Twisted Lizard, and The Waterfront Bakery. If, even after sampling all the great food Chicago has to offer, your little one is still screaming for a Happy Meal, take him/her to McDonald's The Future. Sure, it serves the same burgers and fries as every other McDonald's, but those McDonald's don't have laser beams shooting past as you munch on your Big Mac. Perhaps the most visible treat at Navy Pier (because of sheer size alone) is the Ferris Wheel. At 150-feet, the Ferris Wheel is a replica of the very first Ferris Wheel built for the World Columbian Exposition. If you get to Navy Pier just as dusk does, don't worry: the Ferris Wheel is illuminated at night. A ticket to ride will cost you $3.50, children under 12 and seniors are $3.00, and children under two are free. The Ferris Wheel is open year-round. Acrophobes may want to stick with the musical carousel that is a history lesson in itself; the walls of the carousel illustrate the history of Navy Pier. Tickets are $2.50 for adults, $2.00 for children under 12 and seniors, and free to children

under two – those toddlers get all the breaks, don't they? Of course, what would winter be without at least an attempt at ice skating? From November to March, Navy Pier offers a free outdoor skating experience. This is not a place for show-offs (or Olympians) but rather, a place for individuals and families to come and enjoy the season. Skate rentals are available for $3.50 ($3.00 for children under 12). With so much fun stuff to do, it's easy to while away an entire day here. Just remember, as Navy Pier is located on Chicago's lakefront, it can get a bit chilly in the winter months. Hours vary from season to season. In the summer (May - August), Navy Pier is open Sunday through Thursday, 10:00 a.m. - 10:00 p.m.; Friday and Saturday, 10:00 a.m. - 12:00 a.m. In the fall (September - October), Navy Pier is open Sunday, 10:00 a.m. - 7:00 p.m.; Monday through Thursday, 10:00 a.m. - 9:00 p.m.; Friday and Saturday, 10:00 a.m. - 11:00 p.m. In the winter (November - April: don't forget to bundle up!!), Navy Pier is open Sunday, 10:00 a.m. - 7:00 p.m.; Monday through Thursday, 10:00 a.m. - 8:00 p.m.; Friday and Saturday, 10:00 a.m. - 10:00 p.m.

OLD WATER TOWER
806 North Michigan Avenue, Chicago IL 60611. **The Lowdown:** The Great Chicago Fire in 1871 wiped out nearly everything in its path, but one structure remained as a symbol of hope – the Old Water Tower. Who would have thought that something so practical could look so artistic and hold such sentimental value to the city? Today, visitors can see the medieval influence in its castle-like appearance, but also the practicality in its limestone structure. At the time, the Old Water Tower was an architectural feat. Today, it is still quite a remarkable site to see, and best of all, there are no admission fees and you can drop by to gaze at any time.

WILLIAM W. POWERS CONSERVATION AREA
12949 South Avenue O, Chicago IL 60633. 773/646-3270. **The Lowdown:** If you're looking for a little solitude to get away from the hustle and bustle of city living, The William W. Powers Conservation Area offers that Walden-like way of life. This 580-acre park, right on the Indiana border, offers fishing, boating, cycling, and picnicking in the warmer months and ice fishing in the winter. Still, at any time of year, a stroll through the area can be just as entertaining. There's even a child-designated area. Don't be surprised if you spot a deer, or hear the unmistakable "who" of an owl. What's more, you won't have to pay any admission and there's a free parking lot as well. Open for visitors daily, from 6:00 a.m. to sunset.

WILLOWBROOK WILDLIFE CENTER
525 South Park Boulevard, Glen Ellyn IL. 630/942-6200. **The Lowdown:** In addition to providing their visitors with a unique and entertaining educational experience, Willowbrook Wildlife Center has been helping to preserve the health and happiness of the ill and abandoned animals that surround them. Since 1956, they have opened up their grounds and hearts to the animals that inhabit the area. The main building allows you to

watch over more than 30 different species of wild animals. You can even see the nursery, where these caring folks love and tend to the animals. Throughout the year, you should feel free to walk around and enjoy the scenery or join Willowbrook Wildlife Center for one of the many special events they host. Admission is a suggested donation of $1.00. Open daily, 9:00 a.m. - 5:00 p.m. During the winter (December 1 - March 1), the Center closes at 4:00 p.m.

Participatory Sports

THE CHICAGO SWING DANCE SOCIETY
University of Chicago, Ida Noyes Hall, 1212 East 59th Street, Chicago IL 60637. 312/409-4911. **E-mail address:** swingdance@uchicago.edu. **World Wide Web address:** http://swing.uchicago.edu. **The Lowdown:** Based at the University of Chicago's Hyde Park campus, The Chicago Swing Dance Society is bringing the excitement and fun of this exciting American pastime to the Windy City. Specializing in the Savoy style of swing (also known as the Lindy Hop), The Chicago Swing Dance Society offers classes, workshops, and social dance events for all. Best of all, you can be an absolute beginner; they offer instruction for dancers of all skill levels starting from the novice to the advanced Lindy Hopper wanting to perfect their Swing-outs. As a student-run organization, the Chicago Swing Dance Society has turned into a Chicago institution in all matters of swing dancing. The Chicago Swing Dance Society has made many memorable television appearances including commercials, pilots, and even a stint at a 1998 Bulls playoff game. Their instructors have competed on the national level and can be seen performing and teaching at local colleges and universities, corporate events, fundraisers, and the annual *Dance Chicago* shows. They also host the annual Windy City Lindy Exchange weekend, which draws Lindy Hoppers from all across the nation. Classes are offered five times weekly and comprise a five-week time span. In order to join, you must purchase a pass for a mere $20.00. In addition to some wonderful classes, this pass will also entitle you to attend any of the club-sponsored outings and social dance events at deep discounts. If you want a quick start or have a tight weekday schedule, The Chicago Swing Dance Society also offers affordable fun-filled intensive weekend workshops every quarter. Another great way to enjoy all The Chicago Swing Dance Society has to offer is to drop in on a Friday night Java Jive for a basic swing lesson that's open to all ages, followed by a night of live music and dancing fun! Java Jive takes place every Friday night at Ida Noyes Hall from 8:30 p.m. - 11:30 p.m.

DALEY BICENTENNIAL PLAZA
337 East Randolph Street, Chicago IL 60602. 312/742-7650. **World Wide Web address:** http://www.chicagoparkdistrict. com. **The Lowdown:** Come sunshine or snowfall, Grant Park's Daley Bicentennial Plaza offers a great opportunity to get active. From April to October, 12 lighted tennis courts offer tons of warm weather fun to the tune of just $5.00 an hour. Call ahead to reserve one. If tennis is not your game, try your hand (or legs) at some roller or inline skating. Rental skates are available. In the winter months, Daley Bicentennial Plaza does not let these facilities go to waste. The warm-weather roller rink becomes the cold-weather ice skating rink. The rink is open Monday through Friday, 10:00 a.m. - 10:00 p.m.; Saturday and Sunday, 10:00 a.m. - 5:00 p.m. Admission is $2.00 for adults, and $1.00 for

kids under 14. Ice skate rentals are the same price. Daley Bicentennial Plaza offers numerous special events throughout they year, like Skate With Santa in December. Indoors, the plaza plays host to a number of cultural events and classes; at one point they even offered a series of yoga classes. That said, there is never an uneventful moment around here. Once you've had enough of Daley Bicentennial Plaza itself, you can roam around the rest of Grant Park (see separate listing).

FAMILY GOLF CENTER

221 North Columbus Drive, Chicago IL 60601. 312/616-1234. **Toll-free phone:** 800/409-0888. **World Wide Web address:** http://www.familygolf.com. **The Lowdown:** Whether you're Tiger Woods or Joe Bunker when it comes to golf, Family Golf Center is a fun time! With more than 115 golf centers in operation, Family Golf Center is dedicated to providing quality entertainment and recreation for the entire family. Their outdoor driving range is open year-round and has more than 90 stations. Some of the driving stations are even heated and/or covered, though I wonder if a cheapster could afford to secure one of those spots! The staff is friendly and completely capable of helping players of all skill levels. The range is well-lit, so night time practice is not a problem. But wait, I still haven't told you about the best part: the view. The driving range looks out onto Lake Michigan, offering your practice a glorious backdrop. The cost is $6.00 for 50 balls or $10.00 for 100. If you need to rent some clubs (which I recommend, as all their clubs are in pristine condition), the cost is $3.00 apiece. For even more exciting fun, you can play a round on their beautifully-landscaped nine-hole golf course. Cost is $12.00 per round, Monday through Thursday; and $15.00 per round, Friday through Sunday. If you're visiting in the winter months, just be aware that the course closes with the first frost. Still, they manage to make full use of all their great facilities and prime Loop location. When the pond surrounding the ninth hole freezes, it can be used for ice skating and the rest of the course is often used for cross-country skiing. But just because this is a nine-hole course, don't think there's not a 19th hole. Family Golf Center runs a great restaurant offering light fare and a full bar selection. There's also a full-service pro shop on the premises that will surely suit all your needs. Parking is free for as long as you're inside the facility. Open daily, 8:00 a.m. - 10:00 p.m.

FLEET FEET FUN RUNS

210 West North Avenue, Piper's Alley, Chicago IL 60610. 312/587-3338. **The Lowdown:** Maybe a 4-6 mile jaunt through Chicago is not what you had in mind for entertainment. But if you're idea of fun is talking about mile pace and the latest pair of Nikes on the road, then you'll be in good company on these Fleet Feet Fun Runs. It doesn't matter if you're a resident or a tourist; if your muscles are aching for activity, consider these twice-weekly runs for all levels. Unlike some running clubs, there is no fee to participate in these group runs and it is open to all ages, distances, and paces. The group meets Monday and Wednesday

nights at 6:30 p.m. and Tuesday nights at 6:30 p.m. for women only. Call the Fleet Feet store for more details.

JOHNNY'S ICEHOUSE

1350 West Madison Street, Chicago IL 60607. 312/226-5555. **World Wide Web address:** http://www.johnnysicehouse.com. **The Lowdown:** Chicago sure is a hockey town! Perhaps it's their close proximity to The United Center, but Johnny's IceHouse seems the place where aspiring players want to be. In fact, it is home to the biggest (over 42 teams) and best men's and women's hockey leagues in Chicago. Johnny's can even boast state championship teams in the senior (men's and women's) A and B leagues. With an indoor rink open year-round, players of all skill levels can practice their moves regardless of temperature. For players craving a bit of competition (all in fun, of course), drop by Johnny's IceHouse for some rat hockey. Pick-up games are held daily, from 11:30 a.m. - 1:00 p.m. Games comprise a great mix of players of all ages and skills, making it fair competition for both teams. You can join in for a reasonable charge. If you're a goalie, consider yourself blessed; since there's never enough of them to go around, goalies are invited to play for free. Whether you're just visiting or live here, a game at Johnny's IceHouse is a great way to meet new people. And who knows, maybe you'll even catch a glimpse of a real pro. Well-known for its high-quality maintenance and great ice, Johnny's IceHouse serves as a practice rink for many NHL teams when The United Center is unavailable. After battling it out on the ice, check out the Stanley Club, a private full-service bar and restaurant located on the mezzanine level of the arena.

MARIGOLD BOWL

828 West Grace Street, Chicago IL 60613. 773/935-8183. **The Lowdown:** Marigold Bowl hasn't succumbed to the age of technology. Patrons of this Wrigleyville bowling alley are still expected to keep score with – get this – a pencil and paper. It's the almost-extinct comforts like these that make Marigold Bowl such a great spot. With 32 lanes of bowling fun at your disposal, there's plenty of room to accommodate your group. The best time to visit Marigold Bowl is Wednesday through Sunday, from 9:00 p.m. - 12:00 a.m., when you can bowl for just $.99 a game. For additional fun on a Saturday night, take a break from the bowling and belt out a tune; it's karaoke night in the bar. Plus, you can always spend a few quarters in the arcade. Better still, Marigold Bowl offers free parking all the time. ***$Cash Only$***

McFETRIDGE SPORTS CENTER

3843 North California Avenue, Chicago IL 60618. 312/742-7585. **World Wide Web address:** http://www.chicagoparkdistrict. com. **The Lowdown:** McFetridge Sports Center offers sports enthusiasts an inexpensive place to work out or play. If you're in town on business and your hotel doesn't have a gym, the fitness center at McFetridge is a viable option. The center has lots of free weights and several circuit training machines. The cost is just $2.00 per visit or $15.00 for 25 visits. That's a lot cheaper than a monthly gym membership. The fitness center is open Monday through Friday, 7:00 a.m. - 10:00 p.m.; Saturday and Sunday, 9:00 a.m. - 5:00 p.m. McFetridge's six indoor tennis courts can also be reserved for a nominal fee. Another fun option is their indoor skating rink, which is open year-round. The cost is just $3.00 for adults, $2.75 for young adults (high-schoolers), and $2.25 for children under 13. Skate rentals will cost you an extra $2.50. There's even a pro shop to take care of any unexpected sporting good needs. A free parking lot is an added bonus. McFetridge Sports Center is one of more than 250 staffed locations in the Chicago Park District. To find out about year-round, free events taking place in any of these facilities, visit their Website.

RIIS PARK
6100 West Fullerton Avenue, Chicago IL 60639. 312/746-5363. **World Wide Web address:** http://www.chicagoparkdistrict. com. **The Lowdown:** Let's just talk numbers: Riis Park is comprised of a baseball field, five softball diamonds, 10 tennis courts, three volleyball courts, a swimming pool, a combination football/soccer field, several basketball standards, a track, two horseshoe pits, an archery range, a lagoon where you can practice your cast, and a bike path. For the kids, they've got all of the above plus two playgrounds and three sandboxes. This is truly an overwhelming place. In the middle of Riis Park, there's even a dividing hill that serves as a wonderful sledding in the winter plus an ice rink that is open to the public, often for free. Skate rentals will cost you $2.00 - $3.00, but that's all you'll have to pay for this wonderful, cold-weather activity. There's also an indoor field house, gym, and assembly hall with a kitchen. Overall, Riis Park covers more than 55 acres of land. With all this fun at their fingertips, you can bet that folks in the neighborhood spend much of their time here, so it can tend to get a little bit crowded. Open daily, 6:00 a.m. - 11:00 p.m.

ROLALINE LANES
3713 East 106th Street, Chicago IL 60617. 773/221-0654. **The Lowdown:** What's so exciting about bowling? Everything if you're bowling at the right place. The intimate setting at Rolaline Lanes makes it the perfect cheap place for a date. It is an especially great idea to go when it is time for Candlelight Bowling. This is when Rolaline harkens back to older times and lights the facility solely with candlelight. They also make up a great list of silly rules, like having to skip into position, that make it that much more fun than a regular old string. Cost is under $2.00 per game and $.50 for shoe rentals. Parking is free. Open daily, 12:00 p.m. - 12:00 a.m. ***$Cash Only$***

SLUGGERS WORLD CLASS SPORTS
3540 North Clark Street, Chicago IL 60657. 773/472-9696. **World Wide Web address:** http://www.sluggersworld.qpg.org. **The Lowdown:** Just around the corner from Wrigley Field, you can practice your swing in these good old fashioned batting cages. Located upstairs from Sluggers Bar, Sluggers World Class Sports is no-frills, noisy, and fun. There are a bunch of screened-

in cages, with a few basketball hoops, skee-ball alleys and pinball games wedged into the layout. A mere $1.00 gets you a token good for 15 pitches in any cage: slow, medium, fast, or softball; you can also get six tokens for $5.00. On Monday and Thursday evenings from 6:00 p.m. - 11:00 p.m., as long as there's not a Cubs game on, you can pay just $5.00 for unlimited hitting. Open daily; until 1:00 a.m. on weekends.

WAVELAND BOWL
3700 North Western Avenue, Chicago IL 60618. 773/472-5900.
World Wide Web address: http://www.wavelandbowl.com.
The Lowdown: If you've got the urge to bowl at 4:32 a.m., Waveland Bowl can oblige you. Open 24-hours, Waveland Bowl is one of the city's only alleys that is always at your disposal. And this ain't no run of the mill bowling alley; cosmic bowling and bumper bowling for kids are just two of their unique options. All 40 lanes are equipped with computerized scoring systems, which can be a real lifesaver if you *are* bowling at 4:32 a.m. (no thinking involved). Prices change throughout the week, but prices generally range $2.00 - $5.00 a game. Cozmic Bowling, which usually takes place from 10:00 p.m. - 2:00 a.m., is generally $.50 more expensive. Renting a pair of those lovely, well-worn shoes will cost you an additional $2.50. Free parking is another great reason to make Waveland your bowling alley of choice...any time!

Readings, Poetry, & Literary Events

BARNES & NOBLE
1130 North State Street, Chicago IL 60610. 312/280-8155. ◆ 659 West Diversey Parkway, Chicago IL 60614. 773/871-9004. ◆ 1441 West Webster Avenue, Chicago IL 60614. 773/871-3610. ◆ One South 550 Route 83, Oakbrook Terrace IL 60181. 630/571-0999. ◆ 1550 West 75th Street, Downers Grove IL 60516. 630/663-0181. ◆ 47 East Chicago Avenue, Suite 132, Naperville IL 60540. 630/579-0200. ◆ Other suburban locations. **World Wide Web address:** http://www.barnesandnoble.com. **The Lowdown:** As one of the nation's most recognizable names when it comes to bookselling, Barnes & Noble is always a first stop on author publicity tours. Hence, there's always some sort of reading, author discussion, or book signing going on. Barnes & Noble also helps to get you together with many like-minded individuals, offering a number of book groups that meet frequently. Still, it's not just lovers of Oprah's Book Club that they cater to: events at Barnes & Noble run the gamut from live musical performances to children's storytelling sessions. Best of all, the only price of admission is your own curiosity and interest (plus, probably, a cup of coffee – who can resist that Starbucks aroma?). Drop by to pick up a schedule or visit them online for a listing of upcoming events.

THE BOOK STALL AT CHESTNUT COURT
811 Elm Street, Winnetka IL 60093. 847/446-8880. **Toll-free phone:** 800/678-2242. **World Wide Web address:** http://www.thebookstall.com. **The Lowdown:** Almost more impressive than the selection of books is the number of literary events that take place at The Book Stall. Throughout the year, noted authors stop by to discuss their book and sign copies. even if you can make it to the store at the actual time, the folks at The Book Stall will be nice enough to reserve and autographed copy for you. Author appearances are usually free of charge. At other times throughout the year, you should feel free to join in a discussion group with your peers and thoughtfully talk about what you thought of a particular book. Many of the book discussions even revolve around older publications and classics, so you don't necessarily have to be up to speed on the latest best-sellers. The cost to join in is a $5.00 coupon charge, which can then be used on anything in the store. Why not purchase a copy of the book for next week's discussion? The Book Stall recently expanded their space to attach to the Caribou Coffee location on the corner. They're very excited about this new partnership and you should be too. After all, what goes better with conversation than a cup of coffee? For more information on upcoming events, call or visit their Website. Open Sunday, 11:00 a.m. - 5:00 p.m.; Monday through Friday, 9:30 a.m. - 9:00 p.m.; Saturday, 9:30 a.m. - 5:30 p.m.

BORDERS BOOKS & MUSIC

830 North Michigan Avenue, Chicago IL 60611. 312/573-0564.
• 2817 North Clark Street, Chicago IL 60657. 773/935-3909.
• 2210 West 95th Street, Chicago IL 60643. 773/445-5471.
World Wide Web address: http://www.bordersstores.com.
The Lowdown: You don't need me to tell you about the enormous selection of nicely-priced books, music, and movies at Borders. But what you may not know about is that, virtually every week, Borders sponsors a number of special events including readings, book discussions, author signings, and live music. The best thing is that all of these events are free. Drop in or give them a call to find out about upcoming events. The Michigan Avenue location is open Monday through Saturday, 8:00 a.m. - 11:00 p.m.; Sunday, 9:00 a.m. - 9:00 p.m.

CENTURIES & SLEUTHS BOOKSTORE

743 Garfield Street, Oak Park IL 60304. 708/848-7243.
The Lowdown: This bookstore is for those who profess their bibliophilia to history and mystery. Centuries & Sleuths carries a wide selection of books to satisfy your love for these genres, but they do more than just stock the shelves with them! They sponsor both a Mystery Discussion Group and a History Discussion Group, in which the respective buffs can get together to socialize and discuss their favorite topic. The groups meet on Saturdays; membership is free and open to anyone interested. Centuries & Sleuths also hosts readings and author signings on a fairly regular basis. Authors have included Max Allan and Barbara Collins and their work, *Regeneration: A new life... for a Price;* Wayne Wolf and his book *Heroes & Rogues of the Civil War: Volumes 1-4*; and Sara Hoskinson Frommer and her mystery, *The Vanishing Violinist*. In some cases, the store has "visits" from historical figures of the past such as Napoleon, Joan of Arc, and Elizabeth I. Open Monday, Wednesday, Thursday, and Friday, 11:00 a.m. - 7:00 p.m.; Saturday, 10:00 a.m. - 5:00 p.m.; Sunday, 12:00 p.m. - 5:00 p.m. Closed on Tuesday.

57TH STREET BOOKS

1301 East 57th Street, Chicago IL 60637. 773/684-1300.
The Lowdown: This cozy, quiet bookstore near the University of Chicago in Hyde Park offers free storytelling hours for children. Readings take place Thursday and Saturday mornings at 10:30 a.m. 57th Street Books also offers free author readings and book group meetings throughout the year. Call for more information or a schedule of upcoming events. Open Monday through Saturday, 10:00 a.m. - 10:00 p.m.; Sunday, 10:00 a.m. - 8:00 p.m.

GUILD COMPLEX

Chopin Theater, 1543 West Division Street, Chicago IL 60622. 773/296-1268x26. **World Wide Web address:** http://nupress. nwu.edu/guild. **The Lowdown:** Wicker Park is one of Chicago's burgeoning areas for the young, hip arts scene. This bar and nightclub is at the center of it all, with a focus on avant-garde jazz and rock. Oon Wednesday nights at 7:30 p.m., the Guild Complex, a performance art organization, hosts a literary evening. You never know what you may hear: poetry and fiction readings, songwriters, and many other types of original performance by local and national artists have made up the slate for almost five years. Past performances have featured a Latin evening, with flamenco guitar music and poetry; dramatized stagings of poetic works; rap music; and even a Poetry Video Festival. Admission is $5.00 - $7.00, depending on the bill. Preceding the featured performers, the microphone is open to anyone who wants to try out his or her own new material; these folks also get a reduced admission price of $3.00. The Guild also offers workshops, including the popular Women Writers Conference, on how to write, perform, and publish poetry. Call or visit their Website for schedules.

MAD BAR
1640 North Damen Avenue, Chicago IL 60647. 773/BAR-BAR7. **World Wide Web address:** http://www.mentalgraffiti.org. **The Lowdown:** Sure, you may know Mad Bar as mainly a drinking establishment, but on Mondays and the last Tuesday of every month, this not-so-typical bar transforms itself into a place for poetry readings and appreciation for the spoken word. Mondays at 7:00 p.m. it's time for Mental Graffiti, a free open mike where you'll be exposed to a diverse offering of poetry and music by lots of exceptional performers. Because there is a three-minute time limit, you're bound to see as many as 30 different people hit the stage on any given night. With no said rules intact, the sky is the limit for what these people will do and say, but you can always count on it for being an interesting if not stimulating evening. The last Tuesday of the month (except holidays), Mad Bar offers its patrons "Women Outloud," a spoken word event for women, though men are certainly allowed to come and listen. Open mike events at Mad Bar feature free cover, though you must be 21 years of age. Though there is no dress code for these events, the club does have one. If you plan on staying after the open mike is over, you must adhere to their rule of no sports attire. For more information, call or visit their Website.

TWILIGHT TALES
2446 North Lincoln Avenue, Chicago IL 60614. **World Wide Web address:** http://twilighttales.com. **The Lowdown:** If you can't watch a scary movie alone and still think there are monsters that live under your bed, get ready to have the bejeezus scared out of you! Well, not really. While many of the featured readers tend to focus on the horror, science fiction, and fantasy genres, many other styles are welcome. Music, comedy, and theatrical presentations often make for an enjoyable respite. Most of the featured performers are professional authors who have been working in their chosen genre for years, though the occasional unpublished but promising young author may be featured too. Admission is just $2.00. Readings are held every Monday night, upstairs at The Red Lion Pub (see separate listing), at 8:00 p.m.

WOMEN & CHILDREN FIRST
5233 North Clark Street, Chicago IL 60640. 773/769-9299. **E-mail address:** wcfbooks@aol.com. **World Wide**

Web address: http://www.womenandchildrenfirst.com.
The Lowdown: As the name would suggest, this bookstore carries stock with a feminist perspective as well as children's books. Accordingly their readings and other programs have similar themes. Adult readings generally feature female authors discussing a range of topics from sexuality to the men's movement. The occasional poetry reading and performance art event round out their offerings. Programs are free and they are open to the public. For $3.00, you can receive a one-year subscription to Women & Children First's newsletter, which includes a program schedule. Better yet, save the $3.00 by stopping in and checking out the store. Open Monday and Tuesday, 11:00 a.m. - 7:00 p.m.; Wednesday through Friday, 11:00 a.m. - 9:00 p.m.; Saturday, 11:00 a.m. - 7:00 p.m.; Sunday, 11:00 a.m. - 6:00 p.m.

Spectator Sports

ARLINGTON INTERNATIONAL RACECOURSE
2200 West Euclid Avenue, Arlington Heights IL 60006. 847/255-4300. **World Wide Web address:** http://www.arlington-intl.com. **The Lowdown:** Usually, a day at the race tracks means losing money. If you employ Mr. C's strategy, it can actually be a thrilling way to spend the day *without* spending too much money. In fact, the best part about the whole experience is that you can actually come home with a fatter wallet! You don't need to drop thousands to have fun here. Playing a race for $1.00 - $2.00 can be just as exciting (especially if that 50-1 longshot actually places)! Arlington International is thought – by many – to be one of the world's most beautiful and best racetracks. The six-story grandstand allows plenty of room for you to drop in and enjoy the action. Even when there's no racing at the track, you can still enjoy the thrill of it all at Arlington Trackside, Arlington International's on-site OTB facility. Here, you can enjoy racing from all over the country from the comfort of your own table. There's also a full-bar and full-service restaurant to add to the experience. One tip that I can offer you to keep this fun-filled day within cheap-range: set aside a certain amount of money that you are willing and able to spend and bring exactly that much. Leave your credit cards and bank cards at home, as the lure of an instant money machine can often be too convenient to ignore. Call or visit their Website to find out about upcoming racing schedules up-to-the-minute happenings.

CHICAGO BEARS
1000 Football Drive, Lake Forest IL 60045-4829. 847/295-6600. **World Wide Web address:** http://www.chicagobears.com. **The Lowdown:** Founded in 1920, the Bears have become an indelible part of Chicago's history. As of this printing, the Bears had won nine world championships, made the playoffs 22 times, and sent 24 of their players, one coach, and one general manager to the Pro Football Hall of Fame (a team record). In 1997, the Bears became the first team in the history of the NFL to win 600 games. So what would a trip to Chicago be without a visit to Soldier Field? While tickets can run you over $50.00, there are plenty of seats to be purchased for just over $30.00. Come and see some for yourself: it's Chicago (and NFL) history in the making.

THE CHICAGO BLACKHAWKS
1901 West Madison Street, Chicago IL 60612. 312/455-7000. **World Wide Web address:** http://www.chicagoblackhawks. com. **The Lowdown:** National Hockey League games are infamous for their expensive admission price. Unless you snag rinkside seats, you may end up watching the large TV screens to see the plays, instead of the actual ice they're playing on. So

why is it that hockey fans insist on filling up even the furthest seats if it is difficult to see the game? Well, given the fact that about as much excitement is generated from the fans as from the players, people likely flock to these games for the atmosphere and for the full hockey experience. So, for the best views of the Chicago Blackhawks at the United Center, you may have to dish out $75.00 per game. However, if you're there for the full experience, consider the least expensive, 300-level seats that will cost you only $15.00 per game. You can purchase tickets from the Chicago Blackhawks Ticket Office (312/943-7000), in person at the United Center, or by calling Ticketmaster (312/559-1212, online at http://www.ticketmaster.com).

THE CHICAGO BULLS
1901 West Madison Street, Chicago IL 60612. 312/455-4000. **World Wide Web address:** http://www.bulls.com. **The Lowdown:** The United Center in Chicago is home to some of the most exciting games and entertainment in the NBA. While season tickets can offer regular access if you're an avid game-goer, they're also extremely hard to come by. But you can still enjoy all the excitement the sport has to offer... even on my budget! While courtside and other top seats will cost you anywhere between $50.00 and $85.00, there are still great seats to be had for less than $40.00. Yes you really can catch a game for just $10.00! To purchase tickets, visit The United Center box office, a Ticketmaster outlet, or call 312/559-1212 (online at http://www.ticketmaster.com). For season or group tickets, call 312/455-4000. A word to the wise: tickets sell out quickly so call as soon as possible.

THE CHICAGO CUBS
Wrigley Field, 1060 West Addison Street, Chicago IL 60613. 773/404-CUBS. **World Wide Web address:** http://www.cubs.com. **The Lowdown:** Whether you're visiting Chicago or living here, there are some experiences you cannot miss. One distinctly Chicago activity is a trip to Wrigley Field to watch the Cubs lay America's favorite pastime. While the admission price to see some of your favorite professional sports teams may be skyrocketing, baseball tickets remain comparably affordable, especially if you're there for the atmosphere rather than the game view. Adult, Upper Deck Reserved seating costs just $10.00 for games held between June and August, or on weekends, nights, or Opening Night. Of course, you're bound to be entertained, by players and spectators alike, if you spend the $15.00 for bleacher seats. Even the best seats in the field box cost $25.00, about half as much for the best seating at any other professional sports game. Call 312/831-CUBS for tickets.

CHICAGO FIRE
311 West Superior Street, Suite 444, Chicago IL 60610. **Toll-free phone:** 888/MLS-FIRE. **E-mail address:** firetickets@mlsnet.com. **World Wide Web address:** http://www.chicago-fire.com. **The Lowdown:** Okay, so maybe

hooting and hollering for the Windy City's soccer team isn't your idea of a traditional game day event, but the sport's popularity cannot be denied. It would be hard not to notice the rising attendance numbers at the Chicago Fire games as well. During their 1998 inaugural season, the Fire became the first expansion team to win the MLS cup in their first season. It's an achievement that has drawn people from all over to come and see what all the excitement is about. The season usually lasts from April through September; so it's a great time of year to sit out at Soldier Field and watch this team create some real Chicago history. Tickets run anywhere from $12.00 for FireHouse seating to $23.00 for Premier seating. Tickets can be purchased at your local or online Ticketmaster (http://www. ticketmaster.com), at Soldier Field, or by e-mailing the address above. For more information, call or visit the Chicago Fire Website.

CHICAGO WHITE SOX
Comiskey Park, 333 West 35th Street, Chicago IL 60616. 312/674-1000. **World Wide Web address:** http://www. chisox.com. **The Lowdown:** Whether you're a White Sox fan or not, a day at Comiskey Park is sure to reawaken the hidden child in all of us. It's an especially great way to spend a day or evening if you're traveling with kids. Remember how much you used to love it when your parents took you to root for the home team? Tickets start at just $10.00 and don't run far beyond $25.00. As beer, pretzels, and hot dogs are not included in the price of admission, it's ultimately up to you to decide whether or not to splurge. then again, aren't those really the three things that make the game so worthwhile? Tickets can be purchased at the Comiskey Park box office or by calling 312/831-1-SOX. They can also be purchased at all Ticketmaster locations or online at http://www.ticketmaster.com.

THE CHICAGO WOLVES
2301 Ravine Way, Glenview IL 60025. 847/724-GOAL. **Toll-free phone:** 800/THE-WOLVxES. **World Wide Web address:** http://www.chicagowolves.com. **The Lowdown:** If the idea of a rinkside seat to a Blackhawks game excites you but the thought of paying up to $75.00 is less thrilling, why not try an IHL game. The Tuner Cup-winning Chicago Wolves will provide you with just as much checking and goal-scoring excitement at about half the price. The cheapest of the cheap seats can be had for just $9.00 while the most expensive seats sell for right around $35.00. In between, there are plenty of tickets for $11.00 - $30.00. That's not a lot of dough to see these animals in action. All games are played at Allstate Arena (10550 Lunt Avenue, Rosemont IL), just minutes from downtown. Call or visit their Website to find out the times and prices of upcoming games.

DePAUL UNIVERSITY
1011 West Belden Avenue, Chicago IL 60614. 773/325-7526. **World Wide Web address:** http://www.depaulbluedemons. com. **The Lowdown:** Where else can you watch athletes play for the love of the game instead of their weekly paycheck? With over

15 Division I intercollegiate sports teams, you're guaranteed a game, match, or meet full of talent, heart, and excitement at DePaul University. While the majority of games are free to spectators, some of the more popular sports do require an admission fee. Women's basketball games, held in Allstate Arena, are just $5.00; men's basketball games are $5.00 when held in Alumni Hall and $15.00 when they're played in the United Center. Tickets can be purchased by phone at 312/559-1212 or 800/99-DPAUL), or online at http://www.ticketmaster.com.

LOYOLA UNIVERSITY RAMBLERS
6525 North Sheridan Road, Chicago IL 60626. **World Wide Web address:** http://www.loyolaramblers.com. **The Lowdown:** As part of the Midwestern Collegiate Conference, Loyola University's athletic teams have been providing sports fans with a reason to cheer for years. Loyola University Athletics encompass men's and women's basketball, soccer, and volleyball. They also offer the excitement of cross country and track events, softball, and a golf team. The priciest of Rambler tickets apply to their basketball events, and even these are affordable. You can pick up a pair of courtside bleacher tickets to the men's game for $10.00 or an upper bleacher seat for $8.00. Women's basketball games cost a general admission fee of $3.00.

NORTHWESTERN UNIVERSITY WILDCATS
1501 Central Street, Evanston IL 60208. 847/491-CATS. **World Wide Web address:** http://www.nusports.com. **The Lowdown:** Any sports nut will tell you that college sports can be much more emotional and often times more competitive than a professional game. When it comes to Northwestern University's Wildcats, there is no lack of excitement. Northwestern offers a variety of events to choose from throughout the year including football, basketball, baseball, softball, tennis, and wrestling. With so many things going on, you could drop by every day for a week and have a unique (and inexpensive) experience each time. As Northwestern is well-known for their football team, these are the most expensive tickets. Depending on the game, tickets generally range between $24.00 and $30.00. General admission to a men's basketball game is $10.00 per person. Women's basketball is a lot cheaper – albeit just as exciting – at $4.00 for adults and $3.00 for children. Many other sporting events are free throughout the year.

UNIVERSITY OF CHICAGO DEPARTMENT OF ATHLETICS
5640 South University Avenue, Chicago IL 60637. 773/702-7681. **World Wide Web address:** http://www.uchicago.edu/student/ athletics. **The Lowdown:** Big draws at this NCAA Division III school include football, basketball, and track. Admission to all athletic events is free, except for football. Tickets to football games cost $2.50 for adults and $.50 for children.

UNIVERSITY OF ILLINOIS AT CHICAGO SPORTS
839 West Roosevelt Road, Chicago IL 60608. 312/413-8421. **World Wide Web address:** http://www.uicflames.com. **The Lowdown:** College athletics are some of the most exciting

games to watch. What's more, as their athletes are demanding astronomical salaries, they're an inexpensive option for a night of fun. Sports at the University of Illinois Chicago campus are no different. No matter what type of sport your prefer, UIC has got it. Basketball fans rejoice as men's single regular season tickets can be had for as little as $10.00, with floor level seats costing $25.00. Even better are the tickets for women's basketball, where $5.00 will get you any seat in the house. This same $5.00 ticket price applies to all baseball, softball, volleyball, soccer, swimming, diving, and gymnastics events as well. Men's and women's cross country and tennis tickets are free.

Television Talk Shows

THE JERRY SPRINGER SHOW

NBC Tower, 454 North Columbus Drive, Chicago IL 60611. 312/321-5365. **World Wide Web address:** http://www.universalstudios.com/tv/jerryspringer. **The Lowdown:** If you are looking for high-energy, low-brow entertainment, and you are willing to wait in line for it, then you could be chanting "Jer-*RY!* Jer-*RY!*" along with the rest of the enthusiastic studio audience... for free. An afternoon with Jerry is sure to enlighten; you'll see some of the city's most imaginative characters and hear some of the most colorful language thrown out on the stage of this popular talk show. Jerry's show tackles such timely and important topics as family conflict, intimacy, betrayal, and – most importantly – midget transsexual love triangles. Tickets are free but you must call in advance to register (Monday through Friday, 10:00 a.m. - 2:00 p.m.) and arrive early. Who wouldn't want to arrive early? We all know that most of the action happens in the greenroom anyway. Maybe you could sneak a peek!

THE OPRAH WINFREY SHOW

Harpo Studios, 1058 West Washington Street , Chicago IL 60607. 312/591-9222. **World Wide Web address:** http://www.oprah.com. **The Lowdown:** As one of television's most respected and well-loved talk shows, you can imagine how difficult it is to get tickets to see *The Oprah Winfrey Show*. What's great about Oprah's show is that, unlike many other television talk shows, she doesn't expect you to sit outside for hours on end, just waiting to maybe get a ticket. In order to be an audience member, you must have a reservation; and reservations are only accepted by calling in advance. That's where it can get tricky. If you've ever tried calling for hot concert tickets, you know the frustration that can build when faced with an unending busy signal. Still, when you finally do get through, who can help to ease all that frustration better than Oprah? Get your dialing finger ready and try for your reservations Monday through Friday, 9:00 a.m. - 5:00 p.m. Tapings take place on Tuesday, Wednesday, and Thursday at 9:00 a.m. and 12:00 p.m. The show goes on hiatus during the summer months, so if you were planning a June - August visit, you're out of luck. You should also be advised that kids must be at least 16 to attend the show, and children under 18 will be asked to show proof of age. But here's an added bonus, so bibliophiles listen up. By now, I think we're all aware of Oprah's Book Club. For a writer, being an Oprah Book of the Month is almost as prestigious as winning a Pulitzer Prize. Now, readers can join in the fun. Oprah's Book Club Show is open to regular Joes and Janes like us! Once you've read Oprah's Book selection, all you need to do is write to the show and tell them how the book affected you. If your submission is chosen, you and a few other lucky viewers will sit down to eat with Oprah and discuss the book at length. So, put your reading glasses on and your pen and paper ready; you could be Oprah's next dinner guest. If you're interested in appearing on the Book Club Show, you can send your thoughts to: Oprah's Book Club, P.O. Box 617640, Chicago IL 60661. You can also visit the Oprah Website and fill out an online e-mail submission. In any case, I guarantee that getting a (free) ticket to see a taping will be one of the highlights of your vacation.

Theater

AMERICAN THEATER COMPANY

1909 West Byron Street, Chicago IL 60613. 773/929-1031. **E-mail address:** info@atcweb.org. **World Wide Web address:** http://www.atcweb.org. **The Lowdown:** The mission of American Theater Company, as they put it, is to "explore and celebrate human potential." By presenting four new and/or classic productions each season, ATC works toward its mission. By encouraging freedom, expression, and creativity, American Theater Company productions explore what it is to be human. Works by such classic and contemporary greats at Euripides, Sam Shepard, Thornton Wilder, Eugene O'Neill, and David Mamet are just some of the productions you'll see here. American Theater Company presentations are not just for regular theater-goers; part of their philosophy is that the theater can and should be enjoyed by everyone. At prices like these, theater can be for everyone. Call or visit their Website for a list of upcoming performances. Tickets generally cost $15.00 - $25.00.

THE ANNOYANCE THEATRE

3747 North Clark Street, Chicago IL 60613. 773/929-6200. **The Lowdown:** The Annoyance Theatre's parodies of modern life are always wacky and truly hilarious. With titles like *The Stinky Onion Gang* (a spoof of cutesy, corporate-sponsored children's theater), *That Darned Antichrist* (it's a musical. really), *Coed Prison Sluts* (take a guess), and *Manson The Musical* (need I explain?), performances at The Annoyance Theatre like to go off the deep end... way off the deep end. Sets, costumes, and props are extremely minimal, which actually adds to the fun. What also helps to add to the fun is that The Annoyance Theatre is a BYOB kind of place. So throw a six-pack in the cooler and head out for a night of some truly innovative culture. Many of their plays are offered as double bills, allowing you to see one show for $6.00 or two for $9.00, but ticket prices rarely top $12.00. Shows tend to run in a repertory rotation Tuesday through Saturday, including late-night performances on weekends. Call for a list of upcoming events. *$Cash Only$*

CHICAGO SHAKESPEARE THEATER

Navy Pier, 800 East Grand Avenue, Chicago IL 60611. 312/595-5600. **World Wide Web address:** http://www.chicagoshakes. com. **The Lowdown:** The magic of William Shakespeare is brought to theatrical delight right here at the Chicago Shakespeare Theater. Throughout the year, the Chicago Shakespeare Theater produces a number of shows for all the city to see. While weekend shows can get a bit pricey (just over $40.00) you can save by attending one of their weekday shows on Tuesday, Wednesday, or Thursday, when tickets are just $28.00. Still a bit more than you were hoping to pay? Why not catch a preview show and save $5.00? Or, if you're really into Bill and his plays, buy a three-play subscription for anywhere from

$60.00 - $99.00. Throughout the year, you can also catch a performance in the studio theater. Ticket prices for these shows run right around $30.00 apiece. Prices can vary from show to show. A final option, and one that's a great idea for parents looking to expose their kids to a bit of culture, is Short Shakespeare! This is when one of the bard's many great plays – Romeo and Juliet, for example – is presented in a condensed and easy-to-understand version. Performances take place on Saturday afternoons at different times throughout the year and tickets are just $8.00 for students and kids under 18 and $12.00 for adults. For more information or to order tickets, call or visit their Website.

COURT THEATRE

5535 South Ellis Avenue, Chicago IL 60637. 773/753-4472. **World Wide Web address:** http://courttheatre.uchicago.edu. **The Lowdown:** In residence at the University of Chicago, the Court Theatre is a fully professional repertory theater company. Past players have included Alan Arkin and Ed Asner, as well as the brilliant comic duo of Elaine May and Mike Nichols. Court Theatre performances take place in a modern, arena-style theater arranged into just seven rows, making for an up-close and intimate evening. Accordingly, their tickets don't come as cheaply as you may like; but that doesn't mean there aren't savings to be had. Wouldn't you rather spend $36.00 apiece for tickets on a Saturday night, even for performances of plays by the likes of Edward Albee, Molière, and Oscar Wilde? At the Court Theatre, the savings go to those who can pop out on the spur of the moment. Half-price tickets may be available one hour before any performance. There are also savings for senior citizens: $2.00 off any ticket. Student tickets are $15.00 in advance, and student rush tickets may be available one hour before any performance for only $9.00 (just don't forget your I.D.). The theater is convenient; it's just a 20 minute ride from the Loop. They offer lots of free parking too! For those who prefer to plan ahead, the Court Theatre offers several subscription packages which can also save you some money.

THE GOODMAN THEATRE

North Dearborn (between Lake & Randolph Streets), Chicago IL. 312/443-3800. **E-mail address:** staff@goodman-theatre.org. **World Wide Web address:** http://www.goodman-theatre.org. **The Lowdown:** If you know anything about theater, chances are you know something about The Goodman Theatre. Several of Broadway's biggest hits have started their run here: Robert Falls' revival of *Death of a Salesman*; August Wilson's *Fences* and *The Piano Lesson*; David Mamet's *Glengarry Glen Ross*, *American Buffalo*, and *A Life in the Theater*; and Scott McPherson's *Marvin's Room* have all started here. That said, tickets can sometimes run the risk of being a bit pricey (i.e. $40.00 or more). But, considering the $75.00+ that many theaters charge, this can still be quite a deal. Still, if the thought of parting with that much money for an extraordinary night at the theater isn't within your budget, Mr. C has got the answer: Tix at Six! Drop by The Goodman Theatre box office at 6:00 p.m. on the night of the performance you would like to attend (12:00 p.m. for matinees) and all remaining tickets can be purchased for half-price. Prices don't get much better than that! **NOTE:** At the time the information in this book was being confirmed, The Goodman Theatre was in the process of relocating to the Theater District. While the information reflected here is as up-to-date as possible, you may want to call to verify address, etc.

HOT TIX

108 North State Street, Chicago IL. ◆ WaterWorks Visitor Center, 163 East Peason (at North Michigan Avenue), Chicago IL. ◆ Tower Records, 214 South Wabash Avenue, Chicago IL. ◆ Tower Records, 2301 North Clark Street, Chicago IL. **The Lowdown:** If you enjoy a night at the theater but can't quite afford the always-rising ticket prices, Hot Tix is the answer. Operated by The League of Chicago Theaters, these theater ticket and information centers offer half-price tickets to more than 125 Chicago venues. Tickets are available the day of the performance Tuesday through Sunday. Tickets for weekend and Monday performances (Hot Tix booths are closed on Monday) are available at the State Street location only starting at 5:00 p.m. on Thursday. You take your chances, of course, on what may be offered on any given evening; but among the companies and venues frequently offered are The Steppenwolf, Royal George, Auditorium Theater, Theater Building, Second City, Live Bait, Drury Lane, and Candlelight Dinner Playhouse. You must buy your tickets in person at any of the booths, paying either by cash or credit card. Each branch of Hot Tix is also a Ticketmaster outlet, selling full-price tickets (cash only) to all other events like concerts and sporting events. Open Sunday, 12:00 p.m. - 5:00 p.m.; Tuesday through Saturday, 10:00 a.m. - 6:00 p.m.; closed Monday.

LIVE BAIT THEATER

3914 North Clark Street, Chicago IL 60613. 773/871-1212. **World Wide Web address:** http://www.livebaittheater.org. **The Lowdown:** Live Bait Theatre is so named because they want to lure people in and hook their audiences. They do present some of the best in new local theater work. Ticket prices are generally in the $10.00 - $15.00 range. Mr. C knew there had to be a cheaper way! Well, there is, in the form of two series that offer lower-priced tickets. For you night owls, there's the Late Night series, shows usually offered on Friday and Saturday nights at 11:00 p.m. Tickets for these shows are more affordable at $5.00 - $10.00. Live Bait also offers an Off-Night series. These shows, featuring a variety of local troupes, generally have an 8:00 p.m. curtain on Mondays, Tuesdays, and Wednesdays. Ticket prices range from $5.00 to $10.00 for these as well. And for the best deal yet, consider attending a preview performance of the mainstage shows for free. It doesn't get any cheaper than that!

NEO-FUTURARIUM THEATRE

5153 North Ashland Avenue, Chicago IL 60640. 773/275-5255. **The Lowdown:** During the last decade or so, this ambitious company has written and presented over 3,500 plays. Honestly. How do they do it? Well, most of the plays are only two to three minutes long. In fact, the claim of their hit show, *Too Much Light Makes the Baby Go Blind*, is that you will see 30 plays in 60 minutes! (and they actually do manage to pull it off). Every aspect of this company and their show is given some clever twist. For starters, their home is upstairs from a funeral parlor. Admission is $4.00 plus one roll of a die; in other words, $5.00 - $10.00 randomly. You're asked your name on the way in, and given a name tag with something nonsensical on it instead. Then, there are the mini-plays themselves. There are indeed 30 to choose from, with titles like *Dysfunctional House Cleaning, Leslie the Lobster Speaks Out*, and *Lusia and Diana Can Talk Openly About Sex, But It Is Heather Who Can Say the Big Words With Ease*. These are all developed in advance by the cast, with new titles added each week, hence the prolific volume. The plays are all numbered; the audience shouts out which one it wants to see next, but the actors usually manage to fit them all in anyway. It's a wild, fast-paced, and decidedly different evening of theater, offered Fridays and Saturdays at 11:30 p.m., and Sunday evenings at 7:00 p.m. Best of all, if they sell out, they order out! Pizza, that is (for the audience of course). The Neo-Futurarium Theatre also offers a full season of 8:00 p.m. world premieres that range from interactive versions of *Crime and Punishment* to full-length adaptations of Kafka – all for a heck of a lot less than you'd pay for a movie and popcorn.

STAGE LEFT THEATRE
3408 North Sheffield Avenue, Chicago IL 60657. 773/883-8830. **E-mail address:** SLTChicago@aol.com. **World Wide Web address:** http://members.aol.com/SLTChicago. **The Lowdown:** In the words of the company itself, Stage Left Theatre is "the only theater in Chicago dedicated to raising the level of debate on social and political issues." You can say that again. With a mission statement as in-depth and elaborate as that one, you can only imagine the profundity of their productions. Typical plays deal with the social, moral, and ethical decisions we are faced with every day. Tickets generally range in price from $10.00 - $20.00. In addition to their unique and always-interesting mainstage productions, State Left Theatre offers Downstage Left, a collaborative program that lets interested artists help in the development and production of new plays. For more information on what's happening at the theater, call or visit their Website.

STEPPENWOLF THEATRE COMPANY
1650 North Halsted Street, Chicago IL 60614. 312/335-1650. **World Wide Web address:** http://www.steppenwolf.org. **The Lowdown:** When three young students decided to set up the informal Steppenwolf Theater Company in 1974, it was probably unthinkable to them that the theater would still be around (and prospering) today. But then again, when you count the talent of Gary Sinise among one of the dedicated founders, it's really not that surprising. With an unprecedented amount of critical recognition and acclaim, the Steppenwolf Theatre

Company is one of the world's premiere professional theater companies. Their secret to success is simple: uncompromising excellence. Among the actors who have shown their stuff on the Steppenwolf stage are John Malkovich, Joan Allen, and John Mahoney. Yet, aside from dynamic acting, the Steppenwolf Theatre Company is dedicated to fostering excellence in stage writing and direction as well. It's a formula that seems to work; tickets to many Steppenwolf productions are often hard to come by. While tickets to the main stage productions can sometimes be a bit pricey (around $40.00), there are some budget-friendly options. One hour before the curtain rises, rush tickets go on sale at half price. You can stop by the box office to receive these tickets. In addition to the main stage productions, Steppenwolf offers a number of other entertainment options. Steppenwolf Studio production tickets are usually right around $20.00. These too can be had for half-price (when available) an hour before the performance. The Traffic series is described as a performing arts "intersection," where music, poetry, storytelling, and theater all merge into one place. Tickets are around $25.00. Tickets to the more experimental Steppenwolf Garage shows (held just a few steps away at 1626 North Halsted Street) are just $10.00 apiece. The Steppenwolf Arts Exchange is another branch of the theater, where Chicago is the topic of choice. Tickets are $10.00 each. Each year, in keeping with their mission of fostering talent, Steppenwolf develops and presents four New Play Labs. Four playwrights are selected from around the world and encouraged to work with a group of carefully-selected peers to create and execute a brand-new production.

TOMMY GUN'S GARAGE
1239 South State Street, Chicago IL 60605. 773/RAT-ATAT. **Toll-free phone:** 800/461-0178. **World Wide Web address:** http://www.tommygunsgarage.com. **The Lowdown:** Before Jerry Springer's panel of guests stole the title of the Windy City's scariest group of people, Al Capone and his gangster buddies ruled the town. With prohibition in effect, he and his cohorts set up illegal drinking establishments all over town. Since that time, the speakeasy has been glamorized and has come to be known as one of Chicago's most notable cultural offerings. In the spirit of Capone and his curmudgeons, Tommy Gun's Garage brings the secrecy of good food, drink, and entertainment back to Chicago. This interactive speakeasy is a hilarious comedy and dinner show where you'll become part of the action. Prices fluctuate with the dinner you choose and the night of the week you attend. For the best deals, visit on a Thursday or Sunday, and choose the pasta or chicken ($38.00 per person). If you attend on a Thursday or Sunday, prices range from $38.00 - $43.00; Friday prices are $42.00 - $47.00; Saturday's prices are $45.00 - $50.00. These prices include your admission for the show as well as your dinner (which includes soup or salad, bread and butter, entree, dessert, and a non-alcoholic beverage). If you're looking to come in a large enough group, special prices can be arranged. Shows take place Thursday through Sunday. But, just like any secretive event, you'll need to call so "you's can get da password." You won't be allowed in without it... after all, you could be a copper!

Walks & Tours

BIKE CHICAGO RENTAL & TOURS

P.O. Box 87490, Chicago IL 60680. 312/755-0488. **Toll-free phone:** 800/915-BIKE. **E-mail address:** bikechicago@aol.com. **The Lowdown:** Biking along Chicago's magnificent lakefront (with 18 miles of bike lanes) is the perfect way to tour the city, get some exercise, and enjoy the fresh air. Bike Chicago offers rentals and tours at two different lakefront locations. For $8.00 an hour ($30.00 a day), you can pedal around the city on either a rented mountain bike or a comfortable cruiser bicycle. Bike Chicago also offers kids' bikes, inline skates, quadricycles, 4-wheelers, and even tandem bicycles that can be used by the hour or the day. The tours are open to all ages and all fitness levels, and you'll be able to view the city's architecture, and history in a way that no guided tour bus can show you. Stop by either of their convenient locations at Navy Pier (600 East Grand Avenue) or North Avenue Beach. Bike Chicago is open for business from April through October. Open daily, 8:00 a.m. - 10:00 p.m.

CHICAGO ARCHITECTURE FOUNDATION

224 South Michigan Avenue, Chicago IL 60604. 312/922-3432. **World Wide Web address:** http://www.architecture.org. **The Lowdown:** Chicago is renowned worldwide for its architecture, and the Chicago Architecture Foundation is amply prepared to show you why, through free exhibitions and lectures at their home office, as well as guided tours all around the city. Chicago Architecture Foundation conducts more than 65 different tours throughout the year. While the bus tours can lean toward the expensive side ($15.00 - $35.00 per person), any Cheapster should have no problem affording one of their many walking tours that range in price from free - $10.00. You can save even more money by booking more than one tour at a time. Historic Skycrapers will introduce you to the work of Louis Sullivan and teach you to recognize such famous details as Chicago windows. Modern Skycrapers features the work of Mies van der Rohe and explores post-WWII architectural developments. Both of these tours run daily, 363 days a year. The Frank Lloyd Wright tour takes you through the quiet streets of Oak Park, home to the largest concentration of his designs. It winds up with a stroll through Wright's actual home and studio. The Prairie Avenue Historic District takes you to Clarke House (Chicago's oldest building) and Glessner House (a 19th-century structure by H.H. Richardson). CAF also sponsors Wednesday Lunchtime Lectures at 12:15 p.m. in their lecture hall. These are brown bag affairs and the lecture lasts for about 45 minutes. Lectures are free and open to the public. Recent lectures have such topics as the proposed world's tallest skyscraper, Chicago's new Millennium Park, landmark issues, landscape design, historical neighborhoods, and urban planning. If you don't live in Chicago but are a frequent visitor, Chicago Architecture Foundation offers

a great National Associate membership package. People who live at least 100 miles outside of the city, can become members for as little as $30.00 - $40.00. What does this fee include? It will allow you to go on over 50 tours absolutely free and give you two-for-one admission to the Architecture River Cruise, an activity that was voted the number one tourist activity by local concierges. National Associates will also gain access to the membership hotline, which will provide you with an easy way to make reservations to these popular tours. For further information on tours, times, and prices, give them a call. If you have access to the Internet, visit their Website; when you enter the days that you will be touring the Chicago area, they will provide you with a list of tours that are happening at that time. If you don't get a chance to take one of the tours, you can still enjoy all the CAF has to offer by visiting one of their Shop & Tour Centers in the Santa Fe Center at 224 South Michigan Avenue or in the John Hancock Center at 875 North Michigan Avenue.

CHICAGO BOARD OF TRADE
141 West Jackson Boulevard, Chicago IL 60604-2994. 312/435-3590. **World Wide Web address:** http://www.cbot.com. **The Lowdown:** In a gallery one level above the trading floor, the Chicago Board of Trade will provide a free 30-minute tour which explains the history of the exchange. This above-the-scenes look, including a short film, will show you how the trading of financial futures and agricultural commodities works. Explanations are given every half hour. Please be aware that children under the age of 16 will not be allowed. The Visitors Gallery is open Monday through Friday, 9:00 a.m. - 2:00 p.m.

CHICAGO MOTOR COACH COMPANY
3903 South Halsted, Chicago IL 60609. 312/922-8919. **Toll-free phone:** 800/DDB-USES. **World Wide Web address:** http://www.chicagomotorcoach.com. **The Lowdown:** Want to see the Windy City from a whole new perspective? Hop aboard one of Chicago Motor Coach Company's double decker buses and you can do just that. With stops all around town (Sears Tower, The Art Institute, The Field Museum, Navy Pier, The Water Tower), you can enjoy many popular sites and landmarks. Best of all, you can get off at any stop, explore for as long as you like, then hop back on the next bus to come around – they're only 15 minutes apart. Private tours are also available. The fare for unlimited one-day usage is $15.00 for adults; $12.00 for senior citizens; $8.00 for military personnel in uniform and children under 11.

CHICAGO STOCK EXCHANGE
440 South LaSalle Street (between Congress Parkway & Van Buren Street), Chicago IL 60605. 312/663-2222. **World Wide Web address:** http://www.chicagostockex.com. **The Lowdown:** Here's your opportunity to watch hundreds of people run around like crazy chasing after the almighty dollar. As the second largest stock exchange in America, you'll see plenty of action at the CHX. The fifth-floor gallery is free and open to the public. As you watch, instructional tapes explain what is happening on the

trading floor below. Meanwhile, you can enjoy the lively entertainment of watching all that money changing hands (comfortable in the knowledge that none of your own money. Group tours can be arranged, but due to staff constraints they can only give tours to college groups, investment groups, and the like. It may be worth a call to see if your group qualifies. Open Monday through Friday, 8:30 a.m. - 3:30 p.m.

CHICAGO TRIBUNE NEWSPAPER TOURS

435 North Michigan Avenue, Chicago IL 60611. 312/222-2116. **World Wide Web address:** http://www.chicagotribune.com. **The Lowdown:** For less than the price of a paper (in other words, absolutely free), you can tour the Chicago Tribune's Freedom Center. This houses the newspaper's five-story production and circulation facility. You'll see the paper's 10 offset printing presses (one of the largest press rooms in the world), learn about the history of the *Tribune* and its production, and find out about the telecommunications technology that allows the *Tribune* to print simultaneously in Illinois, Wisconsin and Michigan. I'll bet you didn't even know they could do that. The *Tribune* will conduct tours for up to 50 people, but there must be at least one chaperone for every 15 children. Children under 10 will not be admitted. Reservations are required.

ELI'S CHEESECAKE WORLD

6701 West Forest Preserve, Chicago IL 60634. 773/736-3417. **World Wide Web address:** http://www.elicheesecake.com. **The Lowdown:** The history of Eli's Cheesecake World is about as varied as their menu. It was in 1977 that Eli began serving up cheesecake at his hotspot of a restaurant, Eli's The Place For Steak. This delicious dessert finished off the meals of all the old Hollywood comedians and celebrities who used to traipse through the door: Henny Youngman and the entire Rat Pack were just a few of the patrons. Causing such a stir at the restaurant, Eli decided to make this delicious dessert more accessible to the public and introduced Eli's Cheesecake at the 1980 Taste of Chicago. Since that time, many a local and national celebration have called for the unparalleled quality and taste of Eli's Cheesecake. At the 150th birthday celebration for Chicago, Eli baked the official birthday cake – a 1,500 pound cheesecake; Eli got more festive (and more ingredients) to bake the 2,000 pound red, white, and blue cheesecake served at Bill Clinton's 1993 and 1997 inaugurations; political heavyweights called upon Eli again in 1997 when First Lady Hillary Clinton celebrated her 50th birthday. Now it's your turn to see what all the fuss is about by taking a tour of Eli's Cheesecake World (and taking home a bit of the cheesecake). The cost is just $3.00 for adults, and $2.00 for children under 12. Tours are given Sunday, from 12:00 p.m. - 3:00 p.m.; and Monday through Saturday, from 10:00 a.m. - 3:00 p.m. The daily 12:00 p.m. tour is open for walk-ins, but for any other time you must call and schedule an appointment. If booking a tour for a large group, you must call at least two weeks in advance. For more information, call or visit their Website... and don't forget to send a piece to me!

J.C. CUTTERS

1532 North Kingsbury, Chicago IL 60622. 773/735-9400. **E-mail address:** jccutters@jccutters.com. **World Wide Web address:** http://www.jccutters.com. **The Lowdown:** Why not do it like they did in the old days and tour the city via horse-drawn carriage? Take a step back in time and ride around through the scenic areas of downtown Chicago. Tours encompass the Lakefront, The Magnificent Mile, Washington Square Park, the Gold Coast, the Chicago River, and other locales of historical influence. Tour prices start at $35.00 for a half-hour and the carriages can fit up to four or six adults; when you do the math, it's not too shabby! Hours are Monday through Friday, 7:00 p.m. - 1:00 a.m.; Saturday, 1:00 p.m. - 2:00 a.m.; Sunday, 1:00 p.m. - 1:00 a.m.

JOHN HANCOCK CENTER OBSERVATORY

875 North Michigan Avenue, 94th Floor, Chicago IL 60611. 312/751-3681. **Toll-free phone:** 888/875-VIEW. **World Wide Web address:** http://www.hancock-observatory.com. **The Lowdown:** At more than 1,000 feet above North Michigan Avenue, when one envisions the typical Chicago cityscape, it is this building that they think of. Your adventure begins the minute you step into the building as the world's fastest elevators (they travel at warp speed: 1,800 feet per minute) whisk you all the way up to the 94th floor in a mere 39 seconds. As you enter the admission area, you might be disappointed to see that there's some serious construction going on; don't be deterred, this is actually part of the entertainment. Before entering into this massive structure you have only heard about, you can view the building's blue prints and photographs of the original construction; a five-minute video will further enhance your experience. But wait, you haven't even made it to the observatory yet. Skywalk – which has heated floors for those legendary winters – is a section of the observatory where all the glass has been removed. If you're only in town for a short while, the Windows on Chicago virtual reality kiosks are a great way to see all the sites. Pick and choose from more than 80 sites (including The Art Institute of Chicago, Lincoln Park Zoo, or center court at a Bulls game) and virtually transplant yourself. Six Soundscope machines will let you watch and listen to what is transpiring below. History buffs will love the history walls, where they can observe some of the city's most famous events, from the great fire in 1871 to 1919 White Sox scandal. Though it's easy to get caught up in all this nifty technology and fun, don't forget to glance out at the view. On a clear day, Illinois, Indiana, Michigan, and Wisconsin can all be within your visual field. While I don't often like to pick favorites in any city, I highly suggest making this place a must-see on your list of things to do. Admission is $8.75 for adults, $6.75 for seniors, $6.00 for children under 12, and free to kids under four. Open daily, 9:00 a.m. - 12:00 a.m.

OAK PARK VISITORS CENTER

158 Forest Avenue, Oak Park IL 60301. 708/848-1500. **The Lowdown:** If you're looking to step just outside of the city

for a day, The Oak Park Visitors Center has a number of ways to enjoy this suburb. One-time home to the famous architect Frank Lloyd Wright, there are two main tours that focus on his creations. One focuses on Wright's home and studio; the other is a tour of 13 Wright-designed homes in the Forest Avenue area. Admission to each is $8.00, and $6.00 for senior citizens and children under 18. For a bargain deal, you can purchase a package and get both for $14.00; $10.00 for senior citizens and children under 18. Children under 10 are free at all times. The Visitors Center also offers a self-guided audio walking tour that will take you through one of the "Prettiest Painted Places in America" – The Ridgeland Historic District of Oak Park – where you can view the exteriors of more than 15 "painted ladies." See the evolution of architecture from the early Victorian period, to the Prairie School of Architecture, to the Art Deco craze of the 1950s. Hear the reflections of the famous people who walked these streets, nurtured their creativity, and brought international recognition to this place they called home. Audio tours can be taken daily, 10:00 a.m. - 3:30 p.m. The cost is $6.00 for adults, $4.00 for senior citizens and children. But wait, there's more to see in Oak Park! The Unity Temple tour takes you through this national historic landmark edifice, built in 1905 and dubbed by Wright as his "little jewel." Admission is $6.00 for adults, $4.00 for students and seniors. If you visit on a weekend, that price drops to $5.00 for adults, $3.00 for students and seniors. Oak Park's Pleasant Home Tour takes you around the 1987 estate designed by architect George Maher. This includes the Oak Park & River Forest Historical Society collections displayed on the second floor. Admission is $5.00 for adults, $3.00 for children. One of the most popular tourist spots is the recently-restored birthplace of Ernest Hemingway (http://www.hemingway.org). Come and see the Victorian home where the Nobel Prize-winning author was born in 1899, and learn about his early life. Explore the museum displaying rare photos of Hemingway, his childhood diary, letters, early writings, and other memorabilia. You can also sit back and enjoy videos documenting the author's life and work. Admission is $6.00 for adults, $4.50 for seniors and children. If you want to make an entire day of it (and there's plenty here to do just that), you should think of picking up a combination ticket. For $15.00, you can gain admission to Unity Temple, Hemingway Birthplace and Museum, Pleasant Home & Historical Society, and one of those great audio tours.

SEARS TOWER SKYDECK
233 South Wacker Drive, Chicago IL 60606. 312/875-9696. **World Wide Web address:** http://www.sears-tower.com. **The Lowdown:** Okay, so this view may be a little more expensive than some other skydecks, but it is, after all, one of the world's tallest buildings. The observatory is, in fact, on the 103rd floor of this 110-story giant, located in the financial district. The observatory is open every day of the year and, once you're up there, they won't kick you out until it's time to close. Admission is $8.50 for adults; $6.50 for senior citizens; $5.50 for children ages five - 12; children four and under are free. Open 365 days a year; 9:00 a.m. - 11:00 p.m.

TOUR BLACK CHICAGO

35 East Wacker Drive, Suite 222, Chicago IL 60601. 312/332-2323. **E-mail address:** tbchgo@ameritech.net. **World Wide Web address:** http://www.tourblackchicago.com. **The Lowdown:** Immerse yourself in Chicago's populous African-American culture by allowing Tour Black Chicago to serve as your guide to the city. Each tour highlights prominent black leaders in business, art, sports, government, war, the church, and Chicago society in general. The tour guides will educate and entertain you on both well-known and little-known facts of African American culture in Chicago. You'll see the DuSable Museum of African American History (see separate listing), the Quinn Chapel, the South Side Community Art Center, and the Elliot Donnelly Youth Center, to name a few. You might think you know Chicago, but unless you know its culture, you must try Tour Black Chicago. **Cheap Deal:** Readers who mention *Mr. Cheap's Chicago* will receive a $2.00 discount.

UGLYDUCK CRUISES

401 East Illinois Avenue, Suite 425, Chicago IL 60611. 630/916-9007. **E-mail address:** info@uglyduckcruises.com. **World Wide Web address:** http://www.uglyduckcruises.com. **The Lowdown:** Eat, drink, and set sail! Here is a fun and unique way to see the city while wining and dining. Aboard the Uglyduck, you are free to roam around the spacious decks while gazing back at the Chicago skyline. Or, simply sit back and enjoy the view from your table. Choose from lunch, midday, dinner and moonlight cruise packages. Ticket prices include full buffets (midday, cocktail, and moonlight cruises include hors d'oeuvres), cruise, and entertainment. The meals alone are well-worth setting sail. Menu items include sage roasted chicken, mustard crusted white fish, and vegetable primavera. Prices range from $18.00 to $55.00 per person. Please call for specific times. Cruises depart from Navy Pier.

UNTOUCHABLE TOURS

610 North Clark Street, Chicago IL. 773/881-1195. **The Lowdown:** Besides pizza and big buildings, what is Chicago best known for? Gangsters, of course. This two-hour bus tour will take you to the haunts of some of the city's most notorious mobsters and the sites of all their most news-worthy happenings. Tours cost $22.00 for adults, $16.00 for children (ages 15 and under). You must call ahead to make reservations. Tour times are Sunday, 11:00 a.m. & 2:00 p.m.; Monday through Wednesday, 10:00 a.m.; Thursday, 10:00 a.m. & 1:00 p.m.; Friday, 10:00 a.m., 1:00 a.m. & 7:30 p.m.; Saturday, 10:00 a.m., 1:00 p.m. & 5:00 p.m.

WENDELLA BOATS

400 North Michigan Avenue, Chicago IL 60611. 312/337-1446. **World Wide Web address:** http://www.wendellaboats.com. **The Lowdown:** As a city surrounded by major waterways, Chicago makes the most of its river and lake by offering lots of entertainment options via boat. Wendella Boats is the city's oldest sightseeing boat tour. Started in 1935 by Albert

Borgstrom, Wendella Boats is now operated by the son and grandson of the original founder. Though there are a few different paths you can take, each Wendella tour is narrated by a longtime Chicago expert who knows all about the history and architecture of the city. The boats are equipped with bathrooms and a snack bar, and you are welcome to bring your own food aboard as well. The basic tour is a 90-minute jaunt that traverses both the Chicago River and Lake Michigan. Tours depart several times throughout the day, about 90-minutes apart from one another (tours begin at 10:00 a.m. with the last one leaving at 8:30 p.m.). The cost $14.00 for adults, $12.00 for senior citizens, and $7.00 for children. If 90 minutes is a bit too long, try the one-hour ride on Lake Michigan that departs at 5:45 p.m. Tickets for this journey are $12.00 for adults, $10.00 for seniors, and $6.00 for children. Wendella also offers a two-hour nighttime tour that will give you everything the other tours have and then some! This super-duper tour departs nightly at 7:30 p.m. and costs $16.00 for adults, $14.00 for seniors, and $8.00 for kids. Wendella Boats operate between April and October. Tickets can be purchased an hour before departure. Tours depart from the north bank of the Chicago River at the Wrigley Building. Wendella Boats also operate a RiverBus service. For only $2.00 per person, you can ride this water taxi between Madison Street (near the Sears Tower) and Michigan Avenue and River East (near Navy Pier). For more information, call or visit their Website. *$Cash Only$*

LODGING

| Alternative |

NOTE: Hotel rates can vary based on day of week, season, and special events/holidays. The prices listed in Mr. Cheap's are reflective of the average price you can expect to pay at each establishment. Please contact each location for specific rates.

ARLINGTON HOUSE INTERNATIONAL HOSTEL
616 West Arlington Place, Chicago IL 60614. 773/929-5380. **Toll-free phone:** 800/467-8355. **The Lowdown:** If you're visiting Chicago with the intention of living up the night life and meeting new people, you'll need accommodations that allow you 24-hour access and a friendly atmosphere. Arlington House International Hostel, in Lincoln Park, is just such a place. Rooms are set up in a shared dormitory-style, with some rooms housing up to seven people. This will provide you with a great opportunity to meet other travelers. With a kitchen, free luggage storage, common TV room, laundry room, and private bathrooms, Arlington House International Hostel makes every effort to keep its residents comfortable. Rates run about $40.00 - $60.00 a night for private rooms and $20.00 a night for a semi-private room.

CENTENNIAL HOUSE OF LINCOLN PARK
1020 West Altgeld Street, Chicago IL 60614. 773/871-6020. **E-mail address:** centennialhouse1@aol.com. **World Wide Web address:** http://members.aol.com/centlhouse. **The Lowdown:** Who says you have to sacrifice luxury for the sake of a budget? In this 1891 Victorian house, you'll feel like you've stepped back in time to an era of decadence, yet still feel comfortable with the modern amenities that hostess Fran Ramer provides. You can stay in Elizabeth's Place, a six-room apartment that includes an eat-in kitchen and formal dining room, with up to four other guests; or in Alice's Annex, a three-room suite complete with a kitchenette and dining nook, with up to six other people. Both apartments are fully-furnished and decorated with vintage antiques. Children over the age of six are always welcome. Rates for Elizabeth's Place average $115.00 - $185.00 a night or $650.00 - $1,250 weekly. Alice's Annex can be had for $95.00 - $185.00 a night, or $650.00 - $1,250.00 weekly. If you're planning an extended stay, monthly rates can also be negotiated.

CHICAGO INTERNATIONAL HOSTEL
6318 North Winthrop Avenue, Chicago IL 60660. 773/262-1011. **The Lowdown:** For the truly ascetic, a hostel is *the* way to save big money while traveling. What many folks don't realize, though, is that you don't have to be a foreigner to stay in one. For a mere $15.00 a night, anyone can stay at the Chicago International Hostel, located well uptown on the North Side. Since the hostel is often booked months in advance by foreign

travelers and adventurous students, it's a good idea to reserve early. There's not much to do in the neighborhood, but Lincoln Park is not too far away, and it's just a 25 minute train ride to get downtown. The amenities aren't luxurious by any stretch of the imagination, but towels and linens are provided. They'll also be happy to serve you up a fresh cup of coffee in the morning (for free) before you hit the town. The hostel is open from 7:00 a.m. - 10:00 a.m. and 4:00 p.m. - 12:00 a.m. only. In between, they figure, you'll be gallivanting about the town. That midnight curfew is strictly in effect all week, but on Friday and Saturday nights, doors open again at 2:00 a.m. to let stragglers back in. If you arrive back at the hostel after midnight during the week, or after the 2:00 a.m. "last chance" on weekends, you're probably going to have to wait until 7:00 a.m. to be let inside. Tough as all that sounds, most people who stay here have no trouble complying. Payment may only be made in cash, money order, or traveler's check. No personal checks or credit cards are ever accepted. Hostels certainly aren't the choice for everyone; but if you live the simple life, they can sure save you a lot of money. *$Cash Only$*

FLEMISH HOUSE OF CHICAGO

68 East Cedar Street, Chicago IL 60611. 312/664-9981. **World Wide Web address:** http://www.bestinns.net/usa/il/flemish.html. **The Lowdown:** Believe it or not, it *is* possible to stay in Chicago's affluent Gold Coast neighborhood and keep your budget intact. Forget the mainstream route of a hotel and consider opting for a bed and breakfast; the price *and* the accommodations just might surprise you. The Flemish House of Chicago consists of beautifully-appointed Victorian-style studio and one-bedroom apartments (some even have fireplaces). The high ceilings, antique fixtures, and huge amount of space only add to this place's charm. The Flemish House of Chicago is perfect for any type of trip: romantic, business, or otherwise. Mr. C knows, he's done much of his work from right inside this great place. Owners Mike Maczka and Tom Warnke are two of the city's most hospitable hosts; they've left nothing to chance by stocking extra *everything*! Unlike a traditional bed and breakfast, Flemish House of Chicago has no main sitting area or living room; your continental breakfast is brought to your room the night before and packed away into your fridge. If you decide that you want to leave this place at all, you are within walking distance of Oak Street Beach, the Magnificent Mile, some of the city's best restaurants, and the always-exciting night life at the Rush/Division intersection. Sure, there are plenty of high-priced hotels in the area, but why pay more when a spectacular room and fabulous hosts are awaiting your arrival at Flemish House of Chicago? Tell them Mr. Cheap sent you!

GOLD COAST GUEST HOUSE

113 West Elm Street, Chicago IL 60610. 312/337-0361. **E-mail address:** Sally@bbchicago.com. **World Wide Web address:** http://www.bbchicago.com. **The Lowdown:** Now here is one choice of accommodation that everyone should be clamoring for. If you're a bit tired of the same old hotel/motel grind, choosing a

bed and breakfast can be a pleasurable diversion from the norm. Gold Coast Guest House offers four guest suites in one of the city's most desirable areas. This Victorian townhouse dates back to 1873, just after the Great Chicago Fire. Gold Coast Guest House offers excellent amenities in a beautiful setting. Each of the suites have air-conditioning, ceiling fans, TV/VCR, CD player, hairdryers, and many of your necessary toiletries. You can even choose a suite with a whirlpool tub and additional working space. A 20-foot window-wall faces the B&B's small, lush garden so that guests can bird-watch while enjoying a delicious continental breakfast or relaxing in the living room. Cardinals, sparrows, mourning doves, and finch call the garden's grape arbor home. All this and the tasteful blend of antiques and contemporary furnishings prompted AAA Motor Club to award Gold Coast Guest House a Three Diamond rating! While most B&Bs don't boast such hotel standards as a fitness center, Gold Coast Guest House has an arrangement with the nearby Multiplex Health Club. For a small fee, you can gain an all-access pass to their full-service fitness center. And while there is no business center *at* Gold Coast Guest House,there is a Kinko's a mere two blocks away. Also within walking distance are restaurants, nighttime hotspots, the Lake, the park, and The Magnificent Mile. If you're looking to house more than just yourself and a guest, they'll be happy to rent all four rooms to your corporation. Rates start at just $129.00 nightly per room and range up to $199.00. They also offer special long-term rates to those customers who just can't bring themselves to leave! Garage parking is available for an extra $15.00 per night. Gold Coast Guest House is a non-smoking and pet-free establishment. If you're planning on bringing the brood, kids must be over 12 to stay here. However long your visit, you're sure to enjoy this home away from home in the heart of the Gold Coast.

THE HERITAGE BED & BREAKFAST REGISTRY

75 East Wacker Drive, Suite 3600, Chicago IL 60601. 312/857-0800. **Toll-free phone:** 800/431-5546. **E-mail address:** heritageregistry@ibm.net. **World Wide Web address:** http://www.heritageregistry.com. **The Lowdown:** If you want to experience the city as a street-savvy Chicagoan does, look for accommodations that will allow you to live like one. The Heritage Bed & Breakfast Registry has screened a number of area bed & breakfasts and developed a list of both hosted and unhosted accommodations throughout the city. All you have to do is call The Heritage Bed & Breakfast Registry and let the staff know your needs; they'll do all the work to find you the most comfortable accommodations. Hosted accommodations consist of extra rooms in a house or apartment which are rented out to guests. If you choose this type of lodging, you'll benefit from the insider recommendations provided by your host, as well as the continental breakfasts each morning. Unhosted accommodations are a better choice for individuals seeking privacy; the host hands over an apartment or suite for your own personal use. You won't have a continental breakfast prepared for you with unhosted accommodations, but the host will stock breakfast items in the refrigerator for you. Whichever type you choose,

rates are likely to range between $95.00 and $165.00. Be aware that these bed & breakfasts require a two-night minimum. The Heritage provides full concierge services to all guests including dinner reservations, theater or event tickets, and car or cell phone rental. You'll have all the freedom of being home with the luxury of being on vacation.

THE HOUSE OF TWO URNS BED & BREAKFAST

1239 North Greenview Avenue, Chicago IL 60622. 773/235-1408. **Toll-free phone:** 800/835-9303. **E-mail address:** twourns@earthlink.net. **World Wide Web address:** http://www.twourns.com. **The Lowdown:** Escape from the city without ever leaving Chicago. The House of Two Urns Bed & Breakfast is a winner in Mr. C's book because of its combination of low rates and friendly service. It's the only accommodation of its kind in the ultra-hip Wicker Park neighborhood. The hostess, Kapra Fleming, serves up a home-baked breakfast every morning. She also sells CTA visitor passes to guests and will be more than happy to recommend local eateries and attractions. The bed & breakfast is near theater, bicycling trails, beaches, and a wide selection of restaurants. Room rates generally range from $80.00 - $160.00 per night.

McCORMICK STUDENT VILLAGE
ILLINOIS INSTITUTE OF TECHNOLOGY

3241 South Wabash Avenue, Chicago IL 60616. 312/808-6505. **World Wide Web address:** http://www.iit.edu/~housing/summer. **The Lowdown:** Chicago lodging in the summer can be surprisingly inexpensive if you don't mind a no-frills, alternative residency. McCormick Student Village houses guests in single or double rooms in standard residence halls with shared bathrooms. It may not be glamorous, but it certainly is inexpensive. The lakefront, museums, and theaters are all nearby, you can be downtown with just a short ride. McCormick Student Village opens its doors to you from early June through mid-August. Whether you're looking for single or a double room, a stay here should cost you under $30.00 a night.

THREE ARTS CLUB OF CHICAGO RESIDENCE

1300 North Dearborn Parkway, Chicago IL 60610. 312/944-6250. **E-mail address:** info@threearts.org. **World Wide Web address:** http://threearts.org. **The Lowdown:** Located in the Gold Coast, the Three Arts Club of Chicago is an artists' residence and community cultural center. With a mission to support women artists and to provide diverse cultural programming for the public, it's no wonder the Three Arts Club offers a number of amenities to suit the artist at heart. For any artistic whim you may have, Three Arts Club has the resources to accommodate, including a visual arts studio, two grand pianos, and rehearsal space. The residency provides daily breakfast and dinner, towels, linens, and a coin-operated laundry room. Rates run $45.00 nightly; $250.00 weekly; and $750.00 monthly. Reservations are required and may be made through the housing office. While Three Arts Club is a women-only residence in from September through May, they do allow male residents in the summer.

WOODED ISLE SUITES

5750 South Stony Island Avenue, Chicago IL 60637. 773/288-5578. **Toll-free phone:** 800/290-6844. **World Wide Web address:** http://www.woodedisle.com. **The Lowdown:** For the independent traveler looking to save a few dollars, renting a furnished apartment for your stay just might be the ticket to a budget-friendly visit. Charlie Havens, Sara Pitcher, and friends maintain the 13 apartments that make up Wooded Isle Suites. Think of the money you'll save with your own kitchen; you don't have to rely on innkeepers to prepare your breakfast, nor do you have to dish out big bucks at a different restaurant every day. There is no food provided, but your hosts will supply you with enough coffee and herbal tea necessities to keep you wired for weeks. For entertainment, you can enjoy the urban escape of the courtyard flower garden, or go to any of the many nearby attractions including the Museum of Science & Industry, University of Chicago, The David and Alfred Smart Museum, or the 57th Street Beach. Rates can range from $130.00 a night for a studio apartment to $160.00 a night for a one-bedroom apartment.

Hotels & Motels

NOTE: *Hotel rates can vary based on day of week, season, and special events/ holidays. The prices listed in Mr. Cheap's are reflective of the average price you can expect to pay at each establishment. Please contact each location for specific rates.*

BEST WESTERN GRANT PARK
1100 South Michigan Avenue, Chicago IL 60605. 312/922-2900. **Toll-free phone:** 800/528-1234. **World Wide Web address:** http://www.bestwestern.com/grantparkhotel. **The Lowdown:** This 172-room hotel is often the choice of school groups and European tourists, since it's located near The Art Institute, Shedd Aquarium, Adler Planetarium, and The Field Museum. It's just a few blocks south of the Loop, and close to the charm of Printer's Row shops and restaurants. McCormick Place is also just a short bus ride to the south, so convention-goers also make a point of booking this hotel (sometimes many months in advance). For as little as $99.00 a night, your stay will include an outdoor pool and a small exercise room. Valet parking – with in and out privileges – is available for $15.00. Free coffee and a newspaper are just a few of the perks you'll wake up to. If you're looking to up your amenities (and the price), you can snag one of their suites, which offer all of the above and then some. Kids under 17 are always invited to stay for free. It's two blocks away from the Roosevelt stop on the Howard-Dan Ryan subway line, and taxis pass through the area quite frequently. A word of caution: Though you're still on Michigan Avenue, the neighborhood is far enough away from the Magnificent Mile to get a bit rough at night, so do be careful. For its price and location, this is a great pick if you're in town to see the sights.

BEST WESTERN HAWTHORNE TERRACE
3434 North Broadway Avenue, Chicago IL 60657. 773/244-3434. **World Wide Web address:** http://www.hawthorneterrace.com. **The Lowdown:** If you're in town to catch a Cubs game, you'll want to stay near Wrigley Field; it just so happens that the closest hotel is also one of the most affordable. Some of the hotel's many amenities include a complimentary breakfast and morning paper, a fitness center, and valet parking. Some rooms even come equipped with microwaves and refrigerators. Best Western Hawthorne Terrace is located close to lots of great eateries, and Lincoln Park is not too far away. Rooms start around $120.00 for a standard room and suites can be had for around $150.00.

BEST WESTERN INN OF CHICAGO
162 East Ohio Street, Chicago IL 60611. 312/787-3100. **The Lowdown:** In the hotel business, a well-respected name, prime location, and reasonable price tag are a winning

combination, albeit a difficult one to find. Enter Best Western Inn of Chicago. Located in the heart of the city, the Inn's address makes it less than five blocks from Water Tower Place and the John Hancock Building and less than 10 blocks from the Art Institute, Navy Pier, and Grant Park. All well-appointed guest rooms come with an AM/FM alarm clock and cable television with HBO. If opting for a suite (they can sometime be had for just about $225.00, though they do range up to as much as $400.00), you'll also be treated to a hairdryer and a mini-bar. If you're traveling with kids, it's good to know that Best Western Inn of Chicago offers free accommodations to children under 18 who are staying with their parent or grandparent. Prices fluctuate – as with any hotel – but it shouldn't be hard to secure yourself a room for $150.00 - $180.00 or less at any time of year.

BEST WESTERN RIVER NORTH HOTEL
125 West Ohio Street, Chicago IL 60610. 312/467-0800. **Toll-free phone:** 800/528-1234. **World Wide Web address:** http://www.bestwestern.com. **The Lowdown:** No matter what your reason is for coming to Chicago, Best Western River North Hotel makes an excellent choice of accommodations. Some of the city's most glamorous shopping districts (read: The Magnificent Mile and Oak Street) are just a stone's throw away from this full-service hotel. And let's not forget the great live music venues, nightclubs, comedy clubs, and restaurants: all within walking distance. Did you come here for the culture? The Adler Planetarium, The Field Museum, and Shedd Aquarium are all less than two miles from the hotel. In Chicago on business? The Loop is just a mere six blocks south of the hotel, making this a favorite home away from home for business travelers looking to save a buck or two. If that's not enough, the hotel offers free parking including free in-and-out privileges. Other perks at the River North Hotel are its indoor pool and fitness center. If you're traveling with the family, keep in mind that children under 18 are allowed to stay for free when sharing a room with a parent or grandparent.

CASS HOTEL
640 North Wabash Avenue, Chicago IL 60611. 312/787-4030. **Toll-free phone:** 800/781-4030. **World Wide Web address:** http://www.casshotel.com. **The Lowdown:** "Welcome to the Downtown Chicago without the Downtown price!" That's the saying at Cass Hotel, and it's no lie. You're not likely to find another hotel in this area with rates so low. For one of the cheapest breakfast deals around, drop by the hotel coffee shop for their $1.99 continental breakfast. If it's lunch or dinner you're looking for, many of the city's most popular eating destinations are an easy walk from the hotel. Standard single rooms start as low as $69.00 per night.

CHICAGO TRAVELODGE DOWNTOWN
65 East Harrison Street, Chicago IL 60605. 312/427-8000. **Toll-free phone:** 312/427-7237. **The Lowdown:** Business and leisure travelers with an eye to the economical love this hotel for its reliable accommodations and inexpensive rates. Add to that

its central location – right in the heart of the business district and not too far from McCormick Place, Grant Park, and the Magnificent Mile – and you've got the perfect budget hotel. Rates generally range from $80.00 - $90.00 per night.

CITY SUITES HOTEL

933 West Belmont Avenue, Chicago IL 60657. 773/404-3400. **The Lowdown:** Admit it, when you think of a budget hotel, the first words that pop into mind are *small, cramped, stark*, maybe even *dingy*. Never would you think of a budget hotel that offers suite accommodations and a slew of great amenities. City Suites Hotel must be an exception to the rule, as they offer all the extras you'd find in a fancy hotel without the high price tag. Each suite has its own refrigerator, and each morning you'll be treated to a complimentary continental breakfast as well as a free morning newspaper. The hotel even features a fitness center, a golf course, and conference rooms. Prices generally range from $125.00 - $165.00 per night.

COMFORT INN LINCOLN PARK

601 West Diversey Parkway, Chicago IL 60614. 773/348-2810. **Toll-free phone:** 800/228-5150. **The Lowdown:** This national chain consistently offers great value for the money. And this branch, conveniently located in Lincoln Park (not far from the lake), certainly doesn't disappoint. Both the lobby, and the rooms are beautifully decorated with tasteful paintings, oak furnishings, and dramatic drapery. A complimentary continental breakfast is also provided. To please both the early birds and the late risers alike, breakfast is served from 6:30 a.m. - 10:30 a.m. Meanwhile, there's no shortage of restaurant choices outside the Inn (many of which are profiled in this book), with the eclectic offerings of Lincoln Avenue and Clark Street just a short walk away. Lincoln Park Zoo is around the corner, and Wrigley Field is not far in the other direction. Security in the Comfort Inn is exceptional too, with lobby areas carefully monitored by screen. Plus, while you're far enough away from the downtown hustle, you're close enough to be there with just a quick cab ride. Rates here vary widely, depending on the type of room you want. You could opt for a suite with a Jacuzzi/hot tub for as much as $250.00 a night, or play it on the less luxurious side with a small double for as little as $80.00.

CONGRESS PLAZA HOTEL

520 South Michigan Avenue, Chicago IL 60605. 312/427-3800. **Toll-free phone:** 800/635-1666. **World Wide Web address:** http://www.congresshotel.com. **The Lowdown:** Why does this hotel have such a political-sounding name? Well, it could be because Presidents Grover Cleveland and Theodore Roosevelt have both been guests here, but who knows. Located right across from Grant Park, the Congress Plaza Hotel offers more than 840 spacious rooms (many with city or lake views) at affordable prices. The Congress Plaza Hotel, built in 1893, was originally constructed to accommodate visitors to the World's Columbian Exposition. It's a good thing they've stuck around though, because plenty of tourists and businesspeople alike have been

able to enjoy all the city has to offer with a stay at this hotel. The Sears Tower, The Art Institute, and the Harold Washington Library are all within walking distance. Plus, you're never too far from some of the city's hottest restaurants and nightclubs. If you'd rather spend the night in the hotel, there are three restaurants and two bars to choose from. A complimentary and well-equipped fitness center will also keep you looking your best while traversing the city's hotspots. And, unless your looking for a suite, Congress Plaza Hotel offers some very good room rates. Standard and double guest rooms start at just $105.00 per night, and executive guest rooms start at $125.00. If you were hoping for a view of Lake Michigan, it's going to cost you... anywhere between $145.00 and $185.00 per night, that is. Suites, which start at a still-affordable $250.00, can range all the way up to $750.00 a night!

DAYS INN LINCOLN PARK NORTH
644 West Diversey Parkway, Chicago IL 60614. 773/525-7010. **Toll-free phone:** 888/LPN-DAYS. **E-mail address:** daysinn.lpn@worldnet.att.net. **World Wide Web address:** http://www.lpndaysinn.com. **The Lowdown:** Located just about a mile from Wrigley Field and nestled among the comfortable residential feel of the Lincoln Park neighborhood, Days Inn Lincoln Park North is the highest-rated Days Inn in all of Illinois. Rooms are well-appointed and complimentary continental breakfast is included. Prices start around $80.00 a night (though they can range up to over $200.00).

HAMPTON INN & SUITES CHICAGO RIVER NORTH
33 West Illinois Street, Chicago IL. 312/832-0330. **World Wide Web address:** http://www.hamptoninn-suites.com. **The Lowdown:** You want it all: a clean, comfortable, affordable, and centrally located hotel. The Hampton Inn & Suites has all of these qualities and more. Suites are a particularly good deal for traveling families, as they're quite spacious. Plus, all the excitement of North Michigan Avenue, River North, and the Gold Coast areas are completely within walking distance. Rates are usually between $199.00 and $229.00.

HOMEWOOD SUITES CHICAGO
40 East Grand Avenue, Chicago IL 60611. 312/644-2222. **Toll-free phone:** 800/CAL-LHOMxE. **World Wide Web address:** http://www.homewood-suites.com. **The Lowdown:** If you've got kids and DisneyQuest on your agenda (see separate listing), why not stay somewhere convenient... like in the same building? As part of the Hilton family of hotels, Homewood Suites offers a name you can trust and a price you can count on to be reasonable. In addition to a desirable location (the hotel is within a short walking distance to the Loop, the Magnificent Mile, and some of the city's most laudable restaurants and attractions) and all-suite accommodations, Homewood Suites offers all the amenities you could ask for including both a business center and a fitness center. An indoor pool is also available for your health-conscious or pleasure-seeking fancy. Each suite comes fully equipped with a coffeemaker, hairdryer, iron and ironing board,

VCR, microwave, and refrigerator. But just how much will it cost to enjoy all these luxuries? While prices definitely fluctuate throughout the year, you should have no problem reserving one of these large and comfy living areas for less than $200.00 per night, regardless of season. Homewood Suites is an especially good choice for families looking for something bigger than a shoe box and business travelers on an extended visit.

HOTEL ALLEGRO

171 West Randolph Street, Chicago IL 60601. 312/236-0123. **Toll-free phone:** 800/643-1500. **World Wide Web address:** http://www.allegrochicago.com. **The Lowdown:** In Italian, *allegro* means "fast-tempo" and that pretty much describes the atmosphere at this unique hotel. Each room is creatively designed and extremely colorful. There is even a specialty suite called "Room for RENT", which was actually created by one of the set designers from the Broadway musical *RENT!* Among the other features of the hotel are the weekend packages. Prices start around $199.00 and can get fairly steep depending on the features included in the package. *Mr. Cheap's* recommends the Sheet Music package which includes champagne, chocolate covered strawberries, confetti bubble bath, and a blues or jazz CD. The Cadillac Palace Theatre package is great for those looking for a night on the town (includes 2 tickets to a current show and dinner for two at 312 Chicago). If you just want to spend the evening relaxing, consider partaking of the wine hour served in the hotel lobby.

HOTEL MONACO

225 North Wabash Avenue, Chicago IL 60602. 312/960-8500. **Toll-free phone:** 800/397-7661. **World Wide Web address:** http://www.monaco-chicago.com. **The Lowdown:** Just because you're on a budget doesn't mean you can't live a life of luxury. What better way is there to enjoy the finer things in life than when you're getting them for half-price? The Hotel Monaco takes this philosophy to its hotel. As the name suggests, you'll receive the royal treatment here. The hotel's nearly 200 rooms are designed with a French-deco-inspired motif. As the hotel is close to both North Michigan Avenue and The Loop, they cater to a mix of luxury-seeking business and leisure travelers alike. In the morning, start your journey out right by taking advantage of the hotel's morning coffee service; at night, unwind with the hotel's wine service in the front lobby. And how's this for an amenity? So that you don't get lonesome during your stay, the hotel will supply you with a special friend – a complimentary goldfish in your room! Don't worry, you won't be stuck cleaning the tank or feeding the fish; trained hotel personnel will take care of all that for you. And, If you'd like a friend for your fish (meaning, of course, a second fish), that can be arranged as well. All rooms come with a two-line speaker phone, voice mail, and a fax machine. If you're opting for a suite, you'll be happy to know that they come standard with a two-person jetted spa, VCR, and CD player. Prices start at just $165.00 for deluxe rooms. If you're looking for a great getaway, Hotel Monaco offers a number of specially-priced packages: Mr. C's favorite is the Body, Mind &

Soul package, which includes an overnight stay in a deluxe guest room or suite, a makeover at one of the city's finest department stores, a personal shopping trip, two half-hour massages or treatments at local spas, an in-room gift chock full of aromatherapeutic goodies, two energy bars, a bottle of spring water, and a copy of *Teachings of Buddha*. At $280.00 for a deluxe room and $375.00 for a suite, that's a deal that's good for the body, mind, soul, *and* wallet! Call or visit their Website for other packages or to reserve a room.

HOWARD JOHNSON INN
720 North LaSalle Street, Chicago IL 60610. 312/664-8100. **The Lowdown:** For faithful accommodations, the Howard Johnson Inn never fails. After a tiring day of shopping along North Michigan Avenue, viewing works at the Art Institute of Chicago, or checking out the Adler Planetarium, you can settle down in this well-known chain and know that it's not going to cost you a fortune. Rooms start at just above $80.00 and range up to just over $100.00. Suites and non-smoking rooms are available. As an added bonus, Howard Johnson Inn offers free parking to its guests.

THE MIDLAND HOTEL
172 West Adams Street, Chicago IL 60603-3604. 312/332-1200. **Toll-free phone:** 800/621-2360. **World Wide Web address:** http://www.midlandhotelchicago.com. **The Lowdown:** The Midland Hotel seems to embody quiet sophistication with its opulent lobby, complete with gorgeous chandeliers and gold-leaf ceiling. The guest rooms, though less elaborate, are elegant just the same. For relaxing after a long conference or a day of running around the city, the hotel's Ticker Tape Bar is the perfect spot to unwind. A nice feature for business travelers is the home office guest room which features a VCR, fax, printer, copier, and scanner. Room rates can run the gamut; their Website can offer some great deals if you reserve online. Recently advertised special rates were listed between $99.00 and $139.00.

OHIO HOUSE MOTEL
600 North LaSalle Street, Chicago IL 60610. 312/943-6000. **The Lowdown:** This motel, in the heart of the Near North area, is a good bet for family travelers. Many of the city's most popular family restaurants (The Hard Rock Cafe, Rock 'n Roll McDonalds, Ed Debevic's) are all within walking distance, as is the subway and bustle of North Michigan Avenue. Free parking is another bonus, although the front desk is honest enough to admit that the lot *does* fill up (translation: you'll have to fend for yourself). The motel's five-booth coffee shop has received accolades from the *Chicago Sun-Times* for its huge pancake, sausage, and egg breakfast, which costs only $3.70. The motel is near the entrance to the Eisenhower Expressway, and the neighborhood can be boisterous, but security is good and the switchboard remains open 24 hours a day. All rooms are air-conditioned, with cable television and radio. Prices generally range between $80.00 and $90.00 a night.

PALMER HOUSE HILTON

17 East Monroe Street, Chicago IL 60603. 312/726-7500. **The Lowdown:** Okay, so maybe the Palmer House Hilton is not the *lowest* priced hotel in Chicago; still, there's a lot to be said for this Windy City landmark. First of all, the hotel is nearing its 130th birthday and yet it has managed to retain its original elegance and splendor. All you need do is step foot in the opulent lobby and you will understand what I mean. The ceiling presents a breathtaking barrage of oil paintings and the walls are bejeweled with French-inspired fixtures. The hotel has played host to many famous guests over the years including Charles Dickens and Mark Twain. Although steeped in history, the Palmer House Hilton has also integrated the technology of today to accommodate its guests with the addition of a virtual golf course. Another difference that sets this hotel apart from the rest is that pets are always welcome. In fact, they will be treated just as lavishly as the other guests as they lap up bottled water and nibble on biscuits. At the Palmer House Hilton both canine and human can live in the lap of luxury. Average rates are around $125.00 - $225.00 per night.

QUALITY INN DOWNTOWN

One Midcity Plaza (Madison Street at Halsted), Chicago IL 60661. 312/829-5000. **World Wide Web address:** http://www. qualityinn.com. **The Lowdown:** Looking for a good location and a reliable reputation? Quality Inn Downtown is your place. Located in the heart of Greektown, Quality Inn Downtown allows easy access to some of the city's most popular attractions; the hotel is within walking distance of The Adler Planetarium, Sears Tower, The Art Institute, and the Chicago Symphony. The hotel has all the necessary amenities you could ask for including valet and laundry service, a full-service restaurant, and a lounge. With standard room rates starting at a reasonable $99.00, you can put the rest of your money to good use: forget putting it in the pocket of the hotel and, instead, spend it on some of these nearby must-see places.

A ROOM WITH A VIEW

Toll-free phone: 800/780-4343. **World Wide Web address:** http://www.valuehotels.com. **The Lowdown:** Okay, so this is not an actual hotel. In fact, A Room With A View is not even located in Chicago. This is a service that specializes in finding hotel rooms when there are no rooms available. It seems impossible, but it's true. A Room With A View finds rooms for clients during soldout situations in Chicago, Boston, and New Orleans. Best of all, the service is free. So, if the boss decides to send you to a trade show on short notice, rest assured that you will have a place to rest your head with the help of these folks.

SUMMERFIELD SUITES

166 East Superior Street, Chicago IL 60611. 312/787-6000. **World Wide Web address:** http://www.summerfieldsuites.com. **The Lowdown:** This nationwide chain offers premium accommodations at very affordable prices. If you're planning an extended visit or are bringing along the brood, Summerfield

Suites is an especially great choice of hotel. Some suites offer full kitchens (including refrigerator, oven, toaster, dishes, flatware, and pots and pans), as well as an alarm clock and radio, iron and ironing board, data ports, VCR, and color cable TV. Studios offer microwaves, coffee makers, and small refrigerators. Plus, all guests will be welcome to come in and enjoy some fun in the hotel pool and exercise facility. Additional amenities include a sofabed with each room as well as a complimentary full breakfast buffet. Plus, let's not forget location. Summerfield Suites is just a quick hop, skip, and a jump away from renowned shopping and elegance on Chicago's Magnificent Mile. Other nearby attractions include the John Hancock Center, John G. Shedd Aquarium, Navy Pier, and The Art Institute of Chicago. Prices fluctuate, as usual, with the season. Winter specials can see prices as low as $129.00 for a studio suite, $139.00 for an executive suite, and $149.00 for a one bedroom. Throughout the year, prices can go as high as $239.00 for a room. Still, when taking into consideration the size of these rooms, the amenities you'll receive, and the highly-desired location, this is a more than reasonable price.

WILLOWS HOTEL

555 West Surf Avenue, Chicago IL 60657. 773/528-8400. **Toll-free phone:** 800/787-3108. **The Lowdown:** The Willows Hotel is undoubtedly one of the Windy City's best bargains when it comes to finding clean and comfortable accommodations at a reasonable price. Just a 10-minute cab ride from downtown, the Willows Hotel's Lakeview location makes it the perfect place to enjoy a bit of peace and quiet in the big city. Still, some of Chicago's most popular attractions (Wrigley Field, for example) are within a completely reasonable walking distance. Housed in a gorgeous old building that dates back to the 1920s, the Willows Hotel's distinctive Parisian charm will begin enchanting you as soon as you step inside the lobby: besides the amazing architecture, there's a great old fireplace that makes a cozy spot in which to hunker down on a cold, wintry night. A free continental breakfast and morning newspaper are just two of the amenities included in the nightly room rate, which run anywhere between $110.00 and $180.00.

RESTAURANTS

All Around Town

ANN SATHER
929 West Belmont Avenue, Chicago IL 60657. 773/348-2378. ◆ 3416 North Southport Avenue, Chicago IL 60657. 773/404-4475. ◆ 5207 North Clark Street, Chicago IL 60640. 773/271-6677. ◆ 2665 North Clark Street, Chicago IL 60614. 773/327-9522. **The Lowdown:** For true-blue Swedish dining, a significant part of Chicago's heritage, this famous restaurant has it all. The original Ann Sather in Lake View was formerly a funeral home, but you can't tell now with the way that they have it decorated. The chairs and tables are black, but the restaurant is warmed up by a crystal chandelier, stained glass windows, and red and gold trim. The food will warm you up too, with goodies like three-egg omelettes filled with peaches, cheddar cheese, broccoli, and ham. Or, try one with crab, spinach, and sour cream. If you're watching your cholesterol, you can have any omelette made with just egg whites. Other breakfast musts at Ann Sather are their heavenly homemade cinnamon rolls, and Swedish limpa rye bread, made tangy with anise seeds. Breakfast is served all day, while both the lunch and dinner menus start at 11:00 a.m. (who could eat dinner at that hour?) On the lunch menu, try the Swedish pancakes (ice cream and strawberries are extra), grilled cheese and tomato sandwich, the veggie burger (both sandwiches served with coleslaw), or the Caesar chicken tortellini salad. Add a cup of homemade soup to any salad or sandwich order for just a little extra. For big appetites, Ann Sather offers a long list of dinners under $10.00, complete with appetizer, two side dishes, dessert and beverage. Choices include roast duck, chicken croquettes, and baked meat loaf. Several beers are available; though, for a true Scandinavian experience, you may want to try the potent Swedish glogg, a mixture of spiced sherry, red wine and brandy, with almonds and raisins, served warm. By the way, you can even take home a dozen of those famous cinnamon rolls or a loaf of their limpa bread. Each location opens early (usually 7:00 a.m. - 7:30 a.m.), but call for specific location hours.

BACINO'S
2204 North Lincoln Avenue, Chicago IL 60614. 773/472-7400. ◆ 3146 North Sheffield Avenue, Chicago IL. 773/404-8111. ◆ 118 South Clinton, Chicago IL. 312/876-1188. **The Lowdown:** The Lincoln Park location is the flagship operation for Bacino's. It is here that they first introduced their "heart healthy" pizza more than 30 years ago. Thin and stuffed crust pizzas are the main attraction here, but there are plenty of lighter salads and sandwiches as well. A variety of fresh toppings can be put on (or stuffed into) your pizza including mushrooms, peppers, onions, and broccoli. Sizes come in bambino, small, medium, large, and extra large. Stuffed pizzas range in price from $4.25 for a bambino cheese to $18.80 for a large Bacino's Special (Italian sausage, mushrooms, green peppers, and onions). Thin-crust

pizzas are less expensive (but less filling too!). Prices range from $4.25 for a bambino cheese to $17.80 for an extra-large Bacino's Special Very Vegetarian. Though, there's more than just pizza here; appetizers and salads can really start the meal out right with one of their wonderful desserts rounding out the whole Bacino's experience. If you're not in the pizza mood, Bacino's offers a number of sandwiches and calzones as well. Sandwiches include meatball and Italian beef for $4.25 apiece. Calzones, which are $4.95 apiece, can be stuffed with a variety of ingredients including spinach, sausage, cheese, and herbs. Who knew healthy eating could taste so good? Call for specific location hours.

BILLY GOAT TAVERN *yes*

430 North Michigan Avenue, Chicago IL 60611. 312/222-1525. ✦ 309 West Washington Street, Chicago IL. 312/899-1873. ✦ 330 South Wells Street, Chicago IL. 312/554-0297. ✦ 1535 West Madison Street, Chicago IL. 312/733-9132. **The Lowdown:** The Billy Goat Tavern is a Chicagoland landmark. If you're a first-time visitor, it really is a must (for sheer no-frills atmosphere alone). Anyone who was a fan or who has ever seen some of the earliest episodes of *Saturday Night Live* no doubt knows that the heralded cry "Cheezborger, cheezborger, cheezborger. No Pepsi, Coke! No fries, chips!" originated here. So the legend is told and retold. As you can imagine, the main course here is the cheeseburger (they even come in the double and triple varieties, which you'll probably be pressured to try). Though they do offer other sandwiches (grilled cheese, for example) and breakfast sandwiches in the morning, no visit is complete without trying the cheeseburger. The highest price item on the menu (which, for the curious set, is the triple cheeseburger) weighs in at under $5.00. Sodas are $.95 and under and you can actually purchase a cup of coffee for just $.50! As the names positioned over the bar will tell you, this place has always been a popular spot for journalists on the trail of their next big story (and let's not forget that the North Michigan Avenue location's close proximity to the *Sun-Times* and *Tribune* buildings doesn't hurt either). The place is certainly not going to win any awards for nutrition (especially when you consider that a full bar is positioned directly across from the grill), but it sure is good! For the most genuine experience, visit the North Michigan Avenue location (it is hidden in an underpass, though a sign of the stairway will alert you to its whereabouts). This location is open daily, 6:00 a.m. - 2:00 a.m. Call for other location hours and, as it says on the door, "Butt in anytime!"

THE CORNER BAKERY

222 South Canal Street, Chicago IL 60606. 312/441-0821. ✦ 140 South Dearborn Street, Chicago IL 60603. 312/920-9100. ✦ 1121 North State Street, Chicago IL 60610. 312/787-1969. ✦ 233 South Wacker Drive, Chicago IL 60606. 312/466-0200. ✦ 516 North Clark Street, Chicago IL 60610. 312/644-8100. ✦ 78 East Washington Street, Chicago IL 60602. 312/201-0805. ✦ 676 North St. Clair Street, Chicago IL 60611. 312/266-2570. ✦ 900 North Michigan Avenue, Chicago IL. 312/573-9900. **World Wide**

Web address: http://www.cornerbakery.com. **The Lowdown:**
It seems that just about every corner has a Corner Bakery. With
that kind of ubiquity, you know it's got to be good. All the baked
goods are actually made on the premises, and they're priced to
sell. For snacks, desserts or whatever, The Corner Bakery's
pistachio and chocolate biscotti are a good and inexpensive
choice, as are the giant fudge brownies (sprinkled with
confectioner's sugar). They've got an enormous selection of
freshly-baked breads, with ingredients you probably wouldn't
dare dream of (potato dill, steakhouse rye, chocolate cherry).
What's more, The Corner Bakery is a great place to stop in for a
quick bite to eat-in as well. Most of their sandwiches are in the
$5.00 - $6.00 range and include everything from the basics of
ham and turkey to the specialty sandwiches, like ham on pretzel
and roast beef on olive ciabatta. For a truly wise buy, The Corner
Bakery offers full and half sandwich box lunches, both of which
include homemade bakery chips, whole fruit, and a dessert. Just
make sure you take some home with you – after one taste, it'll
be hard to resist. Call for specific location hours.

EDWARDO'S NATURAL PIZZA RESTAURANT
521 South Dearborn Street, Chicago IL 60605. 312/939-3366.
♦ 1212 North Dearborn Street, Chicago IL 60610. 312/337-4490.
♦ 1321 East 57th Street, Chicago IL 60637. 773/241-7960.
The Lowdown: Despite its yuppie exterior and award-winning
pizza, Edwardo's Natural Pizza Restaurant is not all that
expensive. If you split a pizza, and order an individual salad and
soda, you'll likely part with less than $10.00. Stuffed pizzas start
at $10.95 for a regular size mozzarella, which itself can be
enough to share. Prices go on to $16.95 for a basic large pie,
higher with extra toppings; but one pizza serves four to five
people easily. Thin crust pizzas run up to $19.85 for the large
Edwardo's special, and a whole wheat crust is $.75 extra for
either style pizza. Other pie varieties to try include vegetarian
and pesto. Come on in and taste for yourself what all the fuss is
about.

GIORDANO'S
310 West Randolph Street, Chicago IL 60606. 312/201-1441.
♦ 1840 North Clark Street, Chicago IL 60614. 312/944-6100.
♦ 6836 North Sheridan Road, Chicago IL 60626. 773/262-1313.
♦ 730 North Rush Street, Chicago IL 60611. 312/951-0747. ♦ 236
South Wabash Avenue, Chicago IL 60604. 312/939-4646. ♦ 815
West Van Buren, Chicago IL 60607. 312/421-1221. ♦ 1040 West
Belmont Avenue, Chicago IL 60657. 773/327-1200. ♦ 5309 South
Blackstone, Chicago IL 60615. 773/947-0200. ♦ 5159 South
Pulaski Road, Chicago IL 60632. 773/582-7676. ♦ Other area
locations. **World Wide Web address:** http://www.giordanos.
com. **The Lowdown:** Okay, so maybe Giordano's is a chain, but
only deservedly so. With locations throughout Illinois, Wisconsin,
and Indiana (there's even two locations in the Orlando, Florida
area), Giordano's has long reigned as the home of some of
Chicago's best stuffed pizza. Lauded by food critics everywhere,
even the *New York Times* has called Giordano's "the ultimate
pizza." Considering the fact that Chicago and New York are in a

constant battle for the title of national pizza capital, that's certainly saying something. Giordano's famous recipe comes straight from the Northern Italy kitchen of Mrs. Giordano herself. You can stuff your pie with a variety of always fresh and delicious ingredients including cheese, mushrooms, green peppers, onions, broccoli, pineapple, black or green olives, jalapeños, sausage, Canadian bacon, pepperoni, and shrimp. If you're not in the creative mood, they've got plenty of concoctions ready and waiting for you to try like the tropic delight with cheese, Canadian bacon, and pineapple ($13.25 - $18.45); the veggie with onions, green peppers, and mushrooms ($14.50 - $20.60); or the super veggie with the three above-mentioned ingredients, broccoli, black olives, and tomatoes ($15.75 - $22.35). Average pizza prices range anywhere between $10.75 for a small to $20.60 for a large. While these prices might seem a bit high, let's not forget that this is not your typical pizza. Stuffed pizza translates to more food than you can handle. In fact, when you consider that a small pizza alone can easily serve two to three people and that a large will feed four to five comfortably, a meal at Giordano's could easily weigh under the $5.00 mark per person. If stuffed pizza is not your thing, have no fear because Giordano's bakes up a variety of thin-crust pizzas as well. With the same toppings you can get in your stuffed pizza available to be put on your thin-crust pizza, there's plenty of ingredients to choose from. Thin-crust prices range from $7.15 for a small cheese to $19.45 for an extra-large, four-ingredient design. Giordano's also cooks up a number of traditional appetizers to start your meal out right like stuffed mushrooms, mozzarella sticks, fried calamari, and fried shrimp. Salads range from a basic house to an avocado salad with tomatoes, onions, and olives or a Mediterranean tomato salad with provolone cheese, Genoa salami, black olives. They also serve up a variety of sandwiches such as meatball, ham and cheese, and grilled chicken that are sure to satisfy any taste. There are also a number of basic pasta dishes like spaghetti, chicken parmigiana, and fettucine alfredo for under $10.00. Giordano's is a great place to come with a group who is willing to split a meal, or for travelers with children. Call for specific location hours.

HEAVEN ON SEVEN

111 North Wabash Avenue, 7th Floor, Chicago IL 60602. 312/263-6443. ◆ 600 North Rush Street, 2nd Floor, Chicago IL 60611. 312/280-7774. ◆ 3478 North Clark Street, Chicago IL 60657. 773/477-7818. **E-mail address:** eatcajun@ heavenon7.com. **World Wide Web address:** http://www. heavenon7.com. **The Lowdown:** T-shirts and signs around this restaurant all herald the fact that "People who come back from Heaven all say the same thing: Try the gumbo!" They're right; no meal is complete here unless started out with a cup of the celebrated soup. The gumbo is delicious and meaty. While one cup won't be enough, it is plenty filling. Of the restaurant's three locations, the downtown one is the original and therefore more authentic. But a trip to any of the locations will surely satisfy your craving for Louisiana cooking. While a number of the entrees can reach a bit above Mr. C's limit, there are plenty of

dishes on this large menu that fit a bargain budget. For starters, Heaven on Seven offers a number of tasty appetizers including sweet potato moss, potato-crusted jalapeño poppers, fried Alabama rock shrimp, and Louisiana crab cake. In addition to the already-mentioned gumbo and an always-changing soup of the day, Heaven on Seven offers a turtle soup and a Texas roadhouse chili. A number of salads (served with a cup of soup) are topped with such delectable treats as Southern fried soft shell crab, Creole spiced chicken, and Cajun fried shrimp, chicken, and oysters. Pasta dishes include lots of shrimp concoctions like shrimp voodoo, jerk, remoulade, and ravigote. All these dishes are served with soup or salad and are priced right under $10.00. Of course several Southern classics like Mardi Gras jambalaya, red beans and rice with andouille sausage, fried catfish, and shrimp and parmesan-reggiano cheese grits are here too, and served with soup or salad. Prices range from $7.95 - $10.95. Heaven on Seven's etouffee of the day is also a good choice with soup or salad. If you're new to Louisiana-style Cajun and Creole cooking, Heaven on Seven is a great place to have your first experience. They code the menu for you so you know what to expect from a dish; hot meals are marked with a jalapeño while owner Jimmy Bannos' favorites are underlined. If the meal's still not hot enough for your liking, there are what seems like a million bottles of hot sauce on your table, just waiting to be consumed. If you want to sample the menu, there are plenty of side dishes you can order together to make a meal: jalapeño cheddar corn muffins, black-eyed peas with andouille sausage, collard greens, sweet potato polenta, and jambalaya are just a few of the great options. While I should warn you that the food here can be very filling, I will still urge you to save even the teeniest amount of room for dessert. The dessert menu is comprised of lots of pies including pecan, key lime, coconut cream, and chocolate peanut butter. If you haven't saved room for a slice tonight, ask about taking a whole pie home with you. Call for specific location hours. (North Wabash location *$Cash Only$*).

HI RICKY

3730 North Southport Avenue, Chicago IL 60607. 773/388-0000.
♦ 1852 West North Avenue, Chicago IL 60622. 773/276-8300.
♦ 941 West Randolph Street, Chicago IL 60607. 312/491-9100.
The Lowdown: What can you do when you're craving Thai and your dining companion is dead-set on Chinese? Pay a visit to Hi Ricky, and satisfy both parties. Hi Ricky is an Asian restaurant that serves all varieties of Asian cuisines. But the question is, can all these specialties be done right? Of course! It just takes a couple of great cooks. It's these many different cuisines that make for a large and interesting menu. Test your knowledge of the intricate differences between these foods by pitting a Vietnamese spring roll against a Thai one ($4.75 each). Forget your normal decision between chicken or beef satay, Hi Ricky has got lots of satays to choose from like Thai luk shin (minced pork with garlic and ginger); Malaysian chicken satay that's prepared in a tasty and sweet coconut curry; pork satay in the same coconut curry; tofu satay; Indonesian lamb satay in soy sauce;

Singapore shrimp satay; and Peking duck satay. Each satay is $5.95 a plate, or try the Hi Ricky sampler plate of nine varieties for $8.95. Other appetizers include your basic Asian fare like pot stickers, fried won tons, and stir fried vegetables. Lots of great salads like a Thai omelette salad, carrot and cabbage salad, and Indonesian gado gado salad start at just $1.95 and range up to $6.95. Noodles can be tossed or straight from the wok: pad Thai ($6.75), cashew chicken noodles ($8.45), Malaysian Hokkien noodles ($6.95), and Pat Pong beef noodles ($7.45) are just a few of the choices. Of the many different cuisines you'll find here are Thai, Malaysian, Szechwan, Burmese, Chinese, Indonesian, Vietnamese, and Singaporean. So there's definitely something here to satisfy every craving. Open Sunday, 12:00 p.m. - 10:00 p.m.; Monday through Thursday, 11:30 a.m. - 10:00 p.m.; Friday and Saturday, 12:00 p.m. - 11:00 p.m.

LEONA'S

3215 North Sheffield Avenue, Chicago IL. 773/327-8861. ◆ 6935 North Sheridan Road, Chicago IL. 773/764-5757. ◆ 1936 West Augusta Boulevard, Chicago IL. 773/292-4300. ◆ 1419 West Taylor Street, Chicago IL. 312/850-2222. ◆ 848 West Madison Street, Oak Park IL. 708/445-0101. ◆ 3877 North Elston, Chicago IL. 773/267-7287. ◆ 53rd & Woodlawn Street, Chicago IL. 773/363-2600. ◆ 111th & Western, Chicago IL. 773/881-7700. ◆ 7443 West Irving Park, Chicago IL. 773/625-3636. ◆ 3517 Dempster, Skokie IL. 847/982-0101. ◆ 25th & Western, Chicago IL. 773/523-9696. ◆ 1504 Miner Street, Des Plaines IL. 847/759-0800. **World Wide Web address:** http://www.leonas.com. **The Lowdown:** Family-run since 1950, Leona's has grown into a Chicagoland chain serving almost 50,000 people a week. Not all of the entrees are under $10.00, but the pizza and sandwiches can't be beat for value. Mr. C can't put into words just how huge the carnivorous combo sandwich is; it's comparable to a football (in size only). It's loaded with Italian sausage and beef as well as peppers and sauce. A few dollars more gets you a side dish (try the psychedelic salad) and garnish (choice of confetti corn salad, fresh fruit, or roasted garlic cloves). Of course, what would an Italian restaurant be without pizza? Here, they come with a mind-boggling choice of close to 30 toppings, everything from tofu to turkey breast. Don't forget dessert if you aren't completely stuffed yet. Tempt your tastebuds with Tiramisu, cannoli bread pudding, or a banana split. The buffet (only served at the Taylor Street location) includes your choice of turkey (a whole bird is out on the table for carving), boneless chicken breast, fried eggplant, meatballs, four kinds of pizza, super-fresh broccoli and zucchini, onion rings, and a slew of pasta and regular salads. Desserts like cheesecake, brownie-bottom chocolate cake, and a variety of cookies and truffle-like treats are included in the tab. The whole shebang, all you can eat, is a reasonable $8.95. It's served from 11:00 a.m. until 2:30 p.m., weekdays only.

LOU MALNATI'S PIZZERIA

439 North Wells Street (at Hubbard Street), Chicago IL 60610. 312/828-9800. ◆ 3859 West Ogden Avenue, Chicago IL 60623.

773/762-0800. ◆ 958 West Wrightwood Avenue, Chicago IL 60614. 773/832-4030. **E-mail address:** heylou@loumalnatis.com. **World Wide Web address:** http://www.loumalnatis.com. **The Lowdown:** You certainly can't visit Chicago without indulging in some of their famous deep dish pizza. While many places claim to have the best, few restaurants boast the history that Lou Malnati's does. While Lou has certainly got some hefty competition (with Pizzeria Uno & Due, Gino's East, etc.) there are plenty of Chicagoans who are loyal to Lou. From the opening of their original location in Lincolnwood, Lou Malnati's has had to branch out across the city and several other suburbs to meet the extreme pizza demand. This family-run business now owns 17 stores throughout Chicagoland (8 full service restaurants, 9 carry out & delivery only). Deep dish pizzas start at $4.35 for an individual-sized cheese and increase to just over $17.00 for a large pizza (serves four) with multiple toppings. Thin crust pizzas are just as delicious, though less expensive. While you'd be silly not to order a pizza at Lou Malnati's, they do offer a number of pasta dishes and sandwiches too. Pastas include family favorites like lasagna and spaghetti and are all priced under $7.00. Sandwiches include grilled chicken with a variety of toppings and hamburgers. Items on the kids menu, which include chicken nuggets and mini corn dogs, are under $3.50 apiece. Now that's what I call a family friendly menu. If you're looking for a casual place to enjoy some typical Chicago food, it doesn't get much better (or historical) than Lou Malnati's Pizzeria. Call for specific location hours.

MONDAY'S RESTAURANTS

75 West Harrison Street, Chicago IL 60605. 312/663-3647. ◆ 19 East Jackson Boulevard, Chicago IL 60604. 312/408-1120. ◆ 1201 North State Street, Chicago IL 60610. 312/787-3140. ◆ 120 South Riverside Plaza, Chicago IL 60606. 312/372-9866. ◆ 203 North LaSalle Street, Chicago IL 60601. 312/629-0444. **The Lowdown:** Monday's Restaurants would be best categorized as neighborhood bar/eateries. But they stand out from the crowd with their super-friendly service and rather unusual menu item choices. But don't think that Monday is the only day you can enjoy a meal at Monday's; breakfast, lunch, and dinner are served daily. Some of the breakfast items are basic, like the big Belgian waffles; but real maple syrup and whipped butter make it special. Other offbeat offerings include Ka-Ya-Na, which is scrambled eggs with tomato, onion and feta cheese mixed in, European style, plus a muffin or toast. Several omelettes are on the menu; go for the zucchini with Swiss cheese and onions, or the crabmeat. All breakfast dishes come with fried potatoes, and muffin or toast and jelly. Or, try nova lox and three eggs. The Sunday brunch is $9.95, and well worth it for those with hefty appetites. It's an elaborate, all-you-can eat buffet of eggs, salmon, fresh fruit, breads, and other fixings. Lunches and dinners are just as reasonably priced. Even at dinnertime, there's not much on the menu that tops $10.00. All the Monday's branches have similar – though not identical – menus and decor. But all locations have surely earned Monday's their excellent reputation. Call for specific location hours.

THE ORIGINAL PANCAKE HOUSE

22 East Bellevue Place, Chicago IL 60611. 312/642-7917.
♦ 10437 South Western Avenue, Chicago IL 60643. 773/445-6100. ♦ 1517 East Hyde Park Boulevard, Chicago IL 60615. 773/288-2323. ♦ 2020 North Lincoln Park West, Chicago IL 60614. 773/929-8130. **The Lowdown:** This charming, warm and homey eatery (part of a chain based in Portland, Oregon) gets a vote for friendliest and most efficient staff in town. Even though the folks at The Original Pancake House are obsessively preoccupied with high quality, the breakfast-all-day meals here won't affect your budget too much. You'll be stuffed after a ham and cheese omelette, served with three buttermilk pancakes, all for $7.00. The pancakes are extra-smooth and fluffy, thanks to a special sourdough yeast made especially by the staff. You can also beat the breakfast blahs here by ordering something new. Have you ever tried lacy Swedish pancakes with imported lingonberries ($5.20)? Cherry Kijafa Crêpes are covered and filled with Montmorency cherries simmered in Kijafa sauce ($5.45). Or, how about Hawaiian pancakes, filled with pineapple chunks ($4.85)? Get back to nature with The Original Pancake House's old-fashioned oats, served with cream, for $2.10. And their trademark coffee, brought to you with pure whipping cream if you wish, is $1.25. Potato pancakes are served with applesauce or sour cream for $5.00. Or try The Original Pancake House specialty, the oven-baked apple pancakes served with fresh apples and pure cinnamon glaze, for $6.95. Everything is prepared fresh on the premises according to time-honored recipes. The Original Pancake House does not accept credit cards, which is one way they keep their prices down.

WEST EGG CAFE

620 North Fairbanks Court, Chicago IL 60611. 312/280-8366.
♦ 525 West Monroe, Chicago IL. 312/454-9939. ♦ 50 West Washington Street, Chicago IL. 312/236-3322. **The Lowdown:** You don't have to be a Gatsby to eat at the West Egg Cafe. They serve breakfast, lunch, and dinner, in hefty portions and at reasonable prices. Ingredients are all super-fresh too, and what they do with them gets rather creative. Breakfast is served all day long. Omelettes come with an English muffin and potatoes or tomato slices, priced from $5.00 for your basic cheese version to $6.95 for the Bandito, which is stuffed with chorizo, green chiles, onion, guacamole, and cheese; topped with sour cream; and served with salsa and tortilla. If you think that's a mouthful to say, just imagine what it's like to eat! They devote an entire section of the menu "To Your Health" and offer such things as a breakfast salad (layers of granola, yogurt, fruit, and nuts served with a muffin); Natale's Nature Plate (a veggie pattie with a scoop of cottage cheese and fresh fruit served atop a bed of Romaine lettuce); and Carl's Cool Creation (and egg white scramble with mushrooms, spinach, chicken, and cholesterol-free cheese). Such dare-to-be-healthy dishes won't cost much more than $7.00 a plate. In the pursuit of what they call "eggsellence," West Egg Cage has designed a number of unique and delicious egg plates like the feta frittata, the breakfast burrito, Grandma Meechie's country hash, and the California crêpe. If you're not

feeling much like breakfast, West Egg Cafe is quite proud of their expertise in rotisserie cooking. You can pick up a whole chicken with your choice of dipping sauce, potato, and vegetable for under $10.00. A number of different salads also comprise a portion of the menu, with the San Diego spinach and the Chef James variety taking the prize as two of my favorites. Sandwiches include charbroiled chicken dressed in a number of different ways (BBQ, Creole, buffalo-style) as well as some delicious burgers. More experimental sandwiches include the B.L.T.E. (add the "E" for egg... fried egg, that is!), the Sicilian Po' Boy (grilled veggies with spinach and a basil-pesto sauce), and the West Coast club (turkey, avocado, bean sprouts, bacon, tomato, and cheese on a whole grain bread). For the most part, West Egg Cafe opens early (6:00 a.m.) and closes late (12:00 a.m.), though you'll have to call for specific location hours.

ZOOM KITCHEN
923 North Rush Street, Chicago IL 60611. 312/440-3500. ◆ 1646 North Damen Avenue, Chicago IL 60647. 773/278-7000. ◆ 620 West Belmont Avenue, Chicago IL 60657. 773/325-1400.
The Lowdown: Though I've probably said so elsewhere in this book, one thing I truly enjoy is having all the ingredients at a restaurant laid out in front of me. Because Zoom Kitchen uses only the freshest of foods, they're not ashamed to flaunt them. Picture your high school cafeteria gone retro and you've got a pretty good idea of what Zoom Kitchen looks like. What's best about this place is that you pick the ingredients; if you've been known to pick the onions out of your salad or the tomatoes off your sandwich, there's none of that here. From their "Produce Department'" you can choose a Caesar salad for $4.25 ($5.95 with chicken) or customize your salad for $4.25 ($5.95 with chicken). Ingredients available include a base of mixed greens or Romaine lettuce, plum tomatoes, marinated mushrooms, sweet corn, roasted red peppers, jicama, crystallized pecans, and toasted pumpkin seeds. If you're looking for something with a bit more sustenance, try visiting their "Sandwich Heaven" with choices like turkey breast, low-fat chicken sausage, sliced sirloin steak, meatloaf, turkeyloaf, and grilled yellow-fin tuna. Sandwiches are priced $4.50 - $5.25 and can be served up with a variety of unique condiments such as chipotle or garlic mayo, avocado spread, or cilantro pesto. Several fresh soups of the day and their sirloin chili are always available for $3.25 - $3.50 a bowl. For dessert, freshly-baked pies change weekly and are more of a treat at $2.50 a slice. They even serve up freshly-brewed Intelligentsia coffee, cappuccino, and espresso at prices that are completely within reason. Who wouldn't be willing to pay $2.50 for a delicious double cappuccino topped with lots of foam and cinnamon? Sunday mornings offer an especially good deal with an $8.00 all-you-can-eat brunch buffet. The restaurant itself is wonderfully executed; a metallic theme carries itself throughout and the place is absolutely spotless. Plus, the waitstaff could not be any nicer; quite an achievement considering this is a cafeteria-style place, meaning they're not working for tips (they do have a tip jar though, and it's one you'll feel obligated to contribute to). Call for specific location hours.

Coffeehouses & Afternoon Tea

CAFFE FLORIAN

1450 East 57th Street, Chicago IL 60637. 773/752-4100. **The Lowdown:** Caffe Florian couples old-world Venetian charm with modern day tastes and appetites. The menu encompasses a wide range of cuisines, with a large number of specialty coffee beans and teas arriving from all over the world. More a coffeehouse than a restaurant, Caffe Florian gives even the best of local and national chains a run for their money. It is for this reason that Caffe Florian is popular with more than just the college crowd. Another reason that makes this spot such a popular dining destination is the fact that their deep-dish pizza is some of the best and cheapest in the city. In a city where even the most highbrow of restaurants have a splattering of pies on the menu, that's a pretty bold declaration. Stop in and try some for yourself. Open Sunday through Thursday, 11:00 a.m. - 12:00 a.m.; Friday and Saturday, 11:00 a.m. - 1:00 a.m. This restaurant has no liquor license, but you are welcome to bring your own.

CAPRA'S COFFEE

205 East Ohio Street, Chicago IL 60611. 312/329-0063. **The Lowdown:** Capra's offers more than just delicious coffee. They've got great smoothies, breakfast, and lunch too. The breakfast menu, which ranges in price from $3.50 - $5.25, includes a health-conscious combo of cereal, fruit, bagel, and milk; and good egg and bagel sandwiches too. The menu is limited but then again, Capra's is mainly a coffee shop. The place is immaculate and pretty, dressed in dark green hues with enormous murals lining the wall. But, unlike any coffee shop I've ever been to (and there have been plenty), Capra's offers a unique twist on their lunch menu: it's comprised of a variety of fresh sushi, made daily right along with the coffee. Priced anywhere from $3.95 - $9.50, prices generally roam around the $6.00 - $6.50 point for dishes like California maki (crab, cucumber, avocado, and fish egg) and tekka maki (tuna and cucumber). Capra's makes for a great light meal or a coffee break from the hustle and bustle of the Magnificent Mile, which is just a few short steps away. They've even got a popcorn machine (yes, movie-theater-style) that your kids or companions are sure to get a kick out of. Service is friendly and quick, perfectly suiting its hurried surroundings.

COLOR ME COFFEE

700 East Grand Avenue, Suite 125, Chicago IL 60611. 312/595-5520. **The Lowdown:** Color me impressed! Color Me Coffee offers coffee connoisseurs a variety of coffees from around the world. Sure, it looks like just another coffee stand, but the time and effort that goes into this place is so much more. The owners

themselves even fly around the world, picking up beans in their countries of choice. If you're still not convinced, try a cup before you buy... you won't be disappointed. These exotic and delicious beans can be purchased for under $10.00 a pound – that's less than what you'd pay in the local grocery store. Because it's located by Navy Pier, Color Me Coffee is completely convenient to some of the city's best entertainment. Open Sunday, 10:00 a.m. - 7:00 p.m.; Monday through Thursday, 8:00 a.m. - 8:00 p.m.; Friday, 8:00 a.m. - 10:00 p.m.; Saturday, 10:00 a.m. - 10:00 p.m.

EMERALD CITY COFFEE
3928 North Sheridan Road, Chicago IL 60613. 773/525-7847.
The Lowdown: When one thinks of Chicago they don't often think of Emerald City... but maybe they should. If you know that this coffee house is locally owned by a Seattle transplant, therein lies the secret to the name. Emerald City Coffee serves up a mean cup of Joe in a relaxed and welcoming atmosphere. This brightly-lit space is home to some of the freshest and best-priced coffees, pastries, and sandwiches in the city. Comfortable furniture and a host of board games should keep you entertained for hours. The fact that a couple of guitars are always in place can mean the spawning of some random concert interludes (though, since anyone's invited to join in, you can never count on one particular style). They're open early every day, but especially early during the week, when that morning cup of coffee can make or break your day. Stop in to get your engine revving. Open Monday through Friday, 6:00 a.m. - 8:00 p.m.; Saturday and Sunday, 7:00 a.m. - 8:00 p.m. *$Cash Only$*

FOSTER BROTHERS COFFEE
2 North Michigan Avenue, Chicago IL 60604. 312/630-1133.
• 210 South Canal Street, Chicago IL 60606. 312/441-1412.
• 6441 North Sheridan Road, Chicago IL 60626. 773/262-3002.
The Lowdown: One rule that I adhere to religiously, no matter how cheap the coffee, is quality. Foster Brothers Coffee certainly gives you a quality cup of Joe at a great price. Several flavored and different blends of the day are available, along with all your favorite specialties. The atmosphere, like most other shops, has that well-known Starbucks quality to it. Yet, the feeling here is much more welcoming. Foster Brothers Coffee extends the familial name to the decorations as well; quotes about brotherhood from such writers as Rudyard Kipling adorn the walls as do black and white family pictures. Another great touch? Small reading lamps lining the counter space and fresh flowers on each table, assuring you they take the time to think about your needs. Relaxing music – none of the big band standards that have become the hallmark of so many coffee stops – is the soundtrack of Foster Brothers. Best of all, I was greeted with just about the friendliest service I had seen with.

GOURMAND COFFEEHOUSE
728 South Dearborn Street, Chicago IL 60605. 312/427-2610.
• 1801 South Indiana Avenue, Chicago IL 60616.
The Lowdown: Gourmand doesn't sound like the name of a

shop that Mr. C would frequent, but for baked items, clever sandwiches, and coffee at not-too-crazy prices, this Printer's Row hangout is certainly worth checking out. Their full breakfasts are true bargains. Try one of the specials, which start at $5.55 and include a small coffee and juice. You can choose eggs espresso (eggs steamed with an espresso wand), pancakes, French toast, waffles, or an omelette. A bowl of organic granola, topped with lowfat yogurt is only $3.50. Veggie paella, red beans and rice, or pesto tortellini are other good picks at just $3.50 a plate. Desserts are the real treats here, with a variety of fresh-baked muffins and scones available at $1.60 and $1.85 respectively. Sixty-cent lemon and turtle cookies are the perfect compliment to a chocoloccino, mocha, latte, espresso, cappuccino, or americano, starting at $2.15. Sip to the sounds of blues or jazz, whether in the cozy coolness of the art decorated interior, or out at the sidewalk tables. Gourmand gets a thumbs-up for serving their in-house beverages in glasses or mugs, with refill prices for coffee and iced tea. Friday nights feature open-mike poetry. Since Gourmand is just three blocks west of Michigan Avenue and a five-minute walk from the Art Institute, consider eating here instead of at one of the tourist-crowded eateries on the main drag. Open Monday through Friday, 7:00 a.m. - 11:00 p.m.; Saturday and Sunday, 8:00 a.m. - 11:00 p.m.

JILLIAN'S COFFEE HOUSE & BISTRO

674 West Diversey Parkway, Chicago IL 60614. 773/529-7010.
The Lowdown: From the green-and-white-striped exterior to the fireplace inside, everything about Jillian's is inviting. Let's start with the first half of the restaurant: coffee house. Jillian's Coffee House serves up a mean cup of coffee in all its many forms, from regular old joe to favorite specialty drinks. Cappuccinos, lattes, cafe mochas, and cafe Americanos are all available here, and better priced than the local big-name chains at $1.10 - $2.25 per helping. Jillian's Coffee House also carries a large array of herbal teas at just $1.75 per pot. This is truly a great place to just sit back and repose (not to bring up that fireplace again, but come on, what better way is there to relax... especially during those legendary Chicago winters). Now it's time for the second half of Jillian's operation: the bistro. While the menu is not enormous, it is expertly-prepared and extremely creative. It's certainly enough to make any epicure a regular customer. What caught Mr. C's eye was the individual-sized quiches; while the smoked and dill sounded appetizing, the brie and basil with sun-dried tomato in a mashed potato crust sounded absolutely mouth-watering! Such unusual but delicious salads as poppy seed and fruit; pear, endive, and bleu cheese; white bean and tuna; penne pasta Niçoise; and walnut chicken with buttermilk honey were all well priced. The sandwich menu here is also quite inventive with such offerings as Asian grilled tuna with sesame noodles; ham, cheese, and asparagus with red onion salad; and grilled chicken olivada with cilantro potato salad. For dessert, there are a number of sinful options like the flourless chocolate cake or the orange-cinnamon-white chocolate creme brûlée. On Sunday morning, from 9:00 a.m. - 2:00 p.m., Jillian's offers a great Sunday brunch. What's more, Jillian's

offers a very impressive wine list with not only the usual merlot, chardonnay, and white zinfandel; but pinot noir, viognier, sauvignon blanc, and pinot grigio all offered by the glass for $4.75 or by the bottle for under $20.00 apiece. Bottled beers available include Goose Island, Becks, Warsteiner, and Heffe Weiss; and draft beers offer you a pint of Sam Adams, Guinness, and Bass. Open Sunday, 11:00 a.m. - 9:00 p.m.; Monday through Thursday, 4:00 p.m. - 12:00 a.m.; Friday, 4:00 p.m. - 2:00 a.m.; Saturday, 11:00 a.m. - 2:00 a.m.

JOY OF IRELAND
700 North Michigan Avenue, Chicago IL 60611. 312/664-7290.
The Lowdown: Walk all the way to the back of this Chicago Place shop and you'll find their lovely little café where, Monday through Saturday, you can take a break from shopping with their inexpensive afternoon tea. An all-glass wall will allow you to watch the frivolity unfold along North Michigan Avenue while you sit. Offering hot tea and scones, Joy of Ireland is a quiet place to enjoy a spot of tea or a taste of the old country in a quaint and unhurried atmosphere. Joy of Ireland is also the place for lunch: Monday through Friday, from 11:30 a.m. - 5:00 p.m., Joy of Ireland's chef Paul Pszybylski (who, by the way, was trained at Le Cordon Bleu) cooks up some of the area's most unique delicacies. Scottish smoked salmon, caviar, crab cakes, and roasted ostrich are just a few of the dishes you'll find for under $10.00 (including a side salad). Their daily soups run the range from a lobster bisque or she-crab to a hearty potato leek. Even if you're not starved, they offer a fantastic array of imported cheeses and fresh fruits. But don't think they stop there: real chocolate mousse is just one of the sumptuous desserts you're likely to find. Best of all, you don't have to leave a tip. In fact, the waitstaff doesn't even accept them! If you're feeling overly generous and are so impressed with this place, they will be happy to accept small donations to some of the local charities that they sponsor in lieu of a gratuity. It's nice to know that there are still people who care... and even nicer to know that they're the ones serving you! **Cheap Deal:** The nice folks at Joy of Ireland are willing to extend a 10 percent discount (in the cafe) to you once you tell them you're a *Mr. Cheap's Chicago* reader!

THE SALON AT THE HOTEL INTER-CONTINENTAL
505 North Michigan Avenue, Chicago IL 60611. 312/944-4100.
The Lowdown: To be sure, you'll need a break from the hustle and bustle of shopping the Magnificent Mile. So while you're pondering over which chain coffeeshop or bakery to enter, think of an alternative where you can let your mind relax, as well as your feet. The Salon, located in the posh Hotel Inter-Continental, is an ideal place to sip a cup of tea and munch on a baked delight. The lounge is set up comfortably to appear as a living room would. If conservative is your name, then the Traditional Afternoon Tea is your game. In addition to the pot of tea of your choice, you can add finger sandwiches, freshly-baked raisin scones with Devonshire clotted cream and strawberry preserves, and a selection of fresh pastries. If you're here for a bit more than tea try The Avenue Tea which includes all of the above plus

a plate of fresh strawberries with whipped cream and a glass of Louis Roederer Brut Premier champagne. Traditional Afternoon Tea is $14.50 per person while The Avenue Tea will cost you $23.50 each. Teas are served daily from 2:00 p.m. - 5:00 p.m. and reservations are necessary.

3RD COAST CAFE

1260 North Dearborn Street, Chicago IL 60610. 312/649-0730. **The Lowdown:** 3rd Coast has developed quite a loyal following with its funky atmosphere and great prices. Ostensibly just a coffee shop, catering to the Parcheesi/Ouija board-playing crowd, they actually serve breakfast, lunch, and dinner. You'll find 3rd Coast muffins and munchies in many other coffee shops in the city, but of course the prices are cheapest here at the source. 3rd Coast also beats out other coffeehouses with its atmosphere. Old-fashioned metal milkcrates, worn, circa-1940s ice skates, antique model airplanes, and cases of footballs and baseball gloves from decades past decorate the entire restaurant. Shaded light sconces keep the room mellow, even during the busy evening hours. The cozy marble-topped tables and blue cushioned chairs make this place perfect for a heated game of Trivial Pursuit. In the morning, open your eyes with their homemade scones, available in blueberry, chocolate chip, and raspberry. Muffins are truly enormous and will keep you stuffed until lunch. Other breakfast items include espresso steamed oatmeal and fresh squeezed fruit juices. For lunch and dinner, a very filling and spicy hummus plate, with veggies and warmed pita bread goes or a simple order of salsa and tortilla chips will get you started. On the fancier side, try a grilled calamari salad or a smoked turkey and brie sandwich, both for under $8.00. For your caffeine fix, espresso and cafe au lait are among the offerings. Or, be adventurous and order the delightful iced raspberry coffee. Open Wednesday through Saturday, 24 hours; Sunday through Tuesday, 7:00 a.m. - 3:00 a.m.

UNCOMMON GROUND COFFEEHOUSE

1214 West Grace Street, Chicago IL 60613. 773/929-3680. **E-mail address:** loudcoffee@aol.com. **World Wide Web address:** http://www.uncommonground.com. **The Lowdown:** If you're from Chicago, no doubt you've heard of this place. Uncommon Ground Coffeehouse has received rave reviews for the best coffeehouse in Chicago, the best concert, the best coffee, and the list goes on. Well, add Mr. C's praise to the list. This coffeehouse serves breakfast, lunch, and dinner, but it's not necessarily the menu that keeps the house full. Come here any night and you're likely to hear different live music acts each time. While you may hear an array of musical genres, folk music is generally the main attraction, featuring both local and national acts. Get here early, grab a seat, and enjoy the atmosphere.

Downtown - The Loop

ARTISTS' RESTAURANT
412 South Michigan Avenue, Chicago IL 60605. 312/939-7855. **The Lowdown:** Located in the Fine Arts Building, diagonally across the street from the Art Institute, this mostly-Greek restaurant attracts tourists from the Hilton, actors and students from nearby Columbia College, and everyone in between. Locals recommend the restaurant as *the* place to catch sight of a famous actor or actress; casts from shows at the area's many theaters sometimes come here for a bite after the performance. The open-faced hot roast beef sandwich with mashed potato is one of the restaurant's most popular plates. Among the more innovative menu items are the huge burgundy burger, sautéed with wine and mushrooms, topped with bacon and served with French fries and a pickle; and Pierre's Tuna Volcano, a croissant with tuna, mushrooms, tomato and melted cheddar cheese. Other options include linguine or cheese ravioli, a gyros plate, or souvlaki. Finish off with a potent cup of Greek coffee and a slice of lemony cheesecake. Artists' Restaurant also carries a full liquor license. The restaurant's pretty rose-print wallpaper and faux marble countertop combine for a casual and pleasant atmosphere. It's a good rendezvous for before or after a nearby musical, a concert in Grant Park, or a movie at the Fine Arts Theater next door. Two words of warning, though: the restaurant enforces its $3.00 table minimum, so do be sure and oblige; more importantly, try and remember that wherever tourists abound, so do pick-pockets. A sign in the restaurant warns customers to keep an eye on their wallets and purses, and it's good advice. Open Sunday through Thursday, 7:30 a.m. - 11:00 p.m.; Friday and Saturday, 7:30 a.m. - 12:00 a.m.

THE BERGHOFF RESTAURANT
17 West Adams Street, Chicago IL 60603. 312/427-3170. **World Wide Web address:** http://www.berghoff.com. **The Lowdown:** The Berghoff has long been a staple of good and affordable German cuisine. Founded in 1898, the fact that all of their breads and desserts are cooked right on the premises is just one of the many reasons that makes this place so popular. Start out with one of their traditional German appetizers like bratwurst and knockwurst with potato salad and sauerkraut, or try the creamed herring. The Berghoff house specialties include sauerbraten served with potato pancakes or spaetzels and creamed spinach; wiener schnitzel with German fried potatoes and creamed spinach; and boiled pork shank with new potatoes and sauerkraut. As The Berghoff's food also has a distinctively American flair, you can be sure you'll find such all-American delights as roasted turkey with mashed potatoes and cranberry sauce, and fried shrimp with cocktail sauce. A large sandwich menu barely tops $8.50 in price and includes hot corned beef, hot bratwurst sausage, and broiled whitefish. But not everything

at The Berghoff is so heavy; they've got plenty of pasta dishes and lighter entrees to choose from like shrimp and mushrooms over linguine, broiled fresh vegetable brochette, and mussels with penne pasta. Most entrees are under $10.00 a plate. Everything is delicious and worth at least a taste. But don't forget to finish it all off with one of those homemade desserts!

BLACKIE'S

755 South Clark Street, Chicago IL 60605. 312/786-1161. **The Lowdown:** Tiny but fun, this Printer's Row-Burnham Park neighborhood bar is rich in history. They make a point of running the place, as they put it, free of snobbery and excessive prices. The restaurant has been run by the DeMilio family since 1939, who are still present in conjunction with the Thomas family. In its heyday, Blackie's attracted such celebrities as Tommy Dorsey, Glenn Miller, and even the Three Stooges. After many of the printing companies moved out and Dearborn Station closed in the 1950s, business slowed. Blackie's was rehabbed in the 1970s and is now quite a hopping place once again. You can get a great breakfast for about $6.00. The OJ is fresh-squeezed, and it goes great with any breakfast you choose. For lunch, the all-white meat chicken salad plate and a Caesar salad with albacore tuna are some of the most popular dishes. A six-ounce steak sandwich with grilled onions and mushrooms is served with fries for under $10.00. If you've never stopped in here early enough in the day to grab some of these eats, Mr. C recommends that you do so in the near future. Open Monday through Saturday, 11:00 a.m. - 3:00 p.m.

CAFFÉ BACI

231 South LaSalle Street, Chicago IL 60604. 312/629-1818. ◆ 77 West Wacker Drive, Chicago IL 60601. 312/629-2224. ◆ 225 West Wacker Drive, Chicago IL 60606. 312/251-1234. **World Wide Web address:** http://caffebaci.com. **The Lowdown:** Amidst all the hustle and bustle of the downtown Chicago business world, it can be difficult to find a quiet place to sit down, grab a cup of coffee or a bite to eat, and chat. Luckily for you, Caffé Baci – which is just such a place – has three different downtown locations. While not quite your traditional sit-down restaurant, Caffé Baci is far from a fast food joint. All the food is carefully prepared with only the freshest ingredients, and it's all quite tasty. Choose from one of their many fresh salads, or a salad plate (includes three of their salads) for just $5.75, or try one of Caffé Baci's panini sandwiches, they come dressed in a delightful mix of olive oil and spices. The Torino, a delightful mix of grilled chicken, eggplant, and roasted red peppers, is one of Mr. C's personal favorites. There are plenty of vegetarian panini to choose from as well, like Antonio's ciabatta (fresh mozzarella and artichoke hearts on ciabatta) and the Portofino (sautéed portabello mushrooms with goat cheese and basil in a ginger sauce). If these Italian delights aren't whetting your appetite (you must be crazy, but read on anyway), Caffé Baci offers some traditional American sandwiches as well like roast beef and provolone, and roasted turkey with Swiss. But Caffé Baci is much more than an upscale sandwich shop; each day, they cook up a

number of delicious and fresh entrees that are sure to make your mouth water. For dessert, try one of their fabulous cannolis, or a piece of their always-tempting cheesecake. Of course, there's plenty of coffee beverages here too. Specialty drinks like caffe lattes and caffe mochas start at under $2.00, and you can pick up a cup of regular coffee for just $1.00... who would have thought? If you live in the area, you should keep in mind that Caffé Baci does a pretty big catering business too. Call for specific location hours.

JAKS TAP

901 West Jackson Boulevard, Chicago IL 60607. 312/666-1700.
The Lowdown: While Jaks Tap is certainly a pub to behold (they have one of the largest draft selections in the city), they are also a restaurant to be reckoned with. Though Jaks does offer typical pub fare like chili, wings, burgers, and grilled chicken sandwiches, they also offer an array of items that you would be hard-pressed to find in another beer tavern. Start out with an out-of-the-ordinary appetizer like a plate of hummus and pita bread or a bowl of chicken gumbo. A variety of salads include a house, Caesar, and Cajun-grilled chicken. Jaks Tap puts an inventive spin on many of your run-of-the-mill sandwiches: try a fried catfish Po' Boy on French bread; a Cajun veggie burger with fries, rice and beans, or hummus; or a chicken guacamole sandwich. They keep the atmosphere light and informal by giving their sandwiches such sobriquets as The Gobbler (smoked turkey, Swiss cheese, green onion, and cranberry mayonnaise). Many of the items at Jaks Tap have even crept their way up from the Mexican border, with several quesadillas and burritos finding their way onto the menu. But again, as the name would suggest, people don't always stop by Jaks Tap for the food. With more than 40 beers on tap, everyone's favorite beer is bound to be found at Jaks Tap. Daily drink specials include the micro beer of the day ($3.25 per pint, $12.00 per pitcher) and the frozen margarita of the day for $4.75. Stop in to see which beer is on special. And while you kick back and relax in the comfortable loft-style establishment (Jaks Tap is housed in an old industrial building), you'll see that there's more to take in the just the eye-pleasing decor; you can take in a game of pool or try your hand at a game of darts as well. It's also a great place to go with a large group due to the large, open space and ample seating. Whether you're looking to relax over a beverage, share an inexpensive night out with a friend, or practice all the moves you learned watching *The Color of Money*, Jaks Tap is a choice spot. Open Monday through Wednesday, 11:00 a.m. - 12:00 p.m.; Thursday and Friday, 11:00 a.m. - 2:00 a.m.; Saturday, 5:00 p.m. - 12:00 a.m.

LOU MITCHELL'S

565 West Jackson Boulevard, Chicago IL 60661. 312/939-6800.
The Lowdown: Chivalry is not dead! Lou Mitchell's, a popular diner just west of the Loop since 1923, offers a box of Milk Duds to any lady who has to wait in line for a seat. Prepare to go ahead and lose a few fillings since, at any time of day, you're apt to find a winding line. But the queue moves quickly, and any wait

you may need to endure will surely be worth it. *USA Today* has recommended Lou Mitchell's, and Bisquick named it one of the top 25 neighborhood eateries in the country. To these kudos, Mr. C adds his humble nod. The crowd is diverse; businesspeople, families, travelers from the nearby Union Station and Greyhound bus terminal are just a few of the people you will find here. Different as they may be, they all come for the same thing: Lou's amazingly quick service, cheap prices, and delicious and hearty food. Breakfast is served all day long. Cinnamon raisin bread, baked daily on the premises, is sliced extra thick. A giant mound of hash browns is just $1.50; the popular (and gigantic) fresh fruit salad goes for $3.50. Malted waffles, a neat idea, are served with real maple syrup. A steady supply of marmalade and jam are kept in silver bowls on the tables and countertop. The omelettes all cost $6.00 or more, but the price is easily justified by their size and fluffiness. Lunch and dinner specials change daily, but the most expensive item on the permanent menu is the deluxe albacore tuna salad sandwich, a hefty handful garnished with tomato and cheddar and served with both French fries and cole slaw. Other popular classics include half-pound beefburgers, BLTs, and real sliced turkey sandwiches. All the desserts are homemade. Lou's chocolate chip cookies are loaded with chips and big pecan pieces and the pound cake is extra buttery, while the pie of the day sells for just $1.95 a slice. If you're too full for dessert after your meal, you can always order something to take home with you; not just the desserts, but perhaps a loaf of Greek bread or raisin bread too. If the weather is pleasant, tables are set up on the brick front patio. There's a minimum order of $3.00 per person at Lou's. *$Cash Only$*

MRS. LEVY'S DELICATESSEN

233 South Wacker Drive, Plaza Level, Chicago IL 60606. 312/993-0530. **The Lowdown:** Wouldn't it be great if every neighborhood had a Mrs. Levy? Located within Sears Tower, Mrs. Levy's Delicatessen is a New York-style deli offering great sandwiches, homemade soups, and daily entrees for as little as $2.00 a plate. They also offer an array of delicious soda fountain creations; it's impossible to eat here without drooling over the milkshakes that pass by. Because it's in the Loop (an area catering to the 9-5 business crowd), Mrs. Levy's is only open during the week. And, because it's located within the Sears Tower, most of the clientele work within the building. Drop in for breakfast or lunch and you just may run into Mrs. Levy herself! Open Monday through Friday, 6:30 a.m. – 3:00 p.m.

MY THAI

333 South State Street, Chicago IL 60604. 312/986-0999. **The Lowdown:** Right in the corner of Chicago Music Mart sits My Thai, a fantastic and inexpensive Thai restaurant. The large menu doesn't list a thing over $10.00. Start out with something from the appetizer menu which includes standard favorites like egg rolls, fried wonton, and fried tofu as well as prawn rolls, tod mun, or shrimp and vegetable tempura. Expect the dishes to be big; the menu told me that my order of spring rolls consisted of two rolls. What the menu didn't say, however, was that the rolls

would be two of the longest rolls I had ever seen, sliced into six sections each. Plus, the rolls were wrapped in a thick rice paper, served soft, and cooked so you can actually see and taste the different ingredients: fresh cucumber, bean sprouts, egg, etc. Lots of delicious soups are available too like the spicy favorite tom yum. Other light options include a cucumber salad, beef salad, or bean thread salad. Noodle dishes include the always-popular pad Thai, pad woon sen, and pad see eiw with your choice of chicken or beef. All entrees come with a side of jasmine rice and are priced right at around $5.50. Choose from such well-known meals as pepper steak, sweet almond beef, chop suey with your choice of chicken or beef, or spicy basil leaves. Mr. C went with the chicken rama which, while it often attracts my attention on the menu, never seems to deliver. The dish here is quite a different story; it definitely packed the culinary punch I so often crave. Curry dishes are all $5.50 and encompass your choice of red, yellow, or green. If you're feeling a bit more adventurous, try one of the chef's specialties which include such tasty meals as Siam spicy catfish, seafood curry, and exotic duck. A respectable beverage menu includes lots of wines by the glass or carafe, and more than 10 bottled beers including Kirin, Tsing Tao, and Singha. Open Monday through Friday, 10:30 a.m. – 9:00 p.m.; Saturday, 11:00 a.m. – 9:00 p.m.

SOPRAFFINA MARKETCAFFE

10 North Dearborn, Chicago IL 60605. 312/984-0044. ◆ 222 West Adams Street, Chicago IL 60606. 312/726-4800. ◆ 200 East Randolph Street, Chicago IL 60601. 312/729-9200. **The Lowdown:** Sopraffina Marketcaffe is one of those great little cafeteria-style places where you grab a tray and go to town. They specialize in Italian food and offer a good variety of sandwiches, thin crust pizzas, and pastas. Served on a delicious Italian flatbread, a Sopraffina sandwich is always a good choice for a quick lunch. And at just $5.95 apiece, they're a terrific inexpensive option too. Just a few of the delicious choices are an Assisi (grilled portabello, red onions, watercress, and garlic herb mayo); Parma (ham, gruyere cheese, Vidalia onion dressing); and Portofino (tuna salad, dill havarti cheese, lettuce, and tomato). Pizza varieties are unique and delicious and include such toppings as pesto, Vidalia onions, roasted garlic, and fontina cheese. You can order them in half or whole sizes. Pasta dishes include vegetarian stuffed shells (ricotta cheese, spinach, garden vegetables); gemelli pasta (braided pasta with mushrooms, carrots, sugar snap peas, and a pesto and parmesan cream sauce); and lasagna verdura (roasted veggies with goat cheese in a tomato basil cream sauce). A large cooler and a specialty coffee bar are sure to contain whatever it is you're thirsting for.

TASTE OF SIAM

600 South Dearborn Street, Chicago IL 60605. 312/939-1179. **The Lowdown:** For cheap eats with atmosphere to boot, try Taste of Siam, an easy-to-find and popular spot in Dearborn Park. Not only is it cheap, but the food tastes great too. Beef noodle soup with rice noodles, sprouts, celery, and green onion is a tasty, healthy portion, and worth every penny it costs. Other

inexpensive appetizers include fried tofu, prawn rolls, shrimp and vegetable tempura, and the Siam Platter, a sampler of satay, spring rolls, vegetable tempura, chicken golden cups, egg rolls and prawn rolls. All of these appetizers are big enough to share. Entrees are wonderful and low-priced. Roast duck, pepper steak, ginger chicken , and a mixed vegetable stir fry are just a few of the entree menu's under $10.00 offerings. Thai custard will finish off your meal on a sweet note. If you would like your order prepared any special way (spicier perhaps, or with extra noodles), the kitchen will be happy to oblige you. Because Taste of Siam is so popular, it's a good idea to arrive ahead of the lunch or dinner rush, or to call ahead for reservations. Open Sunday, 12:00 p.m. - 9:30 p.m.; Monday through Thursday, 11:00 a.m. - 9:30 p.m.; Friday and Saturday, 11:00 a.m. - 10:30 p.m.

TRATTORIA DINOTTO

163 West North Avenue, Chicago IL. 312/787-3345. **World Wide Web address:** http://www.dinotto.com. **The Lowdown:** Casual and comfortable, everyone will feel at home at Trattoria Dinotto. The cuisine is Northern Italian and the taste is authentic. Appetizers include bruschetta romana; calamari with marinated tomatoes, chili oil and lemon; and polenta con funghi. For the next course, sample a Caesar salad or antipasto caprese. The pasta dishes are sure to please as well. Some are simple, like farfalle primavera, while others are more daring, like the penne al brevido con gamberetti (rock shrimp, garlic, basil, and spicy marinara sauce over penne). But don't stop there... there are still chicken and veal delicacies as well as a variety of pizzas to try. One thing is for sure, no one will go home hungry. Open Sunday, 5:00 p.m. - 9:00 p.m.; Monday through Thursday, 12:00 p.m. - 10:00 p.m.; Friday and Saturday, 12:00 p.m. - 11:00 p.m.

ZOOP

212 West Van Buren Street, Chicago IL 60607. 312/957-1000. **The Lowdown:** Any way you ladle it, there's no denying that the soups at Zoop are definitely hearty enough to constitute "a meal." On any given day, you'll be faced with more than 10 soup choices (with a thoughtful consideration given to dieters and vegans alike). If just one of these soups isn't enough, they offer a few different combo platters that will allow you to enjoy two and three kinds at a time. Every carton of soup (the portions are large) comes with a delicious baguette as well. Plus, the condiment table is more chock full than any I've ever seen. Be warned that there's not much seating; Zoop is definitely geared toward the take-out and delivery crowd. Still, if you're shopping or touring the area during the week, it makes a great inexpensive and quick lunchtime stop. Open Monday through Friday, 10:30 a.m. - 3:30 p.m.

Far North

NEIGHBORHOODS INCLUDE:
Andersonville ❖ Lakeview ❖ Rogers Park
❖ Roscoe Village ❖ Uptown ❖ Wrigleyville

ANNA MARIA PASTERIA

3953 North Broadway, Chicago IL 60613.
773/929-6363. **World Wide Web address:** http://www.
annamariapasteria.com. **The Lowdown:** These two sisters (Anna
and Maria, hence the name) cook up some mean servings from
southern and northern Italy in a delightfully elegant setting. The
atmosphere here is pure old world. From the brick-lined archway
to the intimate table settings, this is a great place to bring a date
or engage in a quiet evening of catching up with an old friend.
Start out on the light side with one of Anna Maria's soups, salads,
or antipasti; grilled calamaria and marinated portabello
mushrooms are just two of the many choices. Lots of homemade
pastas – including lasagna, manicotti, stuffed shells, and rigatoni
al forno – are priced under $10.00 a plate. Heavier pasta dishes,
like fettucini alfredo or linguini pesto, are a bit more expensive,
though still under $11.00 a serving. You'll spend the most money
when you start browsing the chicken, seafood, and veal menus,
but prices are still excellent! Where else could you find such
dishes as scallops diavola, frutti di mare, chicken marsala, and
veal scaloppine in the $11.00 - $15.00 price range? Dessert is
always a good idea at Anna Maria and Mr. Cheap heartily recommends
ordering up a serving of the tiramisu. Outdoor seating makes for
a particularly pleasing meal in warmer weather. Even with a
decent wine list, Anna Maria welcomes you to bring your own
bottle of choice (though there is a $5.00 cork fee). Open Sunday
through Thursday, 5:00 p.m. - 10:00 p.m.; Friday and Saturday,
5:00 p.m. - 11:00 p.m.

BUCA DI BEPPO

2941 North Clark Street, Chicago IL 60657. 773/348-7673.
E-mail address: famiglia@bucadibeppo.com. **World Wide Web
address:** http://www.bucadibeppo.com. **The Lowdown:** If you
know that the motto at Buca di Beppo is "Italian Dinners and
Sanitary Bathrooms," you can certainly figure out that this is not
a place where pretention reigns. If there isn't already a Buca di
Beppo near you, it's definitely worth a try. Though they have
locations throughout the country, Bucs di Beppo refers to
themselves as a "collection of neighborhood restaurants" rather
than a chain, because each restaurant is so unique in layout and
decor. They specialize in what they refer to as "immigrant
Southern Italian cooking." But what exactly does that mean? It
means that the dinners you'll find here have originated in Sicily,
Campania, Apulia, and other places in southern Italy, and that
the portions are huge – they're meant for sharing. Stop in with a
few friends or bring the entire family. Choose from the many
different meat and pasta dishes, and pass those plates along so
that everyone can try a bit. Eating family-style is always an

intimate experience in itself, and at Buca di Beppo it is a completely casual and fun one too. The first location of Buca di Beppo, which was opened in a basement (hence the origination of the name; "buca" means "basement"), really set the precedent for these casual and fun-filled eateries. Just remember that everything here comes in huge portions, from the plates of food that typically serve two to five people, to the three-liter jugs of chianti which, depending on your party's tolerance, should suit the same number. Best of all, splitting the meal means splitting the bill; a completely filling meal (with plenty of leftovers) can easily cost you under $20.00 per person. The atmosphere alone is worth more than that! Open Sunday, 12:00 p.m. - 10:00 p.m.; Monday through Thursday, 5:00 p.m. - 10:00 p.m.; Friday, 5:00 p.m. - 11:00 p.m.; Saturday, 4:00 p.m. - 11:00 p.m.

FLUKY'S

6821 North Western Avenue, Chicago IL 60645. 773/274-3652. **E-mail address:** info@flukys.com. **World Wide Web address:** http://www.flukys.com. **The Lowdown:** Dining has never been so easy, nostalgic, or cheap. Fluky's brings back memories of hot dog joints from yesteryear; they've even got a drive-through for an authentic evocative experience. This Rogers Park stop has been an institution for more than 70 years. The colorful dining room is one that kids and their parents alike will enjoy dining in, and Fluky's even offers an al fresco dining option when the weather is warm enough. Open Sunday, 7:00 a.m. – 10:00 p.m.; Monday through Thursday, 6:00 a.m. – 10:30 p.m.; Friday and Saturday, 6:00 a.m. – 11:00 p.m.

GOOSE ISLAND BREWING COMPANY

3535 North Clark Street, Chicago IL. 773/832-9040. **E-mail address:** info@gooseisland.com. **World Wide Web address:** http://www.gooseisland.com. **The Lowdown:** Come for the beer, but stay for the food: that's my advice to you concerning this cozy Wrigleyville brewpub. Though Goose Island is widely-known for the beer they brew, they also offer a great menu of traditional and affordable comfort food in a relaxed setting. Much of the food is made to complement the beer selection. Then again, with as big a beer menu as they're offering, you'd be hard pressed to find a beer that *didn't* match up with a certain food. Start out with something as simple as a pretzel with your choice of topping including cheddar jalapeño, parmesan, or classic Bavarian cheese; or opt for something as unique as a Honker's Ale-marinated beef and veggie skewer with sage couscous. The goat cheese pizza is another recommended dish. Sandwiches include a blackened catfish Po' Boy; barbecued pulled pork on an onion roll; and grilled portabello with onions, mushrooms, bacon, or cheese. For your main course indulge in what they call the "World's Finest Fish and Chips" (I'll let you be the judge), turkey mole pot pie, or a BBQ glazed grilled Atlantic salmon. Entrees start at $9.95 and can work their way up close to $20.00 for a filet mignon with lots of extras. Still, this is not your typical pub food because, well, Goose Island is not your typical pub. Open Monday and Wednesday through Friday, 4:00 p.m. - 12:00 a.m.; Saturday and Sunday, 10:00 a.m. - 12:00 a.m.; closed Tuesday.

As we all know how well beer and baseball go together, hours at Goose Island change during the baseball season. Monday through Friday, they are open 11:00 a.m. - 12:00 a.m.; Saturday and Sunday, they are open 10:00 a.m. - 12:00 a.m.

HaSHALOM

2905 West Devon Avenue, Chicago IL 60059. 312/465-5675.
The Lowdown: For a quick break while bargain hunting on Devon, this may be the ultimate place for cheap Israeli and Moroccan eats. Mr. C isn't sure just how the lone waitress managed to calmly handle the giant lunchtime crowd, but she did, and super-quickly at that. His falafel arrived less than five minutes after the waitress took the order, a mean feat for both her and the chef. The falafel was not overly spicy, and was full of crispy, toasted sesame seeds. A side order of baba ganoush was spiked with a good dose of paprika and parsley, and came with plenty of pita bread. Other appetizers include Moroccan Cigars, which are ground beef, pine nuts and hot peppers rolled into filo dough; and matbukha, which is chopped tomatoes cooked with hot peppers and spices. Entrees are served with soup or salad, rice or potatoes, and pita bread, and most are priced under $10.00. Beef or lamb shish kabob, fish a la tveria (whitefish with thina sauce), and lahme (lamb sautéed with pine nuts and spicy cumin sauce, served with hummus) are just a few of the other choices. For lighter appetites, HaShalom offers sandwich plates like the lox platter with one or two bagels; and the falafel sandwich. Sandwich versions of the chicken, lamb, or beef shish kabobs are served with pita, Israeli salad, thina sauce and French fries. There's American-style deli food as well like kosher salami, corned beef sandwiches, or a tuna salad sandwich. Coffee is a mere $.55, though Mr. C prefers dark Israeli coffee for $.85. Cafe au lait is the most expensive beverage at $1.00. With food and drinks so cheap, you can afford to indulge in one of their desserts, like poppyseed cake, baklava, or creme caramel. Open Monday through Friday, 12:00 p.m. - 9:00 p.m.; closed Saturday and Sunday. This restaurant does not have a liquor license, but you are welcome to bring your own. *$Cash Only$*

NHU HOA CAFE

1020 West Argyle Street, Chicago IL 60640. 773/878-0618.
The Lowdown: Among the Vietnamese restaurants on Argyle Street, Nhu Hoa offers something a little bit different: Laotian cuisine. Laotian flavorings bare a striking resemblance to their close neighbors, Thai and Vietnamese, but there are definitely some subtle differences you can taste. Compared to the other places on this block, Nhu Hoa Cafe can get a bit expensive, especially when you delve into the seafood menu. Still, the surroundings are correspondingly more upscale: a pair of lions greet you outside the door, and a giant Buddha statue welcomes you once inside. Meanwhile, much of the vast menu is well within Mr. C's price range. Most of the main dishes range are under $10.00, and portions are certainly ample. Start off with a bowl of keng som kay, which was perhaps the tangiest and tastiest soup Mr. C has ever had. An individual bowl is big enough to be a meal by itself, although there are three larger sizes for couples and

groups to share. For other authentic Laotian fare, try an order of Laos noodles; they're rice noodles with shrimp, chicken, eggs, and bean sprouts mixed in, plus ground peanuts and chilies over the top. For those who enjoy authentically spicy cuisine, there are three varieties of curry: Panang, which is the true style sauce, made with straw mushrooms and chili paste, as well as the more recognizable red and green curries. Whichever you choose, you can apply it to beef, chicken, pork, shrimp, mussels, or squid. There are lots of other items to choose from, including salads and vegetarian dishes. And yet, this is only about one-third of the menu, which covers the full spectrum of Vietnamese cooking as well. Over 150 different examples of it, in fact. These options are a bit less expensive than the Laotian items, as Vietnamese meals consist largely of soups, stews, and rice dishes, but trust me, they're no less filling or tasty. A popular starter is the chim cut quay appetizer: four tiny, whole quail roasted to a crispy brown, with enough for two people to share. There are over a dozen steamed rice main dishes, mixing in such ingredients as grilled beef, shrimp, pork, and lobster meat. Add a Singha, Tsing Tao, or glass of the house wine to your meal. When you're done, try the wonderfully sweet, thick coffees or a fruit milk shake, made with pineapple, avocado, guanabana, and the like. Nhu Hoa also offers lunch specials Tuesday through Friday, 11:30 a.m. - 3:00 p.m. Open Sunday, 9:30 a.m. - 10:00 p.m.; Tuesday through Thursday, 9:30 a.m. - 10:30 p.m.; Friday and Saturday, 9:30 a.m. - 10:30 p.m.; closed Monday.

PAULINE'S
1754 West Balmoral Avenue, Chicago IL 60640. 773/561-8573.
The Lowdown: On just about every block in Chicago, you're bound to come across a reasonably-priced 1950s-style diner. And while I want you to have a wallet-friendly time in the Windy City, I also want you to experience a little diversity. Nonetheless, I couldn't rightfully exclude such a great little diner like Pauline's from this book. From the red vinyl booths to the posters of Hollywood stars of yesteryear that line the walls, everything about Pauline's screams poodle skirts and lettermen sweaters. You almost expect Frankie Avalon to descend from the sky singing his famous rendition of "Beauty School Dropout." As Pauline's is only open until the early afternoon, it's breakfast and lunch that you'll come here for. For breakfast, why not try one of Pauline's famous omelettes with a variety of fillings to choose from. They're nicely priced and did I mention, they're made with *five* eggs? That's right, *FIVE!* If you're part of a duo with a lighter appetite, it might be beneficial (but still oh-so-filling) to split one. Pauline's offers daily specials that can be viewed by checking the blackboard. Pauline's is definitely one of those places where you shouldn't be afraid to take the kids along; they're more than welcome and are guaranteed to love it. Open daily, 7:00 a.m. - 3:00 p.m. *$Cash Only$*

REZA'S
5255 North Clark Street, Chicago IL 60640. 773/561-1898.
World Wide Web address: http://www.rezas.com.
The Lowdown: This longtime Middle Eastern favorite in

Andersonville serves up incredibly large portions of Persian specialties at surprisingly low prices. Many folks call it one of the best deals in town. Reza's Restaurant has a handsome and spacious dining room, done up in natural wood with brass trim. The front of the restaurant even opens up onto Clark Street for refreshing summer breezes. Start off with one of two dozen appetizers, many of which are vegetarian. Falafel, of course, is a must; but try the vegetable casserole, a blend of zucchini, eggplant, carrots, green peppers, and scallions baked in a tomato sauce and served over rice. Entrees consist of lots of lamb, poultry, beef, and vegetarian options. Mr. C opted for what is simply called The Combo: one skewer of charbroiled filet mignon and one skewer of marinated grilled chicken, separated by a mountain of dill flavored rice. Most menu items are available for $11.00 or under. And if you have room for dessert, try a strong cup of coffee and a piece of the homemade baklava or zoulbia, a deep-fried pastry made without sugar. And don't worry about trying to pronounce the names of the Middle Eastern cuisine (it can be excruciating); you can order by number as well. Open daily, 11:00 p.m. - 12:00 a.m.

TIE ME UP NOODLES THAI & ASIAN CUISINE
434 West Diversey Parkway, Chicago IL 60614. 773/404-1145.
The Lowdown: If the name alone doesn't make you curious, my raves about the food here certainly should. Tie Me Up Noodles Thai & Asian Cuisine is a one-room noodle shop that serves up some pretty big portions. For example, an order of spring rolls consists of a dozen tofu delights. Other great (and weighty) appetizers include steamed dumplings, fried tofu, gyoza, and pot stickers. For a new take on a traditional favorite, try the Tie Me Up Rolls. They're enormous and stuffed with shrimp, chicken, crab meat, lettuce, and noodles. Tie Me Up offers a number of great soups including won ton, vegetable, tofu, and tom yum. And, of course, there are oodles of noodles: chicken, beef, BBQ pork, roasted duck, basil, garlic, udon are just a few of the varieties you can choose from. And they're all priced right around $6.00. Tie Me Up also serves some great pad Thai, pad se eu, and crazy noodles. Tie Me Up has a number of entree options as well, with dishes like basil catfish, pad ped talay, and pad woon sen. Desserts include sweet sticky rice and mango, coconut custard, and warm fried bananas. Drop in on a weekday between 11:30 a.m. and 3:30 p.m. and you can take advantage of the Tie Me Up lunch special where just $4.99 will get you an appetizer and an entree. Open Sunday through Thursday, 11:30 a.m. - 10:00 p.m.; Friday and Saturday, 11:30 a.m. - 11:00 p.m.

TIFFIN
2536 West Devon Avenue, Chicago IL 60659. 773/338-2143.
The Lowdown: Tiffin offers some of the most authentic and delicious Indian food in town; and it's cheap too, making it one of my personal favorites. The menu is almost too heavy to lift it's so big, thus increasing everyone's chance of finding the perfect meal. Let's start with the appetizers: samosa (veggie-stuffed pastry), ragara patties (herb and spice stuffed potato patty), and paneer pokoras (cottage cheese fritters) are just a few of the

starters available under $8.00. Vegetarians will be happy to see an extensive menu just for them comprised of such delectable dishes as aloo simla mirch (potatoes and bell peppers in herbs and spices) and kadai paneer (cottage cheese with green peppers, tomatoes, and onions) all priced between $7.95 and $9.95. Chicken curry, mixed grill platter, shrimp masala, and lamb polak are just a sampling of the rest of the massive menu. Some of the most popular dishes are cooked fresh in Tiffin's tandoor. Lamb chops and chicken tandoor are two of the low in fat meals that can be prepared in this traditional clay oven. Conclude the meal with one of their many delicious desserts like the rasmalai (cottage cheese dumpling) or rice khir (basmati rice and milk flavored with cardamom seeds, almonds, and raisins), and I promise you won't be sorry. Open Sunday and Monday, 11:30 a.m. - 9:30 p.m.; Tuesday through Thursday, 11:30 a.m. - 3:30 p.m.; Friday and Saturday, 11:30 a.m. - 10:00 p.m.

WISHBONE RESTAURANT
3300 North Lincoln Avenue, Chicago IL 60657. 773/549-2663.
The Lowdown: One way to find a good restaurant is to follow the crowds, even for a good distance. Wishbone Restaurant always has loyal patrons waiting for a table, especially for the weekend brunch. What are they doing right? The food, of course. It's homemade, scrumptious, and cheap. Rustle up a plate of black-eyed peas and rice with sauce, melted cheese, scallions, and tomato over the top, with salad and a hunk of cornbread, all for under $5.00. Get the picture? Down home cooking is the order of the day at Wishbone. Blackened chicken breast with rice, cornbread, and a vegetable of the day is just $6.50, as is the baked bone-in-ham platter or barbecued pork. Burgers and sandwiches complete the menu, along with the occasionally exotic special, such as chicken and shrimp etoufee. You can order a la carte; or, for $1.00 extra, add your choice of sides like peppered green beans, corn chowder, couscous, or fruit salad. I particularly enjoyed an order of bean cakes, slightly spicy, made with potato, black-eyed peas, and chunks of carrot. Vegetarians will be happy here with dishes such as stuffed acorn squash and eggplant parmigiana. There is a full liquor license, and Wishbone features Southern brews like Dixie Beer. For dessert, finish with a slice of sweet potato pie or peach cobbler. Wishbone Restaurant also serves a breakfast that includes heaping omelette plates topped with homemade biscuits for around $4.00. Open Monday through Friday, 7:00 a.m. - 11:00 p.m.; Saturday, 8:00 a.m. - 11:00 p.m. Closed Sunday and Monday nights. *$Cash Only$*

Lincoln Park

ATHENIAN ROOM

807 West Webster Avenue, Chicago IL 60614. 773/348-5155. **The Lowdown:** Traditional Greek dining is comprised of a variety of Mediterranean specialties: kebabs, lamb, gyros, etc. The Athenian Room offers these favorite Greek foods, with an authentically American spin. Have you ever had your souvlakia with Greek fries? Well, now's your chance. The Athenian Room's specialty is Greek chicken, but it's the gyros that have been called the best in town. The prices are fantastic, with many sandwiches starting below $6.00. Dinners are priced a little higher with the most expensive dish, Alexandros-style steak for just under $12.00. Keep in mind salad, fries, and bread are included with the meal. Open daily, 11:00 a.m. - 10:00 p.m.

bw-3

2464 North Lincoln Avenue, Chicago IL 60614. 773/868-9453. **The Lowdown:** The name of this place is bw-3: it's short for Buffalo Wild Wings and Weck. But what the heck is a weck? It's a wacky name for a casual, comfortable Lincoln Park saloon. bw-3 has the feel of a college hangout, and it definitely attracts a younger crowd. They are no doubt attracted by the large quantities of low-priced bar food: buffalo wings, hamburgers, nachos, and several other unique items have prices like a fast-food joint. Wings, for example (which come in multiples of six) are just $2.99 for a half-dozen, or $5.24 for 12. Every Tuesday, wings are just $.20 apiece! They come glazed in one of eight different sauces including wild, mild, curry, sweet BBQ, and teriyaki. At the least, charcoal-grilled Weckburgers weigh an entire third of a pound. The menu says they are possibly the best burger in America; I'll let you be the judge of that. You can't beat the price for real beef: $3.49 - $4.29 for the basic versions, going up to only $6.29 for fancier sorts like the Swiss and shroom or the black and bleu burger. Sides are extra, but worth it; the French fries are thick slices of deep-fried potatoes, from $2.29 for a regular order to $4.89 for a basket with chili and cheese. Go for it! Chicken breast sandwiches are a good bet, with lots of extras like cheese and sauce available. Now we get to the Mexican side, with homemade chili, chicken fajitas, and buffalitos (stuffed tortillas) comprising just a portion of the menu. If you're looking for a friendly place to pig out, bw-3 is the place. There are plenty of good beers on tap and in bottles, and the place is open nice and late. Plus, with nearly 30 TVs, you certainly won't miss that big game! Open Sunday, 11:00 a.m. - 1:00 a.m.; Monday, 11:00 a.m. - 12:00 a.m.; Tuesday through Friday, 11:00 a.m. - 2:00 a.m.; Saturday, 11:00 a.m. - 3:00 a.m.

BEAT KITCHEN

2100 West Belmont Avenue, Chicago IL 60618. 773/281-4444. **The Lowdown:** Perhaps best known for the variety of great live music presented on its stage Beat Kitchen has an equally eclectic and delicious menu. The name tells you, this is a place for good music and good food. And that goes for light snacks or hearty appetites. The menu starts off, as so many in Chicago do, with pizzas. Nice-sized individual pies are $9.95 each, in several innovative combinations. Thai pizza is decked out with peanut sauce, cucumber, bean sprouts, carrots, smoked chicken, peppers, onions, and jalapeños. There is also a breakfast pizza with eggs, mushroom, green pepper, red onion, bacon, and jalapeño jack cheese. This is pizza? Chomp on hefty sandwiches like Cajun meatloaf served with veggie sauce, blackened chicken breast, or a good old Italian sausage grinder. All come with grilled potatoes and cole slaw on the side. There's an interesting choice of homemade soups, from corn tortilla to chicken gumbo, and salads too, making a meal out of any sandwich. The long, cozy bar features a good selection of domestic and imported beers, both bottled and on tap. Beat Kitchen is also a fun place to see all kinds of live rock and folk music for very little money. Open every day but Sunday, with live music every night; they serve lunches and dinners, with food available until 1:00 a.m.

BROTHER JIMMY'S BBQ

2909 North Sheffield Avenue, Chicago IL 60657. 773/528-0888.
The Lowdown: What a hopping place this is! When they're not raising the roof with live music, they're lowering the price on their great barbecued chow. Outside, all you see is a simple doorway. Inside, this is a huge, high-ceilinged version of a North Carolina roadhouse, right down to the Duke paraphernalia on the walls. There's a long bar area, lots of dining tables and booths, and a stage which features free, live music every Thursday, Friday, and Saturday night. The food consists mainly of burgers, barbecued chicken, ribs, and variations thereof; and you get tons of food for your dough. Three flavors of ribs (spicy, sweet, and dry-rub) come in platters with two side dishes and corn bread, all for $13.95; you sure won't go away hungry. All styles of meat are smoked over hickory wood and there are a dozen of those down-home sides like mashed potatoes, candied yams, collard greens, and baked beans. Plus, Brother Jimmy's serves up some great chili, soups, salads, and Tex-Mex appetizers. On Mondays, $5.95 will get you all the pasta you can eat. Stop by on a Wednesday and enjoy "Wing Night," when $.10 wings and $5.00 pitchers are the specialty du jour. Sunday may be a day for resting for most, but not at Brother Jimmy's. On Sunday, $17.95 will get you all the ribs and draft beer you can eat and drink (drinks keep coming as long as you're eating)! The kitchen serves food until 11:00 p.m. on weekdays, and until 1:00 a.m. on weekends, while the club stays open a bit later. Open Sunday, 11:00 a.m. - 11:00 p.m.; Monday through Friday, 5:00 p.m. - 2:00 a.m.; Saturday, 11:00 a.m. - 3:00 a.m.

CAFE LE LOUP

3348 North Sheffield Avenue, Chicago IL 60657. 773/248-1830.
The Lowdown: In French, Le Loup means wolf. Of course, if you've ever been here, you'd know that by now. The walls of this bistro are crammed with pictures of wolves and other lupine paraphernalia. But don't worry, you won't find "le loup" on the menu; the specialty here is French-Mediterranean. If you're used

to bistro dining, you know that menus at these types of places are often a bit limited. But that's really what makes them so great; it forces you to try dishes you might not order otherwise. Starched white tablecloths and fresh flowers adorn the tables at this popular Wrigleyville spot, and bring with them a distinct air of upscale eating. Appetizers on the French side include escargots de bourgogne ($6.95) and pâté maison ($6.95); Mediterranean treats include hummus and toasted pita bread ($5.95) and spinach and feta cheese filo pockets ($6.95). An ever-changing entree menu includes a number of seasonal specialties, but also sustains a number of customer favorite staples that are very reasonably-priced. Boeuf bourguignon ($11.95), cassoulet ($12.95), and couscous dishes ($12.95) are just a few of the plates you can usually find here. Herbivore dishes like vegetarian crêpes and ratatouille are all priced under $9.00. Couple those prices with your own, you-pick-the-price bottle of wine (there's a minimum $2.00 corkage fee) and you'll be eating like a king. Just don't let the wolves catch a whiff of it! Make sure you grab a seat in the outdoor patio (enclosed and heated in the winter). Open Sunday through Thursday, 5:00 p.m. - 10:30 (closed Monday); Friday and Saturday, 5:00 p.m. - 11:00 p.m. This restaurant has no liquor license, but you are welcome to bring your own.

THE CHICAGO DINER
3411 North Halsted Street, Chicago IL 60657. 773/935-6696.
The Lowdown: Don't look for your average greasy burger and fries at this diner. While trying to shrug off Chicago's reputation as hog butcher to the world, this vegetarian restaurant in Lake View has developed a fine reputation in its own right. The owners are world travelers, which is reflected in the cosmopolitan nature of the menu. This sensibility extends to the cozy wooden booths and tiny tables with pastel floral tablecloths, which lend a romantic air to the place. Try the Future Burger, which is made from basmati rice, couscous, and vegetables and garnished with lettuce, tomato, sprouts, carrots, onion, and pickles all on a whole wheat bun for around $7.00. Add a cup of miso soup for $1.50 more, or a side order of tempeh strips for $1.95. Or, opt for the macrobiotic plate: vegetable, bean and grain of the day plus kale, rice, sea vegetable, pickle, and a choice of tofu or tempeh with miso sauce or gravy. It's as much of a mouthful to eat as it is to describe! The soup of the day or a tossed salad can be added to any entree for just a little bit extra, and most dishes are served with a choice of bread: homemade cornbread, whole wheat pita, seven-grain toast, sprouted English muffin, or walnut-raisin bagel. Lacto-ovo vegetarians and other hard-core vegans can eat here without concern: any dish with dairy cheese can be made with soy cheese as a substitute. If you're not a vegetarian, don't worry about the unfamiliar items on the menu; a handy glossary is provided, and many of these things taste better than you may think. Despite the restaurant's relatively late opening time, it does serve breakfast including tofu scrambles, granola, and French toast. Saturday and Sunday breakfasts offer additional choices like ex-Benedict (grilled tempeh patties on an English muffin, topped with poached eggs

and cheese sauce, and served with home fries). Beverages include herbal teas, carrot, beet, celery, apple or orange juices, soy milk, organic wine, and ciders. The diner has a children's menu, too. Open Monday through Friday, 11:00 a.m. - 10:00 p.m., Saturday and Sunday, 10:00 a.m. - 10:00 p.m.

CLARKE'S PANCAKE HOUSE
2441 North Lincoln Avenue, Chicago IL 60614. 773/472-3505. **The Lowdown:** While there are plenty of all-night pancake houses to contend with, Clarke's is distinctive for its clean, bright white interior and diverse menu. Oh sure, you can get pancakes: German, Swedish, apple, blueberry, carrot, zucchini, raisin, wheat germ, and the list goes on. They're all delicious and priced to devour. But there's more here than breakfast fare. Clarke's serves a variety of sandwiches including Teriyaki chicken, grilled cheese, stir-fried veggies in pita bread, and the San Diego Club (a B.L.T. with ham and cheese). Clarke's goes Mexican with quesadillas and burritos, filled with your choice of chicken, steak, spinach, or vegetables. Their Tijuana pizza is an individual pie made with salsa, onions, Jack cheese, and chorizo sausage. Desserts are a specialty here, from the J.K. Sweets counter at the front of the restaurant. There are also plenty of malts, floats, and shakes to appease your sweet tooth. Open 24 hours.

GOLDEN APPLE GRILLE
2971 North Lincoln Avenue, Chicago IL 60657. 773/528-1413. **The Lowdown:** This is an old-fashioned neighborhood kind of place, decorated with hanging ivy plants, stained glass windows, and a classic revolving-dessert display case by the cash register. The wide-ranging cuisine runs from the familiar (pasta, barbecued chicken) to the unexpected (enchiladas, served with tortillas and refried beans). Despite the dozens of entrees, the focus of the menu is actually breakfast food. All the usuals are here, along with some surprises like banana pancakes and blintzes (cheese, strawberry, blueberry, apple, or peach). Mexican breakfasts, such as chilaquiles (scrambled eggs with tortilla chips, covered with Monterey jack cheese) are also offered. Most everything is priced well under $10.00. There are almost 20 special items just for children, available to those age 10 and under. The diversified menu and quick service should keep everyone content. Open 24 hours.

GOOSE ISLAND BREWING COMPANY
1800 North Clybourn Avenue, Chicago IL 60614. 312/915-0071. **E-mail address:** info@gooseisland.com. **World Wide Web address:** http://www.gooseisland.com. **The Lowdown:** Come for the beer, but stay for the food: that's my advice to you concerning this cozy Lincoln Park brewpub. Though Goose Island is widely-known for the beer they brew, they also offer a great menu of traditional and affordable comfort food in a relaxed setting. Much of the food is made to complement the beer selection: then again, with as big a beer menu as they're offering, you'd be hard pressed to find a beer that didn't match up with a certain food. Start out with something as simple as a pretzel with your choice of topping including cheddar jalapeño,

parmesan, or classic Bavarian cheese; or opt for something as unique as a Honker's Ale-marinated beef and veggie skewer with sage couscous. Like any red-blooded Chicago restaurant, Goose Island offers some mighty tasty pizzas as well; try the goat cheese. Sandwiches include a blackened catfish Po' Boy, barbecued pulled pork on an onion roll, and grilled portabello with onions, mushrooms, bacon, or cheese. For your main course indulge in what they call the "World's Finest Fish and Chips", turkey mole pot pie with horseradish mashed potatoes, or a BBQ glazed grilled Atlantic salmon. Entrees start at $9.95 and can work their way up close to $20.00 for a filet mignon with lots of extras. Still, this is not your typical pub food because, well, Goose Island is not your typical pub. If you're interested in finding out what goes on behind the scenes here (read: how they brew all those delicious beers), Goose Island offers a free tour of their brewery every Sunday at 3:00 p.m. After you've learned about the process, you'll be invited to imbibe some samples with the rest of your group. Tours last anywhere from one to one and a half hours (depending on how thirsty you are I guess). Open Sunday, 11:00 a.m. - 1:00 a.m.; Monday through Thursday, 11:30 a.m. - 1:00 a.m.; Friday, 11:30 a.m. - 2:00 a.m.; Saturday, 11:00 a.m. - 2:00 a.m.

HOGHEAD McDUNNA'S

1505 West Fullerton Avenue, Chicago IL 60614. 773/929-0944. **World Wide Web address:** http://www.hogheadmcdunnas. com. **The Lowdown:** In the DePaul University area, Hoghead McDunna's has an extensive food and drink menu, with lots of great lunch and dinner specials. It's a big, spread-out kind of place, with high ceilings and two large, open rooms. The bar room has a number of tables with a comfy living room area in which to relax. Through the doorway is an even larger dining room, with a stage area to host live bands. Both rooms are dominated by numerous large screen televisions and monitors showing several different ballgames at once. The atmosphere is good for sports fans, but the menu is great for everyone. Hoghead McDunna's offers an eclectic blend of appetizers, sandwiches, and entrees. Half-pound, marinated steak burgers with fries and coleslaw start at just $5.99; with that as a good base, you can add a dozen or so items – including roasted garlic, oak-smoked Gouda, and port wine cheddar – for $.50 each. Other menu items include Cajun blackened tuna on pita bread or a Guinness Stout steak sandwich for $6.99 apiece. Hoghead's give the regular old pizza pie a twist to entice the nouvelle crowd with BBQ chicken and caramelized onions, and grilled eggplant with tomato basil feta cheese. They have an impressive array of beers on tap that include (but aren't limited to) Goose Island Honkers Ale, New Castle Brown Ale, and their very own Hoghead McDunna's Red Chicago. For the best deals, come at lunch time when a separate version of the menu prices everything at $3.99 with the purchase of a beverage. On Tuesday, Hoghead McDunna's has a $1.99 all-you-can-eat spaghetti dinner; and on Thursday they host a $1.99 all-you-can-eat/build-your-own taco bar. Hoghead McDunna's is the kind of place to pig out (and save)!

JOHN'S PLACE

1202 West Webster Avenue, Chicago IL 60614. 773/525-6670.
The Lowdown: There's really no one word you could use to describe the menu at John's Place; American comfort foods are listed right along side dishes from all over the world. The comfortable feeling of the food extends to the decor of this place as well; a wood-burning stove is just one of the homey touches. John's serves three square meals a day, though you're better off going for breakfast if you're looking to avoid a crowd. To tell you the truth, there's not much here I wouldn't urge you to try at least once. Start out with one of three types of chili (vegetable, Los Alamos, or spicy chicken). Light-eaters will enjoy the selection of salads and sandwiches like a Chinese noodle salad, a turkey Cobb salad, grilled tofu, or grilled chicken sandwich. John's burgers (meat, veggie, or turkey) come with your choice of sides and can be generously topped with such ingredients as sautéed mushrooms, pico de gallo, roasted red peppers, and guacamole. A number of John's hearty entrees are priced well under $10.00; a veggie burrito, buckwheat soba noodles, chicken and biscuits, and turkey meatloaf are just a few of the options. Even dinners that are priced above $10.00 don't go much higher than $10.95. As good as the food sounds, it might surprise you to know that it is healthful as well. To drink, John's Place blends up an array of delicious vegan-minded smoothies ($3.50 each). They also mix up a number of delicious specialty cocktails like The Cabo, The Spritzer, and Mr. Marks Lemonade. John's Place is just the kind of restaurant that makes regular customers out of casual diners. Open Sunday, 8:00 a.m. – 9:00 p.m.; Monday through Thursday, 11:00 a.m. – 10:00 p.m.; Friday, 11:00 a.m. – 11:00 p.m.; Saturday, 8:00 a.m. – 11:00 p.m.

LAS TABLAS   yes

2965 North Lincoln Avenue, Chicago IL 60657. 773/871-2414.
The Lowdown: You've had Colombian coffee, but what about their cuisine? With a nondescript storefront that could easily be mistaken for a market or some other retail shop, Las Tablas is one of the city's few Colombian restaurants. As you might have guessed, Mr. C is quite a fan of trying new and inventive ethnic cuisines. In my never-ending quest for finding new foods to try, Las Tablas proved to be a great find. Colombian cuisine is chock full of all my favorites: fruits, vegetables, cheese, and grains comprise most of the menu, so the food is actually pretty healthy as well. For an appetizer, an empanada is a great choice; it's a corn shell filled with ground meat, potatoes, rice, and egg. And at $1.50 apiece, you can afford to taste at least one. Other worthy starters include an aborrajado (a sweet plantain with guava and cheese), a papa choriadda (sautéed potato with cheese, onions, and tomatoes in a choriadda sauce) , or a slice of arepa con queso (corn bread with cheese), all for under $2.00 each. When it comes to entrees, there is really something for everyone here. Tradiciones Colombianas is a mix of beans and rice, plantain, and fried yucca. It is served with your choice of a small salad or a dish of potato and avocado. A dish of arroz con pollo is toppling with chicken, rice, green beans, peas, and carrots. Seafood offerings include red snapper, shrimp, and King fish. Las Tablas

also offers some great two-person deals. For just $22.95 ($12.95 for a single serving), you and your companion can enjoy a fantastic paella filled with chicken, octopus, calamari, sausage, shrimp, clams, and vegetables. Picada is another two-for-one favorite; as Colombia's most popular dish, it is a combination of chicken, rib-eye, pork, New York strip steak, and sausage with plantain, yucca, fried potato, and cornbread. It's a veritable smorgasbord of all your favorites and it's only $21.90. As is the case with any restaurant, the most expensive dishes come from the steak menu. Still, at $11.95 for the specialty of the house, churrascaro, (grilled New York strip steak with plantain, fried yucca, and baked potato) even carnivores will find fantastic prices. Drop in for lunch Monday through Friday, from 12:00 p.m. - 3:00 p.m., when $5.00 will get you a chicken, steak, or vegetarian soup and entree. Open Sunday through Thursday, 12:00 p.m. - 10:00 p.m.; Friday and Saturday, 12:00 p.m. - 11:00 p.m. This restaurant has no liquor license, but you are welcome to bring your own.

METROPOLIS ROTISSERIA
924 West Armitage Avenue, Chicago IL 60614. 773/868-9000.
The Lowdown: Restaurants like Metropolis are among the better things to come from the yuppie revolution. Here you can indulge in fast food that's actually made with real, fresh ingredients and a measure of creativity. Metropolis specializes in rotisserie-cooked chicken and pizza. You can get a half-chicken, cooked to golden brown perfection, with a yogurt-garlic sauce and whole grain bread for under $5.00. Add an extra two side dishes (including real mashed potatoes, polenta, pasta salad, Greek salad, or white bean stew) and make a full meal out of it for just a few dollars more. They also offer the same delicious chicken in a sandwich version; try the Tuscan, which combines roasted tomatoes, sweet peppers, onions, and pesto on crunchy bread with a side of coleslaw. Now, back to the pizza. While $2.25 will get you a delicious slice of veggie-packed pan pizza, I heartily recommend trying the 10-inch pie. You can top your pizza with such extras as chicken, spinach, mushrooms, garlic, sautéed onions, blue cheese, and walnuts. The restaurant's decor is another Italian pedigree: white tile walls livened up a bit with a turquoise, goldenrod, and other Southwestern-hued color scheme. You can order the food for take-out or delivery, order at the counter and bring your food to a table, or sit at the window counter and watch the people walk by. Open daily, 11:30 a.m. - 9:30 p.m.

MICKEY'S SNACK BAR
2450 North Clark Street, Chicago IL 60614. 773/435-0007.
The Lowdown: If you're tired of the typical 1950s-style diner chains that keep popping up across America, try Mickey's Snack Bar on for size. While the atmosphere and decor definitely hearken back to the days of doo-wop and ducktails, the menu and the attitude are an eclectic combination of all the decades since. Like any good diner, you can rest assured that meatloaf, chicken pot pie, and a large selection of pies are on the menu. But, what you might not expect is a variety of ethnic foods like

hummus, eggrolls, and quesadillas. The food is fantastic and nary an item costs more than $7.00. With high-quality food being served at more than reasonable prices, this is the kind of place that should make any loyal cheapster stand up and cheer!

MY PIE

2417 North Clark Street, Chicago IL 60614. 773/929-3380. **The Lowdown:** Actually, the big sign out front reads, My π, which means they must specialize in pun pizza. What are they trying to tell us? Was the cook a math major? Is it impossible for these pizzas to be divided evenly? Maybe. But don't let that deter you from trying these fine deep dish creations. The pizzas are baked to a crunchy finish in a deep pan which is brought to the table (thin pizzas are also available). Order up a basic pizza or add as many toppings as you like: sausage, garlic, Canadian bacon, and many more all for about $1.00 each. Or, try the My Pie Special, which has mushrooms, onions, peppers, and either sausage or pepperoni. You could feed half of Chicago with one of these pizzas! Pizza isn't the only thing on the menu, either. Pasta dinners like spinach fettucine alfredo are available too. There are also burgers, salads, and homemade soups. There are tons of appetizer and snacks like spicy Buffalo wings and stuffed garlic bread made with cheese and real garlic. A large salad bar is not only well-stocked with vegetables and fruits, but also pasta and slices of cheese and pepperoni. Make a meal of it, or add it to your pizza. My Pie runs weekday lunch special that offers all-you-can-eat soup, salad, and pizza for just under $8.00. The restaurant itself, despite its small doorfront, is gigantic on the inside. Since everything is baked to order, service can sometimes be slow; but that's the price you pay for pizza perfection. Though this place is always boisterous, the atmosphere is quite comfortable... especially on those cold winter evenings when the large, open fireplace is lit. Open Sunday, 12:00 p.m. - 11:00 p.m.; Monday through Thursday, 11:00 a.m. - 12:00 p.m.; Friday and Saturday, 11:00 a.m. - 2:00 a.m.

PAPRIKÁSH

5210 West Diversey Avenue, Chicago IL 60639. 773/736-4949. **The Lowdown:** Located in Chicago's Cragin neighborhood, Paprikásh is one of the city's truly authentic Hungarian dining establishments. If you're new to Hungarian dining, be prepared to fill up; Hungarian cuisine is known for its heaviness (as well as its spiciness). Entering the unassuming storefront, you will be amazed to find that the restaurant's slogan, "The closest you can get to Hungary without leaving town" becomes reality. The walls are decked out with Hungarian artwork. Authentic cuisine is what you will find here. Chicken paprikash (a specialty) and Hungarian gulyas are mouth-watering bargains, priced under $11.00. Paprikash also offers a wide variety of Hungarian wines and European beers to complement your meal. Open Tuesday through Sunday, 11:00 a.m. - 11:00 p.m.

PENNY'S NOODLE SHOP

3400 North Sheffield Avenue, Chicago IL 60657. 773/281-8222.
♦ 950 West Diversey Parkway, Chicago IL 60614. 773/281-8448.

The Lowdown: If you're a visitor to Chicago, chances are someone will insist that you have to eat at Penny's Noodle Shop. If you live here, no doubt you already know. Penny's Noodle Shop is a fabulous and popular little cafe around the corner from Wrigley Field (but don't even think about getting in before the game). It serves up a mix of Asian dishes that are wholesome, filling, and well under $10.00. Start off with one of half a dozen appetizers, like Thai spring rolls ($3.75). Unlike the tiny deep-fried finger rolls you may expect, this is a single, soft roll served cold and filled with tofu, cucumber, bean sprouts, and egg. For one person, it could almost be an entree; for two or three, there's plenty to share. The noodle dishes themselves range from pad Thai ($5.25) to barbecued pork ($4.00), thick slices on top of a heap of bean sprouts, egg noodles, greens, cilantro, and ground peanuts. It's served in a deep bowl (especially good if you're chopstick skills aren't up to par), and you can have it as a soup, or without broth. The same option is yours with sliced beef or chicken ($4.00), or pork and shrimp wontons ($4.75). Nothing on the menu costs more than about $6.00. Open Tuesday, Wednesday, Thursday, and Sunday, 11:00 a.m. - 10:00 p.m.; Friday and Saturday, 11:00 a.m. - 10:30 p.m.; closed Monday.

PEQUOD'S PIZZA
2207 North Clybourn Avenue, Chicago IL 60614. 773/327-1512.
The Lowdown: Pequod's offers a very distinct, inexpensive, brick oven-flavored pizza, in a sports bar setting. For appetizers, a tremendous bowl of French fries is $2.35, and a good-sized order of garlic bread is just under $2.00. In keeping with the restaurant's nautical Moby Dick theme, the bread is served on a whale-shaped cutting board. Thin crust pizzas are priced at $6.50, $8.50, and $12.25; deep dish pies go for $8.50, $11.25, and $13.95. For an even better deal, try the lunch special (7-inch pan pizza with cheese and one topping, plus a choice of soda or beer) for $4.45. Not in the mood for pizza? Try mostaccioli marinara, or the Pequod salad with cheese, green peppers, onion, mushrooms, pepperoncinis, carrots, black olives, tomato, and pepperoni. There are also a variety of sandwiches to choose from. The famous Eli's Cheesecake is available plain or chocolate chip. Delivery service is available too. Open Monday through Friday, 11:00 a.m. - 2:00 a.m.; Saturday, 12:00 p.m. - 2:00 a.m.; Sunday, 12:00 p.m. - 12:00 a.m.

R.J. GRUNTS
2056 North Lincoln Park West, Chicago IL 60614. 773/929-5363.
World Wide Web address: http://www.leye.com/restaurants/rj_grunts. **The Lowdown:** R.J. Grunts is well known for two things... award winning chili and an amazing salad bar. If neither of these choices suits you, the menu is full of other options. Start with an appetizer like the hickory BBQ wings or the temperature soup (the price depends on the weather). Move on to one of the many burgers on the menu. Selections include the peppercorn burger (covered with cracked pepper and bleu cheese dressing) and the olive burger (with green olives, black olives, and Swiss cheese). There are also sandwiches galore – Cajun chicken, French dip, tuna melt, etc. If you are looking for something a

little more substantial, why not try the steak fajitas or dive into a bucket of ribs slathered in BBQ sauce. You can wash it all down with one of R.J. Grunts famous shakes in flavors like double chocolate, pineapple, coconut, and peanut butter. Good food, good selection, and reasonable prices are all found at R.J. Grunts. Open Monday through Thursday, 11:30 a.m. - 9:00 p.m.; Friday and Saturday, 11:30 a.m. - 10:30 p.m.; Sunday, 11:30 a.m. - 9:00 p.m.

THE RED LION PUB
2446 North Lincoln Avenue, Chicago IL 60614. 773/348-2695. **World Wide Web address:** http://www.theredlionpub.com. **The Lowdown:** The Red Lion Pub brings a touch of jolly old England to Lincoln Park. With well-worn wooden tables and knickknack-covered walls, The Red Lion Pub is one of Lincoln Park's most popular destinations. The front room is mainly a bar area, with some tables; a more proper dining room is in the back. So, grab a pint of genuine Whitbread Ale or Young's Lager and have a lunch or dinner of true pub food. Start off with some sausage rolls, beans on toast, or Welsh rarebit. One of The Red Lion Pub's most popular dishes is the fish and chips platter: it consists of three large pieces of fish with terrific steak fries. Malt vinegar is served with the chips, another authentic touch. Shepherd's pie, and steak and kidney pie round out the English part of the menu, all of which seems to be done with genuine Anglo spirit. Suffice it to say, if you can't afford a vacation in old England, the Red Lion Pub will do very well for a quick trans-Atlantic experience. Up for a scary story? Another reason that The Red Lion Pub is so well-known around the Windy City is due to the fact that so many people believe it is haunted. Perhaps that's why, every Monday night, upstairs at The Red Lion Pub becomes the setting for the sometimes-eerie Twilight Tales reading series (see separate listing). But, all ghosts aside, The Red Lion Pub makes for a great night out any day of the week.

TWIN ANCHORS
1655 North Sedgwick Street, Chicago IL 60614. 312/266-1616. **The Lowdown:** Famous for serving up ribs since the 30s, Twin Oaks is worth a visit. The menu also offers fried chicken, shrimp, steaks, and sandwiches. Entrees are ample and include French fries, cole slaw, rye bread, crackers, and a dill pickle. This is a very popular spot, so be sure to get there early to avoid waiting in a long line.

AKAI HANA
848 North State Street, Chicago IL 60610. 312/787-4881.
The Lowdown: Akai Hana offers some of the city's freshest sushi and (a limited amount of) other Japanese delicacies at a truly mouth-watering price. Daily specials will let you in on such deals as six-pieces of sushi, a roll, soup, and ice cream (try the red bean) for a mere $10.00. If you're heading out of town for the evening, Akai Hana has got another location in at 3223 Lake Avenue in Wilmette (847/251-0384). Call for specific location hours.

ALBERT'S CAFE & PATISSERIE
52 West Elm Street, Chicago IL 60610. 312/751-0666.
The Lowdown: Window shopping along Oak Street? Finding a spot to eat that won't break the bank can be as difficult a task as restraining yourself from making an impulse purchase. Still, if you're looking for a leisurely place with a menu full of sandwiches and other light fare, Albert's Cafe fits the bill. For late risers, Albert's doesn't start serving breakfast until 10:00 a.m. (9:00 a.m. on Saturdays). While the breakfast menu might seem a bit extravagant with $5.75 French toast and waffles or $7.00 omelettes, the prices don't reach too far beyond this for any meal. Still, their delicious breakfast offerings make Albert's a popular mid-morning pit stop. For a light lunch, Albert's Cafe has a range of offerings including thin-crust pizza, baked vegetarian quiche, and Mediterranean octopus salad. Sandwiches include a turkey club, Monte Cristo, and smoked Norwegian salmon with cream cheese and tomato on a bagel. Albert's entrees include a stir-fried chicken breast platter, tri-color tortellini with cheese and herbs, and fricassee of chicken. All entrees are served with a small side salad and bread and butter. One thing you should come prepared to feast on at Albert's Cafe is dessert. Upon entering the place, you'll come face to face with an enormous cooler (running the entire length of the cafe itself) housing some of your very favorite treats. Albert's Cafe is known throughout the city for their irresistible after-dinner snacks: marble mousse cake, Black Forrest cake, strawberry shortcake. The setting here is very elegant and sophisticated: crisp white tablecloths cover each of the tables. Service is very attentive and the entire eating process runs very smoothly. This is the kind of place you'll want to come back to again and again. Open Tuesday through Thursday, 10:00 a.m. - 9:30 p.m.; Friday, 10:00 a.m. - 10:00 p.m.; Saturday, 9:00 a.m. - 10:00 p.m.

BEN PAO
52 West Illinois Street, Chicago IL 60610. 312/222-1888. **Toll-free phone:** 312/222-0925. **The Lowdown:** Only the freshest

ingredients are used in the dishes served at Ben Pao; and you won't find any of those heavy sauces here either. The emphasis is on presenting traditional Chinese cuisine in a lighter fashion. Start out with crispy garlic tofu or good luck shrimp dumplings. Or sample the satay bar featuring tamarind chicken, portabello satay, and Mongolian beef. For something more filling, Ben Pao has entrees which include seven-flavor chicken, black pepper scallops, Thai basil fragrant beef, spicy shrimp noodles, and much more. The menu seems to go on forever. Veggie lovers should be sure to try Hong Kong spicy eggplant, a house specialty. One thing that cannot be overlooked when speaking of Ben Pao is in the decor; Ben Pao's minimalist design only adds to the places allure (they've even got two waterfalls). In the warmer weather, they offer outdoor seating. Call for hours.

BIG BOWL

6 East Cedar Street, Chicago IL 60611. 312/640-8888. • 159½ West Erie Street. Chicago IL. 312/787-8297. **The Lowdown:** If you're not used to dining alone, let me share a little story with you: as part of my job entails eating at a number of different restaurants in an attempt to compile this book, I am constantly forced to dine solo. Many times, the look of horror, sorrow, or pity that I am faced with when I exclaim "table for one" is enough to make me want to run away. When I entered Big Bowl, there wasn't one bit of this. In fact, the extremely friendly service – from the host staff to the waitstaff – is one of the things that made my dining experience so enjoyable (though, not the main reason). Big Bowl's enormous menu consists of a variety of noodle dishes and entrees with nothing over $10.00. Appetizers include a few different rolls, satays, and flatbread (a kind of pizza-like appetizer). The vegetarian rolls were especially delightful because they seemed to transcend the rules of all the other Americanized Asian restaurants that exist. First off, they were baked which means that the overpowering flavor was one chock full of vegetables, not grease from the fryer. Second, they were filled with better quality vegetables like shiitake mushrooms. Third, instead of the typical (but undoubtedly one of my favorites) peanut sauce, these rolls were served along side a delicious plum-based concoction. My main entrée, a Shanghai chicken noodle dish, was a massive bowl of thick noodles and fresh vegetables, perfectly prepared in a light and flavorful sauce. If you can't find anything on the menu that suits you perfectly, Big Bowl has got you covered. All you need to do is grab a plate, fill it up with the amounts and ingredients you want, and hand it over to the kitchen staff for preparation. Lots of herbal teas and homemade ginger ale make the beverage menu a standout along with the food. While Mr. C tries not to pick favorites, when it comes to quality, quantity, service, and price, Big Bowl comes with the highest recommendation. Open Sunday through Thursday, 11:30 a.m. – 10:00 p.m.; Friday and Saturday, 11:30 a.m. – 11:00 p.m.

CARSON'S RIBS

612 North Wells Street, Chicago IL 60610. 312/280-9200. • 5970 North Ridge Avenue, Chicago IL. 773/271-4000. **Toll-free**

phone: 312/280-7872. **The Lowdown:** People across the country know Carson's as "The Place For Ribs" because it serves some of the best and tangiest you will ever taste. The portions here are generous and each meal starts out with a basket of bread. Be sure to also try the award-winning cole slaw as a mouth-pleasing side dish. For those who like more meat on their bones, Carson's also offers steak, pork chops, and BBQ chicken. Lighter fare includes pulled pork sandwiches, burgers, and salads. Remember to save room for dessert. Choices include cheesecake, chocolate blackout cake, and sundaes. Open Monday through Thursday, 11:00 a.m. - 11:00 p.m.; Friday, 11:00 a.m. - 12:30 a.m.; Saturday, 12:00 p.m. - 12:30 a.m.; Sunday, 12:00 p.m. - 11:00 p.m.

DAO THAI
230 East Ohio Street, Chicago IL 60611. 312/337-0000.
The Lowdown: Just off the Magnificent Mile, this popular spot for Thai has got a ton of appetizer and entree choices for under $6.00 each. These aren't minuscule helpings I'm talking about; the folks at Dao Thai pile your food onto the plate, so there's surely enough to bring home and have for dinner. Not sure what to order? Keep in mind, that the curry dishes are the specialty of the house: hot fried curry, green curry beef, mild curry chicken, and steamed curry fish are just a few of the offerings. If you're still at a loss, the friendly waitstaff will be happy to aid and abet you on your journey into Thai cuisine. Some noteworthy appetizers include the crab rangoon, Thai spring rolls, and shrimp dumplings. The bean cake soup is another delicious choice. Notable entrees include Dao's chop suey, chicken pepper and garlic, basil leaves with meat, and oyster beef. In the warmer months, there's nothing better than taking one of the outside tables and enjoying all the scenery that Streeterville has to offer. The same menu is offered at lunch and dinner, though lunch prices tend to be about $.25 - $.50 cheaper. Dao Thai has a good selection of beers (what tastes better with a plate of pad Thai than a nice, cold Singha?), and some nice wines by the glass or bottle. Though there's plenty of seating, Dao Thai tends to get a wee bit busy during the lunch hours, when local businesspeople head here for a great, inexpensive lunch. Open Sunday, 1:00 p.m. - 10:00 p.m.; Monday through Saturday, 11:00 a.m. - 10:00 p.m.

ED DEBEVIC'S
640 North Wells Street, Chicago IL 60610. 312/664-1707.
The Lowdown: "Make up your mind!" yelled the waiter to a booth full of dawdling teenagers. While the regular customers continued sipping away at their coffee, uninitiated tourists (obviously perturbed) felt compelled to investigate the cause of the disturbance. "What would happen next?" they all wondered. No this is not a scene from the latest newspaper headline "Waiter goes crazy. Attacks table of four!" This is Ed Debevic's, the restaurant where customers eat good old American food on the cheap while being entertained by the (amusing) verbally-abusive waitstaff. The crowd here is an all-encompassing mix of families with rambunctious kids, bachelor businessmen looking for a

close-as-you-can-get-to-home-cooked meal, couples on dates, and the aforementioned tourists. The aforementioned waitstaff consists primarily of out-of-work actors, who pay the rent by slinging hash and harsh remarks. Their antics may be more at home on the stage, but no one seems to mind. Faint-hearted, don't worry. In between outbursts of histrionics, it is very likely that your server will refer to you as "honey" or "sweetie." Now, on to the food! As another one of the many signs proclaims, "If you can find a better diner, eat there." Choosing to eat at Ed Debevic's is easy; it's actually getting in that's the hard part. Once you do get seated, you can grab a juicy hamburger, piled high with tomato and onion, for $5.10. Add a pile of French fries (easily enough to satisfy two) for $2.70. Homemade Windy City Chili is $2.50 a cup. The truly deluxe plate of Mile High Meatloaf comes with real mashed potatoes and gray and a side of fresh veggies. Mom never made it so good! Other fine choices include chicken pot pie and chicken fried steak. Mr. C enjoyed a great roast turkey platter with potatoes and gravy. There are always daily specials, including desserts. All of the pies – including Oreo, coconut, and apple – are always homemade, scrumptious, and reasonably priced. For those of you who are sweet-toothed but small of stomach, they also sell "the world's smallest hot fudge sundae," which is squeezed into something barely larger than a shot glass, for a suitably miniscule $.69. Modeled after the All-American diners of the 1950s, Ed Debevic's is a proud recipient of the Good Coffee Award from the Coffee Brewing Association of America. The high volume of the restaurant requires a new pot (or five) of java to be brewing almost constantly; so rest assured that your cup will be fresh. Ed Debevic's also has a full bar, where they sell (among other things) Ed's own beer, aged in the bottle, at $3.00 a pop. Open until 11:00 p.m. on weeknights, and to 1:00 a.m. on weekends.

EMILIO'S TAPAS SOL Y NIEVE
215 East Ohio Street, Chicago IL 60611. 312/467-7177.
The Lowdown: The best way to enjoy a tapas restaurant is to go in a group. The point of the teensy-weensy plates is to give you just a taste. Since much of the food deserves a chance, you should order up as many of those plates as you desire. Hence, going with an entourage can encourage you to try lots of new things. Emilio's is no exception to the rule. Owner Emilio Gervilla, who was dubbed "The Tapas King" by *Chicago Tribune*, combines fine dining quality with a laid-back atmosphere; there's no pressure to keep eating and eating. You remember those Choose Your Own Adventure books? Emilio's takes that philosophy to his restaurant, except this time it's Choose Your Own Price. If you've got a set amount you're looking to spend, Emilio's can help keep you within your budget. The extensive menu includes almost 20 items for under $6.00 a plate: Emilio's famous potato salad with garlic mayonnaise; grilled eggplant with goat cheese, tomato vinaigrette, and arugula; a Spanish omelette; and cannelloni stuffed with tuna, asparagus, and olives are just a few of the choices. Best of all, even at the under $6.00 mark, Emilio's offers plenty of unique and elegant options; they don't reserve the better meats for higher prices. For $5.95, the cold roasted veal

with olives and sun-dried tomatoes is a great choice, as is the grilled poached squid for the same price. For those who are definitely willing to experiment, the mixed greens with roasted rabbit and vegetables ($5.95) or the sautéed escargot ($4.95) are two on-the-edge choices. If you don't get a chance to try Emilio's Tapas Sol Y Nieve, Emilio's Tapas Lincoln Park is his second restaurant, located at 444 West Fullerton Parkway. 773/327-5100.

FAMOUS DAVE'S
739 North Clark Street, Chicago IL 60610. 312/266-2400. **World Wide Web address:** http://www.famousdaves.com. **The Lowdown:** If you don't know Dave yet, you will. The Great American Rib Cook-Off named his ribs "Best Ribs in America". If you like your food hot and spicy, you're in for a treat at Famous Dave's. From his blackened voodoo chicken and mojo salsa to his devilish hot wings, Dave has mastered the art of high temperatures. In addition to ribs, Famous Dave's serves up a delicious menu of appetizers, sandwiches, entrees, and desserts. How does some of Dave's world famous bread pudding or a hot fudge Kahlua brownie sound? The prices are reasonable and the portions are huge, the perfect combination of good food and value. Once dinner is over, there's an extra bonus: free live blues in the Blue Leopard Lounge. You can make an entire night out of it and still be able to afford breakfast the next morning. If you're traveling into the suburbs for the evening, Famous Dave has staked claims in Naperville, Vernon Hills, and Addison too.

FOODLIFE
835 North Michigan Avenue, Chicago IL 60611. 312/335-3663. **The Lowdown:** Okay, so you're probably asking yourself "What is Mr. Cheap doing in Water Tower Place? A Gold Coast shopping mall anchored by Marshall Field's on one side and Lord & Taylor on the other?" Eating, that's what. Believe it or not, the trendy dining area on the mezzanine level is a relatively cheap place for tourists and shoppers to cool their jets. Certainly, it's unique and worth a look; you can eat very well here and still stay under $10.00 per person. foodlife sure puts all those chain food courts to shame! foodlife is like The Epcot Center of Chicago. They've got food stands for about a dozen cuisines from around the globe, each festooned with the appropriate decor. World-beat music offers gentle rhythms to smooth out the otherwise bustling environs. In all, it feels like you've traveled to some foreign marketplace. Upon your arrival, you'll be greeted and ushered to a table with instructions on the law of the land: this is your table; feel free to walk around, decide what you'd like to eat... as long as this blue card is showing, no one will take your table. You'll even be given your own passport; a temporary credit card that enables you to visit as many booths as you wish, putting together any kind of meal, and pay for the whole thing at the end. Needless to say, there are as many folks wandering around with a sort of bewildered look on their faces, as there are regulars who have the system down pat. Professionals who work in the area have made lunch here a big business, so a trip at dinnertime might provide you with smaller crowds. The

Roadhouse stand has great burgers; an Italian food booth nearby allows you to mix and match from several pastas and sauces at $4.95 for the plate; and you can even try a hefty slice of sweet fennel sausage pizza. I opted for a taste of Mother Earth Grains, where I tried a platter of acorn squash stuffed with vegetables and angel hair pasta. The Mexican place around the corner offered, as its special of the day, a hunk of pan-blackened cod in pineapple salsa, with rice and beans, for $6.50 (about as expensive as any entree gets around here). For just about the same price, you could get a mountainous shrimp and vegetable salad plate at Some Dim Sum. Want a drink with all this? Take your pick from an espresso bar, a juice bar, or a good selection of beers and wines. There are also soups, salads, breads, and of course, desserts. In the end, a surcharge of only 6 percent is added to your bill (for tip), and you may elect not to pay it if you wish. However, Mr. C found the service to be among the most polite he's ever seen. As he heard one food server say to an obvious first-timer, "Just relax and enjoy the ride!"

FUZIO

1045 North Rush Street, Chicago IL 60611. 312/988-4640. **The Lowdown:** From Southern Italy's linguine and meatballs to Shanghai's udon bowl to Thailand's pad Thai noodles with grilled chicken, Fuzio leaves no country unturned when it comes to presenting a global palette of pastas. Everything on the menu is made fresh and with only the finest ingredients; if you don't believe me you can see it all for yourself in their open kitchen. If you're not in the mood for pasta, there are plenty of other plates that are sure to tickle your taste buds. While some of the entrées begin to sneak above Mr. C's limit, most are less than $16.00. The roasted honey-lemon chicken is a good choice; it's a roasted ½ chicken cooked in honey and lemon. It's served up with a delicious helping of veggies and mashed potatoes. Other affordable entrees include breaded sea bass and polenta, boneless pork loin and stir-fried noodles, and a great bouillabaisse for under $16.00. But don't forget to start out with an appetizer. Fuzio makes a delicious focaccia bread that can be topped with toasted garlic and parmesan cheese or caramelized onion, feta cheese, basil, and tomatoes. Baked polenta with grilled portabello mushrooms and Vietnamese chicken spring rolls are just a few of the other options. A variety of salads can also be great as an appetizer or light meal. The décor is very classy; crisp white tablecloths top each of the tiny tables. In the evening, dimmed lights make for a very romantic feel. Though the place can pack 'em in, there's always room for audible conversation. Open Sunday through Thursday, 11:30 a.m. - 10:00 p.m.; Friday and Saturday, 11:30 a.m. - 12:00 a.m.

GINO'S EAST

633 North Wells Street (at West Ontario Street), Chicago IL 60611. 312/988-4200. **The Lowdown:** Though it's moved from its original Streeterville home, Gino's East is still arguably the home of the Chicago-style pizza (Pizzeria Uno has the same claim to fame). Thin-crust pizzas start out at $8.25 for a small cheese and can range up to just under $18.00 for an extra large

supreme. When you consider the bigger-than-average sizes that Gino's offers, you're talking more than enough for a few people. Deep dish pizzas are just a bit more money, with an extra large supreme topping off the menu at $19.99. If you're not used to Chicago-style pizza, Gino's East is a great place to get your first experience. *People* magazine once deemed it the "world's most celebrated pizza"; *Bon Appetit* ranked it among the country's top 10 pizza parlors; and Gino's East has occupied the number one spot for city's best pizza in the *Chicago Tribune* readers poll for several years in a row. If anybody knows good pizza, it has got to be those people!

GOLD COAST DOGS
418 North State Street, Chicago IL 60610. 312/527-1222.
The Lowdown: This is a fast-food joint, granted, but a classy one using the freshest ingredients possible. Remember, Mr. C always says that counter service will save you dough, no tipping required! Don't be put off by the line snaking out the door, filled with businesspeople and families alike, it moves quickly. While you wait, you're more than welcome to read the dozens of praiseworthy newspaper and magazine articles framed on the wall. Dog breeds include the One Magnificent Dog, the plain ol' Red Hot Dog, and the Char Cheddar Red Hot Dog (topped with fresh Wisconsin cheese). Beer bratwursts and Polish sausages are also offered. All sandwiches come with free condiments including mustard, ketchup, relish, onions, tomatoes, hot peppers, pickles, celery salt, and grilled onions. But Gold Coast serves up more than just dogs including chili, turkey sandwiches, and their ever-popular jumbo 1/3 pound char-burgers. And there's more! Recent additions to the menu include gyros, corned beef, salads, meatball sandwiches, Italian beef, and assorted desserts. Open Monday through Friday, 7:00 a.m. - 12:00 a.m.; Saturday, 10:30 a.m. - 8:00 p.m.; Sunday, 11:00 a.m. - 8 p.m.

HUDSON CLUB
504 North Wells Street, Chicago IL 60610. 312/467-1947.
The Lowdown: Hudson Club stands out for offering more than 100 types of wine by the glass. The outstanding food will provide the perfect compliment to whatever libation you choose. The cuisine here can not be easily categorized. It's mostly American with a little Caribbean, Asian, and Mediterranean thrown in for good measure. Hot and cold appetizers range from ahi tuna carpaccio to wood roasted calimari. For the main course, you can sample a wood fired pizza or be a bit more daring and try the oven roasted rabbit or the Chilean sea bass and shrimp. Whatever you decide on is sure to please your palate. Make sure to leave room for one of the decadent desserts like creme brulee, apple brown betty tart, or white chocolate cheesecake. Open Monday through Friday at 3:00 p.m. and serves a limited menu at the bar. Dinner is served beginning at 5:30 p.m. Monday through Saturday; closed on Sunday.

JIA'S
2 East Delaware Place, Chicago IL 60611. 312/642-0626.
The Lowdown: From the contemporary décor to the thoughtfully

prepared food, everything about Jia's is attractive. What's even more attractive is the price! You can start out with any of more than 20 appetizers, soups, and salads, all for well under $10.00. Vegetable, summer, and Thai rolls; gyoza; chicken, beef, and shrimp satay; crab rangoon; soft shell crabs; rice soup with chicken or seafood; and seaweed salad are just some of the many delicious offerings. The not-so-hungry can munch one of Jia's many noodle dishes including pad thai with vegetables and tofu, chicken, or shrimp; Chinese soft noodles with shrimp, chicken, beef, or vegetables; udon noodle; and ramen noodles are just some of the offerings. Jia's stir fry menu include such delectable dishes as sesame chicken, harvest shrimp stir fry, Mongolian beef, and chicken or beef with pea pods. Best of all, most items can be had for less than $12.00. In addition to the many Chinese entrees available at Jia's, the second half of the restaurant leans more toward Japanese cuisine in the form of a sushi bar. All your favorite sushi staples are here: California maki, Namasake maki, sake skin maki, dragon maki, and rainbow maki are all well-priced. Many items can also be ordered by the piece for as little as $2.00 each. Select from tuna, yellowtail, red snapper, oyster, sea bass, and several of your other seafaring favorites. Can't make up your mind? Choose one of the sushi dinners like Jia's six-piece for $10.95. If sushi's not your thing and you're not really feeling the Chinese side of things, Jia's cooks up a limited selection of Japanese entrees as well including chicken, steak, vegetable, and salmon teriyaki as well as shrimp, scallop, and vegetable tempura. Drop in at lunch time for the best savings; that's when tons of your favorite dishes can be had for several dollars less than what they sell for at dinner time. Call for lunch special hours. Open Sunday, 4:00 p.m. – 10:00 p.m.; Monday through Thursday, 11:30 a.m. – 10:00 p.m.; Friday, 11:30 a.m. – 11:00 p.m.; Saturday, 4:00 p.m. – 11:00 p.m.

LO-CAL ZONE
912 North Rush Street, Chicago IL 60611. 312/943-9060.
The Lowdown: While the front door of Lo-Cal Zone sports the word FAT with the familiar red circle-and-slash symbol over it, don't run away for fear of tasteless, boring food. Right across the street from Prada, this tiny health food haven specializes in such traditional junk food as burritos, fajitas, and even soft-serve ice cream. The Zone's motto is "eat here, your body will love it." The aforementioned burritos are about $4.25 each; Mr. C particularly enjoyed the turkey and pepper combination, one of over 10 different varieties. Fat-free, dairy-free mini-pizzas made with soy cheese are only 160 calories each; a lo-cal tuna sandwich is also available. Lo-Cal Zone is also a smoke-free zone. There's not much seating, but most people come in here for take-out anyway. Open Monday through Thursday, 11:00 a.m. - 10:30 p.m.; Friday, 11:00 a.m. - 11:00 p.m.; Saturday, 11:00 a.m. - 12:00 a.m.; Sunday, 11:00 a.m. - 9:00 p.m.

MAGGIANO'S LITTLE ITALY
516 North Clark Street, Chicago IL 60610. 312/644-7700.
World Wide Web address: http://www.maggianos.com.
The Lowdown: Okay, so it's not Little Italy by location, but it

will certainly taste like it. Maggiano's is a family style restaurant with enormous portions and great prices. Some of the many worthwhile appetizers include roasted peppers with olive oil, baked stuffed clams, asparagus in vinaigrette, and mushroom ravioli. Now, on to the entrees. If your server forgets to mention it, keep in mind that the servings at Maggiano's are more than enough for two to three people. If you don't like to bring home leftovers, be sure you order the smaller sized portion of any item. An enormous selection of pasta dishes comprises most of the menu here: shells and roasted vegetables, spaghetti aglio olio, country style rigatoni, and corkscrew vegetables with ricotta cheese are just a few of the delectable offerings. Seafood pasta entrees climb a bit in price, but are well worth the extra pennies for dishes like garlic shrimp with shells and shrimp arrabiata. If pasta's not your thing, there are plenty of chicken choices that are hearty and delicious like roasted chicken with rosemary and garlic. If you're looking for the filet mignon, I must warn you: It's going to cost you. Steak, seafood, and veal dishes easily top $20.00 apiece and even reach as high as $30.00. Obviously, the best way to enjoy a family-style restaurant like this one is with a large group. Maggiano's certainly agrees, and they're willing to offer special prices on family dinners for parties of six or more. For $18.95 per person, you'll get your choice of two appetizers, salads, and pasta dishes that will stuff your group silly. Maggiano's is quite a popular spot, so it's best to call ahead (sometimes well in advance) for reservations. Open Sunday, 12:00 p.m. – 10:00 p.m.; Monday through Thursday, 5:00 p.m. – 10:00 p.m.; Friday, 5:00 p.m. – 11:00 p.m.; Saturday, 3:00 p.m. – 11:00 p.m.

OLD JERUSALEM
1411 North Wells Street, Chicago IL 60610. 312/944-0459.
The Lowdown: Those of you who are new to Middle Eastern cuisine will find it to be a delightful mix of Oriental and Western styles. If that type of fusion sounds appetizing, one place definitely worth checking out is Old Jerusalem. The menu is chock full of light and delicious meals, and nothing is priced above $10.00. For an authentic appetizer, try a plate of feta cheese served with olives and parsley or some rice-stuffed grape leaves and olive oil. Standard plates of hummus, baba ganoush, and tibouli salad are priced under $3.00. The entrees consist of beef and lamb, though Old Jerusalem offers a pretty extensive vegetarian menu as well. The kefta kabob consists of ground lamb patties with tomatoes and onions, while the musaheb is a boneless breast of chicken marinated in vinegar and olive oil. All entrees are served with a plate of Lebanese bread, and many come with a salad and rice pilaf as well. Don't forget to wash it all down with one of their freshly-made juices or a liquid yogurt. They've also got many traditional pastries for dessert, like baklava and fatayer (ricotta filled strudel). This restaurant has no liquor license, but you are welcome to bring your own.

PIZZERIA UNO
29 East Ohio Street, Chicago IL 60611. 312/321-1000. ◆ Pizzeria Due, 619 North Wabash Avenue, Chicago IL 60611. 312/943-

2400. **The Lowdown:** To call these restaurants a Chicago legend (they're the company that first created the deep-dish pizza) is an absurd understatement. Especially since they undertook a nationwide expansion several years ago, making the pizza that made them famous available in outlets across the country. Still, even after all their success, Pizzeria Uno and Pizzeria Due haven't altered the original recipes (food recipes and otherwise) that have made them so famous. These dining establishments remain two pleasant and inexpensive places to dine in the Near North area. While the names are slightly different, both places boast the same menu and prices. Pizza prices start out at right around $4.00 for an individual cheese pie, and can range all the way up to about $20.00 for a large specialty pizza like the Numero Uno which is packed with sausage, pepperoni, mushrooms, onions, peppers, and extra cheese. It's enough food for a month! In between, there are two other sizes and tons of ingredient combinations for you to mix and match. But it's not just pies you're limited to here. Pizzeria Uno and Pizzeria Due offer a good selection of soups, salads, sandwiches, entrees, and pasta dishes too. Like the pizza, all meals are reasonably priced. For the best deals, drop in on a weekday between 11:30 a.m. and 3:00 p.m. for their express lunch. This is when you can get an individual pizza with your choice of soup or salad for just $4.95. Open daily.

REZA'S
432 West Ontario Street, Chicago IL 60610. 312/664-4500. **The Lowdown:** This River North spin-off of the longtime Andersonville staple offers the exact same menu. Reza's serves up incredibly large portions of Persian specialties at surprisingly low prices. Many folks consider it one of the best deals in town. The River North location is a bit flashier than the original Reza's and offers some great outdoor tables for al fresco dining along this quiet stretch of Ontario Street. Start off with one of two dozen appetizers, many of which are vegetarian. Falafel, of course, is a must; but try the vegetable casserole, a blend of zucchini, eggplant, carrots, green peppers, and scallions baked in a tomato sauce and served over rice. Entrees consist of lots of lamb, poultry, beef, and vegetarian options. Mr. C opted for what is simply called The Combo: one skewer of char-broiled filet mignon and one skewer of marinated grilled chicken, separated by a mountain of dill flavored rice. Most menu items are available for $11.00 or under. If you have room for dessert, try a strong cup of coffee and a piece of the homemade baklava or zoulbia, a deep-fried pastry made without sugar. Open daily, 11:00 p.m. - 12:00 a.m.

ROCK BOTTOM BREWERY
One West Grand Avenue, Chicago IL 60610. 312/755-9339. **World Wide Web address:** http://www.rockbottom.com. **The Lowdown:** Even though Rock Bottom Brewery is a chain of sorts (they're based in Colorado and have several locations nationwide), it doesn't have that 'look at me, I'm a recognizable name" quality that so many other chains possess. Rock Bottom is much more inventive when it comes to dishes they offer; plus, everything is prepared with only the freshest ingredients, making

any and every dining experience here consistently good. Plus, being a microbrewery, they give you the chance to take a break from your everyday beer and try something new. If you're really interested, they'll even give you a tour of the brewery. The rooftop beer garden, satellite television, pool tables, and (obviously) fantastic beer selection make Rock Bottom Brewery a great place to just hang out for a few drinks too. Open daily, 11:30 a.m. - 2:00 a.m.

SCOOZI

410 West Huron Street, Chicago IL 60610. 312/943-5900. **The Lowdown:** Yet another Lettuce Entertain You venture finds it way into Mr. C's heart (and stomach). Scoozi is a real everyman place; no one should feel uncomfortable here. The food offering is strictly Italian, though there's nothing pretentious about the menu. A variety of pizzas are available in small and large sizes and include such great toppings as pesto, goat cheese, alfredo sauce, potatoes, and ricotta salata. Fresh pie prices range from $6.95 to $12.95. A variety of great salads include the traditional Caesar and mixed greens as well as your not-so-average spinaci e rucola with spinach, arugula, and sweet corn; or the tagliuzzare with chicken, prosciutto ham, avocado, and gorgonzola cheese. Depending on the appetite at stake, salads at Scoozi can exist as either an appetizer or a light meal. The main entree menu is comprised mostly of pastas. These are available in different sizes and at different prices throughout the day. Some of Mr. C's very favorite bargains are the penne arrabbiata; cappellini Scoozi, which is made with the freshest of vegetables; and the gnocchi in a light tomato cream sauce. While the larger sized portions may seem a bit out of Mr. C's normal price range, there's a whole lot of food going on to these plates. The amount of leftovers certainly justifies the price. Still, while the food is great and the service attentive, what makes Scoozi such a popular place is the atmosphere; there's always a party going on! That said, unless you don't mind an extended wait, it is best to make reservations well ahead of time. Open Sunday, 5:00 p.m. - 9:00 p.m.; Monday through Thursday, 11:30 a.m. - 10:00 p.m.; Friday, 11:30 a.m. - 11:00 p.m.; Saturday, 5:00 p.m. - 11:00 p.m.

STAR OF SIAM

11 East Illinois Street, Chicago IL 60611. 312/670-0100. **The Lowdown:** Housed in an old warehouse-style building, Star of Siam is a traditional Thai restaurant in a modern American setting that is popular with the downtown business types. The open restaurant and unique style of seating make it a great place for large groups of people. The ample portions coupled with reasonable prices make it a great choice for any Cheapster. With traditional Thai crafts lining the walls, the atmosphere is intimate and authentic. The downstairs dining room and upstairs tea room make its setup unique. While they do serve a number of standard Thai foods like pad Thai and hot and sour soups, Star of Siam mixes the menu up a bit with their own unique creations. Open Sunday through Thursday, 11:00 a.m. - 9:30 p.m.; Friday and Saturday, 11:00 a.m. - 10:30 p.m.

SZECHWAN EAST

340 East Ohio Street, Chicago IL 60611. 312/255-9200. **The Lowdown:** *Zagat's* has long considered Szechwan East one of the best Chinese restaurant's in the city, even deeming them "the best" two years in a row. Their lunch buffet is an especially good deal. For $8.95 you can choose from more than 30 different menu items. Pay $12.95 for the same deal on Sunday and you'll get a choice of several other seafood dishes along with a glass of champagne. Then again, is that really a lot when you consider the fact that their dinner menu is comprised of more than 120 items? Even with this abbreviated version, you're sure to find something mouth-watering and delicious. The lunch buffet is available daily, 11:30 a.m. – 2:00 p.m. Open daily, 11:30 a.m. – 10:00 p.m.

TIMOTHY O'TOOLE'S PUB CHICAGO

622 North Fairbanks Court, Chicago IL 60611. 312/642-0700. **E-mail address:** pub622@aol.com. **World Wide Web address:** http://www.timothyotooles.com. **The Lowdown:** Tourists and locals who love the high-rise buildings in Streeterville may want to take a break from equally high prices. Timothy O'Toole's Pub Chicago is the answer. The pub is located on the corner of Ontario and Fairbanks, with an entrance tucked away in the midst of more trendy restaurants and cafes. When you come downstairs you'll find a spacious restaurant area, a large centrally located bar with plenty of seating, and the friendliest staff in Chicago. With 40 TVs, three big screens, and 22 satellite receivers, there isn't a bad seat in the house for watching sports. You'll also find five pool tables, electronic dartboards, NTN interactive trivia, video games, and constant viewing of any major sporting event. In case the sports were not enough to win you over, Timothy O'Toole's Pub Chicago has an extensive and affordable menu. You can pick from a choice of 21 appetizers ranging from the bar classics like buffalo wings and nachos to bruschetta and calamari (prices range from $2.50 - $10.95). From there you can move on to the dinner menu which includes 21 different sandwiches, nine different burgers and chicken sandwiches (including a veggie burger), nine different salads, and 20 different entrees (including steaks, ribs, chicken dishes and 2 new pastas, all ranging in price from $6.95 - $24.95). To wash it all down, Timothy O'Toole's Pub Chicago has a large beer, wine, and martini menu that includes over 20 bottles of imported and domestic beers, 16 draft beers (including the O'Toole's Copper Ale house brew, and a full service bar featuring the famous Holy Water, made with 12 liquors and three juices. Open Sunday through Wednesday, 11:00 a.m. - 2:00 a.m., and Thursday through Saturday, 11:00 a.m. - 4:00 a.m.

TUCCI BENUCCH

900 North Michigan Avenue, Chicago IL 60611. 312/266-2500. **The Lowdown:** From the same folks that brought you foodlife (see separate listing) comes this great little spot right across the street. Posing as a floral-encased Italian villa, Tucci Benucch offers friendly service and good food at one of the city's most prestigious addresses. Almost instantaneously upon seating, two

kinds of bread are dropped onto your plate from a communal straw basket. One is a flavorful focaccia, the other a rustic and crusty Italian. Browsing through the menu, you'll see lots of typical Italian entrees, all hearty and good. Appetizers include grilled bruschetta ($4.50), stuffed grilled eggplant and goat cheese ($5.25), and ravioli al forno ($5.95). They also offer a good selection of salads (in both small and large sizes) including a baby lettuce salad with caramelized walnuts, gorgonzola, and balsamic vinaigrette ($4.50); and a chopped salad with chicken, pasta, bacon, gorgonzola, and tomatoes in a mustard vinaigrette ($5.95 - $9.95). Tucci Benucch has got a lot of fine pasta dishes as well, many for under $10.00. Baked spaghetti with ricotta cheese and alfredo ($9.95), five cheese ravioli ($9.95), angel hair pasta with grilled pesto vegetables and low-fat marinara ($9.95), and a plate of shells with meat sauce, meatball, and sausage are just a few of the choices. Tucci Benucch takes a unique approach to thin crust pizza with lots of extraordinary toppings; goat cheese, sun-dried tomatoes, pesto, and olives ($8.95); portabello mushrooms, asparagus, oven-dried tomatoes, and asiago cheese ($9.25); and roasted chicken, broccoli, oven-dried tomatoes, pesto, and mozzarella cheese ($9.50) are three such varieties. As I had been stuffing myself silly with pizzas all week, I opted for a light lunch of minestrone soup ($2.95) and a small spinach-goat cheese salad ($4.95). The minestrone was great, chock full of vegetables, pasta, and flavor. While there was just over a dollop of goat cheese atop the salad, that in itself was rich enough to constitute a meal. Topped with oven-dried tomatoes and pine nuts, and dressed in a mustard vinaigrette, it is definitely a meal I would recommend. As an added savings bonus, bring the kids along. For just $4.95 kids can get their choice of cheese pizza, spaghetti with meatball, or buttered noodles. Open Sunday, 12:00 p.m. – 9:00 p.m.; Monday through Saturday, 11:00 a.m. – 9:30 p.m.

South Side & Hyde Park

ARMY & LOU'S   *yes*

420 East 75th Street, Chicago IL 60619. 773/483-3100. **The Lowdown:** For more than 50 years, this South Side institution has been serving up traditional Southern food to the Windy City's politically-astute. Perhaps this is because the restaurant's original owner, Army, was a rather politically-minded writer for *The Defender*. Or maybe it's just because the food is so delicious. Whatever the case, don't be surprised to see some of the city's most well-known politicians, including the mayor, drop in for a smattering of butter-soaked corn bread and some black-eyed peas. If you're a fan of fried food, you're a fan of Army & Lou's. All food is made from scratch and they use only the freshest ingredients. This doesn't mean, however, that your diet won't take a licking. Fried chicken and catfish are two of the restaurant's most popular dishes. All the rest of your favorite Southern dishes are here as well: the award-winning Louisiana-Style Gumbo is a must-have, though you'll have to pay a little extra for it since it's priced at $13.95. Other Southern dishes include smothered chicken, cornish hen, and two center cut pieces of porks chops. Desserts here are as rich and filling as the entrees, but well worth the splurge. The sweet potato pie at Army & Lou's is the ultimate. Army & Lou's is open for breakfast as well and has great daily specials under $10.00. Just be sure and get there early, as the place can really fill up. From the bright red awning and sign outside to the overly sanguine dining room, the atmosphere at Army & Lou's is warm and inviting. The leisurely pace evokes the essence of a sleepy Southern town. Army & Lou's offers a great opportunity for spending some quality time with a group of friends and is sure to make your Chicago experience a warm and welcoming one. Open daily 9except Tuesday), 9:00 a.m. - 10:00 p.m.

DIXIE KITCHEN & BAIT SHOP   *yes*

5225 South Harper Court, Chicago IL 60615. 773/363-4943. **The Lowdown:** The popularity of this restaurant/bait shop has resulted in the opening of a second location to satisfy the suburban masses in Evanston (see separate listing). Serving up Cajun and Creole delights like gumbo, Po' Boy sandwiches, jambalaya, and fried green tomatoes, Dixie Kitchen & Bait Shop combines great food with a flair for Southern hospitality. The vintage decor in this tiny, one-room establishment makes it feel like you've been transported back in time. The red and white checkered tablecloths and painted wooden chairs offer a minimalist charm and appreciation of the simple life. Still, while there are plenty of other Southern-styled juke joints around town, few offer the authenticity of Dixie Kitchen & Bait Shop. For example, the corn bread that is served with each meal has small bits of jalapeño thrown in for good measure. Neighborhood locals flock here, as do true-blue Southern transplants who are yearning for a taste of home. It's this type of true Southernization that makes the place so great. They even offer their own Dixie Kitchen hot sauce that will surely accompany any meal delightfully. Delicious desserts include a to-die-for peach cobbler. But what's it like to dine in an actual bait shop? You'll just have to see for yourself. Open Sunday through Thursday, 11:00 a.m. - 10:00 p.m.; Friday and Saturday, 11:00 a.m. - 11:00 p.m.

HEALTHY FOOD LITHUANIAN RESTAURANT
3236 South Halsted Street, Chicago IL 60608. 312/326-2724. **The Lowdown:** While the name might seem to say it all, Healthy Food is probably not what you would expect. Instead, the "healthy" part of the name refers to the fact that all the Lithuanian fare is made with the freshest ingredients and, most importantly, made from scratch. If you're unfamiliar with Lithuanian cuisine, it is comprised of lots of grains and dairy products. (Don't worry carnivores, there's meat on the menu as well!) The food must be pleasing to a variety of palates, because Healthy Food has been around since 1938. While Healthy Food does serve all three meals, it is for the earlier two that they attract the most attention. Typical breakfast fare has gone healthily wild at this Bridgeport spot; instead of your typical Bisquick-concocted pancake, try one of their buckwheat or wheat germ incarnations. For an even sweeter treat, try a blynas (a cheese-filled pancake) with fruit. One great traditional dish to try if you're there for lunch is the kugelis, a potato pudding with grated potatoes, bacon, and onion. Meals are usually accompanied with a basket of black rye bread, a traditional Lithuanian staple (white bread is only cooked on special occasions), and soup or salad. Don't forget to wash it all down with one of their great fruit and wheat germ shakes. The decor is warm and inviting, and the service is friendly. Eating here is definitely a pleasurable experience, and you can easily have an entire meal for under $10.00. Open Sunday, 7:30 a.m. - 5:00 p.m.; Monday through Saturday, 7:00 a.m. - 7:00 p.m. *$Cash Only$*

HONG MIN
221 West Cermak Road, Chicago IL 60616. 312/842-5026. **The Lowdown:** If you're roaming around Chinatown with no money in your pocket or food in your stomach, Hong Min should be a most welcome sight. While the decor does not aim to please (at these prices, who cares?), the food certainly does. Many consider Hong Min one of Chinatown's finest eateries and, after one taste, it's easy to see why. The dim sum is one dish you have to try here! With late night hours, Hong Min is a great option any time of day. They offer free parking for two hours, which is plenty of time to stuff your face silly. Open daily, 10:00 a.m. - 2:00 a.m. This restaurant has no liquor license, but you are welcome to bring your own.

KING WAH
2225 South Wentworth Avenue, Chicago IL 60616. 312/842-1404. **The Lowdown:** If you're looking for a truly delicious

Chinatown experience, King Wah is a great place to start. With a decor that is modern and sophisticated and a menu that is always fresh and cooked to order, King Wah is a pleasure for the eyes and stomach alike. And the larger-than-average portions are great to split between two people. For lovers of dim sum, you've come to the right place. The staff is friendly and will be happy to help you in choosing a meal. While there are plenty of traditional and everyday Chinese meals found on the menu, King Wah also offers a large number of specialty dishes that you'd be hard-pressed to find elsewhere in the city. Make it a true adventure and try something out of your comfort zone. Open Sunday through Friday, 11:00 a.m. - 10:00 p.m.; Saturday, 11:00 a.m. - 11:00 p.m.

MELLOW YELLOW
1508 East 53rd Street, Chicago IL 60615. 773/667-2000.
The Lowdown: Donovan would be proud of the self-described "laid-back spot" that is Mellow Yellow. Serving up a variety of traditional American sandwiches and entrees, Mellow Yellow is a great place to kick back and relax in the Hyde Park area. But you certainly cannot stop by without trying some of their famous chili. They serve their chili with meat or veggies, and can prepare it in one of five special ways. The rotisserie chicken, cooked to perfection, is another great dish to try. For under $7.00 you get chicken, coleslaw, and a side order. If you drop in early enough on a weekday, you can even take advantage of some of the fantastic Mellow Yellow dinner specials. I don't think there's too many other places in town where entire meals can be had for as little as $5.00. You'll be mad about it! Open Sunday through Thursday, 9:00 a.m. - 9:00 p.m.; Friday and Saturday, 8:00 a.m. - 10:00 p.m.

West of Town

NEIGHBORHOODS INCLUDE:
Bucktown ❖ Greektown ❖ Wicker Park

THE BABALUCI
2152 North Damen Avenue, Chicago IL 60647.
773/486-5300. ◆ 1001 West Golf Road, Hoffman Estates IL
60195. 847/843-3663. **The Lowdown:** There's a reason this
Bucktown eatery attracts more than just the neighborhood
crowd. While the upstairs piano bar and complimentary valet
parking are all amenities that could easily draw a crowd, Mr. C is
willing to bet it is the authentic Sicilian food that brings 'em in. A
direct translation of the restaurant's name (which means
"snails") does not begin to tell you what kind of eats you'll
encounter here. You can start off with a great antipasti like
roasted goat cheese with spicy marinara; grilled shrimp with
artichoke hearts, prosciutto, and spinach; or grilled octopus with
garlic and oil. A number of fresh salads mix in a variety of unique
ingredients (pine nuts, pancetta, and frizelle) and Italian spices
with your more traditional greens and veggies. As you might
expect from an Italian restaurant, there are plenty of pastas at
your disposal: tricolor rotini with pecorino, gorgonzola, fontina,
and parmesan cheeses; veal-stuffed pasta with pine nuts and
pecorino cheese; and spaghetti alla carbonara are all priced well
under $10.00. Entrees are a bit more expensive, but all weigh in
at under a still-reasonable $15.00. The veal Babaluci with sun-
dried tomatoes, artichoke hearts, and spinach is a good deal; as
is the grilled Italian sausage with polenta. Don't forget about that
piano bar; it's a great way to while away the after-dinner hours.
Weekends bring live entertainment, with an emphasis on jazz
and blues performers. Open Sunday, 4:00 p.m. - 10:00 p.m.;
Monday through Thursday, 11:30 a.m. - 11:00 p.m.; Friday,
11:30 a.m. - 12:00 a.m.; Saturday, 4:00 p.m. - 12:00 a.m.

GREEK ISLANDS
200 South Halsted Street, Chicago IL 60661. 312/782-9855.
The Lowdown: One of the largest and best-known spots along
Greektown's restaurant strip, Greek Islands manages to be
showy and reasonably-priced at the same time. Sure, you may
have a little trouble pronouncing some of the dishes (can you say
"youvarelakia" or "tzatziki" without stumbling or stuttering?) but
that's all the more reason to welcome the pleasant and
knowledgeable nature of the waitstaff. The enormous menu
encompasses some of the most traditional and delicious Greek
recipes: try the combination plate with roast lamb, mousaka,
meatballs, dolmades, and mixed veggies to get a little taste of
everything. The kokkinisto (braised lamb in a tomato sauce) is
another good bet. For the most part, entrees don't reach much
above $10.00. Greek Islands even offers a number of good wines
by the bottle for right around $14.00 a pop; domestic and
imported beers are well-priced too. While you're there, you can
even pick up a bottle of olive oil or fresh fish flown in directly

from Greece. Free valet parking is available too. Open Sunday through Thursday, 11:00 a.m. - 12:00 a.m.; Friday and Saturday, 11:00 a.m. - 1:00 a.m.

LEO'S LUNCHROOM

1809 West Division Street, Chicago IL 60622. 773/276-6509. **The Lowdown:** It may sound like an truck-driver-filled greasy spoon, but Leo's Lunchroom is actually part of the young, and artsy rebirth of Wicker Park. It puts a hip spin on traditional diner food, without touching traditional diner prices. From a good old grilled cheese on whole wheat bread to hot pastrami on rye with scallions and cream cheese, Leo's will fill you up cheaply. Try the chili – regular or vegetarian – or the big, fresh julienne salad with ham, turkey, cheddar and Swiss cheeses, tomatoes, cucumbers, mushrooms, eggs, and onions. Everything here gets a modern, homestyle touch. Corned beef hash isn't your average ground up mystery; you get diced chunks of tasty beef, mixed with sautéed potatoes, with two eggs (any style) on top. Daily specials offer even more artistic touches, like their Southwestern French Toast (in which flour tortillas are given the French toast treatment), filled with sweet ricotta cheese, and topped with fresh raspberries. Speaking of breakfast, the biscuits and gravy here just can't be beat; the only drawback being you'll have to wait until the weekend to get them. Leo's eclectic dinner menu offers a number of always-changing daily and weekly specials that offer even better savings from the regular prices. There is outdoor seating in the back, which helps with crowd control when weather permits. If you're eating inside, the lunch counter is certainly the best seat in the house. Here, you'll get a good look at the haywire collage of pictures from seemingly every TV show known to man including autographed pictures of some of the celebs who've found their way to this downscale scene. Open every day but Monday, 8:00 a.m. - 10:00 p.m. This restaurant has no liquor license, but you are welcome to bring your own. *$Cash Only$*

MANNY'S COFFEE SHOP AND DELI

1141 South Jefferson Street, Chicago IL 60607. 312/939-2855. **World Wide Web address:** http://www.mannysdeli.com. **The Lowdown:** It might feel like you've been transported to the Lower East Side of New York when you drop into Manny's, the home of good old fashioned corned beef sandwiches, chicken soup, and other great Jewish delicacies. It's a cafeteria-style deli, which means you need to leave all ideas of fancy decor at the door; Manny's looks like it hasn't been updated since the early 1950s – but that's all part of the charm! The antedated atmosphere is what helped to bring Manny's Coffee Shop to the eye of Hollywood. Manny's Coffee Shop set the scene for 1987's *The Big Town*, where "The Arm" (Matt Dillon) plans to gamble his way to the top. Ambiance aside, the food here may be as close as Chicago gets to a real Old World Jewish noshery. Corned beef is the traditional yardstick, and it measures up well; $6.95 gets you a hefty handful that will take a while to finish. All the other hot sandwiches are here including brisket of beef, pastrami, tongue, and reubens. On the cold side, try the chopped liver sandwich or the nova lox with cream cheese. Hot dishes include meatloaf, half-chicken, beef stew, and more. Manny's also offers a bunch of daily specials. These never change, sure and steady as the old man sipping tea in the booth next to you. Tuesdays always offer stuffed cabbage; Wednesdays, count on chicken pot pie; Fridays, gefilte fish. And don't forget the daily side dishes, like overcooked spaghetti (how else should it be cooked?), or kasha and bowties. Any day, you can add things like knishes or crispy potato pancakes on the side, too. Chicken soup is always on the menu and can be filled with matzo balls, kreplach, noodles, or rice. Whiel everything is worth a try, you'll want to stick with the corned beef for the truest experience. And since the set up is cafeteria-style, there's no need to worry about a tip. At the cash register, you'll see another old-time touch: the glass counter displaying cigars, candy and sundries for sale. While I can't exactly tell you what a sundry is, I can tell you that they're available here. If you park across the street and get your ticket validated at Manny's, you'll only have to pay $2.00. Open Monday through Saturday, 5:00 a.m. - 4:00 p.m; closed Sunday.

MUNCH
1800 West Grand Avenue, Chicago IL 60612. 312/226-4914.
World Wide Web address: http://www.munchinc.com.
The Lowdown: Munch is the kind of place that aims to make you a regular, and I'd be surprised if they didn't succeed. The tiny, two-room restaurant serves up some hearty American comfort food for three square meals a day. Breakfasts and weekend brunches are probably Munch's busiest times, and with good reason. The hearty and thoughtfully-prepared morning dishes include traditional egg plates and omelettes as well as pancakes and French toast. The biscuits and gravy are always a popular meal, and the scrambled egg and veggie crêpe is an item that certainly dares to be different. There's really not anything on the menu that tops $6.00. The comfort food continues into the lunch hour, with a variety of reasonably-priced items. Start out with a cup of chili and then move onto the main course; salads include good old mixed greens along with chopped chicken and Mediterranean pasta. Sandwiches don't get much more expensive than $7.00 and include such treats as the creamy club wrap (turkey, bacon, tomatoes, spinach, and scallion cream cheese) and the San Francisco melt (portabello mushroom, roasted red peppers, spinach, tomatoes, basil aioli, and melted Havarti). The dinner menu keeps much of the lunch menu but extends it to include several appetizers and entrees as well. Some of Mr. C's favorite starters include the blackened chicken quesadilla as well as the daily risotto. While entrees tend to get a bit more pricey, it pays to know that the most expensive item on the menu – the New York strip steak – is just $15.00 (including a vegetable). I had the dijon crusted pork loin and was not disappointed. Whatever time of day you pop in, you can be sure there'll be plenty to munch on here. This location does not have a liquor license but you are welcome to bring your own. Open Sunday, 9:00 a.m. - 3:00 p.m.; Tuesday through Thursday, 10:00 a.m. - 9:00 p.m.; Friday, 10:00 a.m. - 10:00 p.m.; Saturday, 9:00 a.m. - 10:00 p.m.

THE NORTHSIDE CAFE

1635 North Damen Avenue, Chicago IL 60647. 773/384-3555.
World Wide Web address: http://www.northsidechicago.com.
The Lowdown: Reflective of the area it inhabits, Northside Cafe is a trendy spot for an artsy crowd. Whether you drop in for a quick drink and a bout of people-watching or a full-fledged meal, you're bound to have a great time. Taking a typical pub menu to new heights, Northside Cafe has established itself as a neighborhood institution. Lauded by many as one of the best bars in the city, it can be difficult to find a quiet moment at the Northside, but that's all just part of the fun. For starters, hummus; pizza bread with goat cheese, sun-dried tomatoes, and fennel; or warm tomato foccacia are always a viable option. The Northside salad menu, which ranges right around the $8.00 mark, is well-known throughout the city with The Northside Salad (grilled Cajun chicken, mixed greens, apples, and tortilla strips) and The Northside Tuna (grilled tuna steak with mixed greens, apples, and tortilla strips) being two of the more popular choices. Northside Cafe serves up some great sandwiches too, like a ham and jack cheese sub, three-cheese, and grilled catfish varieties. Entrees include several pasta dishes for under $9.00 and the prototypically expensive New York strip steak weighing in at under $12.00. But what the Northside Cafe is probably best known for is their delicious, half-pound burgers. Topped with all your favorite veggies and cheeses, burgers are priced right around $6.00. For the not-so-hungry, they even offer a miniature version of the half-pound classic burger. A large and varied beer and wine selection includes Leinenkugel's, Sprecher, and Sierra Nevada on tap and a nice selection of wines by the bottle and glass. The Northside Cafe also serves up some of the city's most famous margaritas with mango, strawberry, and blue curacao being at the top of the favorite flavor list. Open Sunday through Friday, 11:00 a.m. - 1:30 a.m.; Saturday, 11:00 p.m. - 2:30 a.m.

RODITY'S

222 South Halsted Street, Chicago IL 60661. 312/454-0800.
World Wide Web address: http://www.roditys.com.
The Lowdown: In the heart of old Greektown, Rodity's is a most welcoming sight of a restaurant. Both the exterior and interior are bright and inviting, as is the budget-friendly menu. Since the early 1970s, Rodity's has been a preeminent name in authentic Greek dining. Appetizers include such favorites as homemade yogurt, tzatziki, and eggplant salad. The Greek tradition continues as we move to the entree menu, with moussaka (eggplant and ground beef), pastichio (macaroni and ground beef), and spanakotiropita (spinach and cheese pie) starting out the menu at well-under $10.00. A variety of seafood offerings – including swordfish, whitefish, and halibut – do not top a $14.00 price cap. For those non-adventurers out there, try the Greek version of an American standard with a feta-topped hamburger. Be sure to save room for some dessert; creamed caramel flan, rice pudding, and chocolate-layered custard cake are just a few of the choices. Rodity's offers a number of daily specials (though they stay the same from week to week) that will afford you even

more of a variety and savings. They offer a good selection of wine and beers too. Open Sunday through Thursday, 11:00 a.m. - 12:00 a.m.; Friday and Saturday, 11:00 a.m. - 1:00 a.m.

SANTORINI

800 West Adams Street, Chicago IL 60606. 312/829-8820.
The Lowdown: It's hard not to believe the hype: with enthusiastic accolades from Phil Vettel, Pat Bruno, *Zagat*, and various other foodies, Mr. C decided to try Santorini for himself. Located right near the heart of Greektown, it's only appropriate that Santorini serves up Greek cuisine. But this isn't your everyday Greek cuisine; Santorini's menu is comprised of what can only be described as some of the city's *best* Greek cuisine. Start out with a soup, salad, or appetizer (there are lots of traditional Greek dishes like tzatziki and saganaki), then move on to the entrees. Santorini offers a good selection of vegetarian meals including a vegetable kebob, vegetarian moussaka, and spinach pie. Santorini prepares a number of pasta dishes too. Heartier meals include keftedes (charcoal-grilled meatballs with tomato sauce and goat cheese) and lamb stamnas (lamb crêpes stuffed with veggies and cheese). But the food that Santorini is best-known (and most heralded) for is their seafood; unfortunately, this is where the menu also accrues the highest prices. Though, with several dishes available for under $13.00, seafood prices can still be considered reasonable. The red snapper is always a popular choice, as is the whole black sea bass. Just remember that you can't leave without a cup of Greek coffee (and you thought *your* coffee was strong) and one of their delicious desserts. If you're dining with a group, Santorini offers a number of family style dinner options for anywhere from $14.95 - $29.95; it's a great deal. A glass of wine will cost you a bit more, but not much; there are plenty of bottles to choose from in the $15.00 - $20.00 range. Another thing that makes Santorini such a popular place to eat is their late night hours... as if you needed another reason to come here! Open Sunday through Thursday, 11:00 a.m. - 2:00 a.m.; Friday and Saturday, 11:00 a.m. - 1:00 a.m.

SILVER CLOUD BAR & GRILL

1700 North Damen Avenue, Chicago IL 60647. 773/489-6212.
The Lowdown: "Food like Mom would make, if she was gettin' paid!" So goes the saying at Silver Cloud Bar & Grill; and they're right. Specializing in down-home American cooking with a twist, Silver Cloud Bar & Grill could easily be your home away from home while visiting the Windy City. With a large offering of lunch and dinner items, Silver Cloud makes a stop worthwhile any time of day. Start out with one of their delicious appetizers like the self-proclaimed White Trash Nachos; it's a not-so-healthy mix of Fritos, chili, and cheese. For the more discerning taste, the baked goat cheese and spicy marinara sauce can be a well-received option. New England crab cakes and spinach dip are two other popular options. A variety of dishes like linguini marinara, chicken pot pie, meatloaf, and beef stroganoff can be had for well-undr $9.00. Pricier items like marinated pork chops with sweet potato casserole, fillet of salmon, and New York strip steak

top the menu between $12.95 and $15.95. Considering all entrees are served with your choice of soup or dinner salad and a variety of vegetable sides, this is still a great deal. Lighter appetites will appreciate the enormous sandwich menu with such favorites as tuna melts, jerk chicken sandwiches, sloppy Joes, and catfish Po' Boys. The "just like Mom made" delicacies extend to the dessert menu as well with such childhood classics as S'mores, Rice Krispy treats, and root beer floats finding their way onto the menu. Silver Cloud Bar & Grill also has a terrific weekend brunch menu that includes biscuits and gravy, eggs Florentine, and eggs Benedict. Brunch is served on Saturday and Sunday, 10:00 a.m. - 4:00 p.m. In keeping with the neighborhood, Silver Cloud has a kind of artsy feel to it. Not only is the food prepared in an aesthetically-pleasing manner, but the walls are decorated in such a way as well. Lots of local artists have been happy to lend their work to Silver Cloud for display. Silver Cloud has got a pretty impressive bar menu as well. Hard-to-find beers like 3 Floyd's Pride & Joy, Seven Sisters' Cider, and Rogue Stout are all on tap for just $3.50 a pop. Bottled beers range from the forgotten-since-your-college-days Schlitz Long Neck to the über-yuppie Leffe Ale. Decide for yourself which one tastes better with a heaping plate of meatloaf! Open Sunday, 10:00 a.m. - 12:00 a.m.; Monday, 5:00 p.m. - 1:00 a.m.; Tuesday and Wednesday, 11:30 a.m. - 1:00 a.m.; Thursday and Friday, 11:30 a.m. - 2:00 a.m.; Saturday, 10:00 a.m. - 3:00 a.m.

UNCLE MIKE'S PLACE
1700 West Grand Avenue, Chicago IL 60622. 312/226-5318. **The Lowdown:** As it's often less crowded than some of the other nearby eateries, Uncle Mike's Place is a good alternative. They only serve breakfast and lunch. But, believe me when I say that you won't go hungry after chowing down on their Old Fashioned Farmer's Breakfast: three eggs scrambled with ham, onion, peppers, and potato, with Swiss cheese melted over the top. They also have a great selection of pancakes with various toppings from fruit to chocolate chips and French toast, starting around $3.00. On the lunch side, I enjoyed a huge salad plate of several mixed greens, avocado and other veggies, cheese, and strips of grilled chicken on top. The sandwich menu has close to 30 choices including Santa Fe chicken (with mango and salsa), steak on pita, Southern style catfish, and breaded perch. For $1.00 extra, you can complement your sandwich with fries, cole slaw, potato salad, or a fruit cup. If you have an overactive appetite, stop in for one of the ample lunch specials, served daily from 11:00 a.m. - 3:00 p.m. These are actually dinner-sized portions which include soup or salad, a side vegetable, and rice or mashes potatoes. Open Sunday, 6:00 a.m. - 3:00 p.m. Monday through Saturday, 5:00 a.m. - 3:00 p.m. *$Cash Only$*

WISHBONE RESTAURANT
1001 West Washington Boulevard, Chicago IL 60607. 312/850-2663. **The Lowdown:** One way to find a good restaurant is to follow the crowds, even for a good distance. Wishbone Restaurant always has loyal patrons waiting for a table,

especially for the weekend brunch. What are they doing right? The food, of course. It's homemade, scrumptious, and cheap. Rustle up a plate of black-eyed peas and rice with sauce, melted cheese, scallions, and tomato over the top, with salad and a hunk of cornbread, all for under $5.00. Get the picture? Down home cooking is the order of the day at Wishbone. Blackened chicken breast with rice, cornbread, and a vegetable of the day is just $6.50, as is the baked bone-in-ham platter or barbecued pork. Burgers and sandwiches complete the menu, along with the occasionally exotic special, such as chicken and shrimp etoufee. You can order a la carte; or, for $1.00 extra, add your choice of sides like peppered green beans, corn chowder, couscous, or fruit salad. I particularly enjoyed an order of bean cakes, slightly spicy, made with potato, black-eyed peas, and chunks of carrot. Vegetarians will be happy here with dishes such as stuffed acorn squash and eggplant parmigiana. There is a full liquor license, and Wishbone features Southern brews like Dixie Beer. For dessert, finish with a slice of sweet potato pie or peach cobbler. Wishbone Restaurant also serves a breakfast that includes heaping omelette plates topped with homemade biscuits for around $4.00. Open Monday through Friday, 7:00 a.m. - 11:00 p.m.; Saturday, 8:00 a.m. - 11:00 p.m. Closed Sunday and Monday nights. *$Cash Only$*

Suburban Chicago

AKAI HANA
3223 Lake Avenue, Wilmette IL 60091. 847/251-0384. **The Lowdown:** Akai Hana offers some of the city's freshest sushi and (a limited amount of) other Japanese delicacies at a truly mouth-watering price. Daily specials will let you in on such deals as six-pieces of sushi, a roll, soup, and ice cream (try the red bean) for a mere $10.00. Call for hours.

BLIND FAITH CAFE
525 Dempster Street, Evanston IL 60201. 847/328-6875. **The Lowdown:** Longtime fans of this Evanston institution will tell you that yes, vegetarian dining can be delicious. In fact, several prestigious magazines (*New City Chicago*, *North Shore Magazine*) have deemed Blind Faith Cafe the absolute "Best Vegetarian Restaurant" in the area. What makes Blind Faith such a unique eatery is the fact that, while the food is prepared with traditional vegetarian and macrobiotic staples (tofu, tempeh, and seitan), it's prepared with a distinct international slant. From Mexican specialties to Italian delights, this restaurant aims to please those looking for a healthy yet still inventive meal. To drink, Blind Faith Cafe has got a great assortment of fresh juices and smoothies and a menu of organic beers and wines. A wonderful dessert menu keeps the vegan in mind, with many of the items prepared in a completely non-dairy fashion. Open Sunday, 10:00 a.m. - 9:00 p.m.; Monday through Saturday, 10:00 a.m. - 10:00 p.m.

BUCA DI BEPPO
604 North Milwaukee Avenue, Wheeling IL 60090. 847/808-9898. ◆ 90 Yorktown Shopping Center, Lombard IL 60148. 630/932-7673. ◆ 15360 South 94th Avenue, Orland Park IL 60461. 708/349-6262. **E-mail address:** famiglia@bucadibeppo.com. **World Wide Web address:** http://www.bucadibeppo.com. **The Lowdown:** If you know that the motto at Buca di Beppo is "Italian Dinners and Sanitary Bathrooms," you can certainly figure out that this is not a place where pretention reigns. If there isn't already a Buca di Beppo near you, it's definitely worth a try. Though they have locations throughout the country, Buca di Beppo refers to themselves as a collection of neighborhood restaurants rather than a chain, because each restaurant is so unique in layout and decor. They specialize in what they refer to as "immigrant Southern Italian cooking." But what exactly does that mean? It means that the dinners you'll find here have originated in Sicily, Campania, Apulia, and other places in southern Italy and that the portions are huge – they're meant for sharing. Stop in with a few friends or bring the entire family. Choose from the many different meat and pasta dishes, and pass those plates along so that everyone can try a bit. Eating family-style is always an intimate experience in itself, and at Buca di Beppo it is a completely casual and fun experience too. The first

location of Buca di Beppo, which was opened in a basement (hence the origination of the name: "buca" means "basement"), really set the precedent for these casual and fun-filled eateries. Just remember that everything here comes in huge portions, from the plates of food that typically serve two to five people, to the three-liter jugs of chianti which, depending on your party's tolerance, should suit the same number. Best of all, splitting the meal means splitting the bill; a completely filling meal (with plenty of leftovers) can easily cost you under $20.00 per person. The atmosphere alone is worth more than that! Open Sunday, 12:00 p.m. - 10:00 p.m.; Monday through Thursday, 5:00 p.m. - 10:00 p.m.; Friday, 5:00 p.m. - 11:00 p.m.; Saturday, 4:00 p.m. - 11:00 p.m.

CAFE SALSA
9932 West 55th Street, Countryside IL 60525. 708/352-5100.
The Lowdown: Heralded as the best Mexican restaurant in Chicago by the *Chicago Tribune*, Cafe Salsa offers delicious and authentic Mexican food. Stop by for lunch and you'll be treated to a variety of tasty quesadillas – cheese, chicken, steak, wild mushroom, chorizo, seafood – for under $8.00 apiece. Each one is a meal in itself. They also offer a large list of soups (roasted corn chowder, black bean chowder); you can purchase a cup for just $1.95. Most entrees are served with refried or charro beans and Spanish rice and include such dishes as tacos, burritos, chimichangas, enchiladas, flautas, and tamales. They're all stuffed with a variety of fresh meats and veggies, and barely anything tops $10.00. Lunchtime at Cafe Salsa also includes a wide selection of fajitas, pastas, sandwiches, and wraps along with some heartier entrees like chicken in mole sauce, carne asada, and Mexican shish-ka-bob. Dinner time can get a bit more expensive, though the menu doesn't change all that much. You can still feast on your favorite tacos, burritos, et al, though prices will probably be a $1.00 or so higher. With dinner comes a wider selection of entrees. While the dinner specialties at Cafe Salsa can reach up to $15.00 or so, there's still plenty to choose from in the $5.00 - $12.00 range. Cafe Salsa even offers a great and inexpensive kids menu. But wait, don't forget the beverages! Cafe Salsa is well-known for their 16-ounce margaritas and their selection of more than 50 premium tequilas. They have a good wine list, which includes several bottles for under $15.00 apiece. Bottled beers – both domestic and imported – are $2.35 - $3.10; and drafts start at just $1.40 a mug. If that weren't enough, they offer great drink specials every day of the week, like $3.50 Tequila Tuesday, when any tequila well drink (including the house margarita) is just $3.50.

THE CHICAGO DINER
581 Elm Place, Highland Park IL 60035. 847/433-1228.
The Lowdown: Don't look for your average greasy burger and fries at this diner. While trying to shrug off Chicago's reputation as hog butcher to the world, this vegetarian restaurant in Lake View has developed a fine reputation in its own right. The owners are world travelers, which is reflected in the cosmopolitan nature of the menu. This sensibility extends to the cozy wooden booths

and tiny tables with pastel floral tablecloths, which lend a romantic air to the place. Try the Future Burger, which is made from basmati rice, couscous, and vegetables and garnished with lettuce, tomato, sprouts, carrots, onion, and pickles all on a whole wheat bun for around $7.00. Add a cup of miso soup for $1.50 more, or a side order of tempeh strips for $1.95. Or, opt for the macrobiotic plate: vegetable, bean and grain of the day plus kale, rice, sea vegetable, pickle, and a choice of tofu or tempeh with miso sauce or gravy. It's as much of a mouthful to eat as it is to describe! The soup of the day or a tossed salad can be added to any entree for just a little bit extra, and most dishes are served with a choice of bread: homemade cornbread, whole wheat pita, seven-grain toast, sprouted English muffin, or walnut-raisin bagel. Lacto-ovo vegetarians and other hard-core vegans can eat here without concern: any dish with dairy cheese can be made with soy cheese as a substitute. If you're not a vegetarian, don't worry about the unfamiliar items on the menu; a handy glossary is provided, and many of these things taste better than you may think. Despite the restaurant's relatively late opening time, it does serve breakfast including tofu scrambles, granola, and French toast. Saturday and Sunday breakfasts offer additional choices like ex-Benedict (grilled tempeh patties on an English muffin, topped with poached eggs and cheese sauce, and served with home fries). Beverages include herbal teas, carrot, beet, celery, apple or orange juices, soy milk, organic wine, and ciders. The diner has a children's menu, too.

CROSS-RHODES
913½ Chicago Avenue, Evanston IL 60202. 847/475-4475.
The Lowdown: Cross-Rhodes is one of Evanston's most popular spots for a healthy, delicious, and inexpensive meal. They serve up some delicious Greek cuisine (souvlaki is the house specialty) in hearty portions, seven days a week. Even with the popularity of this place, Cross-Rhodes has maintained its comfortable atmosphere where everyone is welcome. Plus, all the food is carefully-prepared with healthy ingredients, making Cross-Rhodes one of the few places where you can find a meal that is healthy and cheap! It is certainly a gem in Evanston. Open Sunday, 4:00 p.m. - 9:00 p.m.; Monday through Saturday, 11:30 a.m. - 10:00 p.m. *$Cash Only$*

DIXIE KITCHEN & BAIT SHOP
825 Church Street, Evanston IL 60201. 847/733-9030.
The Lowdown: The popularity of Dixie Kitchen & Bait Shop's Chicago location (see separate listing) has resulted in the opening of a second location to satisfy the suburban masses here. Serving up Cajun and Creole delights like gumbo, Po' Boy sandwiches, jambalaya, and fried green tomatoes, Dixie Kitchen & Bait Shop combines great food with a flair for Southern hospitality. The vintage decor makes it feel like you've been transported back in time. The red and white checkered tablecloths and painted wooden chairs offer a minimalist charm and appreciation of the simple life. Still, while there are plenty of other Southern-styled juke joints around town, few offer the

authenticity of Dixie Kitchen & Bait Shop. For example, the corn bread that is served with each meal has small bits of jalapeño thrown in for good measure. Neighborhood locals flock here, as do true-blue Southern transplants who are yearning for a taste of home. It's this type of true Southernization that makes the place so great. They even offer their own Dixie Kitchen hot sauce that will be sure to accompany any meal delightfully. Delicious desserts include a to-die-for peach cobbler and other sinful treats that are not to be missed. But what's it like to dine in an actual bait shop? You'll just have to see for yourself. Open Sunday through Thursday, 11:00 a.m. - 10:00 p.m.; Friday and Saturday, 11:00 a.m. - 11:00 p.m.

LOU MALNATI'S PIZZERIA

6649 North Lincoln Avenue, Lincolnwood IL 60645. 847/673-0800. ◆ 1050 East Higgins Road, Elk Grove IL 60007. 847/439-2000. ◆ One South Roselle Road, Schaumburg IL 60163. 847/985-1525. ◆ 85 South Buffalo Grove Road, Buffalo Grove IL 60089. 847/215-7100. ◆ 131 West Jefferson Avenue, Naperville IL 60540. 630/717-0700. **E-mail address:** heylou@ loumalnatis.com. **World Wide Web address:** http://www. loumalnatis.com. **The Lowdown:** You certainly can't visit Chicago without indulging in some of their famous deep dish pizza. While many places claim to have the best, few restaurants boast the history that Lou Malnati's does. While Lou has certainly got some hefty competition (with Pizzeria Uno & Due, Gino's East, etc.) there are plenty of Chicagoans who are loyal to Lou. From the opening of their original location in Lincolnwood, Lou Malnati's has had to branch out across the city and several other suburbs to meet the extreme pizza demand. This family-run business now owns 17 stores throughout Chicagoland (8 full service restaurants, 9 carry out & delivery only). Deep dish pizzas start at $4.35 for an individual-sized cheese and increase to just over $17.00 for a large pizza (serves four) with multiple toppings. Thin crust pizzas are just as delicious, though less expensive. While you'd be silly not to order a pizza at Lou Malnati's, they do offer a number of pasta dishes and sandwiches too. Pastas include family favorites like lasagna and spaghetti and are all priced under $7.00. Sandwiches include grilled chicken with a variety of toppings and hamburgers. Items on the kids menu, which include chicken nuggets and mini corn dogs, are under $3.50 apiece. Now that's what I call a family friendly menu. If you're looking for a casual place to enjoy some typical Chicago food, it doesn't get much better (or historical) than Lou Malnati's Pizzeria. Call for specific location hours.

MAMA THAI

1112 Madison, Oak Park IL 60302. 708/386-0100. **The Lowdown:** One look at Mama Thai's menu will make your mouth water. Here the food is as authentic as you will find outside of Thailand. The owner and her family have worked hard to make it that way. No matter what you decide on from chicken satay to seafood curry, you will not be disappointed. The traditional like pad Thai and ginger chicken are offered as well as other delicacies like pepper steak and the Mama Thai Noodle

Special (crispy egg noodles mixed with carrots, pea pods, mushrooms, bamboo shoots, and seafood in a special gravy). Open Tuesday through Thursday, 11:30 a.m. - 9:30 p.m.; Friday and Saturday, 11:30 a.m. - 10:00 p.m.; Sunday, 12:00 p.m. - 9:00 p.m.

UNCLE LOU RESTAURANT
246 North Cass Avenue, Westmont IL 60559. 630/515-8889.
The Lowdown: Not sure if you are in the mood for Chinese or Japanese food? Problem solved... head over to Uncle Lou's where you don't have to make the decision. Here you will find Asian cuisine at its best. Start out at the sushi bar where you can pick from eel, sea urchins, octopus, tuna, or other sea creatures. Move on to orange beef, empress chicken, or mu-shu pork. Shrimp in lobster sauce is one Mr. C's personal favorites. There's also a bounty of vegetables and rices to taste including eggplant in garlic sauce and Uncle Lou's special fried rice. For the best of both worlds, Uncle Lou is the perfect compromise. Open Monday through Thursday, 11:30 a.m. - 9:30 p.m.; Friday and Saturday, 11:30 a.m. - 10:30 p.m.; Sunday, 11:30 a.m. - 9:00 p.m.

VILLA MARIA RISTORANTE
9237 Ogden Avenue, Brookfield IL 60513. 708/485-6010.
The Lowdown: From the moment you step foot inside the bright and cheerful dining room, you'll feel right at home at Villa Maria Ristorante. Located just 15 miles southwest of Chicago, Villa Maria offers delicious and thoughtfully-prepared Italian food. Whether you drop in for lunch or dinner, a meal at Villa Maria is always sure to be a treat. A large menu of appetizers includes stuffed artichokes, baked and raw clams, oysters Rockefeller, and broiled octopus. Less exotic offerings include stuffed mushrooms, mozzarella sticks, and potato skins. As you might expect from an Italian restaurant, a number of great pasta dishes comprise a portion of the menu. But what you might not expect is that, even with prices that run mainly in the $7.00 - $12.00 range, all dishes come with soup or salad. Villa Maria's house specialties, which include beef pezzetini and steak pizzaiola, are priced under $12.00 apiece and come with soup or salad and your choice of potato or pasta. The rest of the menu consists of steaks, veal, chicken, and seafood. All entrees are served with soup or salad and an additional side, and there's not too much that is priced beyond $15.00. But wait, prices do get better than this! Stop by Villa Maria for lunch and you'll get just as wide a selection at an even cheaper price. How about a New York strip steak for $8.95 or pasta for under $5.00? You probably couldn't get a better deal if you were making it yourself. The lunch menu also includes an array of salads, sandwiches, and pizzas, making this a great place where a variety of appetites can get together to "do lunch." Call for hours.

ALPHABETICAL INDEX

CASH ONLY

BRING YOUR OWN

Is your favorite cheap spot missing?
Do you have comments or suggestions?

Chicago has a lot to offer. If you've got a
bargain-priced store, restaurant, hotel, or
entertainment activity, let us know about it!!
Or drop us a line to let us know what you
do or don't like about the book.

CHAPTER HEADING:

_____

NAME OF BUSINESS/ORGANIZATION:

_____

ADDRESS:

_____

_____

PHONE:

_____

WHAT'S SO GREAT ABOUT THIS PLACE?

_____

_____

_____

_____

COMMENTS:

_____

_____

_____

_____

YOUR NAME & ADDRESS:

_____

_____

_____

_____

Clip this page and send to:
Mr. Cheap's® _Chicago_
c/o Adams Media Corporation
260 Center Street
Holbrook, MA 02343
E-mail: mrcheap@adamsmedia.com